Chief Bender

ALSO BY ROBERT PEYTON WIGGINS

The Federal League of Base Ball Clubs:
The History of an Outlaw Major League,
1914–1915 (McFarland, 2009)

Chief Bender

A Baseball Biography

ROBERT PEYTON WIGGINS

McFarland & Company, Inc., Publishers
Jefferson, North Carolina, and London

LIBRARY OF CONGRESS CATALOGUING-IN-PUBLICATION DATA

Wiggins, Robert Peyton.
    Chief Bender : a baseball biography / Robert Peyton Wiggins.
        p.   cm.
    Includes bibliographical references and index.

    ISBN 978-0-7864-4229-4
    softcover : 50# alkaline paper ∞

    1. Bender, Charles Albert, 1883–1954.   2. Indian baseball
players— Pennsylvania — Philadelphia — Biography.   3. Philadelphia Athletics (Baseball team)— Biography.   I. Title.
GV865.B36W54   2010
796.357092 — dc22   2009035182
[B]

British Library cataloguing data are available

On the cover: Charles Bender at Columbia Park, Philadelphia
(National Baseball Hall of Fame Library, Cooperstown, New York)

Manufactured in the United States of America

McFarland & Company, Inc., Publishers
  Box 611, Jefferson, North Carolina 28640
    www.mcfarlandpub.com

To Deborah
and Dale

Bender was one of those baseball naturals who come along once in two or three decades.

— J. Taylor Spink, editor of the *Sporting News*

Of all the men I ever handled during my 52 years as manager, if there was one game I simply had to win, I'd want The Chief to pitch it for me.

— Connie Mack, manager of the Philadelphia Athletics, 1901–1950

If what you did yesterday still looks big to you, you haven't done much today.

— Charles Albert Bender

Table of Contents

Preface

When first I explored the possibility of writing about Charles Albert "Chief" Bender some six years ago, I was surprised to find that no comprehensive biography of the Chippewa pitcher had been written in the fifty years following his death. This seemed surprising in that he was the most successful Native American major league baseball player and was the first American Indian inducted into the Baseball Hall of Fame. The discovery of numerous interviews and recollections of Bender in the *Sporting News* between 1942 and 1953 reinforced my interest in the project. My wife and son are members of the Choctaw tribe, and that fact further contributed to an interest in the Native American ballplayer.

In an era of baseball populated by such characters as John McGraw, Ty Cobb, and Rube Waddell, little attention has been paid to Chief Bender. Several dozen American Indians of various blood reached the big leagues in the first two decades of the twentieth century. Jim Thorpe was certainly the most well known of these, but Chief Bender was the best baseball player of the group.

I completed a preliminary 168-page manuscript about Chief Bender in 2004. At about the same time, I also began to assemble information for a much larger project, *The Federal League of Baseball Clubs*. McFarland expressed an interest in both volumes. About this same time William Kashatus' book on Bender, *Money Pitcher* (2006), was released. The Bender manuscript was put on hold and I concentrated on getting the Federal League book ready for publication. Just after I returned to work on my Bender book, there appeared yet another biography of Bender, Tom Swift's *Chief Bender's Burden* (2008).

Of course, I was concerned that there would be little demand for a third biography of Bender, but I reserved final judgment until I read both books. In the end, my McFarland editor and I believed that my manuscript, a traditional biography with detailed coverage of the entirety of Bender's baseball career, had much to contribute to the story.

1

Though the internet has made a large number of historic publications available through one's home computer, travel is still a necessity when utilizing contemporary sources. I would particularly like to thank the staff of the library at the National Baseball Hall of Fame at Cooperstown, New York, and the Cumberland County Historical Society in Carlisle, Pennsylvania, for graciously providing access to their archives. I am also grateful to the Pennsylvania State Archives in Harrisburg for microfilm access to Philadelphia and other Pennsylvania newspapers, the State Library of Virginia for microfilm of the *Richmond Times-Dispatch* and *Washington Post*, as well as the Society for American Baseball Research (SABR) and the University of Virginia Library system for access to ProQuest, a source of several major historical newspapers. I would be remiss if I did not mention the free internet access granted by paperofrecord.com for the entire *Sporting News* archive through 2003 and LA84 Foundation, which is in the process of loading all issues of *Sporting Life* to its on-line research sports library that already includes reprints of *Baseball Magazine*. The Library of Congress has made a plethora of high resolution historic baseball photographs available to the public on its web site.

A special thanks is due some individuals who went well out of their way to assist in my search for photographs: Richard Tritt, photo curator at the Cumberland County Historical Society; Margaret Baughman, photograph collection librarian for the Cleveland Public Library; and Andrew Newman of the National Baseball Hall of Fame and Museum.

Prologue: The Chief

As the time neared for the first pitch of the fourth game of the 1913 World Series, all streets leading to Shibe Park in Philadelphia were jammed with people who had no chance of getting in, but would hang around the ballpark just to hear the noise. Hundreds of baseball fans, or "bugs" as they were often known in those days, filled the rooftops overlooking the twelve-foot right field fence of the ballpark. The Philadelphia Athletics had a two games-to-one lead over the despised New York Giants of manager John McGraw, and the hometown faithful were optimistic that it would become a two-game lead with their team's most reliable big-game pitcher on the mound. That pitcher was the big right-hander, Charles Albert Bender, a one-half Chippewa from the White Earth Indian Reservation in Minnesota, who had pitched for Connie Mack and the Athletics since 1903. He is known in the record books as "Chief," an appellation often assigned to Native American ballplayers by white society.

Bender was an imposing figure on the mound. At 6'2" and 185 pounds, he was tall for a ballplayer in his era and Charley used a high leg kick and an overhand delivery that made him seem even bigger on the mound.

Though Bender was one-half European, the *Washington Post* described his facial features as "wholly Indian. His hair is coal black and his complexion swarthy, his nose straight and long. His eyes are brown-black and are exceptionally clear and penetrating."[1]

Charles Bender had beaten the Giants in Game One to belie rumors that the Chippewa had been paid to lose the games he pitched against New York. Athletics manager Connie Mack was confident the veteran would earn Philadelphia a commanding three games-to-one lead in the Series.

Mack called "Albert" Bender his most reliable pitcher, but the hurler would struggle on this fall afternoon. Over the first six innings, the great Athletics pitcher allowed but two hits, both singles by burly New York catcher Larry McLean. Wrote the *New York Times*, "To New York fans it seemed incredible that the crafty, resourceful red man could again humble the Giants as he did in the opening game."[2]

Fans atop row houses opposite right field, Shibe Park, 1913 World Series (George Grantham Bain Collection, Library of Congress).

By the fifth inning it appeared the Athletics had the game wrapped up with a 6–0 lead and their best big-game pitcher shutting down the opposition with ease. Bender worked slowly and methodically, possessing marvelous control as he "flirted with the corners of the plate." The Chief escaped the fifth inning due to Rube Oldring's sensational catch of pinch-hitter Moose McCormick's vicious line drive with two runners on base. Rube was off at the crack of the bat and snared the ball in his undersized glove just inches off the grass. He kept on running in toward the infield to keep the New York base runner on third. The Giants' rally died when the runner on first, Claude Cooper, attempted to steal second base. Catcher Wally Schang made a feint toward third to freeze the runner there and then fired the ball to Eddie Collins, who applied the tag just before Cooper reached second base.

Celebrated baseball correspondent Hugh Fullerton noted, "By the sixth it was evident Bender was fading. His fastball no longer had jump on it and he was relying more and more on curves and 'slows.' Still, with six runs it looked hopeless for New York."[3]

The New York seventh started harmlessly enough. In his earlier at-bats, Silent George Burns looked miserable against the big hurler, backing away from Charley's wide breaking curveballs. Bender had him backing out again, but when Burns saw the ball was going to catch the plate, he lunged with his bat and hit a little pop fly just out of the pitcher's reach for an infield hit. Bender laughed heartily when Red Murray swung and missed a pitch by more than a foot. Moments later Murray got his revenge with a single to right. One reporter wrote, "Murray's comment directed at Bender after Red had reached first base was lost in the roars from the Giants' bench."[4] After Art Wilson struck out, the Chief got two quick strikes on the next batter, Fred Merkle. Bender threw an off-speed pitch on a 3–2 count and Merkle's bat sent a vicious line drive into left field. The sphere split the outfielders, hit the Shibe Park turf and bounced into the left field bleachers for a home run. Three runners scored to cut the Athletics' lead in half.

As the hometown bleacherites grew increasingly restless and vocal, some even cried for the "Indian's" removal. Mack did not move from his position on the bench.

The Giants continued their assault against the beleaguered Athletics pitcher in the eighth inning. Buck Herzog singled to left. Larry Doyle "shot a greaser" at second baseman Collins, who slipped as he caught the ball. Eddie hopped up quickly and threw to shortstop Jack Barry in time to force Herzog at second for the first out of the inning.

The next batter, Art Fletcher, rapped a hot grounder back at Bender. The agile hurler gathered it in and turned sharply, but he made a perilously wide throw to Barry, who had to change direction and make an off-balanced bare-handed stab at the ball.

"It made me gulp when I saw where the ball was going," related third baseman Frank Baker, "because the 'Chief' had put all his speed into it and it would have rolled a mile had it gotten away. Barry stuck his bare hand into the ball and it pretty nearly tore it off, but he saved the old ball game right there."[5]

If not for Bender's wide throw, the Athletics would have had a double play and the side would have been retired, but as it was, the only out was the force on Doyle. The next Giants batter, George Burns, doubled before Tillie Shafer tripled home two New York runs that narrowed the Athletics' lead to 6–5.

"It looked as if the great pitcher was done for," declared the *Times*. With the tying runner dancing off third base and the crowd growing more anxious, team captain Harry Davis, Bender's mentor since he was a rookie, walked out to confer with the tiring pitcher. Collins and Barry moved in and patted Bender on the back for encouragement. Meanwhile, Connie Mack sent coach Ira Thomas out to tell Reggie Brown, who was warming up, to get ready to come into the game.[6] However, Mack was not convinced he was ready to give up on his money pitcher just yet.

Before the World Series began, Mack had called Bender to his office at

Shibe Park and told him, "Albert, I am counting on you to win this Series."[7] The proud pitcher was not about to be knocked out of such an important contest. Bender declared he would stay in the game and Davis returned to the bench as the huge crowd held its collective breath.

Despite five runs and several hard hit balls off Bender in two innings, Connie Mack stood by his right-hander. Eddie Collins corralled Red Murray's sharp grounder and threw the Giants outfielder out at first to retire the side.

Many years later, Bender told a reporter, "Why, in my day, and up to a few years ago, it was considered a disgrace to get knocked out [of a game]. It happened once in a while, of course, but I know when I was knocked out, I felt like crawling into a cave to hide."[8]

In the ninth inning, an unshaken Bender set the side down in order. Doc Crandall, a pinch-hitter, grounded out to second, Merkle flied harmlessly to right, and "Harvard Eddie" Grant, pinch-hitting for the pitcher, fouled out to Schang on a full count. The next day the Athletics wrapped up the World Series championship with a victory in New York. Chief Bender's two victories against New York made him the first pitcher to win six World Series games.

Among the hundreds of thousands of Americans following the World Series, there were some who had a particular interest. The focus for these people was Chief Bender, who had become a popular symbol for the Native American population. Many fans followed the progress of the 1913 World Series games on bulletin boards prominently displayed outside the offices of major newspapers throughout the country. A wire service story out of Portland said that about fifty blanketed Indians from the reservations of Oregon and Washington traveled as far as five hundred miles to a place where they could get the latest news of the game. "On Tuesday the Indians all wanted Philadelphia to win because Chief Bender was pitching and many whooped at the news of his victory," read the report.[9]

Charles Albert Bender joined the Philadelphia Athletics in 1903 when he was two months shy of his nineteenth birthday. During the course of his baseball career, he had to overcome subtle as well as overt discrimination to become one of the top pitchers of the Dead Ball era. A product of Carlisle Indian School, Bender won 212 games over sixteen seasons, largely for Connie Mack's club. While Charles was with the Athletics, he led the American League in winning percentage three times, tossed a no-hitter in 1910, and was one of the early World Series stars, posting a 2.44 earned run average in five career Series. A dependable pitcher with a good fastball and an overhand curve, Bender was Mack's "go to" starter, often given the ball for the big game against the opposing team's best hurler.

Although baseball was enormously popular in the early decades of the

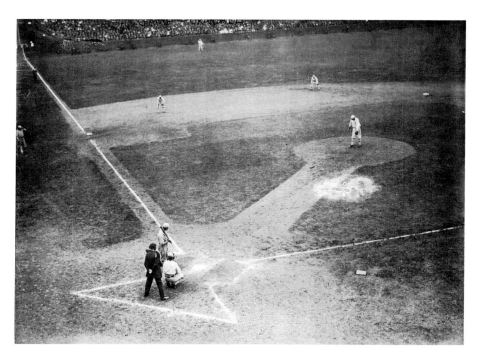

Chief Bender pitching to pinch-hitter Doc Crandall in the ninth inning of Game Four, 1913 World Series, at Shibe Park (George Grantham Bain Collection, Library of Congress).

twentieth century, the reputation of the game, and particularly that of baseball players, was not entirely respectable. While Christy Mathewson, or "the Christian Gentleman" as he was called, was the best-known exception to this rule, Chief Bender also belonged to the group of unusually upstanding players.

Attendance at the ballparks increased when Bender pitched. At first fans may have come out because they were curious about the "Indian" on the mound. Over time, they came to like Bender and larger crowds became common whenever the Chippewa pitched.

Aside from his baseball career, Charles excelled at several other sports, became an excellent trap shooter, loved fishing and hunting, and became accomplished at golf and bowling. In a series on the stars of baseball that appeared in 1942, J. Taylor Spink, editor of the *Sporting News,* wrote, "Bender was one of those baseball naturals who come along once in two or three decades...."[10]

"A natural competitor, he became so adept at golf that many professionals felt he missed his real calling, and at billiards he was proficient enough to provide even the famed Willie Hoppe with an interesting evening."[11]

Grantland Rice had come to that conclusion twenty-five years earlier when Bender was in his final major league season as a pitcher.

> We ran across Chief Bender a few days ago down to Pinehurst. The Chief is leading a rasping existence. In the forenoon he finished in the money in a big trap shooting tournament; in the afternoon he collected at a round of golf. That night we watched him again, this time playing a first-class game of billiards. Bender is undoubtedly one of the best all around performers in the land. He has the knack of doing everything well, and a big part of his success comes from his cool, keen judgment and his amazing temperament — a temperament or a disposition a cyclone couldn't upset. At the closest part of the hardest game nothing can change the placid calm of his bearing. We know of no man in the span of sport who takes the break of the game as it comes with Bender's eternal poise.[12]

Napoleon Lajoie was perhaps the American League's greatest hitter when Bender debuted in 1903. Thirteen years later, the former Cleveland star and manager paid high praise to Mack's standout hurler. "They tell me Mathewson was a very wise pitcher," he said, "but if he had anything on Chief Bender I am glad I have never had to bat against his offerings. Bender when in his prime had a world of stuff, but even after he lost a great deal of it he was still a wonderful pitcher, because he knew every trick of the profession. Once he discovered a batter's weakness, that batter was lucky to hit him safely with a shovel. His control was usually perfect, and under fire he was at his best. Pitchers like Bender are rare birds in baseball."[13]

"I was a high ball pitcher," Bender explained. "I had a hop to my fastball. When I started pitching, I didn't need a college course to convince me that a batter could not get a solid wallop at a ball on the edge of the shoulder line."[14]

Hall of Fame umpire Billy Evans worked behind the plate in many a game pitched by Bender between 1906 and 1914. "If ever a pitcher used his control to the utmost advantage it was Bender," Evans declared. "If a batter had a weakness and most of them have, Bender played up to it all the time.

"I have often heard him say to some player who didn't like a fastball inside, 'Don't hug that plate too close today for I have plenty of speed and you can expect to see the fast one breezing under your chin all afternoon.'"[15]

As he developed, Bender expanded his pitching repertoire. "I relied mainly on the fastball, a curve and a change-up and I knew where the ball was going," he explained. "But I learned how to throw all the other stuff that was popular then, and, except in name, those tricky pitches of today are about the same."[16]

Bender came to the major leagues at the time when hurlers used a variety of trick pitches, most of which would be outlawed by the end of the second decade of the century. Charles was known to use a "shine" ball and the so-called "talcum" pitch, whereby one side of the ball was rubbed with talcum powder, which caused the ball to drop when thrown. Amidst numerous doctored pitches, the spitball, emery ball and others, there was little notice.

As he began to rely less on his fastball, Bender's most successful pitch became his "nickel curve," which he is said to have developed just in time for his best years with the Athletics. Batters complained the pitch "came in fast and then dropped." Charley would teach the pitch that would become known as the slider to succeeding generations of pitchers.

An all-around player, Bender appeared in several games in the infield and outfield and Connie Mack employed him as an occasional pinch-hitter. He also was a proficient sign stealer, practicing this art from the coaching box or on the bench between starts. After his playing career, Charley employed his knowledge of the pitching art as a manager, coach and scout.

Though "Chief" Bender was a trim, healthy specimen during his playing days, he was plagued by numerous stress-induced maladies that probably contributed to an alcohol problem later in his baseball career. Almost annually, poor health and sore arms interrupted his mound duties for the Athletics. Bender was under immense pressure to succeed as well, not only because of his fiercely competitive nature, but because he was "supposed to fail" due to the Native American blood that flowed through his veins.

"Mr. Mack thought I was the coolest pitcher he ever had," Bender revealed years after his playing days were over. "I was cool, on the outside. On the inside, I burned up. I couldn't eat for three hours after a game."[17]

Comparing Bender's statistics with those of Eddie Plank, the Athletics pitcher with whom the Chief is often connected, Eddie had far more work during the time period (1903–1914) in which the two anchored the A's pitching staff. During those twelve seasons, Plank pitched 3,586 innings compared to 2,613 for Bender, pitched in 496 games to the Chief's 385, and started 425 of them compared to 289 starting assignments for Charles.

After winning 180 games prior to his thirtieth birthday (May 5, 1914), Bender went 32–28 in his thirties. Pitchers of that era often wore out in their thirties since off-season conditioning was virtually unheard of and sore arms became more frequent as a pitcher aged.

Bender admitted he spent little time on off-season conditioning. "Practically all I did was hunt and fish, but in those days it was not impressed on our minds that we should prepare ourselves for the future."[18]

Following World War I, Bender chose to accept a managerial job in the minor leagues rather than hang on as a second-line pitcher with a major league club. Through 1927, he continued to take a turn on the mound and won ninety-one games in the "bushes." The Chief managed eight different minor league clubs, coached the U.S. Naval Academy baseball team for six years, served as pitching coach with the Chicago White Sox, New York Giants and Philadelphia Athletics, scouted for the Athletics and the Yankees, and even spent part of a season barnstorming with the House of David independent baseball team.

Connie Mack, the long-time Philadelphia manager for whom Bender played twelve seasons, wrote in 1950 that the Chief was one of the top half-dozen pitchers in the history of the game. Mack is also reported to have said that Bender was the greatest "money pitcher" he'd ever coached and "the thinkin'est pitcher I ever saw."

"The Chief was the same in a million-dollar game as he was in a dollar game," Mack told the *Sporting News* near the end of his career as a manager. "He never showed any nervousness or tension. But the bigger the stakes, the better he always was.

"Of all the men I ever handled during my 52 years as manager, if there was one game I simply had to win, I'd want The Chief to pitch it for me."[19]

This was high praise indeed from the man who managed such great pitchers as Lefty Grove, Eddie Plank and Rube Waddell, all inductees in the National Baseball Hall of Fame.

◆ 1 ◆

From the Reservation to Carlisle

There was little to suggest that young Charles Bender would have a life any different than the other mixed-blood boys on the reservation. Even those who were sent to the white man's schools to become "good Indians" often returned to the reservation to spend their lives as common laborers or struggling with the poor soil on their allotment just to eke out a living. Much of White Earth Reservation's native population accepted government subsidies and large numbers of the people descended into a life of idleness. Because the land was poor, there were few opportunities for young men, and drunkenness was already a problem on the reservation when Charles was a child. However, young Bender had two things most of his fellow tribesmen did not have — a drive to succeed through education and athletic prowess.

Charles Albert Bender[1] was born on May 5, 1884, in Crow Wing County, Minnesota. He was the son of Mary Razor (Indian name: Pay shaw de o quay[2]), a full-blood Chippewa, and Albertus Bliss Bender,[3] a homesteader-farmer of German descent. Charles was a member of a large family that included brothers Frank, John, James, Fred, and George, and sisters Mary (Maud), Anne, Elizabeth, and Emma.[4] Because the Bender homestead was at Partridge Lake,[5] twenty miles east of Brainerd, Minnesota, that town has been mistakenly referred to as the birthplace of Charles Albert.

Mary Razor was a member of the largest tribe of Native Americans north of Mexico, the Ojibwe. The word "Chippewa" was used in treaties with the U.S. Government and became the tribal name used south of the Canadian border. The relationship between the two names for the tribe becomes more apparent if an "O" is placed in front of the word Chippewa, making it O'chippewa.[6]

Before the rush of white settlers into their territory, their tribal lands spread from the shores of the Great Lakes across Minnesota to the Turtle Mountains of North Dakota. Although strong in numbers and occupying a large area, the Chippewa were not prominent in English history before the American Revolution because of their remoteness from the European settlements.

Through a series of treaties beginning in 1854, the United States Government began to create reservations on which the Native Americans would be confined. When Charles Albert was about four years old, the Bender family moved to the White Earth Reservation in northwestern Minnesota. The reservation was established by a treaty with the Mississippi band of Chippewa in March 1867. It was supposed to be an isolated reservation upon which to relocate the Woodland Indians of Michigan, Wisconsin, and Minnesota. However, many of the Native Americans refused to move there and others took a look at the disagreeable land before returning to their ancestral homes. White Earth Reservation encompassed about 1,300 square miles, but most of that land is no longer Indian-owned due to allotments and tax forfeiture losses in the early twentieth century.

The Dawes Severalty Act of 1887 allowed the president of the United States to break up Indian lands, previously held in common by the tribe, into small allotments to be parceled out to individuals. Unassigned lands would then be made available to white homesteaders. The legislation dictated how the allotments were to be distributed:

> To each head of a family, one-quarter of a section; To each single person over eighteen years of age, one-eighth of a section; ... and to each other single person under eighteen years now living, or who may be born prior to the date of the order of the President directing an allotment of the lands embraced in any reservation, one-sixteenth of a section....[7]

Full ownership would only come to the Native American land holder after the federal government held the allotment in trust for twenty-five years. The goal of the Dawes Act was to assimilate the American Indian population into white society by encouraging the destruction of the tribal association, but in the end it produced a class of Americans who became dependent on federal assistance.

The Benders settled on reservation land in what would become Gregory Township, Mahnoman County. Because of Mary Bender's Ojibwa blood, the Benders were allotted a plot of 160 acres of prairie within the White Earth Reservation. Eventually, allotments to the family's mixed-blood children swelled the family's land holdings to twenty-three 80-acre sections. The Bender's land on the White Earth Reservation was mostly prairie with an occasional marsh and was of poor quality for the growing of crops. Charles once commented that things "didn't work out very well under the Bender system of tilling the soil and we had a hard time of it."

Charles, or Albert as he was most often called in his early years, later remarked that as a youngster he spent much of his idle time throwing stones. "And that," Bender said, "is how I laid my foundation as a pitcher."[8]

It is probable young Charles Albert Bender attended reservation schools at White Earth and Pipestone. His sister Anna wrote that she spent three years at the boarding school at Pipestone before she and Albert were sent to another boarding school in Philadelphia.

At the age of seven, Albert became a farm laborer for hire, earning a dollar a day. It wasn't a promising proposition. A short time later, young Charles' life changed dramatically when a recruiter from the Educational Home boarding school in Philadelphia paid a visit to White Earth Reservation looking to enlist bright Native American children.

"In Philadelphia at that time was a wealthy woman, a Mrs. Cox, who supported and conducted a school for Indian boys from 7 to 15 years of age," Bender told an interviewer in 1942. "...There were so many of us at home and so little to feed us that mother didn't mind giving me up."[9]

"Of course I had to come East by train," Bender later related with a measure of embellishment. "I had never seen a train and we left the reservation at night. Standing on the platform with the kerosene headlight rushing towards me, I thought the big reflector on the approaching locomotive was the moon driving down the track to destroy us. Frightened, I took out for the prairie grass and scrub growth to hide. It took the reservation three days to find me and put me on the train."[10]

The Educational Home was originally a boarding school operated by the Episcopal Church for destitute white children. It began taking in Native American children in 1884 when it merged with another Episcopal school named Lincoln Institute that was funded by the government's Indian Department. Once at the school, the young Native American students would not be allowed to return home until they were at least twelve years old unless dismissed for disciplinary reasons.[11]

Charles Albert, his brother John, and sister Anna were among twelve children between the ages of seven and fifteen that were enrolled at the Educational Home on July 15, 1891. Anna was sent to the girls' boarding school on 11th Street and the boys were taken to the Education Home on Forty-ninth and Greeley Avenue. Among the Benders group of White Earth recruits was Charles Roy, who would one day pitch in the major leagues for the Philadelphia Phillies.

Though Bender said he never had an "Indian name," the school registered him both as Charles and "Mandowescence," an Ojibwa word meaning "Little Spirit Animal."[12] Perhaps Charley had not remembered the childhood word because the use of Chippewa names may have been discouraged by his Caucasian father, or it could have been used because an Indian name was required for admission to the school in order to qualify for funding by the Indian Department.

Conversation in native language was forbidden in the government-supported boarding schools, though this probably was not a problem for the

Bender children, who came from a home with a European parent. The children received a rudimentary education as well as training in a number of useful trades. The underlying purpose of the school, like all government-sponsored boarding schools for Native Americans, was to eradicate the children's tribal identities so "they may grow in wisdom for the good of society and the prosperity of true religion."[13] The superintendent promoted music as the school's main extracurricular activity and deemphasized sports.

Later in life Charles Bender spoke fondly of the Educational Home. "Lincoln Institute was a grand school and we had a great time. There were about 125 Indian boys. I worked in the laundry to help pay my way. I learned to play ball watching the older boys. They had a good club. Why, we even made our own baseballs from core to cover."[14]

Despite the superintendent's wishes, the older boys organized a baseball team and played against amateur and semi-pro clubs in the area. Charley's favorite player on the Home's team was the pitcher, a Mohawk named Louis Bruce. Seven years older that Charles, Bruce would one day become a teammate of Bender's on the Philadelphia Athletics.

"At that time — I was 8," Charles recalled, "I had an idea that I wanted to be a catcher, but the idea lasted only until I got hit between the eyes with a ball. In those days we didn't have mitts like they have now. My catcher's glove was a dress glove with the finger tips cut off."

Those early days at the school laid the groundwork for Charley's lifetime love of shooting and hunting. "I stayed at Lincoln Institute for five years," he recalled, "going to school nine months and roaming the fields with a fishing pole or gun the other three months. Our favorite sport was to go to the river and shoot bullfrogs."[15]

When he reached the age of twelve, Charles Albert, or "Al" as he was often called, returned home to White Earth. "Mrs. Cox furnished me with the money for the trip," he said, "and packed some lunch for me."

Before he left Philadelphia, Bender paid $3 for a rifle at a hardware store. Accompanied by another Indian school student named Seymour Fairbanks, the boys got off the train each time it stopped and did some shooting. After three days, Charles Albert reached Detroit, Minnesota, but he had no money left, so Fairbanks paid the stage coach fare to White Earth Reservation. Bender said he still had to walk the final twenty-nine miles to his family's home with his prize rifle over his shoulder.[16]

Life at White Earth was a faded memory to Charley and quite different from what he experienced in Pennsylvania. The family's log home was overcrowded with children, porous to the elements, and extremely hot in the summer. He hardly remembered his youngest siblings. A brother named George was born while he was away at boarding school and his oldest sister, Emma, now had a child of her own.

Anna Bender's homecoming was different than her brother's but was no less traumatic. She later recalled that the days at the Education Home were the happiest of her childhood, especially the summers out of the city. In her final year in Philadelphia, Anna was confirmed in the Episcopal Church. A few years later, she wrote about her return home to White Earth.

> I seldom heard from my parents and was so young when I came away that I did not even want to go home except that other students went to theirs. How miserable I felt when the time came to go....
>
> When I arrived at the station, I was met by my mother who had with her my two younger sisters, and two young brothers whom I had never seen. They greeted me kindly but they and everything seemed so strange that I burst into tears. To comfort me, my mother took me into a store and bought me a bag of apples....
>
> As we gathered around the table later a great wave of homesickness came over me so that I was unable to eat for the lump in my throat, so I put my head down and cried good and hard, while the children looking on in surprise.
>
> When my father returned from work he greeted me kindly but scanned me carefully from head to foot. He asked me if I remembered him, but I had to answer "No." He talked to me kindly and tried to help me recall my early childhood, which proved unsuccessful. At last he told me I had changed greatly from a loving child to a stranger and seemed disappointed which only added to my lonesomeness.[17]

Charley Bender's relationship with his father was far from ideal. That summer, thirteen-year-old Charles and his brothers were worked from dawn to dusk to keep the farm going. Years later Charles gave a hint of his dad's impact during a speech at a father-and-son dinner at the First Baptist Church in Chester, Pennsylvania. "As far as myself," he said, "I was raised without the benefit of a father's encouragement and had I been so blessed, as you boys are, I might have been able to have avoided many of the mistakes that have been my part and parcel through the years."[18]

Charles Albert's break from his Minnesota parents came when his father sent him and brother Frank to the lake for fresh water. "He handed me the pail," Bender recounted for the *Sporting News*. "I was a bit slow in starting. 'Get along,' he shouted, and when I didn't move as quickly as he wanted, he gave me a terrific kick in the pants. The bucket flew out of my hand and I fell flat on my face.

"My brother Frank said nothing, but walked over, picked me up, brushed me off and put the pail back in my hand. We started off for the lake at a fast pace."

As the boys neared the lake, Frank chastised his younger brother. "Are you going to stand for that kick in the pants from father?"

When Charles Albert didn't say anything, his brother completed his thought, "I wouldn't. Let's run away!"[19]

Leaving home seemed like a good idea at the time and the brothers walked some twenty miles to the house of Frank's godfather. The runaways were not warmly welcomed, but they were allowed to spend the night in the barn. When Albertus Bender did not come after them or send for the boys, they decided they were on their own and got jobs working in the fields at White Earth Farm. It is unknown whether Charley ever saw his father again after that kick in the pants. He rarely returned home as an adult, and it has been suggested that Albertus was an absentee father for considerable stretches until he and his wife Mary ultimately separated.

While Albert and his brother were working at White Earth farm, an opportunity arose that would change the direction of both their lives. "Miss Alice Parker, a teacher from the Carlisle Indian School, came through looking for boys," explained Charles Albert. "Frank and I jumped at the chance to go to Carlisle."[20]

That decision would set Charles Albert Bender on a course to become one of the most famous Native Americans in the United States. Alice Parker was part of a network of recruiting agents on reservations around the country assigned to provide the Carlisle School with a steady flow of new students.

From July 1896 to 1902, Charles Bender attended Carlisle Indian Industrial School, the first U.S. Government off-reservation boarding school exclusively for American Indian children. The Carlisle School and Haskell Institute in Kansas were the most prominent among a number of federally operated boarding schools implementing the U.S. Government's education policy toward Native Americans.

The Carlisle Indian School, established in 1879, provided an educational setting for more than 12,000 Native American students until it closed in 1918. Created and directed by Captain Richard Henry Pratt, the school's purpose was to eradicate the traditions of young Native Americans and indoctrinate them in western values, language, dress and religion. By eliminating the Indian identity, Pratt believed that his "civilizing" mission was saving the man.[21]

Enrollment at the Indian school began to swell as more tribes' children were recruited. The original group of eighty-two grew to a yearly average of 1,000 students, which required more living and classroom space. The students built an administration building, a gymnasium for athletics, shops for industrial training, and a chapel on the grounds. In January 1896 a trolley line was completed from the town of Carlisle to the school and construction of a forty-foot-wide street and driveway alongside the rails was underway.[22]

The Bender brothers traveled to Carlisle by train and, after their arrival at the railway station, they probably departed Main Street and walked toward the school along the same road they would take on trips to and from the school to "Outing" homes and day trips out of town.

Charles Albert Bender was two months past his twelfth birthday when his relationship with the school began with a descriptive statement that was completed and periodically updated for all students.

Charles A. Bender[23]
Address: White Earth Agency
Attended Carlisle 7/5/1896 — 5/14/02
Father: Albert Bender (German), Mother: living, full blood Chippewa.
Height at arrival: 5' 3"
Weight: 101 lbs.
Graduated class of 1902. Captain of baseball team 1901-02.
Also: expelled for "treachery to baseball team"
Entered school at grade 4. Attended Dickinson Prep School in Carlisle.
Married: Marie (German-American)
Owned a house in Philadelphia.

Bender's brothers Frank, John, and James were students at Carlisle at various times while Charley was there. The Indian school's files of students indicate that James Bender joined Charles and Frank at Carlisle on September 5, 1896. It also states he was expelled in March 1900, but no reason was given. The younger Bender children, Annie, Elizabeth, Emma, Fred, and George, would attend the Hampton Normal & Agricultural Institute in Virginia.

"When we reached school," recalled Charles, "the first thing they gave us was a bath, then clean underwear and a room. It wasn't long before I was installed in the regular routine, which was very strict because of military regulations."[24]

Uninitiated students were given white people's haircuts and those with only Indian names were required to select a new one from the school's approved list of English names. They were forbidden to speak their native language and members of different tribes were mixed together to discourage traditional communication. Blue military-style uniforms and kepis were issued to the boys, and the girls dressed in Victorian style dresses. Shoes were required; no moccasins were allowed.[25]

Discipline was strictly enforced, military style. The boys and girls were organized into companies commanded by student officers. The children marched in formation to and from their classes, to the drill field for daily activities, and to the dining hall for meals. The school's curriculum was mostly vocational and the students were to serve three-year terms without leave.

Charles Bender recalled the day's schedule went as follows: "Reveille was sounded at 5:45 A.M. The students were required to appear for roll call at 6:30; then came breakfast, and the cleaning of quarters (rooms) and setting up exercises in the gymnasium."

Manual training was an important phase of the program and from eight to noon the young braves practiced a trade. There were classes in carpentering, wheel righting, blacksmithing, painting, printing and farming.

Pratt Avenue Entrance, Carlisle Indian Industrial School (Cumberland County Historical Society, Carlisle, Pennsylvania).

After lunch, the students assembled in classrooms for three hours of study in the basic curriculum of that time — reading, writing and arithmetic. Bender's primary education at the Philadelphia school gave him a distinct advantage over many of the newer students. As his adult life would confirm, Charles was a good student with a hunger for knowledge.

Four o'clock was the assigned time for the school's sports teams to begin practice. There was a military drill and dress parade every night at six followed by the evening meal. Seven to eight P.M. was designated for study, and then the students had recreation time in the gym until lights out at nine o'clock. Three shifts of male students were assigned to guard duty overnight starting at nine P.M. and concluding at six A.M. Bender said the guards "carried a Civil War musket with nothing in it."[26]

A court system was organized in the hierarchical style of a military justice system, with students deciding the consequence for an offense. The most severe punishment was confinement to the guardhouse. The old guardhouse, built by German Hessian prisoners during the Revolutionary War, still stands.

Bender remembered "there wasn't much time to play — only two hours

Students relaxing on the lawn at the United States Indian School just after the turn of the twentieth century (Benjamin Johnston Collection, Library of Congress).

between 4 and 6 — and 30 minutes of this time was lost in changing from uniform to play-clothes, but we managed to have plenty of fun. I was too small for any of the large teams, but managed to make the class clubs.

"In the summer we 'hired out' for work at the neighboring farms. The first year I went to Penn Manor and worked as a house boy at $4 a week for Joseph E. Beck. The next summer I remained away from Carlisle and went to work for Eleazer Doane in Buchmanville. I went to the country school, walking three miles each way."[27]

Instead of returning the Native American children to their natural families during the summer, the detribalizing process continued with the placement of students with non–Indian families. An "Outing Program" was required for all students, usually for three months, though some of the young Native Americans remained with their Caucasian families year-round and attended local public schools with their white "siblings." Families chosen for the program were usually Quaker or Pennsylvania Dutch that lived in the area between Lancaster and Philadelphia. The participating families received cheap labor for their farms or businesses in exchange for strict adherence to the outing code's principles, which dictated that students were to learn English and "the customs of civilized life." Field agents from the Indian school made periodic visits to verify that patron families kept a report of any violation of the program's rules that included: "Does pupil bathe as often as rules require (once a week)? How does pupil use evenings and Sundays? Has pupil used tobacco or spirituous liquors in any form? State what pupil bought with money expended...."[28]

A first-hand account of the outing experience was printed in the Carlisle School's weekly newsletter on June 30, 1899: "Frank Bender who is on a farm not far from Philadelphia says by letter to his teacher that although the work of the farm requires long hours, he finds some time to read and study. He began shorthand before he went out and he practices some, while for his books to pick up at odd times he has *The Last of the Mohicans*, and *Thrift* by Smiles. He likes his place and the people are kind and nice to him he says."[29]

In 1899 Colonel Pratt hired Glenn S. Warner away from Cornell University at an unheard of salary of $1,200 to coach football and baseball. Since Warner was older than most of his fellow students when he participated in sports at Cornell, they called him "Pop." Glenn played guard on the football team, was the school's heavyweight boxing champion, played baseball, and earned a law degree from Cornell in 1892.

Pop Warner soon realized the Indians were exactly the kind of players he had hoped to coach. "They are born lovers of the game," he later commented. "They have speed and skill in use of hands and feet. They also have highly developed powers of observation, handed down through generations."[30]

Warner was a one-man coaching staff in his early years at the Indian school. Pop's first Carlisle football team in 1899 went 7–2, with wins over the traditional football schools Pennsylvania, Columbia, and the University California. The team traveled to San Francisco and defeated a previously unbeaten and unscored on California team, 2–0, in one of the first intersectional collegiate contests. The Indians' only losses that year were to two of the top teams in college football, Harvard and Princeton. In 1900 Carlisle (6–4–1) had wins over the University of Virginia, 17–2, and Maryland, but suffered four losses to Ivy League schools.

"I also tried my hand at football — I was a substitute end — but I didn't care for the game," admitted Charles Bender. "I hated to practice. All the Indian boys hated to practice. Pop had a hard time of it. How he ever succeeded in turning out great teams is more or less a mystery."[31]

Bender said the football team was quickly reduced to about thirty lads, averaging twenty years of age. Back then, re-substitution of a player in a game from which he had been removed was not allowed, and it was not uncommon for the first team to play through the entire thirty-five-minute halves. Seldom did more than five substitutes get into a game.

Bender did play during the daily scrimmages. However, the seventeen-year-old Chippewa was too slender to be thrown into games against the college football giants of the day — Penn, Harvard and Cornell. During one 1901 gridiron skirmish, Charley suffered multiple rib fractures that warranted a trip to the hospital.[32] That season, the Indians won five games, lost seven and played a scoreless tie with Washington & Jefferson.

"Stirring up the Indians against the 'palefaces'

The 1901 Carlisle Indian School track team. Charles Bender is the tall lanky individual on the far right of the front row, in the foreground, in this image published in the March 6, 1903, *Redman & Helper* (Cumberland County Historical Society, Carlisle, Pennsylvania).

was Warner's best stock in trade when it came to arousing them," Charles added. "We hated to be ridiculed."

Although the Indians' first win over Cornell came in October of 1902, several months after Bender left the school, Charles remembered that the night the team arrived in Ithica, the papers came out with a story that read, "Warner and his circus have arrived. They may not be able to play football, but they can wear fancy headdress."

"Pop showed the boys the clippings, played upon their pride, got them good and mad — and did they whip Cornell!" Bender said.[33]

While a student at Carlisle, Charley Bender ran track and played both baseball and football for Warner. Years later, Bender said all he learned about the national game of baseball was taught to him by Pop Warner, who had been a pitcher at Cornell until he threw his arm out.

Warner first spotted Charley Bender when he was a lanky sixteen-year-old throwing a ball along the sidelines of the athletic field. Pop saw potential in the athletic Chippewa and put him on the varsity baseball team. Though Bender was a hard thrower, he was far too inexperienced to trust on the mound and was relegated to playing first base and right field.[34]

"In 1900 I first met Pop Warner," recalled Bender. "I was only a skinny kid, weighed 140 and was about five feet eleven inches. Pop allowed me to pitch to the batters on the first team and I thought I was the biggest guy in school. In 1901 I made the regular club."[35]

Bender recalled many years later that he beat Mercersburg, 10–1, in the first regular season game he pitched, but accounts by Carlisle newspapers suggest different. The first mention of Charles Bender as a pitcher by the *Carlisle Daily Herald* came the day after his appearance in relief of Arthur Pratt in the loss to Princeton on April 12, 1901. Charley's first victory came on May 1 against Lebanon Valley College by a score of 13–8. "The visitors put up a splendid game and when in the second," wrote the *Daily Herald*, "they scored seven runs, it looked as if they might take the Indians' scalps, and young Bender pitched the entire game in a very creditable manner, striking out eight men."[36] Nonetheless, there is little doubt Bender's memory was clouded when he later told J. Taylor Spink, "There has never been a thrill to match that first victory for Carlisle."[37]

A week later, a team from Gettysburg, Pennsylvania, rolled into Carlisle to oppose the Indians' best pitcher, Louis Leroy. The visitors' pitcher was a tantalizing left-hander named Eddie Plank, who dominated the Carlisle nine. Only two hits were made by Warner's team, one of them by Charley Bender, who played the field that afternoon. Bender would win another game for the Indians on June 21 when he pitched the 5–4 Carlisle victory against Bloomsburg Normal in the next-to-last contest of the season.[38]

One of the more interesting characters on the Carlisle School's athletic teams was Louis Leroy, a half Stockbridge (descended from Algonkian-speaking tribes, primarily Mohicans) from Ormo, Wisconsin. Four years older that Charles Bender, Leroy was a baseball pitcher and halfback on the football team.

An item from the *Indian Industrial School Newsletter* (June 2, 1899) reported the results of a recent baseball game won by Carlisle, 6–2. "It is said that the Dickinsonians looked at close of the game as though a cyclone had struck their rooters and that the players had all been invited to a funeral. Two large dogs did their part in rooting, however. It was a fine game. LeRoy as pitcher and Roberts as catcher make a fine combination."[39]

Coach Glenn "Pop" Warner, Carlisle Indian School (1899–1903, 1907–1914) (Chicago History Museum).

Leroy was so talented he wanted to pitch professionally and he ran away from school four times to achieve his goal. School records indicate Louis was first enrolled on March 30, 1899, and ran away on November 22. At age nineteen, he re-enrolled on January 25, 1900, and a few days later, the school newsletter reported, "Louis LeRoy is with us again. He has had many and varied experiences since he left Carlisle last year, and is now ready to settle down to steady, hard work and study."[40]

Though twenty years of age, the Native American Leroy was still bound to the boarding school unless he graduated or was expelled. His plight was not a unique one. Hundreds of male students fled the school, many of them repeat offenders. Members of the baseball team were especially susceptible to the temptation to desert the school and play for pay with one of the many thriving semi-pro clubs in the area. Because of his repeated disappearances, Louis became known at the school as the player with a "$10,000 arm and ten-cent head."[41]

In June 1901, the baseball team was returning home from a road game when their train made a stop in Lancaster, Pennsylvania. Pop Warner discovered that Leroy was missing when his team was about to board the train and continue to Carlisle. The coach went into town in search of the wayward right-hander. He looked up the manager of the Lancaster professional team, but the man had no Indian players. He had, however, just signed a promising Italian pitcher. Warner found the "Italian pitcher," Leroy, at a rooming house and forced him to return to Carlisle. Once they were back on campus, Leroy was thrown in the old guardhouse to cool his heels.

Actually, Louis "cooled his heels" in the guardhouse from mid–June to early September, when he was released in time for the start of football season. Leroy was supposed to play in the Indians' backfield in a game against the University of Michigan on November 2 when he and another running back slipped out of the team's hotel in Detroit and disappeared.[42]

During the summer of 1901 Charles Bender spent his "outing" working on the farm of Dave Hertzler at Williams Grove. It was during that "outing," pitching hay on the farm, that Charley received his first professional baseball opportunity. He was offered $5 to pitch a game for a semi-pro team in Dillsburg, about eighteen miles from Carlisle, against the Churchtown community club.

His account of the Churchtown game was one of Bender's favorite stories when he became a speaker on the banquet circuit.

What a game that was. I struck out 21 batters, hit a home run with the bases loaded — but lost the game. We played in a hay field, with a cabbage patch in left and stones for bases. The catcher set a new record for assists, and I guess it still stands. Believe it or not, he dropped every third strike, but threw out 19 of 21 at first base.

The score was 9 to 5 in the last of the ninth when, with three on, I tied it up with a hit that got lost among the cabbages. But we lost in the tenth.

I worried about losing because I wasn't sure of getting the $5, so I kept right on the heels of the manager from the field to the boarding house where we dressed. He slammed the door in my face, but I camped right there until he came out.

Eventually he came out. He had a hat full of coins, mostly pennies—$3.20, he explained, because the collection had been low, the expenses high. But, the manager promised, "I'll give you the $1.80 the next time I see you."

They say this is a small world, but I've been looking for that fellow for more than 50 years, and haven't found him yet.[43]

Bender eventually received the $1.80 he was owned by the Dillsburg manager. Charles told the story of the Dillsburg game at a banquet honoring the 1941 Montgomery-Delaware County League baseball champions and within a month after the story's publication the Chief received a bag of coins—Indian-head pennies, a three-cent piece and a couple of 1875 dimes. The package was postmarked Dillsburg, Pennsylvania.[44]

With Louis Leroy gone, Charley Bender was made captain of the Carlisle baseball team for the 1902 season. Bender was the best pitcher Warner had, but the Indians were a bad baseball team, winning only four of their nineteen games. Charles pitched well enough against the Dickinson College nine to win on April 19, but his support was not sufficient to give Carlisle the game. Students from both schools were there in force and "rooted vociferously" for their respective teams. Bender struck out nine of the Dickinsons and allowed only two hits, but the Indians lost by a score of 2–1.[45]

That May, a quirk of fate ended Charley's tenure at the Indian school. Impressed by his performance against them two weeks earlier, Dickinson College sought to recruit the pitcher for its baseball team. Carlisle had a two-week break in its schedule and allowed Bender to join the Dickinsons to get in some extra work on the mound.

At the time rules regarding eligibility for collegiate athletics were inconsistent, at best. Some of the Dickinson players, as was a common practice, were attending prep schools but played ball on the college team. Sometimes, college football and baseball players even played professional ball in the off-season under pseudonyms. Therefore, Bender didn't give it much thought when he was farmed out to the Dickerson baseball team. "You must understand that anything went in those days as far as athletics were concerned," he said.

"Carlisle and Dickinson were scheduled to meet in a dual track meet," Bender recalled. "The star sprinter of the Dickinson team also was the star pitcher on the baseball club. He told Captain Cannon of the baseball team that he was sick and could not make the trip. Cannon then asked me to go."

After the Dickinsons won a couple of events in which Bender participated, the slight could not be overlooked by the leaders at Carlisle. "The officials at Carlisle immediately charged me with being a party to the deception," Charles Albert explained. "I was brought up on the carpet and ordered out of school."[46]

There has been no other explanation for Bender's expulsion by the Carlisle Indian School that May, but the fact remains that Charley continued a close relationship with the school for many years. Despite the blight on his record, Bender is listed among the graduates of the class of 1902.

On his own for the first time since entering the Indian school when he was twelve, Bender played semi-

Carlisle Indian Industrial School, Class of 1902; #5 "Charles Bender" (Cumberland County Historical Society, Carlisle, Pennsylvania).

pro baseball that summer with the Harrisburg Athletic Club to earn a living. So as not to jeopardize his eligibility to play football for Dickinson in the fall, Bender signed and played under the name Charles Albert. Bender said he earned "$160 a month and expenses" during his time as a semi-pro.[47]

Bender, or "Albert," did not experience success in his first couple of mound assignments for the Harrisburg A. C. On June 12 he gave up ten hits in a 9–3 loss to Norristown, but he was a good deal more successful three days later, according to the *Harrisburg Telegraph*. "When Albert was substituted, the Maryland Athletic team could do nothing with him." The score was tied 7–7 when Albert came to mound in the fifth inning and the final count read 8–7, Harrisburg.[48]

A raw talent, Bender had not excited professional baseball scouts when he played at Carlisle, but that changed after Charles Albert pitched against the Chicago National League club in Harrisburg on June 17, 1902. In the lineup that day for the Colts, as the Chicago team was known in those days, were Joe Tinker, Johnny Kling and Bobby Lowe. Bender, or "Albert," allowed the major leaguers only six hits, Tinker and Kling drawing goose eggs. The local crowd of about 3,500 anxious fans watched as a tall teenager with Native

American features displayed the poise of a major leaguer. However, the semi-pro talent on the Harrisburg club could not score against Colts pitcher Jim St. Vrain. Charles Albert found himself behind early when his left fielder let a fly ball get by for a double with two runners on base and he lost 3–0.[49]

Davy Jones, the center fielder on the Chicago club that day, told his manager, Frank Selee, that "the Indian was the best pitcher they faced in a month, but Selee wasn't interested for some reason."[50]

Someone who was interested was a minor league manager named Jesse Frysinger, who recommended the young pitcher to Connie Mack, manager of the Philadelphia club in the two-year-old American League of Base Ball Clubs. "Albert" continued to pitch for the Harrisburg A.C. for the rest of the summer and reinforced the impression that his success against the major leaguers was not a fluke.

On June 22 Bender took the mound against the Cuban X Giants, perhaps the best of the numerous black teams in the country. Newspaper stories from that time were filled with the prejudices of the writers, which was apparent from the report of the game. In the article that read "H.A.C. should have won...," the Harrisburg newspaper concluded, "they were robbed by the dirtiest base ball playing ever seen in this city." The reporter complained that several times the X Giants' third baseman tried to spike the Harrisburg first baseman and once he deliberately pushed him over.

The Harrisburgers lost, 4–3, though "the visitors tried to find Albert's curves but he kept them guessing and several of the darky sluggers gimply fanned."[51]

Two weeks later, Charles Albert got his chance against the only club that could rival the Cuban X Giants for the top spot among African American teams in the eastern United States. Sol White's Philadelphia Giants were in their first year of existence and within a year they would establish supremacy among black baseball teams.

Charles Albert had pitched well enough to beat the Cuban X Giants and was even better against the Philadelphia Giants. The lanky Chippewa pitched no-hit baseball for nine innings, but the score was knotted at 1–1. The Giants had scored their run in the fourth inning after a walk to Sol White, a dropped throw by Bender's first baseman, another base on balls and a passed ball. The Philadelphia Giants won the game in the tenth when John Manning reached base on an error and scored on Jap Payne's extra-base knock.

"It should not have been (a) hit and would not have been had a regular fielder been covering the position," wrote the *Harrisburg Telegram*. "Gallagher misjudged the ball and it went past him, the runner on first base coming home."[52]

Bender was able to save a little money during his time with the Harrisburg A. C., but Albert did later write that he "had to scratch to make ends meet during the winter."[53]

At some point in the latter half of 1902, Charles Albert Bender signed a contract to play with the Philadelphia Athletics in 1903 for $1,800. The specific details about Charley's first contract with the Athletics are sketchy, but according to the story Bender told J. Taylor Spink in 1942, "When Jess Frysinger, scout for Connie Mack, called me aside and asked me if I would like to sign a contract with the Athletics, I was so excited I didn't even ask the terms. I read the figures—$300 a month—and thought I had taken my first step to become a millionaire."[54]

Bender returned to Dickinson in the fall with the intention to join practice with the football team. "After one week, the dean called me in his office and gave me the bad news," Charles recalled. "He told me that the athletic director of Carlisle had called and said that they would sever all relations with Dickinson if I was allowed to play. That meant the end of my schooling."

> I went into town, bought a double-barreled shotgun, some shells, a few clothes and went hunting at Williams Grove.... It was the finest vacation I ever had. I walked seven miles a day to go shooting, either at the North or South Mountain. In December, I went into a jewelry store to learn clock making. Then the day of all days came, when I set off for Jacksonville, Florida, and the Athletics' training camp.[55]

During his professional baseball career, Bender returned to Carlisle on many occasions until the Indian school closed in 1918. He was a hero to the Native American students and his baseball exploits were recounted in *The Arrow*, the school's student-published newspaper. Charles also helped instruct the baseball team on occasion.

Charles Albert Bender was not the first Carlisle Indian to play Organized Baseball. A Seneca named Jacob Jimmerson starred in both football and baseball at the Indian school before he signed a contract to play for the Philadelphia National League club in 1898. Unfortunately, he came up with a sore arm during spring training and never pitched in a regular season major league game. Charles Leroy joined the Buffalo (New York) Eastern League club in 1902, although he would not play in the major leagues until almost three full seasons after Charles Bender made this debut with Philadelphia Athletics.[56]

Several members of the Carlisle baseball team would follow Bender to baseball's major leagues,[57] though none attained anywhere near the success of the Chippewa pitcher from Minnesota. Chief Bender became the most prominent product of the Indian school's goals for the administration to point to until Jim Thorpe's Olympic experience in 1912.

Despite the condemnation of the school's detribalization policy, Charley

Bender would not have become the hero to the nation's Indian population had he not attended the Carlisle School. Without the educational opportunities afforded him because of his Indian heritage, Charles would probably have spent his life in the world of his European father as a laborer or a poor farmer.

◆ 2 ◆

Connie Mack's A's

Baseball was THE American game in the first two decades of the twentieth century. Amateur and school boy baseball flourished at an extraordinary level. The northeastern part of the United States was swarming with amateur baseball teams, and the game was the country's most popular participant sport just as it was the biggest spectator sport on the professional level. The Pennsylvania Amateur Baseball Association sponsored by the *Philadelphia Inquirer* fielded more than 250 teams with 4,000 players.

Philadelphia was a booming metropolis and the nation's third largest city in the early 1900s. It was also home to two major league baseball teams, though the National League's Phillies fell on hard times during the war with the American League.

In 1900, Connie Mack, manager of a minor league team in Milwaukee, was persuaded by Ban Johnson, president of the newly formed American League, to invest in a team to be formed in Philadelphia. This was in direct opposition to the National League Phillies, who had been playing ball there since 1883. The new club in town was called the Athletics, a popular nickname for local teams since 1859.

Though he had a franchise, Mack needed investors. Johnson suggested Connie contact Benjamin F. Shibe, part owner of the A. J. Reach Company, manufacturers of baseball equipment. The new league's president also convinced millionaire coal magnate Charles Somers to join the Philadelphia endeavor. The Philadelphia group organized a corporation with Shibe, as the largest stockholder, club president.

With the investors on board, Connie addressed the urgent need for a ballpark to host his club's home games. "What I know about Philadelphia I learned from walking the streets of the city," he said, "inspecting every vacant lot. We were in such a hurry to get started that we thought we might have to take a city playground."

Mack and Shibe eventually settled on a site at Twenty-ninth and Oxford streets, but, as Connie Mack recalled, "We had just five weeks left after leasing the park to put up stands in order to keep the franchise. It didn't take us very long to construct a single-decked wooden grandstand...."[1]

The site for the new American League park was in the heart of Brewery-town, a north Philadelphia neighborhood located three miles northwest of Independence Hall. The new owners took out a ten-year lease on the vacant property bordered by Twenty-Ninth Street, Columbia Avenue, Thirtieth Street, and Oxford Street. A single-decked grandstand would have a seating capacity of only 9,500, mostly in the bleachers. The wooden grandstand extended down both sides of the infield from home plate; open bleachers continued from the grandstands along both foul lines.[2] Confined within a city block, the A's ballpark had the smallest dimensions in the American League. The hastily constructed ballpark was called Columbia Park and would serve as the home of the Athletics through the 1908 season.

Born Cornelius McGillicuddy, Connie Mack was the son of Irish immigrants, the third of seven children. Cornelius was attracted to baseball at a young age, and played the infield and outfield before becoming his hometown team's regular catcher. However, his father wanted him to stay at home and work in the local shoe factory. After the East Brookfield team won the Central Massachusetts championship in 1883, Cornelius joined his boyhood friend and battery mate William Hogan to play with the Meridian team in the Connecticut State League for the 1884 season at $90 a month. Adopting the shortened name of Connie Mack, he later played for Hartford in the Eastern League. At the end of the 1886 season, Mack was sold to Washington of the National League.[3]

In the days Connie was a catcher for Washington, the rules were far different than those adopted by the turn of the century. Pitchers used an underhand delivery, stood fifty feet from the batting box, and seven balls were required to draw a walk. A batter could even tell the pitcher where he wanted the ball pitched to him.

While he was playing for the Senators, Connie married Margaret Hogan, sister of his friend Willie Hogan. Margaret gave him three children, Marguerite, Roy and Earle, before she died at the age of twenty-six.[4]

Mack was an avid supporter of the National Brotherhood of Professional Players and the revolt that led to the formation of the Players' League (1890) in protest of the National League's ceiling on salaries. Connie signed with the Players' Buffalo club and got a taste of ownership, investing his life savings of $500 in the team. He lost it all when the league folded after only one season.

Assigned to Pittsburgh in 1891, Mack replaced Al Buckenberger as manager during the 1894 season, but the Pirates gave Connie his release following the 1896 campaign. The Milwaukee club of Ban Johnson's Western League was also making a change, and in 1897 Mack became the field manager and ran the business affairs for the team. Connie's years in Milwaukee gave him the opportunity to learn about the business of baseball. Mack's connection with Johnson led to the offer to organize the Philadelphia entry in Ban's new "major league" in 1901, and Connie began a fifty-year reign in that city, both in the dugout and front office.[5]

Mack began his first season in Philadelphia owning twenty-five percent of the city's American League club and eventually he became the principal owner. With baseball his only business, gate receipts and concession sales were the sole sources of capital he had to run the club. Connie did not take much money out of the game for personal benefit and later financial problems forced him to break up two of the greatest teams ever assembled.

"Behind the saintly, grandfatherly appearance of the 6'1" 150-lb., erect Mr. Mack, there was a complex personality, a blend of patience and impetuosity, kindness and stubbornness, tightfistedness and generosity," wrote Mack biographer Norman L. Macht. "He never raised his voice and seldom confronted a player in front of his teammates, but he could put a man in his place with a cutting sarcastic comment. He disdained swearing, but did sometimes cut loose with a salty barrage. To strangers of any age who approached him in a hotel lobby or dining room, he could be courtly and pleasant."[6]

From the start of his tenure as manager of the Athletics, Connie Mack did not wear a baseball uniform. Even on the hottest of days, he wore a three-piece suit and starched shirt collar while directing a game. Fifty years later, he still dressed the same way, even when it went out of fashion. After Connie reached the bench, he rarely left it, coaching the entire game from there. (There was no dugout at Columbia Park or in most major league parks in the early days.)

When the National League refused to grant equal status to the upstart American League in 1901, the new league's owners went about plundering the older circuit's rosters by offering higher salaries. The American League raiders were aided by the National League's salary cap that mandated a player could earn no more than $2,400 for the baseball season. According to the *Spalding Guide*, seventy-four active National League players jumped to the American League, most of them for the promise of higher wages and no salary cap.

Connie Mack raided the cross-town Phillies for the nucleus of his 1901 team. His biggest prize was one of baseball's greatest players, Phillies star second baseman Napoleon "Larry" Lajoie, who jumped to the Athletics for an offer of $4,000 in salary. Two of the Phillies starting pitchers, Chick Fraser and Bill Bernhard, also signed to play for Connie Mack, and veteran third baseman Lafayette Napoleon Cross was pilfered from the Brooklyn National League club. Catcher Mike Powers, outfielder Dave Fultz, and first baseman Ralph "Socks" Seybold were brought to the A's from Mack's 1900 Milwaukee club.[7]

Connie Mack also developed new avenues for recruits not often explored by most baseball clubs. Before the turn of the century, professional baseball was an opportunity the young sons of immigrants used to escape the poverty suffered by their peers. There were few collegians in the game in 1900; men like Christy Mathewson, a graduate of Bucknell, Pittsburgh's Ginger Beaumont from Beloit, and Brooklyn's Hughie Jennings, who had a law degree from Cornell, were exceptions. As baseball salaries increased in the early 1900s, generational Americans and more collegians began to appear on major league rosters.

Mack shrewdly tapped this unique source for players. He worried that signing college players would drive up salaries, but continued to scout eastern schools for talent, even when observers and fellow managers like Hughie Jennings ridiculed the practice. Among Connie's first players who had attended college were Eddie Plank, Gettysburg College; Mike Powers of Notre Dame; Andy Coakley, Holy Cross; and Dave Fultz, a Columbia law school graduate. When Detroit traded Ira Thomas to Philadelphia in 1908, the catcher was apprehensive about "going to Connie Mack's team of college boys." Part of the reason Mack traded the talented and illiterate Joe Jackson in 1908 was that he did not fit in with his college-educated teammates.

The inaugural American League season began in Philadelphia on April 26, 1901, when an immense crowd swamped little Columbia Park. The announced attendance was 10,524, but almost an additional 4,000 made it inside. The *Washington Post* reported:

> As early as 12 o'clock the big gates were besieged by impatient hundreds, and when the flood gates were opened a half hour later the stream of humanity surged into the American League Park, filling the stands to overflowing and circling the outfield six deep.... Those who were not lucky enough to find seats quickly availed themselves of the limited accommodations offered by railings, until even these were exhausted. The fence around the park itself was then attacked by daring climbers, and a convenient ledge about ten feet from the ground was quickly lined by enthusiastic fans.[8]

Despite Lajoie's three hits, the Athletics lost the game to Washington, 5–1, but the American League had won the hearts of Philadelphia fans. Three members of the Athletics Opening Day lineup, Socks Seybold, Lave Cross and Doc Powers, would remain with the club long enough to experience two American League championships.

Connie Mack was dissatisfied with his options at the first base position and wound up with outfielder Socks Seybold at the first sack for the first month of the season. Mack remembered a Philadelphia-born player named Harry Davis from his days as manager of the Pittsburgh club and persuaded him to join the Athletics that May.

Davis' father died when Harry was five and the youngster was sent to

Girard College, actually a Philadelphia institution for orphans and fatherless boys. There, young Davis became a catcher for the Girard baseball team. After graduation, he got a job as a bank clerk and later worked for the Pennsylvania Railroad. He played ball for the Pennsy team, a strong independent outfit, and soon was signed to a contract with Providence of the Eastern League. Davis bounced around between National League clubs and the minors during the late 1890s until he finally decided to settle down in a more secure position as an accountant with the Pennsylvania Railroad. In 1901 Harry accepted Mack's offer and became the Athletics first baseman for the next ten seasons. After the A's released Lave Cross in 1905, Davis became team captain and held the post until he moved to Cleveland as manager in 1912. Harry's nickname in the clubhouse became "Jasper," a moniker picked from a popular minstrel song of the day.[9]

Davis became a leader on the field who could take charge of the team as acting manager when Mack was away. Harry coached first base when not batting and after he became captain he would position the team's fielders dependent upon the batter, pitcher or game situation. Connie Mack would still make the decision on pitching changes, but it was up to Davis to implement them from his first base position. Harry became a mentor for many of the young players who were central to the Athletics' dynasty in the second decade of the century. He picked keen observers of the game like Tully Hartsel, Charles Bender and later Jack Coombs for base coaches. These coaches were so adept at reading the opposing team's signals, their work became an integral part of the A's success.

Over the first month of the 1901 season, the Athletics outdrew the Phillies, but attendance tailed off thereafter and they attracted only 206,319 fans (28,600 less than the Phillies) for the season. Yet the thrifty owners still managed a tidy profit. Though the Athletics drew well throughout the remainder of the decade, the little ballpark's meager seating capacity could not support enough people to suit Mack or team president Ben Shibe. The park's gates often had to be shut after all the seats had been sold, leaving thousands of fans on the outside. This was especially a problem during the championship seasons of 1902 and 1905.

The 1901 Philadelphia Athletics finished in fourth place, and a year later, reinforced with three more stars from the cross-town Phillies, a championship seemed possible. Mack again raided the Phillies' roster, signing right fielder Elmer Flick, shortstop Monte Cross, and pitcher Bill Duggleby.

During the spring of 1902, the Philadelphia National League club obtained injunctions to prevent former Phillies Napoleon Lajoie (who batted .422 with the Athletics in 1901), Bill Bernard and Chick Fraser from playing professional baseball in Pennsylvania with any team other than the Phillies. Mack recalled that, upon hearing the news while in spring training at Chapel Hill, North Carolina, "I felt as though they had swept my ball club right from under me."[10]

Essentially, the players became free agents who could negotiate with the Phillies or any American League club not based in Pennsylvania. Pitchers Fraser, a twenty-game winner for the A's in 1901, and Duggleby went back to the Phillies shortly after the 1902 season began. The Pennsylvania Supreme Court's decision could only be enforced within that state, so three of the former Phillies—Lajoie, the best second baseman in the game; Flick; and seventeen-game winner Bernard—signed contracts to play for the Cleveland American League franchise. Monte Cross, for whom the National Leaguers expressed little interest, remained with the Athletics. Connie Mack would have to reconstruct his team after only one season. Building around Plank, Lave Cross, Seybold, Powers and Harry Davis, Mack assembled not only a competitive club, but a pennant winner.

After the injunction, the only reliable pitcher left to the A's was rookie left-hander Eddie Plank, who had been signed fresh off the campus at Gettysburg College in 1901. Cleveland sent Mack a catcher, Osee Schreckengost, and Boston chipped in pitcher Pete Hustling.

Prior to the 1902 season, Mack signed a small package of dynamite in 5'5" Tully Hartsel, who jumped from the National League's Chicago Orphans, with whom he batted .335 in 1901. The lefty hitting outfielder led the American League in runs scored, bases on balls, and stolen bases in his first season with the A's. Hartsel would be Mack's leadoff batter for ten seasons and capitalized on his size to lead the American League in walks five times.

Acting on a tip, Mack signed second baseman Danny Murphy, who was playing in Norwich, Connecticut. Murphy batted .336 with Norwich in 1901 and was hitting .462 after 49 games a year later when he was purchased by the A's. While he was no Napoleon Lajoie, Murphy anchored Connie Mack's infield and batted a robust .313 in his rookie season. In his first game with the Athletics on July 8, 1902, in Boston, Murphy made six hits in six times at bat, one of which was an inside-the-park home run off Cy Young. Danny would prove to be a solid player for Philadelphia through the 1913 season.

Mack and Shibe also made improvements on Columbia Park before the club's second season. The left field bleachers were extended twenty-five feet, which greatly increased the seating capacity. In 1902 the club's attendance would be more than double that of the previous year.

A week after he jumped the American League's Baltimore franchise in July 1902 to become manager of the New York Giants, John McGraw had plenty to say about what he thought of Ban Johnson's American League. McGraw's remarks were printed in the newspapers and in *Sporting Life*:

I say the American League is a loser and has been from the start and I got out of it because there is no money to be made in it and because it is dominated by a clique who use every effort in behalf of the Chicago, Boston and Philadelphia clubs.... The Philadelphia Athletic Club is not making any money. It has a big white elephant on its hands. The grounds are leased for ten years at the rate of $7000 a year and the principle backer of the club has had all that he wants of it, because he cannot see a penny coming in at the gate. No money was made last year and no money will be made this year.[11]

Connie Mack's response was published in the newspapers.

McGraw says that the Athletic club is a white elephant, that is, not making any money; that it did not make any last year, and that its principal stockholder has all that he wants of it. There is a quick way to settle this. I will bet McGraw $1000 — and I think that I can get the coin — that the Athletics made money last year and are making money this year. Insofar as the dissatisfaction of Benjamin Shibe, the principle stockholder, is concerned, that is another lie out of the solid. Not once has Mr. Shibe shown any feeling in the matter other than pleasure with the result of his investment. It is a 100 to 1 shot, and he is thoroughly satisfied.[12]

The press quickly played up McGraw's remark. One Philadelphia cartoonist pictured a crowd in Columbia Park feeding peanuts to a white elephant. In his autobiography, Mack described the decision to adopt the white elephant as the insignia for his club: "Boys," I said, "we accept McGraw's appellation. We will name our Philadelphia A's the White Elephants."[13]

The turning point in the 1902 American League pennant race came that June when Connie Mack convinced the highly talented but troublesome George "Rube" Waddell, who was pitching in California, to join the Athletics. Waddell pitched for Mack at Milwaukee in 1900, so the A's manager was aware of the baggage that accompanied the zany left-hander. When Rube began having second thoughts about leaving the Los Angeles Looloos that summer, two Pinkerton guards were hired to escort the pitcher from California to Philadelphia.

Though Rube did not pitch his first game with Philadelphia until July 1, the temperamental hurler compiled twenty-four victories and led the league in strikeouts. Mack, realizing that the Athletics' regular catcher,

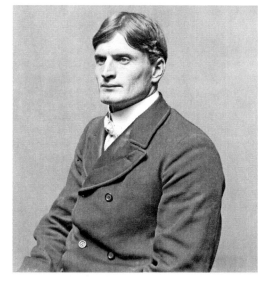

George Edward "Rube" Waddell, studio portrait (circa 1901) (Chicago History Museum).

Mike Powers, wasn't compatible with Waddell, made Osee Schreckengost Rube's personal receiver. The two free spirits became a solid battery for as long as the pair remained with the club.

With Waddell's pitching and a solid offense, the Athletics won sixteen of seventeen games at one point in August to take a firm hold on first place. But by the beginning of September, Boston had pulled within one game of the first-place Athletics.

The Mackmen came charging back, wining two from Boston as Plank and Waddell beat Bill Dinneen and Cy Young. The Athletics returned home and swept three straight games with Washington, after which Boston came to town for a series in which they had to win three of the four games to stay in serious contention. In the first game, Rube again defeated Young. The clubs split the next two contests before Waddell came back to win the final game of the series, virtually assuring Philadelphia the American League championship.

When the rebuilt A's clinched the 1902 American League flag on September 25, a fan presented the club with a blue field flag with a white elephant in the center and stars and stripes in the corner. The banner was to fly over Columbia Park until the championship pennant was received from the American League, but the elephant flag was so popular it continued to be displayed for years.[14]

Mack had given Philadelphia its first baseball championship since the Athletics of the old American Association finished first in 1883. Eddie Plank won 20 games and Husting contributed fourteen victories. Six A's batted over .300, including stocky outfielder Socks Seybold, who also slugged sixteen home runs, partly due to the cozy dimensions of Columbia Park.

A parade to honor the American League champions was held on Broad Street. Connie Mack and the players rode in open carriages and some 350 clubs, organizations, and bands participated.

Sporting Life reported, "All along the parade route of the parade every inch of standing room was taken up and every window, fence top, tree, pole or other place of vantage was occupied by sightseers."[15]

Among the most memorable entrants in the parade were several effigies of Mugsy McGraws, hay-wagons of "Rubes," and the prominent black baseball club known as the Philadelphia Giants, "who carried their canes with a highly regimental air." There were numerous marching bands, including the Katzen-jammer Band, which played the official tune of the affair, "Hail! Hail! The Gang's All Here."[16]

The National League champion Pittsburgh Pirates challenged the Athletics to a series of exhibition games following the regular season. For a while, it looked like the fans' dream of seeing the two major league champions play one another would come about. In the end, there was still fear of "player robbing" (wooing players to jump leagues) when teams visited rival cities.

Instead, Pirates owner Barney Dreyfuss agreed to have his club face a contingent of all-stars from the opposing circuit in a best-of-five series, beginning in Pittsburgh on October 7. There was no big purse at stake or a trophy to win. Dubbed the "All-Americans," the American League assembled a squad that included first baseman Harry Davis, shortstop Monte Cross and outfielder Tully Hartsel of the Athletics. The All-Americans also recruited Nap Lajoie, but baseball's premier second baseman would not appear in games played in Pittsburgh because he still risked arrest if he took the field in a Pennsylvania city.

The Pirates won the series with two victories to one for the All-Americans and there was one tie. The only American League win was Cy Young's 1–0 shutout in the fourth contest. The series was poorly attended, partly due to dreary weather, and those games have received little attention as the first on the field break in hostilities between the warring leagues.

Near the end of 1902, the National League, losing money and players, grew weary of the war with the American League and sued for a peace agreement. A National Agreement was concluded in January 1903, in which the National League acknowledged the major league status of the American League and both circuits agreed to respect player contracts of the member clubs.

On November 1, 1902, Mack speculated about his club's prospects for 1903: "Our only weakness is in the box. The loss of Husting was a blow. But I think I will be able to get together a good staff. Albert Bender, the Indian, who pitched for Harrisburg this year under the name of Albert, should help us."[17]

♦ 3 ♦

Walking on Air

Charles Bender began his major league baseball career in 1903 at the age of eighteen without ever having played in the minor leagues. His first spring training with the Philadelphia Athletics would be in Jacksonville, Florida. Young Charles traveled to the port of New York City, where the 310-foot steamship *Arapahoe* was loading passengers.

"I can still see the ship as it stood at the dock," Bender recalled years later. "It looked like a ferry boat to me. As I walked up to the gangplank, I heard someone say: 'There's the big chief.' I looked up and saw three young fellows—Harry Davis, Monte Cross and Danny Hoffman—staring at me from the top deck. That's how I got the nickname of Chief."

That first ocean voyage was a rough experience for the rookie. Bender acknowledged, "If it hadn't been for Harry Davis, who took me in tow, told me what to do and looked after me like a father, I think I might have died—or at least have been quite seasick. Harry was so good to me. I almost learned to worship him, I took his advice on anything and everything."[1]

The team's facilities in Florida were a far cry from what training camps would become years later. "Connie put us up in the Casino," Bender remembered. "It had been a big gambling hall the year before. Five or six of us slept in a room made by erecting partitions in the big barn-like structure. There were four rooms in all. Our beds were cots and our 'private baths' were pitchers and wash bowls."

"We trained at Phoenix Park that spring," he added. "What a spot! We dressed in the attic of a two-story house and our lockers were nails in the wall. Our only shower bath was a hot sulphur spring that ran up through a pipe and came down on our heads in a steady stream."[2]

Baseball clubs did not have a great deal of money to spend on training facilities in those days. Mack had an arrangement with a second-rate establishment called Wolfe's for the players' meals. Bender believed Wolfe's was where the term "baseball steak" originated.

Every time we ordered a steak, Wolfe would walk back to the kitchen and shout: "One baseball steak!" The next thing we would hear would be the sound of the mallet hitting the steak. It was a wooden block with small spikes in it and served to mash and at the same time cut the meat.

Osee Schreck and Rube Waddell were with us and it was in Wolfe's that Schreck first nailed a steak to the wall. It created quite a commotion and for a time it looked as if we might lose our eating place, but Connie smoothed things over. We weren't as fortunate a few years later when Schreck did the trick in a swanky New Orleans hotel and we were invited to leave — and the evacuation order stuck.[3]

At ten o'clock on the last day of February, the Athletics loaded into electric cars for the twenty-five-minute trip to the baseball field for their first practice. When the A's were divided into two teams for scrimmages a few days later, there weren't enough position players to field two complete squads, so Connie Mack donned a uniform and played first base, thereby encouraging good work from each side.[4]

Waddell wasn't present for workouts when spring training began; Rube and his roommate, Osee Schreckengost, left for Orlando prior to the start of camp. The eccentric pitcher tried alligator wrestling at a city park, and then the pair went swamping. Rube was injured when he reached into the water and a gator bit a chuck out of his hand. The left-hander arrived back at camp with a bandage on his right hand. Things were never routine or quiet on the club as long as Waddell and Schreck were around.

Bender also recalled that Rube attempted to commit suicide that spring after he saw the girl he was sweet on with another man.

Rube said he was heart-broken. He started to cry, leaped dramatically to his feet and exclaimed: "I'm going to kill myself. I'm going to jump off the dock and drown."

He rushed out of the place with Schreck at his heels. He raced to the dock, ran to the end and jumped in. But the tide was out and instead of the usual four or five feet of water, there was only about six inches of water and two feet of muck.

Rube hit the muck head-first, buried himself and almost choked to death before Schreck and some dockhands could drag him out. He didn't threaten to commit suicide by drowning for some time. Waddell could swim like a fish — in water, but not in mud.[5]

An opening on the club's pitching staff was available for "Albert" Bender because Mack needed a replacement for right-hander Bert Husting and his twenty-seven starts in 1902 for the A's. A star college athlete in football and baseball for the University of Wisconsin, Husting left baseball following the 1902 season to pursue a law career. Another pitcher, Andy Coakley, was coaching at Holy Cross and would not be able to join the Athletics until the collegiate baseball season concluded.

What the Athletics had in Charles Albert Bender was a talented but raw pitcher who was a dedicated student of the game. The teenager threw a variety of curves and had great control for one so young, but most impressive was Bender's fastball that came toward the plate "first like a cannonball and next just edges by the plate."[6] Professional baseball clubs did not employ pitching coaches at that time, so Bender was tutored in his craft by Harry Davis and catcher Schreckengost.

After two weeks of workouts, the *Philadelphia North American* reported, "In the afternoon Bender and (Clarence) Quinn did the pitching and their work was excellent. Bender particularly distinguished himself. He had lots of speed, fielded his position finely, and was warmly congratulated by Mack for his performance."[7]

Before the team left the South, Connie Mack reiterated, "I think I will be able to put together a good staff. Albert Bender, who pitched for the Harrisburg A. C. last season under the name of Charles Albert, should help us." Charles Albert's teammates called him "Big Chief" that spring. Gradually, it was shortened to "Chief" and the sobriquet stuck for the remainder of Bender's life.

As a result of the recent peace agreement between the American and National leagues, the pre-season would be completed with a series of interleague exhibition games between the Athletics and the Phillies. The two teams were scheduled to play four games at the Phillies' home park and three at Columbia Park, but on the eve of the first game, the Athletics players went on strike. Since the players' contracts did not include compensation for preseason exhibitions, the A's, through team captain Lave Cross, announced they would not play unless they received twenty percent of the gate receipts. The press was hostile toward the players, calling them "Mercenary" and "Foolhardy," while the *Sporting News* editorialized, "It is unfortunate that the players should cheapen themselves by wishing to be rewarded for doing their duty."[8]

The players finally agreed to forego a share of the gate and play a five-game series in return for a portion of money derived from exhibition games played during the regular season. The defending American League champion Athletics then went out and lost four out of the five games to the lowly Phillies, a seventh-place club in both 1902 and 1903.

The opening game of the city series on April 6 drew only 5,600 shivering fans to Columbia Park. For nine innings, Rube Waddell matched zeros with the Phils' Fred Mitchell, who had played for the Athletics in 1902. Waddell allowed two runs in the top of the tenth and the American League castoff, Mitchell, completed his shutout in the bottom of the frame.

The second game, played at the National League park on Broad Street and Huntington Avenue before 6,640 fans, resulted in another ten-inning victory for the Phillies. Athletics shortstop Monte Cross was ejected from the game in the third inning for throwing the ball during a violent argument with umpire Gus Moran. Charles Bender was sent in to play shortstop and, on his very first chance, the rookie booted a ground ball and made a wild throw that led to two Phillies runs. Charley's failure to make a play on a ground ball in the eighth, "another chance that Monte would have smothered," allowed the Phillies to score the tying run, and two innings later three singles, "two of which went right by the paralyzed Bender," gave the Nationals a 6–5 victory.[9]

Charles Albert's troubles afield led *Sporting Life* to editorialize, "The Athletics' Indian pitcher, Bender, in practice can play short field like a house a fire; but when it comes to a real game — well, it's too painful for Athletic rooters to dwell upon."[10] Bender never played shortstop for Connie Mack again, though he did manage to get into three games at first base during the 1903 season.

The National Leaguers also won the third game in ten innings. Bender relieved "Highball" Wilson and pitched well but to no avail. Charles Dryden referred to Bender as "Chief" in his report of the affair for the *Philadelphia North American*.

> The aborigine's debut was eminently successful. He developed terrific speed and Powers had all he could do to hold him. One wicked inshoot narrowly missed hitting (Shad) Barry in the head. The moleskin hero went down as though he were once more on the gridiron....
>
> Only three safeties were made off Bender in his five innings of service, but these were bunched in the eighth and resulted in two unearned runs. The "chief" sent two men to base on balls. His handling of two bunts and lightening throws to first and second, mark him a fielding pitcher far out of the ordinary.[11]

Rube Waddell came back to win game four, but the Athletics lost the fifth and final game in ten innings. Charley did get a tune up for the regular season in an exhibition game at Jersey City on April 17. The Eastern League Skeeters were no match for Bender and the Athletics, falling 13–1.

The Athletics opened the 1903 regular season in Boston on Monday, April 20, which was also Patriot's Day for the locals. The teams played a morning game before a disappointing crowd of 8,376 fans and the Bostons beat Rube Waddell, 9–4.

Eddie Plank started the afternoon game for the A's with almost 20,000 Beantown fans on hand. Over the first six innings, Cy Young allowed only one Philadelphia base runner. After Plank was knocked out of the game in the fifth inning, eighteen-year-old Charles Bender took the ball in his first major league game for what appeared to be a mop-up task.

"Golly, I was scared," recalled the rookie hurler. "My first major league game and against Cy Young!"[12]

"Bender, the young Indian, was sent among the cruel palefaces," reported the *North American*. "He had a uphill job to start with, making his debut in swift company at a time when the game was apparently dead and buried. The way he behaved puts a new red goose feather in his head dress.... Bender fanned such sluggers as Ferris and Freeman, fielded his position, and made a hit."[13]

The Athletics were down 6–0 when they came to bat in the seventh inning, and Boston's Cy Young appeared to be in complete control. The *Sporting News* reported that a storm of singles and triples (one hit drifted into the overflow standing in front of the left field wall for a ground-rule triple) by the A's produced six runs in that round, "Cy's name was changed to Sigh, and the score was tied. Further swatting off the offerings of Young and Hughes in the two remaining rounds produced enough runs to win the game especially as the Indian Bender, who had been substituted for Plank early in the contest, had served a stop notice on the Boston's batting."[14]

In the ninth inning, Charles Albert singled for the first of his 243 major league hits and came around to score on base hits by Hartsel and Davis. Though the rookie gave up a run to Boston in the ninth, Philadelphia's 10–7 victory gave Bender his first major league win.

The always low-key Connie Mack congratulated his young pitcher simply, saying, "Nice work, Albert." Charley admitted, "That night I felt like I was walking on air."[15]

At the time Charles Bender came to the major leagues, pitchers had a distinct advantage over batters, because, unlike today, a fresh white ball was only in play for a short time. Umpires were not allowed to replace a banged-up ball and fans had to return balls hit into the stands. As a result, pitchers had the advantage of working much of a game with a baseball darkened by use, dirt, saliva, and scrapes, either accidental or by design. As the innings wore on, batters were attempting to hit a ball softened from the beating it took during a game. Although pitchers benefited from the "dead" ball, a mis-shapen ball often took odd bounces on the way to an infielder. Furthermore, the infields of that day were not the manicured rugs of today, but were full of rocks, pebbles and divots. When a new ball was put into the game, pitchers and infielders quickly smeared it with dirt to make it easier to grip.

Baseball games in the first decade of the twentieth century featured singles, bunts, sacrifices, hit-and-run plays and stolen bases. Batters choked up on the bat and attempted to punch the pitch between the infielders. They seldom swung for the fences since the strategy of the era dictated the game be played one base at a time. As a result, outfielders played very shallow and occasionally threw runners out on force plays. Extra-base hits were not the norm and a home run hit over the outfield fence was a rare occurrence.

When major league teams went on the road in 1903, they usually took a squad of only about fourteen or fifteen players, including pitchers. Ballparks did not have locker rooms for the visiting teams, forcing players to dress at their hotel and ride to the park in open horse-drawn carriages called "tally-hos." Sometimes, the opposition's procession served as fodder for overzealous home team supporters.

The Athletics played their formal home opener on April 22 and a crowd of 13,578 watched Philadelphia beat Boston, 6–1, behind Rube Waddell's pitching. Before the contest, American League president Ban Johnson presented the 1902 championship pennant to the Athletics.

When the New York American League team came to Columbia Park a week later, the Gotham press was driven to hyperbole when they first spotted Connie Mack's new Native American pitcher. "Of all freakish baseball organizations, the palm must be awarded to Mack for his collection," noted the *Evening Sun*.

> In his pitching department, he has Rube Waddell, a fellow whose eccentric ideas cannot be explained. Then he has an Indian, a real live Indian, one with red skin and straight black hair that looks like a wig made from a horse's tail. His name is Bender, a good name for a pitcher, at that. Well, this fellow is just six feet three inches in a baseball uniform. If he gets his loose jointed bones piled right he probably would touch a seven foot mark. He warmed up today, and his antics were great to anybody that has a sense of humor. His right foot he raises before he delivers the ball. It wriggles just like a toy snake that's worked by a spring in the tail. His foot hides his face to the batter. That's puzzling, to begin with. Well, that's the fellow Connie Mack had a mind to trying out against the Griffithsons.[16]

When young Bender took the mound for his "tryout" that afternoon, the joke was on "the Griffmen." The *North American* noted, "The pitching of Bender delighted the crowd, which cheered him on to do his utmost. He employed speed and a curve over which he had excellent control.... On several occasions he had himself in a hole — three balls and no strikes — but the tall, dark boy pulled himself together and made the Yorkers hit it."[17]

Charles Bender would get his first complete game major league win, a 6–0 shutout against the Highlanders that afternoon. Charley struck out three, allowed only four hits, all singles, and no opposing batter made it as far as third base. He did, however, hit two batters and walked one. The losing pitcher was the New York manager and future Hall of Famer Clark Griffith.

"The New York players were simply powerless before his erratically speedy delivery," wrote the *New York Times*. "He was somewhat erratic, but this only augmented his effectiveness. The New York players had a wholesome fear of his wicked in shoots, as he gave Ganzel a terrific shot in the back in the second inning. He also hit Williams, and compelled most of the other batsmen to dodge some of his curves that went nearer their persons than the plate."[18]

"It looks from Bender's two attempts as if the Indian was assuredly a success now," pronounced the *Sporting News*. "That's strange, for Bender was far from being considered a star when he pitched for Carlisle, Dickinson and the

Harrisburg A. C. last year. He has all the ear marks of a comer, and has shown in the tight places that he has been in, that he is not lacking in sand."[19]

On April 29, in another game against the Highlanders at Columbia Park, Connie Mack sent Charles up to pinch-hit against left-hander Jesse Tannehill with two out, the bases filled and three runs needed to tie the score. After he took two called strikes, Bender lined the third pitch he saw for a single, driving home two of the runners.[20] Philadelphia lost the game, 5–4, but Charles fortified his manager's respect for him as a hitter, and Bender would be used as a pinch-hitter several times over the next eight seasons.

Now in Connie Mack's regular pitching rotation, Bender pitched three times during the first week in May. He lost closely contested games with Boston's Bill Dinneen and the Highlanders' Jack Chesbro. Then on May 7, his teammates made it easy for the rookie, scoring 19 runs, and Bender coasted to a victory over Washington.

After that good start, the next couple of weeks were quite frustrating for the young pitcher — in more ways than on the field. On May 12 in Chicago, Albert took a 2–1 lead into the bottom of the ninth inning with first place in the American League on the line. However, the White Sox tied the score on a double, a sacrifice bunt and a sacrifice fly by Eddie McFarland. The game then moved on to the tenth inning.

The first Chicago batter, Cozy Dolan, walloped a long drive into left field, but the speedy Danny Hoffman hauled it down after a long run. Charley's respite did not last long when the next batter, Fielder Jones, laced a drive that went to the left field fence for a two-base hit. Up next was the Chicago manager, Nixey Callahan, who had replaced Danny Green in the lineup after the latter was drilled in the back with a Bender fastball earlier in the game. The contest was decided moments later when Callahan lined a Bender pitch to center that Pickering, in his haste to make a quick play to the plate, let the ball go between his legs.

Two days later, the Athletics concluded the Chicago series and took the train to St. Louis for a game the next afternoon. During the nighttime trip aboard a Pullman car, Bender left his sleeping compartment to visit the washroom. He left his wallet in a coat left hanging on the rail that supported the curtain. When Charles returned to his bunk, he discovered that his wallet containing ten $10 bills was missing. When the train reached its destination, the St. Louis police searched the Pullman's passengers but the cash was not found.[21]

Charles Dryden, who was described by his employers as "the *North American's* baseball expert and humorist," wrote an account of the theft for his paper. "Big Chief Bender of the Chippewas, has lost his wampum belt, valued at $100, and the mishap entailed no end of trouble. The Indian's wealth got away from him in a Wabash sleeper early this morning. All hands were routed from sweet dreams while the train was passing through the flooded district of East St. Louis."[22]

Two days later, Charles Albert lost a 2–0 decision to the Browns in St. Louis when a wild throw by his catcher let in the only runs of the contest. To add insult to Charley's woes, an unflattering and derogatory cartoon accompanied Dryden's account of the stolen wallet in the May 28 edition of the *Philadelphia North America*. A famous New York-based editorial cartoonist named Charles Nelan portrayed the nineteen-year-old ballplayer as a sinister character, dressed in rather slipshod Indian costume, on his hands and knees in the aisle of a railroad passenger car looking for his "wampum belt."[23]

Bender's personal losing streak had reached four games when he took the mound in Washington on June 2. On that day Charley won another easy game over the lowly Senators, 12–3. That victory started him on a five-game winning streak during which he would allow only one run in each of the final four games.

Wrote a reporter in the *Washington Post*, "In his last game here the young chap stood up like a statue under a perfect bedlam of war whoops and Indian yells from the bleachers and grandstands that would have shaken a hardened veteran at the game. Yet never a kink appeared in one of his long straight black hairs. He appeared to get just a little cooler as the game progressed, and in the most trying places pitched his best ball."[24]

On June 18, the Athletics traveled to Toledo for an unusual Sunday game. Because Sunday baseball was illegal in Detroit, the contest would be considered a home game for the Tigers. Bender defeated the Bengals, 7–3, before a crowd of 4,500.

Existing "blue laws" in Philadelphia and much of the East prohibited the playing of professional baseball on the Sabbath during the entirety of Bender's career with the Athletics. These laws were a collection of ordinances dating back to 1794 that regulated drinking, gambling, and other unsavory activities that might take place on the Sabbath. The only American League cities that permitted Sunday baseball were Chicago and St. Louis. (Detroit lifted the ban in 1911.) In order to reap the benefits from large weekend crowds, Shibe and Mack worked to legalize Sunday professional baseball games until the City of Philadelphia made it legal in 1935.

Drinking alcoholic beverages at the ball game was also prohibited. Although there were no beer sales at Columbia Park, a large number of taverns were scattered throughout the neighborhood and ten or so breweries were located only a few blocks from the ballpark. Oftentimes during an afternoon game, a western breeze would push the smell of fermenting mash and freshly brewed beer over the top of the grandstand into the environs of Columbia Park.

Andy Coakley, who had been coaching the Holy Cross team, joined the

Athletics in Chicago on June 20. The natty collegian, considered the "Beau Brummel" of baseball, was purchased a year earlier by the Athletics based on the recommendation of D. A. "Denny" Long, former owner of the Toledo Mud Hens and an associate of Ban Johnson. Long was an astute judge of baseball talent and sold several players to Connie Mack and other professional clubs. Long said that the most money he ever received for a player was the $1,750 he garnered for Andy Coakley, who went on to become a twenty-game winner for the Philadelphia Athletics in 1905.[25]

Coakley became Charles Bender's roommate when the Athletics were on the road. Andy played for Holy Cross in 1901 and 1902 when their baseball coach was Jack Pappaleau, a teammate of the celebrated American Indian outfielder Louis Sockalexis at the school in 1895 and 1896. Later, as coach, Jack told Coakley and the other players of Sockalexis' prowess in baseball, track and football while at the school.[26]

During the summer of 1903 a reporter interviewed Charles Bender for a biographical profile to be published in the *Washington Post*. The scribe's observations of the rookie hurler in the piece entitled "Athletic Pitcher Bender Promises to Become a Celebrated Twirler" gave an idea of the young Chippewa's attitudes at that time. The word "Chief" was never mentioned in the piece, as Charles Albert was usually referred to as "Bender" or "The

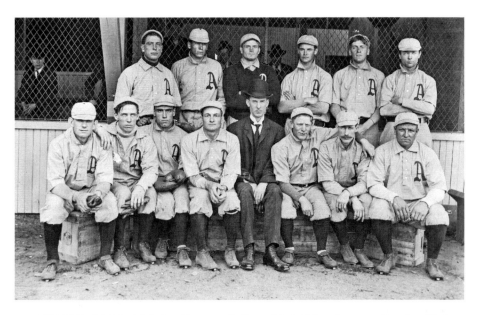

1903 Philadelphia Athletics: Top row (left to right): Schreckengost, Bender, Waddell, Henley, Hoffman, Davis. Sitting (left to right): Murphy, Plank, Powers, L. Cross, Mack, Hartsel, M. Cross, Seybold (Chicago History Museum).

Indian" in the papers outside of Philadelphia during his first couple of seasons with the Athletics.

"It's pretty hard work to get Bender to tell you much about himself," wrote the *Post* reporter. "He's a sort of stoic. Modesty is his characteristic trait. He is not a talker; rather, he impressed the chance acquaintance as the typical Indian, quiet, reserved, and thinking every minute.....

"If you ask him for a picture, he laughs at you. That's about the only time he ever does laugh much. He is not famous as a conversationalist. In true Indian fashion, he wraps himself in his blanket of modesty and does not say much, but 'ugh.'"[27]

Bender's best game in 1903 came on July 21 at Columbia Park against the St. Louis Browns. "Wee Willie" Sudhoff matched Bender's scoreless pitching except in the third inning, when the Athletics scored the only run of the contest on Seybold's two-out single. Bender faced only twenty-eight opposing batters and only three Browns reached base, two on singles and one on a walk. Bender's dominance was also evident from his seven assists, one more than his infielders combined.

"Mr. Bender, with faultless support, pitched the smartest game of his career," pronounced Charles Dryden. "He had the Browns in the Haunted Swing all the way. One man reached third base.... Mr. Bender wild-pitched him there in the sixth with one out, and the next two skied. In all but two rounds the side perished in order. That is pitching much."[28]

The Athletics held first place in the 1903 American League standings until June 23 when a 6–5 loss in St. Louis allowed Boston to edge ahead in the standings. By the end of July, the American League pennant race had evolved into a two-team affair between the Athletics and Boston. A stretch of six straight games between the two contenders beginning in Philadelphia on August 5 would go a long way in settling the championship.

Philadelphia went into the first game of the crucial set trailing Boston by 2 games. Waddell lost the opener, putting the home team's hopes on the shoulders of the club's youngest pitcher on August 6.

Bender was matched against the venerable Cy Young, on his way to a twenty-eight-victory season. After allowing a first-inning run, the younger hurler held the Boston nine in check over the next five innings while his teammates amassed seven hits and four runs. There was a scary moment in the fourth when one of Charley's fast ones knocked Boston shortstop Fred Parent out cold. For a few moments, Parent lay there while no one seemed to know what to do. Freddy soon revived himself without medical aid and, "after his head had been screwed on straight," he wobbled down to first base.

Philadelphia took a 4–3 lead into the eighth inning and, with skies threatening, Boston was retired without scoring. When the final out in the eighth was registered, umpire James Hassett decided it was too dark to continue play. Young stood patiently on the mound while Boston manager Jimmy Collins protested the umpire's decision to call the game, but to no avail.

"It was pretty dark at that moment, but the gloom was nothing to the black cloud that settled upon the alabaster brow of James Collins," wrote the *North American*. "Now, the 9861 spectators did not grumble. They had seen the game pass successfully beyond the rain check period, and were satisfied. The only ones who would have liked to remain longer were a wagonload of gamblers the police pinched and hauled away during the sixth round."[29]

Charley's effort was wasted when Eddie Plank was routed, 11–3, in the series finale. It got worse after the teams moved to Boston. Before a large crowd of more than 15,000 on Saturday, Boston again beat the A's, 11–6. Philadelphia went on to lose all three games in Beantown and fell 6 games out of first place. Bender didn't start any of the games in Boston, but took the mound the following Thursday in Chicago and stopped the bleeding with a 5–1 triumph over Doc White and the White Sox.

On August 21, Waddell allowed three hits while defeating the Tigers, 1–0, in the opening game of a doubleheader in Detroit. Rube then pitched the nightcap as well, losing 2–1. His thirteen strikeouts in the two games boosted Rube's total to a record 302 for the season. He would not pitch another game for the Athletics in 1903.

Waddell was on the team's train when it left Detroit, but he was nowhere to be found when the players reached Cleveland. Rube remained missing for his scheduled start on the twenty-fifth. When he finally showed up the next day, an angry Connie Mack fired him, though the next day he changed the lefty's status to suspended for the reminder of the season.[30]

Eventually, Mack forgave Rube, and after he signed a new contract for the 1904 season, the manager allowed Waddell to have September off so he could perform in vaudeville. In May 1903, a St. Louis theater manager had signed Rube, at $40 a week, to perform on the stage following the baseball season. On September 4, Waddell left for St. Louis to begin his commitment as an actor in a melodrama entitled *The Stain of Guilt*. A Chicago critic who saw the show wrote, "The stain of guilt for this play will have to rest partly upon the man who wrote it and partly upon whoever hired Waddell."

"Rube's role required that he throw the villain off the stage," Bender chuckled. "On the night I saw the play he threw him into the bass drum in the orchestra pit. After the show, the Rube and I had some drinks with the villain. The villain was very fed up with things, and Rube wore out about four of them that year."[31]

Without Waddell, any chance the Athletics had for the pennant was lost. Philadelphia would eventually finish the 1903 season in second place, 14 games behind Boston.

Elijah Edward Pinnance, an Ojibwa from Ontario, Canada, became the first full-blood North American Indian to pitch in a regular season game in the major leagues when he made his debut for the A's against Washington on September 14, 1903. When the A's built up a 13–0 lead after seven innings, Connie Mack decided to get a look at the new Indian pitcher Harry Davis had recruited from the Tomahawk League of Michigan. When Umpire Connolly announced the new pitcher's name, it sounded to most of those in attendance as "peanuts." The fans took the cue and called the newcomer "Peanuts" the rest of the game. The A's pitcher retired the side in order in the eighth, but gave up the Senators' only run in the ninth.[32]

When Pinnance was asked by a Washington reporter about the nickname, he answered, "Why should that name annoy me? I'll be roasted more or less, and from what I've been able to observe, the roasting process vastly improves the peanut."[33]

Following his effort against Washington, Pinnance pitched in only one other major league game. He threw five innings in the A's final game of the season at Columbia Park.

Bender finished his rookie season with a 17–15 won-lost record. Though he issued only 65 bases on balls in 270 innings pitched, Charley led the American League in hit batsmen with 25 victims. The rookie took to task something Harry Davis told him that first spring with the Athletics.

"Kid," he said, "whenever you get two strikes on a batter and no balls, throw the next one at his bean. Don't be afraid. You'll never kill anyone when you throw at 'em. But don't throw behind 'em or you'll surely hit 'em."[34]

A sports columnist named T. P. Magilligan wrote that he saw Bender intentionally hit batters on more than one occasion. According to Magilligan, the most notorious of these incidents occurred in August 1903 when the A's pitcher drilled the Browns' Bobby Wallace in the ribs. Bender was peeved because he was down by five runs on the scoreboard and the Browns' Hunter Hill had run him over in a play at home plate in the top of the inning. "He had Bobby ducking that day and after throwing two at his bean finally landed on Bobby's side," wrote the scribe. "...Bender declared after the game that he hit Wallace unintentionally, but the fans were up in arms against the Squaw man, and only the timely intervention of the police saved the Indian from serious injury."[35]

American League umpire Billy Evans related that Bender often warned opposing batters not to "hug the plate too close" or they would find a fastball heading toward their chin. It was not an idle threat.[36]

Eddie Plank led Connie Mack's pitching staff in 1903 with twenty-three victories. Gettysburg Eddie, along with Charles Albert Bender, would form the nucleus of Connie Mack's pitching staff from 1903 through 1914.

Edward Stewart Plank would win 285 games as a Philadelphia Athletic in his thirteen years with the club. The lanky left-hander had outstanding command of his pitches and was a finesse pitcher, mixing a fastball with his "cross-fire," a sidearm curve that dissected the plate at such an angle it could rarely be hit hard.

An apt description of Eddie Plank's pitching style was attributed to the left-hander's teammate, outfielder Tully Hartsel:

> Now Plank, there was a specimen! Reminded me of a spider, all lanky and stretched out, with limbs goin' every which way. And that's before he threw the ball! As a leadoff man myself, I can tell you he used to drive batters batty! Me, I had patience so's I'd wait out those kind of pitchers. But most guys were so anxious to hit, that by the time Eddie got ready to toss the damn thing, they were tight as an over-wound watch. Very deliberate fellow. Took his job as seriously like a banker. His smile muscles musta withered after childhood cause I never saw him smile. Like warm up pitches he hardly ever threw; why use 'em if ya don't have to?[37]

The Boston Americans and the Pittsburgh Nationals, champions of their respective leagues, agreed to play a championship series following the 1903 regular season. The Cubs and White Stockings played a lengthy fourteen-game post-season series in Chicago; the Browns and Cardinals met seven times in St. Louis; and the Cleveland Americans beat Cincinnati six games to three in another inter-league set. The Athletics were given the chance to exact revenge for the loss of their pre-season exhibition series with the Phillies.

Charles Bender got the starting assignment for the Athletics in the opening game of the fall city series on September 30. The A's trailed, 3–2, going into the bottom of the eighth inning when the Athletics exploded for five runs off Phillies pitcher Bill Duggleby, making Bender a 7–3 winner.

Bender started two more times in the seven-game series. He won game four, 5–0, made two hits and also stole a base. By the time of the seventh and final game on October 8, the Athletics had the series wrapped up with four wins against two for the Nationals. This time, "Bender was batted fiercely and four errors were made behind him."[38] The Athletics lost, 13–6, but picked up $200 per player for the series.[39]

"That fall Connie paid my way to Foston, Minnesota," Bender remembered fondly. "He called me in and handed me $300 for the trip home and back. It was a very fine thing to do, for I know the club did not make much money. Mr. Mack is full of these deeds."[40]

Just before Thanksgiving, Charles arrived in Carlisle and rented a room at Lockwoods' on East Main Street. Three months later the *American Volunteer* reported, "Bender, who is spending the winter here, is fast developing into an expert billiard player. Although he has been playing a little more than a year he makes the most difficult shots and only a few days ago made a run of nineteen."[41]

In March 1904, Charles Bender returned to the Indian school to help coach the baseball team. Following the 1902 season, coach Pop Warner chose to deemphasize baseball in favor of track and football recruitment, which left the baseball players to fend for themselves. Bender worked with captain Lloyd Nephew and the rest of the team until it was time to head for spring training with the Athletics. The A's left from Philadelphia on March 12 for the train ride to Spartanburg, South Carolina.

En route, the Athletics' train stopped off in Washington, D.C. The *Washington Post* noted that Connie Mack "now has five Indians on his reservation ... Bender, Bruce, Pinnance, Waddell and Schreckengost."[42] It is interesting to speculate about the writer's motives for listing Rube and Schreck with the three Native Americans.

The isolated training site in South Carolina presented fewer distractions for Rube Waddell and the other wayward spirits on the club than Florida the previous year. When the A's left Spartanburg, the team was in good shape and the prospects for the season appeared promising. That perception didn't last long. Bender's training was cut short when he was disabled with a case of the mumps.

The first order of business after the club returned to Philadelphia was the pre-season series with the Phillies. Bender pitched and hit a triple in the 14–6 Athletics victory on April 6, but he lost the seventh game, 3–1, despite striking out eleven Phillies. The Athletics did manage to win the 1904 city series, 5 games to 3.

Bender scattered seven hits to beat Jack Chesbro and the Highlanders at New York's Hilltop Park in the Athletics' fourth game of the season. Charley took a shutout into the ninth inning before a hit batsman led to New York's only score in the A's 5–1 victory. After that, the fortunes of that game's starting pitchers went in opposite directions. Chesbro won an incredible 41 games for New York that season, though it still wasn't enough to gain a pennant for the Highlanders.

After his victory over Chesbro, Charles did not appear in a game again until he pinch-hit for Waddell in a 2–0 loss to St. Louis on May 17. Two days later, Bender pitched a complete game in a 4–3 loss to the Browns.

Although Bender appeared to be a hale and hearty specimen during his playing days, he was plagued by poor health in several of his seasons with the Athletics. When Bender became ill, Connie Mack wanted him to see a doctor, but Charles would only shake his head. "I'm sick, but I don't need medicine," he would say.

Once Mack went to check on his ailing pitcher at his hotel room and found that Bender was not there. No one knew where Albert had gone. When Bender was missing all night and then did not show up the next day, the manager became worried. For two days the club searched for Albert. Just before Mack was about to notify the authorities, he learned Bender was back in his room.

"I went away where it was quiet and where I could be alone," explained Bender. "When an Indian is sick he doesn't want any noise around and he just wants to let nature take its course in curing him."[43]

The particulars of the story as related by columnist Frank Menke are uncertain, but it sounds like something Bender would say and do. That was his way. The Chippewa spurned doctors and medication, hiding himself away until he felt better. Charley played much of the 1904 season while suffering with abdominal pain that was later diagnosed as appendicitis.

During Charley's month-long absence from the starting rotation, Connie Mack only used three pitchers—Waddell, Plank, and Weldon Henley. Waddell and Plank won fifty-one games between them, but the rest of the team's pitchers won only thirty more that season and the Athletics dropped to a disappointing fifth-place finish. With a roster limit of sixteen players, injuries and illness forced Connie Mack to perform a balancing act all season.

Poor seasons by several players exacerbated the Athletics' problems. Shortstop Monte Cross batted an anemic .189, and the club's two catchers, Schreckengost and Powers, hit .186 and .190, respectively. Center fielder Ollie Pickering got off to a horrible start at the bat and was replaced by Danny Hoffman. Then Hoffman was hit in the eye by a pitch thrown by Jesse Tannehill and wound up playing in only 53 games.

In its 1904 post-season analysis, the *Sporting News* reflected, "Not a single day from the start to the finish of the season did not Manager Mack have one or more of his men in his private hospital. Lave Cross and Eddie Plank were the only members of the Athletics who went through the season without missing games on account of illness or injury.... Harry Davis and Hoffman, two of the Athletics' best men, missed nearly half the entire season nursing injuries. Bender was on the sick list more than three-fourths of the time...."[44]

Louis Bruce, Charley's hero when he attended Lincoln Institute back in the 1890s, joined the Athletics on June 20, 1904, having graduated from the University of Pennsylvania Dental College a week earlier. Bruce had pitched and played the outfield the previous two seasons with Toronto, largely to pay his college expenses. In 1902 he led the Eastern League in winning percentage among pitchers with an 18–2 record. The following season, Lou won 13 of the 18 games he pitched and his batting average of .358 was the second highest mark in the league.[45]

Bruce was a pitching candidate for the Athletics, but with a well-stocked rotation of Waddell, Plank, Bender, and Henley, Mack used the rookie as a utility man "on account of his prowess with the stick and his skill as a fielder."[46] The 5'5" outfielder debuted in a loss to Boston at Columbia Park on June 22, batted .267 in 30 games for the Athletics, and even pitched scoreless innings in two games that year. In the end, Connie Mack didn't think the undersized Bruce had sufficient big league skills and the young man of Mohawk heritage did not return to the majors after that one season.

At mid-season, the *Sporting News* editorialized, "Had Bender, who is called the 'Right-handed Waddell' by the Athletics' catchers because they say he has exactly the same curves, shoots and speed as the Rube, except, of course, that he delivers the ball with the other hand, began well in the spring, Manager Mack and his players are of the opinion that he would have made a record this year unequaled — by any other twirler. Ill health made it impossible for him to do this, though Manager Mack expected him to do wonders from now to the end of the season."[47]

Charles did perform remarkably on occasion. On June 14, Bender ended a personal three-game losing streak when he defeated Cleveland 4–0, permitting only one safety, a hit by Billy Lush. Bender had already struck out seven of the Naps when the game was called after Cleveland batted in the fifth inning. As storm clouds rolled into the area, the Naps attempted to delay play, but the rain storm broke just as the third out was recorded in the bottom of the fifth.

On July 13, Charles Albert shut out Chicago on three hits at Columbia Park, after which the *Chicago Daily Tribune* declared "that bronze statue in the center of the diamond was invulnerable." The only chance the White Sox had to score was in the fourth inning when Nixey Callahan tripled with no one out. Bender induced the next batter to ground to Monte Cross, who held the runner with a bluff and then threw to first for the out. George Davis fanned and Jiggs Donohue grounded out to end the threat. With thirteen whiffs, Charley tied an American League record for strikeouts in a single game. Bender's strikeout record stood only two days before Fred Glade of the Browns bettered the mark by two against Washington.[48]

"Indian Bender, I see, fanned 13 of the boys and hit nobody," wrote W. A. Phelon, Jr., for *Sporting Life*. "It is, in fact, far more unusual for Bender to pitch a game without whanging a paleface than for him to accumulate a strikeout record."[49]

Though Phelon's report rang of sarcasm, Chicago manager Nixey Callahan's reaction to Bender's milestone was laced with bitterness and anger. "He hates any white man out-side of the Athletics," he said. "You remember that game last season when he hit four of us? Well, whenever he hit a man he stood and grinned, and never made a movement to help or condole with the victim. But when a foul tip hurt his catcher he was in like a flash to see if he were injured. I called him an uncivilized demon, and when I came to bat he sent one at my head that would have taken my coco off if it had hit me."[50]

On August 1, Bender threw another shutout, beating St. Louis, 4–0, and allowed only four hits, all singles. After hanging around in fifth place for

much of June and July, the Athletics won ten of twelve games on their western road trip and pulled within two games of first place upon Eddie Plank's
3–1 win against Cleveland. Immediately thereafter, they lost three straight
games at home.

Connie Mack "trotted out his invalid Indian Chief" to break the Athletics' slump in the third game of a series with Detroit. Bender responded in
grand style after allowing two runs in the first inning, by out-pitching the
Tigers' George Mullin, 7–4. Despite the heroic effort in a game late in the
season in St. Louis, Charles Albert did not win another game after defeating
the Tigers on August 26, going 0-4-1 the rest of the year.

Any hope Philadelphia had for a pennant ended in mid–September when
the A's best hitter, Harry Davis, broke his hand and Rube Waddell suffered a
shoulder separation during a run-down play on the base paths.

One of Bender's best efforts in 1904 came in a game he did not win. On
September 27, only one week after being hammered in an 11–1 loss in Boston,
Bender took the ball in the second game of a doubleheader in St. Louis. The
Browns' Willie Sudhoff and Bender dueled for ten innings without either
team scoring. The Athletics managed eleven hits compared to six off Bender,
including two each by John Heidrick and Tom Jones. The Chief walked only
one batter and had eleven strikeouts, including whiffs of Heidrick, Wallace
and Hines in the ninth. The game ended in a tie upon being called by Umpire
King because of darkness.[51]

The Athletics made their final trip to Detroit at the end of September.
On October 1, Bender lost the second game of a doubleheader to George
Mullin, 2–1. However, Charley didn't leave Detroit empty handed.

On October 3, 1904, Charles Albert Bender married twenty-one-year-
old Marie Clements of Detroit. He was introduced to her at the home of a
mutual friend while the Athletics were in the city playing the Tigers during
the 1903 season and, despite their racial differences, the Chippewa and the
white girl hit it off. Following their first meeting, the future Mrs. Bender anx-
iously followed the career of her beau in the newspapers. They planned a
quiet wedding to coincide with the Athletics final visit to Detroit in the 1904
season.[52]

The newlyweds departed Detroit the following Tuesday for Washington, where Charley would make his final start of the season on Friday. On
October 7, the new bridegroom took the mound in the second game of a doubleheader in the Capitol City. By pre-agreement the contest was to be called
after the seventh inning. For six innings Bender dominated the Senators and
took a 2–0 lead into the home team's final at-bat. With two out and a runner on base, Bender struck out the opposing pitcher, Case Patten, to apparently finish the contest. However, catcher Osee Schreckengost could not corral
the pitch and the ball landed at the batter's feet. Patten kicked the ball away

from Schreck and took off for first base, arriving there safely. The Athletics protested, but Umpire King claimed Osee was the one that kicked the ball. Bender walked the next batter to load the bases, after which the light-hitting Hunter Hill slapped a single to center field. Hartsel came up with the ball quickly and threw to home in an attempt to prevent Patten from scoring the tying run. Upon seeing the throw heading toward the catcher, the lead runner, Patsy Donovan, "loitered going home until Patten got at his heels, thus blocking the catcher in getting Hartsel's throw." The throw sailed past Osee and all three runners on base scored. Bender and the Athletics were suddenly the losers, 3–2.[53] Some honeymoon!

Immediately upon completion of the baseball season, the newlyweds took off for their honeymoon trip to the Dakota wilds. They stopped along the way in Cleveland where Charley fitted Marie with a hunting outfit. The couple then continued on to their destination of Devils' Lake, the largest natural body of water in North Dakota and home to some of the best duck and goose hunting in North America.

"He taught me how to shoot, hunt and fish," Marie told Philadelphia reporter Ed Pollock fifty years later, "and many years later he taught me to play golf. I went with him on most of his hunting and fishing trips. I loved it."[54]

Because of physical ailments, Bender started only twenty games during the 1904 regular season, though he relieved on the mound in nine others. Partly due to illness, Bender slipped to a 10–11 record. During the off-season, Charles finally consulted a physician, who determined that he had been suffering from appendicitis for nearly a year.

Charles Albert had a busy fall and winter. The newlyweds set up housekeeping in Carlisle, where Charley again delved in the jewelry business to develop a trade that could provide for his family after his days as a ballplayer were over. That December Bender entered Todd Hospital in Carlisle where he underwent an appendectomy.[55]

Like Connie Mack and many of the A's players, Charley and Marie would eventually establish their home within walking distance of Columbia Park. The area surrounding the ballpark had all the necessities of everyday life — economic housing in the large number of row houses, groceries, bakeries, clothiers, and plenty of taverns. Trolley lines on Columbia and Twenty-ninth Street made the entire city accessible.

Emil Beck, one of the young boys in the neighborhood back then, remembered, "Rube Waddell, Chief Bender and a lot of others lived in the area. You could often see Connie Mack and some of the players walking through the neighborhood. We used to chase after them as they walked to the ballpark."[56]

Though Charles loved children, he and his wife were destined not to have any of their own. Mrs. Bender would remain out of the public eye while her husband became one of the most famous residents of Philadelphia. Marie's mother conceded that Charles was a "fine fellow" and "a fine husband," but she told a reporter her son-in-law was adamant about not discussing his day's work after he came home. "I've heard the rest doing it, and he scowls, and I say, 'Now, stop that.' ...Then he would smile at me."[57]

♦ 4 ♦

The Native American Baseball Player

During the course of Hampton Institute's Indian Day in 1914, Fred Bender, a student and brother of the famous pitcher, spoke about the importance of education and participation in government for the advancement of the American Indian population. Young Bender's thesis seems strange when contrasted with the attitudes of the twenty-first century, but he spoke for many of that generation of Native Americans educated in the white man's schools.

"I am proud of the fact I am an Indian and glad that our problem is a hard one," he concluded, "and glad that we have been handicapped by unwarranted prejudice, because all of these have tended to make our march toward progress a hard one. The obstacles thus placed in our way have made the Red man a stronger people because he has had to overcome them."[1]

Charles' formative years were spent in the same environment as his younger brother and both had little attachment to the ways and traditions of their mother's people. Had it not been for his Chippewa blood, Charles Albert Bender may have spent his life as an uneducated white boy and he was grateful for the opportunities athletics at the Carlisle Industrial School afforded him. A proud man, there is nothing to suggest Charles ever thought of himself as a victim, even though he knew the road toward acceptance and success in white society would be difficult. Unlike many Native Americans, Bender did have an understanding of the white man's customs and his athletic prowess put him into a position to counter his detractors.

Bender did not refer to the racism and prejudice against Native Americans in his many interviews and, in fairness, that discussion would have been met with derision in the era in which he lived. In the midst of the 1905 baseball season, *Sporting Life* editor Francis Richter quoted the Chippewa pitcher, "I avoid notoriety when I can. I do not want my name presented to the public as an Indian, but as a pitcher."[2]

The Native American baseball player held a unique appeal for the white fans, children and the press. Indian ballplayers received substantial attention because they were the only "uncivilized savages" the eastern fans had ever seen in person. Many whites at that time were old enough to remember the battle of the Little Big Horn ("Custer's Last Stand" in modern-day lore). The renegade Geronimo had only surrendered in 1886 and the tragedy at Wounded Knee occurred in 1890.

Native American ballplayers were at the bottom of baseball's social order when Charles Albert Bender broke in with the Athletics in 1903. There were no Latin Americans in the major leagues and it would be more than forty years before African Americans or dark-skinned Latinos could play in Organized Baseball. In 1901, Baltimore Orioles manager John McGraw claimed that his new second baseman, Charlie Grant, was an American Indian, and gave him the name Chief Tockohama. It was said that the owner of a rival club, Charles Comiskey of the White Sox, protested that the player was really of African descent and Grant's career in the majors was finished before it started.

Although Charley Bender was half European, contemporary accounts either suggest or state that the pitcher was a full-blood Indian. While it was his pitching skills that made him stand out, Bender's baseball success became inseparable from his ethnicity. In virtually every newspaper story or magazine article about his on-the-field exploits, Charles is referred to first as an Indian or the Chippewa pitcher. Even his plaque on the wall of honor in the National Baseball Hall of Fame and Museum begins with the words "Famous Chippewa Indian."

American Indian baseball players were often dubbed "Chief." Many detested the appellation because they felt "chief" was a term of honor and reserved for the hereditary leader of the tribe, thus was inappropriate for a common ballplayer. As time went by the nickname became viewed as a sobriquet with racial overtones.

Charles Albert Bender signed autographs as "Charles" until later in life when he began to scrawl "Chief Bender." During his playing days, Bender stoically doffed his cap to war hoops for the "Chief," and when he opened a retail business in Philadelphia, it was named Chief Bender Sporting Goods Company. Charles did not state publicly that he disliked the nickname and he would eventually accept it for his professional identity.

Bender was often subjected to the stereotype of the period. Baseball writers in his time could hardly resist the urge to utilize the racist cliché, and even newspaper pieces favorable to Bender often suggested a subtle form of racism when compared to the sensitivities of today.

Newspaper writers of that time reinforced the stereotype of the undisciplined Indian. Though he lamented the decline in Chief Bender's pitching prowess, a sports columnist named H. C. Hamilton wrote in 1917, "Strong, healthy, quick, drilled in outdoor sports by inherited rivalries, the Indian never has been able to completely fathom the white man's game of baseball. Many hundreds of the copper skinned men have called, but very few of them have reached the pinnacle of perfection in the majors."[3]

Bender had the fortune, or misfortune, to play in the major leagues when sportswriters used humor and imagination within their stories, and the master of that style of writing was the *Philadelphia North American's* Charles Dryden. No player, manager or owner was exempt from Dryden's whimsical pen. Dryden came to Philadelphia from the *New York American*, where he had so angered Andrew Freedman of the New York Giants with his accounts

Charles Albert Bender did not like his picture taken when he first came to the major leagues. This may account for the menacing look he is giving the *Chicago Daily News* photographer in this picture from the 1905 season (Chicago History Museum).

the owner barred him from the park to stop his stories. Charles continued to cover the games from a telegraph pole outside of the park with even more humorous accounts that served to make Freedman the joke of New York.

J. Taylor Spink recalled that Dryden wrote a piece about the time "a mad dog went foaming and yowling across the field at the Polo Grounds and Charles wrote a paragraph saying the dog had been bitten by John McGraw."[4]

Dryden was one of the first, if not the first, sportswriter to refer to Charles Bender in print as "Chief," using the sobriquet during the city series with the Phillies in the spring of 1903.[5] Dryden was famous for designating nicknames for players and he was the first to call Cubs manager Frank Chance "Peerless Leader." Once he moved on to Chicago, Dryden noted for his readers that White Sox pitcher Ed Walsh was "the only man in the world who could strut standing still."[6]

More troubling is the use of hackneyed language by baseball writers from Bender's time that smacks of racism by modern standards. After Bender escaped a ninth-inning jam on Opening Day in 1905, Dryden was led to write, "That was about the closest squeak Charles Albert ever did meet up with, and when it was all over the 15,211 ladies and gents swallowed their hearts on the way home, and forgave the dusky child of the forest. In eight spectacular rounds he had won a new turkey feather for his head piece, and then for a wind-up came within half an inch of letting the champions scalp him alive."[7]

After Bender hit two inside-the-park home runs during a game in May 1906, *Sporting Life* commented, "Despite the fact that he is educated and civilized, Big Chief Bender, with a war club in his hands, is a menace to paleface pitcher."[8] Later that same season, a *Washington Post* reporter described a relief appearance by Bender as a Wild West shoot-out: "Bender tried his primeval pellets, but his pale-faced brethren were next to his arrows, and the gallant red man had to succumb with the others."[9]

A *New York Times* reporter described Bender's strikeouts as Yankee scalps dangled from his good brown arm. "Lo, the poor Indian!" exclaimed the *Times* following the Highlanders' victory on September 4, 1908. "Paleface luck outweighed aboriginal skill, and Big Chief Bender, from the Philadelphia tribe, was dispatched to the happy hunting grounds by the Yankee bucks...."[10]

By 1910 Bender was recognized as one of the top hurlers in the game, but still endured racist epithets by fans and the press. A wire service report just before the World Series harkened back to the Indian wars of the previous century. "Big Chief Bender, the wily redskin of the Athletics, who has been lying in ambush spying on the Cubs, has expressed his opinion the Chicago team won't have a chance when it meets the Athletics."[11]

One of the most naïve prattles degrading Bender's heritage was posted prominently on the front page of the *New York Times* at the height of the pitcher's success. "Bender is the biggest man of his tribe tonight," the *Times* reporter wrote in his account of the final game of the 1911 World Series, "and at some far-off reservation, when they get the news, the aborigines will pass the news from wigwam to wigwam, and the squaws will tell the little papooses that if they grow up and be good Indians maybe someday they will be like the great Chief Bender and become heap fine flingers."[12]

In May 1913 a "biographical" article by Chicago sports columnist Harvey T. Woodruff entitled "Career of 'Chief' Charles Albert Bender, The 'Good Indian' of Baseball" was reprinted in newspapers all across the nation. Though the gist of the piece was favorable to Bender, it included nonsense typical of that time, including a story that "Mostly tradition is authority for the statement that young Bender secured a baseball from an Indian officer on the Chippewa reservation, fashioned a baseball bat from a war club handed down from a venerated chief, and showed aptitude for baseball as a youngster." The author did concede that when asked about such stories "Charles Albert just smiles that bland smile familiar to all big league fans and says, 'If it will help your story any, I'll not deny it.'"[13]

The Woodruff article was accompanied by several crude cartoon drawings, one of which depicted Charles in full headdress astride a paint pony with several scalps dangling from his belt. (The caption read, "1910 his best year with 23 scalps to his credit.") Another cartoon depicted a baby Bender juggling several small round objects while secured in a cradleboard leaned against a tree. "Heap Big Ball Player," read the caption, "(Bender) Played catch with his mother's beads when a papoose."

While Bender appeared apathetic about the tall tales written about his life, he was extremely protective of the privacy of his Caucasian wife. When a local newspaper ran a "report" that said a fair Hiawatha beamed down upon Mr. Bender from the pavilion during the opening game of the 1907 season, the *Philadelphia North American* reported Charles' objection to the story. "Inasmuch as the late Mr. Hiawatha was a male Indian and Mrs. Bender is a beautiful young white woman, Charles Albert failed to appreciate the well-meant compliment. Ugh! The Big Chief has spoken."[14]

Perhaps Charles Bender's most violent encounter with racism came as result of a case of mistaken identity. Particularly dark-skinned Native American ballplayers, like the Giants' John "Chief" Meyers, suffered additional abuse because they were perceived to be of African American blood. A Cahuilla Indian, Meyers endured taunts of "nigger" from fans who thought him too dark of skin. Bender became a target of that same bigotry in Washington, D.C., during the 1907 baseball season. It was not because he was an Indian, but due to his complexion.

Hugh Fullerton reported in his sports column that while the Athletics were in Washington for a series with the Nationals, Bender went to a café and ordered seltzer lemonade. The proprietor walked over and told the well-dressed dark-skinned man to "Get out now. Go quietly. You're not allowed." A suddenly annoyed Bender repeated his drink order and refused to leave.

According to Fullerton, the proprietor signaled two burly waiters who rushed toward the ballplayer. "A straight left laid one on his back; a right jab bounced the other among the rare bric-a-brac. The bartender joined and sat down in a costly vase. The proprietor leaped forward and bit the wall so hard he knocked a picture down and smashed it...."

Within a few moments, Bender was tossed onto the sidewalk. The disheveled Chippewa picked himself up, dusted off his suit and muttered, "If they'd have waited a minute I'd told them I was an Indian."[15]

Bender and fellow Native American ballplayers were undoubtedly subjected to numerous instances of racism during the normal activity of everyday life. One incident that was documented occurred just weeks after the A's won the 1911 World Series. Bender and fellow pitchers Jack Coombs and Cy Morgan were in Atlantic City performing on the vaudeville circuit. The *Philadelphia North American* reported that a man said to be from Alabama was checking into Young's Hotel when he saw the three ballplayers in the lobby. The Southerner banged his fist down on the desk and exclaimed, "I will not stay at a place like this!"

When hotel manager Walsh asked what the problem was, the man replied that he would not "linger in a caravansary that had among its guests a person of color."

The manager replied, "Why that man's an Indian. He's Chief Bender of the World's Champion Athletics. The best is none too good for him."

According to the *North American*, "The Southern man looked as cheap as cold potatoes. He inquired for the bar and asked Manager Walsh to accompany him."[16]

Bender was not the first American Indian to suffer prejudice while a major league ballplayer. That burden fell on Lou Sockalexis, who played for the Cleveland National League club from 1897 to 1899. It is said a player of Sioux heritage named James Madison Toy broke into the major leagues with Cleveland's American Association team a full ten years before Sockalexis made his debut. However, Toy did not acknowledge his Indian heritage and wore a handlebar mustache, which gave him the appearance of a European. Because Toy kept his Indian ethnicity a secret, Sockalexis was referred to as the first Native American to play professional baseball until the early 1960s when Baseball Hall of Fame historian Lee Allen endorsed Toy as the first American Indian major leaguer.[17]

Sockalexis was a product of college baseball, a rarity among all races in the 1890s. Son of a high-ranking member of the Penobscot tribe, Louis grew up on Indian Island, a reservation in Maine. He attended St. Mary's, a Catholic school in Van Buren, and participated in a number of athletic activities, including skating and track.

Sockalexis played baseball at Maine's Ricker Institute in 1894 and that summer was a teammate of Mike Powers on a team sponsored by the Poland Spring Hotel. Powers was captain of the Holy Cross team and convinced Lou to join him at the Worcester, Massachusetts, institution.[18]

Sockalexis had not graduated high school when he enrolled at Holy Cross, but requirements for college athletics were less formal at that time. Louis became a huge favorite with the students, batting .436 and .444 in his two years with the Crusaders, and decades later he would be inducted into the school's Hall of Fame.

When Mike Powers transferred to Notre Dame in December 1896 to begin his medical studies, the house diary of Holy Cross charged that Powers received "a bribe from the Notre Dame University and had too small a spirit to refuse it.... Other small spirits may imitate ex–Captain Powers."[19]

Two days later, Sockalexis became one of the "small spirits" and followed Powers to Notre Dame. Louis was only at South Bend for a month before he was expelled for public drunkenness after he and another Notre

Dame player went on a drinking spree in town. Mike Powers contacted Pat Tebeau, who was more than willing to take him for his club in Cleveland.[20]

The Cleveland National League club signed Sockalexis for $1,500 and he made his major league debut for the Spiders on April 22, 1897. Though he lacked polish as a fielder, Sockalexis had a strong arm and his throwing ability distinguished him from fellow players. Louis was larger than the average player of that day, standing almost six feet tall and weighing 195 pounds. He was nicknamed "Sock" by his teammates.

When the Penobscot outfielder reached the big leagues, the "Indian Wars" of the West were still fresh in people's minds, and among the white population there was a deep-seated prejudice against Native Americans. Contemporary accounts indicate that Sockalexis was subjected to jeers, war whoops and catcalls on his first trip around the league.

It should be said that a great degree of verbal abuse was used by fans and players alike during that time in an attempt to rattle and intimidate the opposition. The brand of baseball played in those days was described as "rowdyism." Players not only verbally abused one another, they attempted to injure opposing players on the base paths with the sharpened spikes of their shoes and pitchers intentionally threw at batters as a common practice. Players engaged in fisticuffs with umpires, fans and opposing teams.

However, rampant racist behavior by fans was not necessarily the norm, as demonstrated in the column of D.C.R. in the *Sporting News*. "Sockalexis, the Indian of Indians, made his initial bow and captivated the spectators by his fine exhibition of playing. He did more at the bat than the rest of the club together and in the field was invincible." There was no mention of any negative treatment by the fans and the author only talked about the player's ethnicity in a positive light and even admitted "In contrast with some of the other Cleveland players, he is every inch a gentleman, educated and refined."[21]

The Spiders of 1897 were a team riddled with injuries and Sockalexis quickly earned a starting role. Even before the start of the season, some newspaper reports already were referring to the Cleveland team as the Indians. On May 1, the *Washington Post* reported, "Sockalexis, the big medicine man of the Indians covered himself with glory today. In his four times at bat he made four hits, one a three bagger when the bases were full."[22]

A small group of Penobscot Indians in traditional tribal dress, including Chief Francis, appeared at Sockalexis' game against the New York Giants on June 17. The Polo Grounds fans went "wild when Louis waved to his redskinned-brothers parading through the third base grandstand."

Socks stepped in to bat against future Hall of Fame pitcher Amos Rusie and walloped a pitch from the Hoosier Thunderbolt over the right field ropes for a home run. Sockalexis only managed a single in his remaining at bats, but no matter, Cleveland won, 7–2.

Louis appeared on his way to an outstanding major league career when he went on a night of protracted drinking on the Fourth of July and could not play for two days. Manager Tebeau ordered his players to keep Sockalexis out of the saloons, but Socks tried to elude his watchdogs one night by climbing out a second-story window of the team's hotel. Instead of escaping, he fell two stories to the ground, wrenching his right ankle. The injury cost Louis his right field job, and he would never again play regularly in the National League. Newspapers even began to refer to Sockalexis as "Pain-in-the-Face."[23]

His teammates soon turned against Sock and accused him of indifference to the rules and shirking on fly balls to right field. The Cleveland club's president fined the wayward player $25, $50 and $100, respectively, for three separate occasions that Sockalexis was found to be intoxicated. Furthermore, he was suspended until the team's doctor certified that Louis was no longer on the bottle.[24]

"The eminent Sockalexis is off the reservation," began one particularly naive editorial.

> The charms of the white man's fire water has stirred the blood he has derived from his primitive forefathers and the doughty red man will excite the rooters no more for a long time.... Your savage is always a savage in some in some respects. One of the more important of these is, he cannot be educated up to the proper Christian sense of the extreme beauty and importance of money. Hence the savage, however carefully he may have been kicked into shape by civilization, would never rise to the dignity of a pawnbroker or a sugar magnate. He simply hasn't that kind of an intellect.[25]

Sock finished the 1897 season batting .338 in 66 games (the second most games for a Cleveland outfielder that season). The following year, Lou struggled against left-handers, batted just .224 in twenty-one games, and continued to play subpar defense. Prior to the 1899 season, Sockalexis signed a Spiders contract with the provision he abstain from alcoholic drink. After only seven games, Socks was released outright. By 1903 the Penobscot was out of baseball, working as a laborer and suffering from the effects of alcoholism. Louis died in 1913 and is buried on Indian Island, Maine, where his grave is marked by a granite monument with an inscription on a bronze plaque.

Prior to the 1915 American League season, the Cleveland club, known as the Naps, needed a new nickname following the departure of Napoleon Lajoie, and on January 17 the *Cleveland Plain Dealer* announced that a new name had been selected for the team. The article indicated that club president Charles Somers invited the city's baseball writers to make the selection.

Indians was their choice, "It having been one of the names applied to the old National League club of Cleveland many years ago."[26]

Initially, there was no mention of Sockalexis, but a day later the *Plain Dealer* amplified on the choice of the name Indians. "Many years ago there was an Indian named Sockalexis who was the star of the Cleveland baseball club.... The 'fans' throughout the country began to call the Clevelanders the 'Indians.' It was an honorable name, and while it stuck the team made an excellent record. It also serves to revive the memory of the single great player who has been gathered to his fathers in the happy hunting ground of Abenakis."[27] The legend of Louis Sockalexis was assured.

As the second high-profile Native American to play major league baseball, Charles Bender did not experience the fate of or the degree of torment suffered by Sockalexis. Perhaps it was because he did not speak out against prejudice like other Native American players, namely Chief Meyers, who maintained he was treated as a foreigner in his own country. Perhaps this was because Charley was an outstanding player on a successful team who had the support and tutelage of highly respected baseball men like Connie Mack and Harry Davis. Though he often appeared aloof in his early years in the American League, Bender was generally quiet and a gracious man who handled racial taunts passively.

"The young man boasts exceptionally good habits," observed the *Washington Post* in a profile of Bender during his rookie season. "He is a heavy sleeper and a hearty eater. He does not know the taste of tobacco and lets the 'fire water' alone. He never was known to take a drink of an intoxicant. Good judges of baseball material that have watched him predict a great future for the youngster."[28]

A reporter wrote of Bender during the 1905 season, "He is well liked by his fellow-players, who will tell you the 'Chief,' as they call him, is a fine fellow. On the road he continually remains about the hotel where the team is sojourning and either immerses himself in a book or quietly sits in a chair listening to the chat and small talk of his teammates. He very seldom joins them or takes part in the conversations being taciturn and non-talkative to a fault, and having all the unemotional qualities of his race."[29]

Billy Evans was an American League umpire during nine of Charley's twelve seasons with the Athletics and later wrote that when Bender walked onto the field, he was always greeted with the wild war whoops. "However, the more the fans yelled the better he pitched," noted Evans.[30]

It was said children even followed Bender in the street whooping and performing rain dances. Occasionally, he would answer the whoops by cupping his hands around his mouth and shout, "Foreigners! Foreigners!" But most often, Bender responded to derisive chants and war whoops from the fans by making the "Indian sign" (placing a hex on the opposition) or doffing his cap.

"Unless angered because of some turn of affairs," noted Evans, "Bender always wore an engaging smile that caused you to immediately admire him."[31]

On the field Native American ballplayers had to put up with verbal abuse that went beyond the usual dugout insults. However, it does not appear from period sources that Bender received more abuse from opposing ballplayers than did his teammates, at least not after his rookie season. Of course, he had that intimidating inside fastball to express his displeasure to the offenders when they came to bat. During his rookie season, batters quickly learned not to get too comfortable at the plate when Charley was pitching. Bender was known to dust a batter with an up and in fastball, and stand on the mound with a big smile as his victim picked himself up from the ground.

During a 1903 game between Philadelphia and New York, Bender was subjected to a barrage of insults from Highlanders manager Clark Griffith. When the physically imposing Bender threatened the 5'6" squirt of a manager with a public thrashing unless he ceased, Griffith prudently decided to hold his tongue.[32] This didn't end efforts to rattle the young pitcher, but thereafter the New York manager would designate one or more of his players to goad the Chippewa pitcher.

Charles Albert was aware of the Native American stereotypes in those days and personally did everything possible to deflect that image. Bender was tolerant of the fans, unyielding to the opposition and suspicious of newspaper men. Though he eventually became very comfortable talking to writers and even welcomed their inquiries, during his playing days he was very wary of the press.

Bender the ballplayer did not seek fame and recognition at first, just the respect of his manager and teammates. Later, Charles Albert reluctantly accepted the acclaim, but handled it professionally despite his young age.

Wrote one reporter who interviewed Bender in 1905, "In conversation he speaks quietly and slowly and his voice is modulated a very low pitch.... When he is interrogated he will look at you with those brown-black eyes as if pondering over in his mind the answer he is going to give you. Sometimes you will wait as long as thirty, forty or fifty seconds for a response and the pause becomes embarrassing. Then will come the answer, slow and terse and couched, in immaculate English, the language of a gentleman and scholar."[33]

"On the field Bender is one of the quietest players in the game ever known," noted a reporter for the *St. Louis Star Chronicle* in 1907. "If you ever find a fan who says he heard Charlie Bender 'sassing the umpire,' put him down as a man who has mixed up his pitchers. In defeat or victory, Bender is the same earnest, thoughtful, quiet and conscientious twirler. The game is a serious business with him."[34]

Bender once explained, "The reason I went into baseball as a profession was that when I left school, baseball offered me the best opportunity both for money and advancement.... I adopted it because I played baseball better than I could do anything else, because the life and the game appealed to me and because there was so little of racial prejudice in the game.... There has been scarcely a trace of sentiment against me on account of birth. I have been treated the same as other men."[35]

Apologists have suggested Bender's statements were designed to appease the white fans and the baseball establishment. However, when one takes into consideration the overt bigotry and prejudice a Native American would experience upon an attempt to invade any area of white society, Bender's assessment of Organized Baseball may not be as unrealistic as it appears on the surface.

Rarely was there anyone in the game — ex-teammates, the opposition, umpires, players he managed, or the press — that related anything negative about Chief Bender. Many of Charley's teammates became lifelong friends and he was widely respected by men he played with and against. Rube Bressler, Bender's roommate while a rookie with the Athletics in 1914, described Charley as "one of the kindest and finest men who ever lived."[36]

◆ 5 ◆

A Pennant for Brewerytown

During the 1929 baseball season, a Philadelphia sportswriter asked Chief Bender what he thought about Athletics pitching ace "Lefty" Grove. "Grove is a great pitcher," he said. "A king of speed ballers. But I think Rube Waddell had something on the present Mack pitcher. Grove throws like the immortal Rube. His fastball actually hops a couple of inches as it reaches the plate.... I was thrilled every time I saw that old Rube out there on the mound. I honestly think his curves broke at an angle. He had a sharp breaking drop that seemed to stop dead, then fall. Grove, when he reaches his peak, may be as good as the Rube."[1]

He was christened "George," but everyone knew the fire-balling southpaw as "Rube" Waddell. In 1904, Waddell struck out 349 batters, which stood as a modern major league record until 1965. Rube was exceptional in his first four seasons with Connie Mack's Philadelphia Athletics, winning 98 games—that is, when he was predisposed to pitch.

Connie Mack was aware of Waddell's odd disposition when he offered Rube the opportunity to play with the A's in June of 1902. During the pitcher's years with the Athletics, Mack had to endure such Waddell stunts as mimicking an automated man in a store window, wrestling an alligator, leading a marching band, and acting in vaudeville. If a fire engine, parade, or circus happened to pass Columbia Park, Waddell was likely to join the excitement in the streets while dressed in his baseball uniform.

In his later years, Chief Bender told many a story about old Rube. "We roomed once right next to a fire house and one day out came the big fire engine — on behind clung Waddell," he recalled in 1942. "So we raced to the fire. Smoke was pouring out of an apartment house. And through the smoke came Waddell, carrying an unconscious woman on his shoulder. He had gone up to the third floor to get her!"[2]

The pious Connie Mack sought to keep his players away from hard liquor, did not tolerate profanity, and imposed a curfew on his men. With Waddell around, the manager had limited success in the enforcement of any of these rules, as Bender related during an interview with J. Taylor Spink of the *Sporting News*.

> I remember the year Connie hired a bodyguard for him, a big burly fellow who had been a constable. The constable lasted about two weeks. Harry Davis and I were sitting in front of the Euclid Hotel in Cleveland one night. It was about 11 o'clock. A hansom cab drew up and Rube Waddell stepped out. He reached into the cab, pulled out the constable and tossed him over his shoulder. The bodyguard weighed at least 230. Rube carried him into the hotel.
>
> "Gettin' in a bit early, aren't you, Rube?" asked Davis.
>
> "Gettin' in, hell," replied the Rube, "as soon as I put down this drunk, I'm startin' out for the evening."
>
> That, of course, was the last of the constable — when Connie heard about it.[3]

Waddell was known for a good heart and a heroic nature, but he also had a malicious side. On February 7, 1905, in Lynn, Massachusetts, Rube prevented a fire by carrying a burning stove out of a store and throwing it into a snow bank. It was an even more amazing feat that he did not burn his hands.[4]

Three days later, Waddell was sought by police for assault. He had arrived drunk at the home of his wife's parents in Lynn and became enraged when they made a comment about payment of his "board bill." Waddell hit his father-in-law with a flatiron and when the mother-in-law tried to intercede with a broom, Waddell hit her with a chair. The family's Newfoundland dog leapt at the assailant to protect his owners and bit the pitcher on the left arm. Rube grabbed his trunk and took off down the road, leaving a trail of blood from his bleeding wound.[5]

The following Friday in Philadelphia, Waddell expressed surprise when reporters asked him about the assault on his in-laws. "Nothing in that yarn," he replied. "You see my arm is all right and no dog has bitten me. No, you don't suppose I would do such a foolish thing as pitching flatirons at the heads of my wife's parents, do you? Why, that's all foolish nonsense."[6]

The press or no one else appeared to buy Waddell's version. It would be up to Connie Mack to straighten things out.

The Athletics opened their 1905 spring training in New Orleans during the week of Mardi Gras. There could only be one reason to go there at that time of year with a crew that included Waddell and Schreckengost — to make more money from large crowds that would attend their games with the local Southern League team.

The A's contingent arrived late in New Orleans because of a freight train wreck that held up their train for eight hours. The players were forced to take the field against the Pelicans with no warm-up and were beaten, 7–2. Bender gave up four runs in the first three innings, but he did not throw hard or use his curveball. After three games with the New Orleans club, Mack moved his team north to Shreveport for practices.[7]

Two weeks into spring training, a Philadelphia sports scribe sent his report to the *Sporting News*. "Bender is once again strong and robust when a year ago he was in bad shape physically. The operation on Bender for appendicitis three months ago has restored the big Indian to perfect health and made a new man of him."[8]

The Athletics arrived back in Philadelphia on April 1 for an eight-game exhibition series with the Phillies. The weather was good for that time of year and 15,000 squeezed into Columbia Park to watch the renewal of the city rivalry. Bender shut out the Phillies, 4–0, in the series opener. Francis Richter of *Sporting Life* wrote, "Bender, the big Indian twirler, was in wonderful form for this early in the season and his effective work with men on bases prevented the Phillies from making the circuit in the nine innings. Bender used curves and speed, and eight of the Phillies were retired on strikes."[9]

The city games were split evenly, each team winning four. Though the Big Chief lost in his other start against the National Leaguers, the newspapers were enthusiastic about the Athletics' pitching prospects for 1905.

Charles Bender also had the honor of pitching the regular season's opening game, April 14, at Columbia Park. Despite chilly weather, the opener was a gala affair, with around 10,000 in attendance. The opponent was defending American League champion Boston, its players sporting red socks for the first time. Bender won a narrow 3–2 verdict over Cy Young.

Two of the three Athletics runs were largely due to the efforts of the starting pitcher. Bender walked to open the fifth inning and scored on Hoffman's double. Two frames later Bender smote a double with no one out. When Hartsel struck out, the Red Sox catcher saw Charley off the bag and whipped a throw to second. Bender took off for third and landed there safely.

"Hoffman fouled to left," wrote Charles Dryden of the Chief's run-scoring dash. "It was a short drive, but Bender took the gamble, and cantered home neck and neck with Burkett's wide throw."

Charley mowed down the champions for eight innings, limiting them to two hits and no runs. Then, in the ninth, a hit, a safe bunt, and three bases on balls nearly cost Bender the game. With two out, two runs in and the bases loaded, reserve infielder Bob Unglaub came up to pinch-hit for Young. The count went to three balls and two strikes, which meant another wide one would force in the tying run. Bender recalled that a couple of pitches were fouled off and then, "The next one I threw hard, low, and over the outside corner."[10]

Unglaub dropped his bat and started for first base, but he stopped abruptly when umpire Silk O'Loughlin shouted "Strike," making Philadelphia the winner. The *North American* reported, "Mr. Unglaub showed extreme fatigue, with a touch of petulance, when the arbitrator called him out.... Some of the war correspondents aver the ball that fanned Unglaub was a little off-side — perhaps an inch and a half. Now do be easy with Silk (the sole umpire for the game), who has looked at nothing but pool and snow balls for six months."[11]

Despite missing five weeks with what was described as kidney trouble, Bender finished the 1905 regular season with an 18–11 record. Mack never hesitated to pitch him in important games, both as a starter and a reliever. Three of his victories that season came in relief and Charley held the lead in three games for other starting pitchers.

An article that appeared in the *Washington Post* at mid-season attributed much of Bender's success during in 1905 to the spitball.

> This year Bender is particularly effective on account of his complete mastery of the spitball, and Mack claims that neither Howell nor Chesbro has worked havoc with this menace to the batter than has Bender....
>
> It is the terrific speed that Bender uses that has made his spitball so effective and Manager Mack tells of several instances where Bender would pitch this delusive ball for the batter's waist and it would take a sudden slanting drop, usually finishing up about the catcher's knee. It was this terrific momentum that Bender gives to all his curves and fastballs that causes them to take sudden and unexpected shoots and drops.

The article also quoted Charles Bender, saying, "The spit ball, I feel confident, has done me harm. I have made a resolution to give it up and will depend hereafter on speed, control, and change of pace...."[12]

Through the first three months of the season, the American League pennant chase was a nip-and-tuck contest between two teams, the Cleveland Naps and the Chicago White Sox. The heavy-hitting Naps (a nickname honoring player-manager Napoleon "Nap" Lajoie) established a big lead by the end of June and at one point held a 100-point advantage in the standings over the third-place Athletics.

On July 6 the A's returned home for a rematch with the Bostons after winning two of three games in the New England city. Andy Coakley beat Boston that afternoon and the next day Rube Waddell squared off against Cy Young at Columbia Park. Waddell began the top of the eighth inning trailing, 1–0. In that frame, Boston shortstop Fred Parent rapped a hard bouncer back to the mound that caromed off the back of Rube's pitching hand. Mack came onto the diamond and was assured by Waddell that he could still pitch. But after the next batter singled on the first pitch, Mack waved for Bender to replace Rube and Charles got out of the eighth without allowing an opposition score.

Philadelphia picked up a run to tie the game in the bottom of the inning, and the Chief sat the Bostons down in the ninth and tenth. In the bottom of the latter frame, Young walked two A's, Cy's first bases on balls in thirty innings of mound work. Danny Hoffman singled home the winning run and the Athletics' faithful erupted in celebration.[13] Philadelphia was now within a game and a half of first place.

"Charles Albert seems to be better going than coming," commented Charles Dryden. "He couldn't get started well on the front end of games of late, but as a finisher the Carlisle jeweler is great."[14]

The next afternoon, hoards of Athletics fans, afflicted with pennant fever, descended on small Columbia Park for a Saturday doubleheader with Boston. The grandstand filled well before game time and Ben Shibe allowed thousands more to stand around the outfield and along the baselines, twelve deep. An announced crowd of 25,075 got inside the park and another five to six thousand ticketless fans milled around outside. During the twin bill, fans disrupted play several times, and mounted policemen had to be called in to maintain order.

Due to the reduced amount of playing field, the two teams amassed a total of sixty-four hits in the two games and an unheard of fifty baseballs were used. With the A's down, 8–3, in the first game, Bender relieved Eddie Plank in the fifth and "The Chief" managed to get ejected while at bat in the ninth inning for throwing dirt on Umpire O'Loughlin.[15]

Weldon Henley salvaged a split of the doubleheader in the night cap with an 11–4 victory that concluded after eight innings because of darkness. Two weeks later Henley pitched a no-hit, no-run game against the seventh-place St. Louis Browns. The right-hander's masterpiece was the first no-hitter in the short history of the Athletics.

Cleveland's chances for the pennant were doomed that July when Nap Lajoie developed blood poisoning from a severe spike wound. Cleveland faltered and the Athletics surged into first place on August 2. Although Lajoie eventually recovered from his injury, Cleveland was not a factor for the remainder of the season.

After the Naps faded from the top spot, a new threat to the Athletics' pennant aspirations emerged in the Chicago White Sox. Chicago battled the A's through September, and the Sox were just three percentage points out of first place when they arrived at Columbia Park for a crucial series over the final three days of the month. The A's little ballpark was packed for the games and the playing field was again ringed with the standing-room-only crowd. "All the roofs tops looking down into the field were crowded," wrote R. H. Little, "and people leaned excitedly out of the windows of all the surrounding buildings cheering the Athletics on to victory."[16]

Eddie Plank won the first game, 3–2, on a fluke play in the seventh inning. With Hartsel on second base, Harry Davis punched a single to short left field. The hit wasn't deep enough to score Tully, but the ball struck Hartsel's mitt, which was left lying in the outfield when he came off the field between innings. Due to the glove on the field, Tully was able to score the winning run. Charles Bender won the next day in a cakewalk, 11–1.

"Charles Albert Bender, an estimable, highly respected Chippewa red man who showed his savage instincts by leading the remorseless massacre from the pitcher's box, was the idol of the multitude," wrote Little. "When he posed in front of the crowd, scowling at the shrinking Chicago batsmen, the crowd cheered. When he bent down and ground the ball into the dirt he received deafening applause, but when in a proud masterful manner he spat on the ball and wiped it on his shirt, he received an ovation...."[17]

As reported by the *Chicago Daily Tribune*, the "Carlisled son of the forest" was in trouble only once, when a pair of doubles in the fifth inning led to the Sox's only run. "The crafty Indian passed the bad paleface (Ed McFarland), got Tannehill in the box, and struck him out. Whereas a mighty shout went up. That was Bender's best stunt."[18]

With Waddell on the shelf with a sore arm, Plank came back with only one day's rest in the series finale and lost by one run in a contest with Chicago's George Owen. The three games with Chicago drew 64,899 and an estimated 10,000 ticket seekers were turned away.

After the pivotal series in Philadelphia, the White Sox stayed close to the Athletics in the standings, but never caught up. On October 5, the Athletics played a doubleheader with Washington before a big Thursday crowd of 7,734 in the nation's capitol. Winning both games from the last-place Senators would leave the Athletics only one victory away from the pennant. "Due to the ardent rooting for the Athletics," reported the *Washington Post,* "Philadelphia must have turned out a large party for these games."

In the first contest, Bender made three hits, including a triple with three runners on base, and pitched an 8–0 shutout. Andy Coakley started the night cap, but was behind 3–0 after only two innings with Case Patten, Washington's best pitcher, on the mound. In his account for the *North American,* Charles Dryden went into persiflage reminiscent of Thayer's "Casey at Bat" when Bender entered the game as a pinch-hitter.

> The faithful Mack following from Philadelphia grew glum and a chill crept down the spines of the war correspondents. A ray of light shone athwart the dismal scene when Monte drew a pass in the third, Scheck went out, then Andy Coakley crossed behind the plate, towel in hand, hiking out for the shower bath to Jake's star dressing room.
> Behind the paleface flinger who skidooed came the Indian, loose and lanky and trailing his war club on the dusty path.... Squaring his long, flat feet at the plate, Charlie blazed away and a triple bumped the distant fence.
> Monte scored and Charlie Albert plunged into third base like a bundle of old clothes. His chin caught and the rest of him flopped over and landed limply in the dust.... Topsy's triple sent the Indian home and ... the bow-legged Lave batted in another run and the score was tied."[19]

Bender took the slab and was touched for a run in the third inning. The big pitcher came right back and pasted a double in the fourth that scored two more A's base runners, but the Washingtons regained the lead in the fifth and added another tally in the sixth.

With the A's down by a run in the eighth and final round, Bender and Hartsel went out, but Lord doubled, Davis tripled and Lave Cross singled to plate the winning run. Catcher Osee Schreckengost doubled to make the final score 9–7.

Overall, Bender's credits for the day included two wins, seventeen strike-outs, two triples, a double and one single. Charley batted in seven runs and scored two in the fifteen innings he played that afternoon.

The *Washington Post* pronounced "An American Aborigine has practically won the pennant of the American League in America's greatest sport."[20]

Washington routed Coakley and Waddell the next day in a game that could have clinched the pennant, but it didn't matter. As it turned out, another A's victory was not necessary as the White Sox lost to the St. Louis Browns. The Athletics had won their second American League championship, and when they returned to Philadelphia the evening of October 7, a huge crowd had gathered at the Pennsylvania Railroad station to greet them. As the players appeared on the platform, the assembled fans began to cheer. Most of the players chose to escape the crowd by exiting to the street through the baggage room, but Bender and Rube Waddell attempted to work their way through the multitude. Several policemen were required to extricate the two trapped pitchers from the throng and then escorted the players to waiting street cars. However, the souvenir seekers ripped Rube's uniform and tore a baseball glove belonging to Harry Davis from his grasp.[21]

"Why should we play this upstart club (Boston), or any other American League team, for any post season championship?" John McGraw had sneered during the 1904 season. And Giants owner John T. Brush announced: "There is nothing in the constitution or playing rules of the National League which requires its victorious club to submit its championship honors to a contest with a victorious club in a minor league."[22] The Giants flatly turned down Boston's challenge for a World Series meeting.

In 1905, it was a different story. With the public and press expressing indignation over the Giants' snub of Boston the previous year, McGraw agreed to play the American League champion after clinching his league's pennant on October 1. The World Series between the Giants and the Philadelphia Athletics would be a best of seven games contested under guidelines prescribed by none other than John Brush, who had sabotaged the event a year earlier.

Connie Mack's club would be handicapped going into their games with the Giants because of a silly prank that cost the Athletics the services of Rube Waddell for the World Series. Back on September 8, Waddell lasted only two innings in the final game of a series in Boston. The Athletics won anyway and the team left for Philadelphia that evening. After taking three out of four games in the Boston series, the players were in a festive mood during the trip and were breaking the straw hats worn by teammates and club officials. According to fashion dictates of the time, straw hats were meant to be worn during the spring and summer, but not after Labor Day.

The A's had to change trains in Providence, Rhode Island, where the dapper Andy Coakley rejoined the team after a day's visit with his family. When Waddell spotted Coakley's straw hat, he attempted to snatch it in order to punch out the top.

"In those days," recalled Manager Mack, "the players carried their own suit rolls and there was a special compartment on the outside for spiked shoes. When Coakley saw Rube coming, he tossed the bag at Rube. The spikes caught Rube on the chin. He lost his temper, made a rush for Coakley, tripped over the suit roll and fell on his (left) arm."

"It was a hot night and he sat next to the open window," added Mack. "The next morning he could not raise his arm high enough to put on his collar."[23]

The bizarre incident at the Providence train station cost the Athletics a 26-game winner for the balance of the season and the World Series. In late September, Waddell told Mack that he was able to pitch. The A's manager inserted him into games against Chicago and Washington, but the left-hander was ineffective on both occasions and he was summarily removed. Though the newspapers reported that Waddell left that game in Boston on September 8 because of a sore arm, Connie Mack always said the problem arose because he slept with his left arm exposed to an open window on the train ride that evening. Despite the loss of their top pitcher, the Athletics managed to win the American League pennant by two games over the White Sox.

Philadelphia, with a short-handed pitching corps, would be going into the World Series against a New York Giants pitching rotation that included Christy Mathewson (31 victories), Joe McGinnity (21 wins), Red Ames (22), Dummy Taylor (15) and Hooks Wiltse (14). New York would use only two of its "big five" pitchers in the Series, but that duo was more than sufficient.

The *Philadelphia North American* erected a large gong in front of Broad Street Station to ring when an A's batter made an extra-base hit against the Giants. The gong was to ring once for each Athletic double, twice for triples and three times for a home run. Unfortunately, the Philadelphia fans only heard the bell ring on five occasions (for five doubles) during the Series.[24]

During the first decade of the century, professional gamblers were conspicuous in the stands and around the ballparks. On the day of the first game of the World Series, the historic Continental Hotel was awash with gambling activity. A Philadelphia syndicate wagered $5,000 even money that the A's would beat the Giants, and individuals bet amounts exceeding the annual salary of many a major league baseball player. Paddy Leedon, a local "sporting man," put up $2,000 even money the A's would win and his brother bet an additional $1,500 at the same odds.[25]

The *New York Times* reported that John McGraw wagered about $400 at even money with Philadelphia rooters. It was also written that New York players Boileryard Clarke, Mike Donlin, and Bill Dahlen also succeeded in getting a few bets down.[26]

In recognition of the first World Series game in Philadelphia on October 9, Giants owner John Brush had special uniforms made for his team. They were jet black, with white peaked caps and stockings and a large white NY on the front of the shirts.

A crowd of 17,955 baseball fans, about 6,000 above seating capacity, squeezed into the little wooden park at Twenty-ninth and Columbia for the first game. Special policemen held back a portion of the overflow crowd standing on the field behind the foul lines, and a large number of spectators were perched atop the fences.

When the Giants arrived upon the field a few minutes after two o'clock, they were greeted with cheers from the small but vocal New York contingent. Players from the opposing teams intermingled, shook their opposing numbers hands and engaged in friendly conversation.

"I will never forget the impression created in Philadelphia and the thrill that I got personally when the Giants suddenly trotted out from their dugout clad in uniforms of black flannel trimmed with white," recalled McGraw. "The psychological effect of being togged out in snappy uniforms was immediately noticeable upon the players. The Athletics in their regular season uniforms appeared dull alongside our champions."[27]

Among the Athletics, at least Chief Bender was confident. Just before game time, a grasshopper lit on his shoulder and Charley immediately took it as an omen for good luck. He assured his teammates that Philadelphia would be victorious that afternoon.[28]

Just before the game began, McGraw went to home plate for the pre-game talk with Athletics captain Lave Cross and Umpires Sheridan and O'Day. As the Giants manager walked up, Cross presented him with a miniature white elephant on a pedestal. McGraw accepted it and bowed in mock courtesy as the crowd laughed. John then posed for a photograph with the elephant in his hands.[29]

Left-hander Eddie Plank, a twenty-five-game winner for the Athletics, opposed Mathewson in the opening game. The two hurlers were not strangers. They had met in Pennsylvania college competition when Eddie pitched for Gettysburg and Matty for Bucknell. The A's lefty had not won a decision in their match-ups and it was to be no different on that day. The contest was scoreless until the fifth inning when the Giants broke through for two runs, an outburst ignited by a Mathewson single.

In the home half of the fifth, Seybold's line drive hit Mathewson in the groin. The Giants ace staggered, but he managed to pick up the ball and threw

New York Giants manager John McGraw holding the white elephant sculpture presented to him by the Athletics prior to the first game of the 1905 World Series (Cleveland Public Library).

Socks out at first. The pain was so severe Christy had to be helped to the bench. During the delay, McGraw ordered McGinnity to warm up, but Mathewson insisted on continuing and returned to the mound. He retired the side and continued to dominate the A's batters inning after inning. With Mathewson contributing a key sacrifice in the ninth, New York added another run, and the Giants ace pitched masterfully throughout, finishing with a four-hit, 3–0 victory.

The second game was played at New York's Polo Grounds on a cold October 10 afternoon. The park was jammed with almost 30,000 spectators and a ring of "in-the-money" fans watched from their horse-drawn carriages in distant center field. Connie Mack called on his twenty-one-year-old right-hander, Charles Albert Bender, for the most important game the Athletics had played to this time in their history.

"The grandstand was packed until those standing in the rear were almost forced over the walls," recorded the *New York Times*. "Men and women clamored and climbed for seats. Women walked with utter disregard for conventionalities on the tops of seats and jumped from one to another in their struggle for points of vantage. The bleachers were a mass of excited humanity. Men stood, sat, and hung to the roofs of the stands, in the eaves, and even on the top of the fence."

A little before two o'clock there was a wild dash onto the field for the boards that had been laid for the overflow crowd. Eventually the crowd down the baselines stood fifty deep in a solid line from the end of the right field bleachers around to the bleachers in left field.[30] Policemen mounted on horses were brought in to make sure the fans stayed in their designated places. Adding to the madness were the horns, whistles, megaphones, and rattles that contributed to the noise just as the game began and when the Giants put runners on base. If that wasn't enough delirium for the opposing pitcher to deal with, thousands of fans feverishly waved blue flags each time the Giants threatened to score.

Expressionless, Charles Bender went about his pre-game regime as usual, playing catch and batting out fly balls, all the while abstaining from the traditional ballplayer chatter. An inquiry from the press box about how he felt elicited the response, "(I) am all right," and that was the extent of Bender's conversation.[31]

New York's "Iron Man" Joe McGinnity retired the Athletics in the top of the first inning without any scoring. As Bender arrived at the mound chewing a large wad of gum, the crowd greeted him with Indian yells from all around the grounds. "Heap much bumps, Bender" became the cry.[32]

Bender's first pitch to lead-off batter Roger Bresnahan was a strike, but the speedy catcher whacked the next offering, a head-high pitch, into left field for a double. The hit pushed the noise level even higher as the fans anticipated an early lead for the Giants. However, the poised Athletics pitcher retired the next three batters easily. Browne attempted to bunt and popped out to first base, Turkey Mike Donlin fouled out, and Dan McGann went down on three empty swings, the first of nine Giants to strike out.

The Big Chief got into trouble again in the second inning when he walked Dahlen with one out. With Devlin at bat, Bender made several throws to first base, where Bad Bill was taking a big lead. First base Coach McGann kept complaining that the A's pitcher was using a balk move, but Umpire O'Day disagreed. Dahlen eventually stole second base, after which Devlin also drew a walk. The threat fizzled when the base runners attempted a double steal and Schreckengost's throw to Lave Cross nailed Dahlen at third base.

The Athletics took the lead in the top of the third inning. Schreckengost grounded to the second baseman, but first baseman McGann dropped the throw for an error. Bender bunted the base runner over to second and, with two outs, Bris Lord's single over second drove in Schreck with the first run. Charley allowed only one base runner over the next four innings, and Schreck threw that man out when he attempted to steal second.

"Bender, the tall, gaunt, swarthy aboriginal speed incubator, bent himself to his uttermost...," reported the *Times*. "Bender had speed, control, curves, slants, twists, and everything else on the boxman's calendar. New York could do nothing with him."[33]

A *New York Sun* reporter gave due credit to Bender's catcher. "Sometimes the Indian, trying to send the ball around the batter's neck, whisked it through dangerously high, but at those Schreck reached up quick as a flash and pulled the ball down as if it were the easiest thing in the world for him."[34]

The Giants still trailed only 1–0 when Mike Donlin doubled into the crowd in right-center field to open the home half of seventh inning. McGann struck out for the third consecutive time and the next two batters went out easily. The Athletics sealed the verdict in the eighth with two more runs. Schreck occupied first base, but there were two out and Hartsel was down to his last strike. McGinnity's next pitch sailed into the hitting zone and Tully met it with solid wood. The ball shot over the third baseman's head into a vacated part of left field. Osee never slowed down and turned third just as Mertes threw the ball toward home plate. The Giants had a good chance to get the runner, but the throw bounced off Schreck's back and rolled away from the catcher. Moments later Hartsel skipped home on Lord's base hit.

The Giants raised the home fans hopes in the ninth by putting the first two batters on base via an error and a walk, but Bender retired the next three batters on a pop-up and two harmless grounders to gain his first World Series victory.

Working with only two days' rest, Mathewson returned to the mound for Game Three and again befuddled Philadelphia's batters, permitting only five hits and one walk. Dan McGann was the Giants' offensive force in the 9–0 romp with two singles, a double, and four runs batted in.

Bender intently studied Mathewson's work during the Series. "I learned how to pitch a fadeaway watching Matty," he said. "It took quite a time to master the delivery, but I finally made it with constant practice and fine control."[35]

The dominance of pitching continued in Game Four when McGinnity and Plank combined to allow only one run and nine hits. The Giants scored that run in the fourth inning, largely due to errors by the A's shortstop and third baseman. The 1–0 triumph increased New York's lead in games to three to one.

It was left to Charley Bender to extend the Series in the must-win Game Five, played at a hostile Polo Grounds. McGraw countered with the redoubtable Mathewson, who would be pitching with just one day of rest. Christy again was up to the challenge, allowed only six hits and walked no one.

The two pitchers put matching zeros on the scoreboard until the bottom of the fifth inning. In that frame, Bender suffered a brief loss of control and walked Mertes and Dahlen. Art Devlin's bunt advanced the runners and Mertes scored on a sacrifice fly by Billy Gilbert. Bender intercepted the throw from the outfield and whipped the ball to Lave Cross at third in time for the tag on Dahlen. It was a nifty play by the Chief, but he now trailed, 1–0.

That was the game's only run until the home half of the eighth. Bender walked Mathewson and the Giants pitcher scurried to third base on Roger Bresnahan's double. George Browne smacked a scorcher back to the mound, but the ball caromed off Bender's hands. Monte Cross reached the ball in time to throw the batter out, but Matty scored. Charles Albert pitched well, but his three walks all figured in the scoring. The Athletics never threatened in the late going as the Giants pitcher retired the final ten batters he faced. Bender was nearly as good, yielding just five hits, but he went down to a 2–0 defeat that gave McGraw and his Giants the World Series championship.

Mathewson was phenomenal in his three starts against the Athletics. In the space of six days, he pitched three shutouts and allowed only fourteen hits. The Giants' "Big Six" struck out eighteen and walked only one batter in twenty-seven innings. All five games of the Series ended in a shutout.

It had to be fresh on the mind of Connie Mack that during the war between the two leagues, he had Matty's name on a contract for the 1901 season, but the pitcher jumped back to the Giants. "That hurt more than anything," Mack remarked. "Why that big fellow should have been pitching for me."[36]

The Athletics' .161 team batting average was the lowest ever for a World Series and the two teams combined .185 is also an all-time low. As losers, each player on the Athletics was to receive only a 25 percent share of the total amount allocated for the players. However, the rules for the Series had called for too great a gap between the winning and losing shares, so fifteen individual players made side agreements with their opposing counterparts to split their shares fifty-fifty. By spurning these side agreements, only McGraw, Mathewson and Bresnahan walked away with a full winners share of $1,142. Some Giants subsequently tried to wriggle out of their deal, though with limited success.[37]

In the end, each of the A's received a far greater payday than they expected. Prior to the Series, Ben Shibe notified American League president Ban Johnson that the Athletics wanted to have the club's percentage of the receipts for the first four games of the Series divided among the players. In addition to the $380.47 they received from the National Commission, each Philadelphia player got an additional check for $451.75 as his share of the $8,131.49 chipped in by management.[38]

Addie Joss, star hurler for the Cleveland American League club, claimed Bender's work during the Series against the Giants signaled a new method of pitching.

"There was a time when it was the accepted theory that one of the requisites of the first-class pitchers was the ability to keep the ball around the batter's neck," Joss wrote in his newspaper column later in the decade. "Bender had the advantage of the gathering gloom, and this, coupled with his ability to keep his fastball low, proved a stumbling block for the aggressive Giants. Members of both teams say the big fellow was unhittable on account of this, which goes to show how much harder it is to hit the low ball than the high one."[39]

After the Series, the Athletics, minus Lave Cross, Davis and Lord, went on a barnstorming trip and played games in seven cities in seven days. It was said the champions cleared a neat sum for the week's work and the *North American* chipped in $1,000 from the sales of a souvenir book celebrating the champions.[40]

On the evening October 23, Philadelphia staged a great parade down the length of Broad Street to celebrate the Athletics' American League pennant. Amid fireworks and countless banners and flags, the more than 10,000 participants and a large number of floats and vehicles dwarfed the parade of three years earlier. Chief Bender, Andy Coakley and Eddie Plank rode in one of the eight automobiles provided for the players and team officials. Among the impersonators from a local Mummers club was a Pennsylvania "hayseed" for Rube Waddell, a scalpel-wielded operating room physician for Doc Powers, a white-cloaked ghost for Scheckengost and a war-whooping Indian for Bender. The Mummers also borrowed an elephant from the Philadelphia zoo, although the zookeepers drew the line at giving the pachyderm a coat of white-wash.[41]

♦ 6 ♦

"I Will Devote My Time ... to the Match Shooting Business"

Reporters at spring training in Montgomery, Alabama, were optimistic about the Athletics' chances of repeating as American League champions in 1906. One Philadelphia scribe wrote, "Another encouraging report from the South is that Bender, who a year ago was in bad health, is now big and strong and in grand shape physically. In his first game the Indian struck out six men in the two innings he pitched and only one hit was made off him."[1]

The only noteworthy personnel change by the defending American League champions was at third base, where there was a vacancy after forty-year-old Lave Cross was sold to Washington. The move cleared the way for Harry Davis, Mack's most reliable confidant on the team, to officially be named team captain.

Competing for Lave's third base job was Reuben "Rube" Oldring, whose contract was purchased from the Montgomery Southern League club during the 1905 season. Despite his commitment to the Athletics, Rube played eight regular season games and two exhibition contests at third base for his home-town New York Highlanders that October. Rube batted .300, with a triple, a home run, and four stolen bases in his brief stint with the New Yorkers.

At the conclusion of the 1905 season, the Highlanders' Clark Griffith attempted to draft Oldring. The player's contract, however, was owned by Philadelphia and the New York club had to give up any designs on Rube.[2] Oldring was born in the same month and year as Charles Bender; the pair would become roommates and remained lifelong friends.

Poor weather in the South limited the Athletics' practice time during spring training, and when they returned home for the 1906 Philadelphia series the first of April, the team was greeted with snowy, frigid conditions. The first two games against the Phillies were canceled due to the wet and cold.

Once the city series finally began, the Athletics won the first two games behind the pitching of Waddell and Plank. Bender got his turn in the third contest. Opposing Bender was the veteran Tully Sparks, who "pitched superbly" and held the Athletics to only two hits. Bender was good as well, scattering six hits, and he became the winning pitcher when the A's scored the only run of the day on a wild throw by the Phillies third baseman.[3]

The Athletics dominated the pre-season city series, winning four of the five games with the National Leaguers. Andy Coakley could have won the only game the A's lost except for sloppy fielding by his teammates.

Following the games with the Phillies, Connie Mack took his team to Atlantic City for the week-long break before the regular season opener in Washington. During their time in the resort city, Mack divided the Athletics into two squads for daily afternoon scrimmages. Unfortunately, Rube Oldring broke an ankle in one of the practice games the day before the regular season opened. Rube had won the third base job during spring training but now would be lost until July 25.[4]

The Athletics opened the 1906 American League season on April 14 in Washington, D.C. against the Nationals, as the team was now called. Dressed in their road uniforms of Quakers grey, the A's joined the home team for a pre-game parade around the grounds as a band on hand for the festivities played "Dixie." For the second straight year, Chief Bender drew the Opening Day pitching assignment and the Athletics beat the Nationals, 4–3. Charley was dominant for the first eight innings and Washington was only able to make the score close because of a Monte Cross error in the ninth inning. With two out, light-hitting catcher Mike Heyton brought the home fans to their feet with a two-run double. However, Bender induced pinch-hitter Joe Stanley to roll out to second base for the final out. The *Washington Post* observed, "Bender is in mid-season form."

On April 29, 1906, the New York ban on Sunday baseball was temporarily lifted so the Highlanders and Athletics could play a benefit game for the victims of the San Francisco earthquake. The teams raised $5,600 and also worked out a trade. Connie Mack traded outfielder Danny Hoffman, who had been complaining about his loss of playing time, to the Highlanders for the rights to a former A's outfielder, Dave Fultz.

A Brown graduate with a law degree from Columbia, Fultz batted .302 for Mack's 1902 champions and then was sold to New York in 1903. Although the thirty-one-year-old outfielder declined to rejoin the Athletics because he wanted to practice law, the *Sporting News* reasoned that Mack felt he had to get rid of Hoffman because "harmony in a club was more essential and more of a winning factor than the best individual player that ever lived."[5]

In 1906 four ex–Carlisle Indian School students would play in the major leagues: Bender; Minnesota Chippewa Frank Jude, an outfielder who played in 80 games for Cincinnati; Charlie Roy, who pitched seven games with the cross-town Phillies; and Louis Leroy. Leroy finally escaped the Carlisle School for good in December 1901 and joined the Buffalo Bisons of the Eastern League the following spring. He was picked up by the New York Highlanders in September of 1905 after winning eighteen games with Montreal during the Eastern League season.

Louis made his major league debut on September 22 and held the Chicago White Sox to only six hits in a complete game 5–2 victory. "Leroy showed pitching ability of an unusually high order," reported the *New York Times*. "He depended a great deal upon the wet ball, which he delivered with telling effect. Speed was not conspicuous in his delivery, but curves and drops appeared to be his stronghold."[6]

The game between the Athletics and Highlanders at Hilltop Park on May 4, 1906, featured a match between Leroy and his old Carlisle classmate, Charles Bender. The Athletics tagged Louis for two early runs and it appeared the defending champions were well on their way to a victory.

"For four innings," reported the *New York Times*, "Bender's pitching was troublesome, only one scratch hit being made off his delivery…. But the Indian became nettled at the rulings of Umpire Evans on balls and strikes, and the climax was reached in the fifth inning, when he vigorously protested a decision of Umpire Hurst…."

The trouble began when a Highlander base runner attempted to steal second. When Tim Hurst called an opposition runner safe, Bender exploded. He threw his glove down and uncharacteristically berated and kicked at the umpire. Charley was thrown out of the game and Waddell came on to retire the side, but Eddie Plank took the mound for the sixth and was touched for four runs in two innings.

Though Leroy retired the A's in order in the top of the fifth, he was removed for a pinch-hitter in the very inning Bender was ejected. The two Carlisle alumni were out of the game with the score tied at 2–2. (New York eventually won, 6–2.)[7] That contest would be the only meeting between Bender and Leroy as major leaguers.

Angry at his ejection and the roasting he received from the Highlanders' bench jockeys, Bender asked Mack if he could have another shot against the New Yorkers the next day, which also happened to coincide with the pitcher's twenty-second birthday. Some 6,000 bugs braved the threat of bad weather to come out for the day's game, delayed in the second inning when the steady drizzle turned to rain for about fifteen minutes. Bender not only defeated the Highlanders on only six hits despite the slippery field, he drove one of "Buffalo Bill" Hogg's curveballs into deep right field for an inside-the-park home run that sent two base runners around to score in front of him.

Reported the *New York Times*, "The advent of the big Indian in the box for Philadelphia after his display of temper the day before made him a mark for the jeers of the crowd, but before the game ended they were applauding his good work in the box and at bat.... Had he been perfectly supported the home team would have been shut out."[8]

Bender's most remarkable game as a hitter came on May 8 when Philadelphia was playing the Boston club at Huntington Avenue Grounds. Though the Athletics were having their way with Boston starting pitcher Jesse Tannehill, Connie Mack was having a hard time finding people to play in the field. In the sixth inning he decided to put in one of his best pitchers, Charles Bender, to play left field. That substitution would spell Tully Hartsel, who was overworked because of the ball club's recent rash of injuries to position players.

In his initial at-bat, Charles Albert connected with Tannehill's first pitch and drove a long fly ball that bounced into the overflow crowd of people that was allowed to stand in the deepest environs of right field. While Bender was racing around the bases, right fielder Buck Freeman retrieved the ball from among the feet and threw it in to shortstop Freddie Parent. The relay was late and Bender slid under the catcher's tag attempt for an inside-the-park home run. Most often a ball hit into a crowd of standees was ruled a ground-rule double, but Umpire Sheridan allowed the four-bagger because the fans did not interfere with Freeman's play on the ball and the Boston club did not question the decision.

Left fielder Bender came up to the plate for a second time in the eighth inning with a runner on second base and Philadelphia leading, 9–2. There was a two-ball, two-strike count when Bender's bat made solid contact with a Tannehill pitch. The sphere flew on a line into center field and shot past Larry Stahl's leaping attempt. By the time Stahl caught up with the ball, Bender, a former track athlete at Carlisle, was already nearing third. A good throw might have nailed Charley at the plate, but the relay throw was off-line and Bender crossed the plate with his second inside-the-park home run in as many at-bats.[9] As soon as he crossed the plate, Bender's teammates surrounded him in celebration.

Recounting his baseball career years later, Charles rated that game among his most memorable. Bender would hit just three more home runs in his sixteen-year major league career.

Two days later, Bender took the mound in Huntington Avenue Grounds and defeated the Bostons, 5–1. Philadelphia was in first place at the time and in the midst of an eleven-game winning spree. Charley won three games during the streak, running his record to five wins out of six decisions.

Cleveland stopped the Athletics' winning streak on May 21. Despite having struck out thirteen opposing batters, Waddell was pulled for a pinch-hitter in the bottom of the ninth inning with the score knotted at a run apiece. Bender took over for Rube and pitched hitless ball over the next three innings. By the fourteenth inning, daylight was fading and it was doubtful the game could continue after that inning.

Bender started the fourteenth by striking out Bill Bradley, and next up for the Naps was their left-handed-batting catcher Harry Bemis. Bemis swung at Bender's first pitch and lifted a high fly ball to left field. Hartzel moved back to the fence, but he could only watch as the ball sailed out of the ballpark, across Broad Street, and landed among the trolleys awaiting the end of the contest. Cleveland rookie right-hander Harry Eells retired the Athletics in the home half of the fourteenth to secure the win for Cleveland.[10]

A couple of days later, Waddell showed up at the ballpark with a swollen left thumb. The southpaw explained that when he jumped out of his carriage before it collided with a delivery wagon, his thumb got caught in the whip socket. Chief Bender's recollection of his teammate's injury was quite different. "What happened was that he actually had been driving in his buggy, but an ice wagon had blocked the road. So Waddell took a sock at the ice man and made the mistake of hitting him with the thumb out."[11]

Rube returned to pitch in less than two weeks but was not effective. The injured thumb bothered Waddell for much of the season and he finished the year with a un–Rube-like 15–17 won-lost record. The Athletics managed to stay in first place until June 1, when a loss to the Highlanders dropped the club into second place.

Connie Mack often used Bender and Waddell in relief when the starting pitcher faltered, and over a period of two days in late June 1906, the Chief relieved in three consecutive games against the Nationals at Washington's League Park. The doubleheader on June 29 was played in sweltering summer heat that was so bad shortstop Monte Cross was forced to leave the second game due to heat prostration. After pitcher Andy Coakley was tagged for three runs in the seventh inning of the first game, Mr. Mack ushered Bender into the game. The Athletics were only up two runs when Andy departed, but Bender held the Nationals at bay for the final two innings to preserve Philadelphia's victory. Bender succeeded two Philadelphia pitchers in the second game with the Athletics down by five runs, but his team's late rally fell short by one score. In the next day's game, Waddell began to complain about the heat around the sixth inning and Bender came on to save the game with three shutout innings in the A's 6–5 win.

A rain-out of the home game with New York on July 3 forced the Athletics to schedule an Independence Day doubleheader at Columbia Park. After the Mackmen won the first game, Bender pitched well but lost to Al Orth and the Highlanders, 2–1, in the nightcap. It would be the Chief's last appearance on the mound for a while. Newspaper reports indicated he was "debilitated by bowel problems."

On July 5, rookie right-hander Jack Coombs blanked Washington, 3–0, in his first start with the Athletics. Tom McGillicuddy recommended the four-sport star at Colby College to his brother and the Athletics signed

Coombs to a contract in the winter of 1905 on the condition he would join the team following his graduation the following spring. Coombs was an intelligent ballplayer who employed an outstanding fastball and a deceptive curve thrown out of an intimidating sidearm delivery.[12]

Less than two months after he reported to the Athletics, Coombs hooked up with Joe Harris of the Boston Red Sox in one of baseball's most memorable games. On September 1, 1906, the Athletics and Red Sox battled through twenty-four high pressure innings. Jack Coombs pitched the entire game and finally won the duel. He allowed one run in the marathon, struck out eighteen batters and triumphed, 4–1.

"Bender has just returned from a seashore resort, where he had gone to get rid of a chronic attack of cholera morbus," reported the *Sporting News* on July 28. "He has got rid of it all right but lost about 25 pounds in weight."

The same article included the tidbit: "(Andy) Coakley, who has been ailing all season, was granted a vacation to go to the Vermont hills for a couple of weeks to recuperate, but instead of going away to rest and build up, he was secretly married the night before he left and his bride has gone with him to New England."[13]

During Bender's absence, the Athletics regained first place and eventually took a seven-game lead over the White Sox. They then visited South Side Park in Chicago for a five-game series beginning on August 5. Bender was routed in the first game, 10–2, and the Athletics lost all five contests. The Chief lost again, 7–4, to the Browns in his next effort and was uncharacteristically wild with his pitches in both August starts.

While Philadelphia lost eight straight games, Chicago won nineteen games in a row during the first three weeks of August to fly past the Athletics in the standings. Plank was hurt and couldn't pitch at all, Bender was ill, and Waddell was inconsistent due to his injured thumb. Danny Murphy and Socks Seybold were also on the shelf due to injury. On August 4, the Athletics were resting in first place with a record of 59 wins and 34 losses. The club went 19–33 the remainder of the season, along the way enduring a major-league record 48 consecutive innings of play without scoring a run.

On September 4, Bender made his final start of the season, a win over Washington. The Athletics were in third place, four-and-one-half games out of first, but two days later the club suffered the first of three straight losses that finished their pennant chances for good. When the A's left for a twelve-game road trip September 16, Bender and several other veterans were left at home.

Playing ball under the name of Sullivan, a junior at Columbia University named Eddie Collins appeared in his first game for the Athletics in Chicago on September 17. Sullivan, who played shortstop that afternoon, got one hit off Ed Walsh and struck out twice. Collins would go on to play twenty-five years in the major leagues, bat .333, and gain induction into the Baseball Hall of Fame.

Chief Bender's hitting improved each season after joining the Athletics and in 1906 he had his best season at the plate to date. He batted .253 with 25 hits in 44 games, legged out four doubles and slugged three home runs. It was a remarkable performance for a pitcher, in that American League batters as a group hit for a .249 average. Charley also filled in as a substitute outfielder in four games. Bender appeared on the mound in 36 games, won 15, lost 10, and held the lead for the Athletics in three other games as a substitute pitcher.

On December 13, 1906, Connie Mack sold pitcher Andy Coakley to Cincinnati. A twenty-game winner in 1905, he slipped to 7–8 a year later. Coakley struggled through two more seasons in the major leagues before embarking on a thirty-seven-year career as baseball coach at Columbia University. Columbia's baseball team still plays its games at Andy Coakley Field.

Though he returned his signed 1907 contract to Connie Mack in early February, Charles Bender was a no-show at the club's training site in Marlin, Texas, that March. Bender never made it to Marlin, and the *Philadelphia Inquirer* reported on March 13 that the Chief was in Dallas and would stay there until the Athletics arrived to play a series of exhibition games in that city and Fort Worth. Charley saw his first action on March 17 when he and newcomer Rube Vickers led the A's rookies and substitutes, or "yannigans" as they were called in those days, to a 2–0 victory over Dallas.

Reported the *Inquirer*, "Bender only cut loose a few times, but that was enough for the home team. Half the Texans stood with one foot in the batter's box and the other in an encouraging position towards the bench as if the quicker they could get back to the bench the better it would be for them."[14]

That spring Mack moved Rube Oldring to the outfield. "I had a powerful arm and in fielding the ball at third I often threw over the first baseman's head," Rube acknowledged. "As result, I was charged with 16 errors in 59 games that year (1906)."[15]

The following spring, Rube's 1907 contract bore a note from Mack: "From this day on, you are my center fielder. You will have all the room you want and will not have to throw the ball over anybody's head."[16]

Mack did not play Oldring in center field only because of his strong arm; Rube had the ability to get a good jump on the ball, he was fast, and he made few errors. Rube would lead the American League in fielding percentage three times. In 1913 he stole 40 bases, and he hit fourteen triples in 1910 and again in 1911.[17]

The highlight of the spring was to be a seven-game exhibition series against John McGraw's New York Giants at the home park of the Southern League's New Orleans Pelicans. The games would bring the excitement of major league baseball to the South and the two teams could make a little money in the process. The Giants beat Coombs and the Athletics, 4–3, on March 27 in the first game of the series—then things became interesting.

In the first inning of the second game, the Giants became incensed when umpire Charles Zimmer did not call a balk on Eddie Plank's feint toward third base. McGraw and catcher Roger Bresnahan reviled the umpire and raised such a ruckus Zimmer ordered them out of the game. Policemen ushered Bresnahan out of the park, but McGraw fled to the protection of the Giants bench. The New York manager declared he would pull his men off the field if the umpire did not reverse the ejection. Zimmer awarded the game to the Athletics by a 9–0 forfeit score. That afternoon, McGraw complained that Zimmer, a former National League catcher who lived in New Orleans, was making calls favorable to the Athletics so Mack would use his influence to get him an arbiter job in the Southern League.

A big holiday crowd was on hand for the next day's game, but the Giants refused to take the field as long as Zimmer was the umpire. McGraw's crew was given five minutes to assume their positions on the field and at the expiration of that deadline Zimmer again forfeited the game to the Athletics.

In an effort not to disappoint the crowd, the Giants agreed to play if Joe Rickert, a player on the New Orleans club, was allowed to officiate the contest. The Athletics proceeded to pound the New Yorkers, 7–0. Especially pleasing to the Athletics had to be the five runs they scored off Christy Mathewson before his departure after four innings on the mound.

New York sports reporter Joe Villa quipped that after "the sportsmanlike gentlemen from Harlem" were whitewashed "McGraw took to his bed with cramps while the rest of the series ended in a farce that will do the National League here a world of harm."

"It is the general inference that McGraw, realizing he was dead lucky to win the first game from the Athletics," Villa added. He "was leery about the rest of the series and picked a row that would break things up so effectually that the fading World's Champions would either get another umpire who would fear them or could duck out of the series altogether."[18]

New Orleans correspondent Will Hamilton did not mince words. "It is not exaggerating to say that this was the dirtiest deal ever given any town and it is doubtless the most cowardly trick the dirtiest and rowdiest of all base ball managers ever pulled off."[19]

After the Pelicans owner barred the gates of Athletic Park to McGraw's team prior to the game of March 30, he wired his club to return home and replace the Giants for the final two games of the series against the Athletics. Since the New Orleans club was also obligated to play in Alexandria, the Athletics loaned a few players to the Pelicans so those games could proceed as scheduled. Harry Davis sent Bender, Dygert, Coombs and Plank to Alexandria, after which those players would rejoin the A's in Philadelphia on April 3.

Because of the games Connie Mack had scheduled with the Giants, he insisted the city series with the Phillies be pushed back until his A's finished their business in New Orleans. The National Leaguers were annoyed at Mack's demand and the angry Phillies polished off the Athletics in four straight games when the two clubs finally met.

Though the *Sporting News* reported that "the Indian has gained something like 28 pounds in weight ... and says he has never felt so good and strong in his life," Chief Bender was not ready for the start of the season. He didn't pitch in New Orleans against the Giants or in the city series. He would only appear on the mound as a relief pitcher during the first week of the season.

The Opening Day game on April 11 was played in frigid weather with 10,000 souls braving the conditions at Columbia Park. Jack Coombs and Cy Young completed nine innings with the game tied, 4–4. Young retired and Jesse Tannehill replaced him on the mound for the Red Sox, but Mack stayed with Coombs. It was beginning to get dark by the fourteenth inning when Coombs weakened and Boston scored four runs to win the game.

Conditions had not improved for the season's second game two days later. Only 4,000 shivering, half-frozen spectators showed up for the Saturday game, a day that usually guaranteed the biggest gate of the week. Rube Vickers started for the Athletics, but the gale that blew across the field made it impossible for him to control the ball and he was removed after only one inning. Waddell took over with Philadelphia down, 1–0, and Tully Hartsell socked a ball over the right field fence with two teammates on base to give the Athletics the lead. Waddell took a 4–2 lead into the ninth inning and retired the first two batters. He got two strikes on Charlie Armbruster and then Rube wasted four pitches out of the strike zone trying to whiff the Boston batter. After walking Armbruster, Rube's next pitch hit Billy Sullivan square in the back.

According to the *Sporting News* "That was too much for Captain Davis ... (who) promptly called time and motioned to the bench for Bender to come out. Waddell begged Davis not to take him out, saying he would fan out (Jimmy) Collins in short order, but Captain Harry said nay and to the bench he had to go. Bender showed the form he was in this spring by putting three across the plate so fast that Collins couldn't see one of them. Three balls was all the Indian flung and the game was over."[20]

Four days later, Waddell again took a 4–2 lead into the ninth inning, this time against the New York Highlanders at Hilltop Park. After a walk and a single, Mack removed Rube and brought in Bender "amid war whoops from the excited palefaces."[21] This time the move backfired. New York scored three times off the Chief to win, 5–4. Angry about being removed from the two games, Waddell walked out on the team and, on April 27, Mack suspended the troublesome left-hander.

Bender was prepared to take the Monday afternoon off for the first game of a series in Washington on April 29. However, he forgot to check with Ban Johnson. The American League president notified the Washington management that there would be no umpire present for the day's game and two players should be selected to officiate. The home team picked Piano Legs Hickman and Connie Mack selected Bender, who was not expected to pitch until the final game of the series. With the two players acting as substitute arbiters, the A's won, 2–1. The *Washington Post* complained that "there was considerable dissatisfaction with the umpiring," and the *Washington Herald* chimed in, "(Washington manager) Cantillon objected strenuously to one of Bender's decisions at first base, but otherwise the sub umps had a rather easy time of it."[22]

The regular umpire showed up for the next day's game and the Chief got his afternoon off. However, Bender performed no better on the mound in his start on Thursday than he had as an umpire, departing after the fifth inning, trailing 4–1.

Plagued by a sore arm and poor health, Bender was hardly spectacular early in the 1907 season. He was routed in successive starts against the Tigers on May 18 (the A's lost, 15–8) and May 22 (lost, 6–5). On May 30, Boston beat the Big Chief, 6–4, at Columbia Park, his fourth successive losing effort. Connie Mack pulled Bender from the starting rotation and gave him almost a month off.

When water therapy for Bender's lame right arm prescribed by the club's physician provided little or no improvement, Connie Mack allowed trainer Martin Lawler to apply his own methods to the pitcher's ailing limb. In less than a month Bender's right arm regained its strength of old and he embarked on the most successful string of games during his career as a major league pitcher. Unfortunately, the arm problems returned in September and Bender spent the final weeks of the season on the invalid list.[23]

Philadelphia held first place the last week of April, but the Athletics were hurting. Bender and Plank were both out for a while as were second baseman Danny Murphy and shortstop Monte Cross. By late May, Philadelphia had fallen to fifth place. Mack had no choice but to take back a repentant Waddell and immediately put him on the mound.

Ultimately, the chase for the 1907 pennant became a close affair. The defending World Series champion Chicago White Sox jumped out in front during the early part of the season with the Athletics and Detroit Tigers in close pursuit.

In the seventh inning of a game against Chicago at Columbia Park on June 4, Chief Bender pinch-hit for a future Hall of Fame second baseman.

The A's were trailing, 6–5, but had landed runners on second and third with one out. The White Sox elected to intentionally walk catcher Schreckengost and have Doc White pitch to the youngster Eddie Collins instead. Connie Mack ordered Bender to pinch-hit for Eddie and the move almost paid off. Charley smashed a line drive toward right field, but second baseman Frank Isbell leapt, caught the ball, and jogged to the base to easily double up Rube Oldring, who was well on his way to third base. Bender finished the game at second base, the only time he played that position in a regular season ball game. He had no chances in the field and finished his major league career as a second sacker without a fielding average.

The Athletics lost, 10–6, and Connie Mack was very dissatisfied with his team's sloppy effort, especially with the infield play of third baseman Jack Knight, who committed his twenty-first error in forty games. Mack got the man he had long coveted on June 7 when Jimmy Collins, the former player-manager of Boston, was acquired in a trade for Knight. Collins had once been the best third baseman in the game, but at thirty-seven his skills were waning and his performance was adversely affected by the knee injury he sustained in 1906.

On July 10, the Athletics traveled to St. Louis for a game with the Browns the following day. They were without their manager, because Mack stayed in Chicago "on business." In those days, teams did not employ coaches so it was up to the team captain or another player to take over the club in the absence of the manager. On this occasion, Mack named catcher Osee Schreckengost acting manager. In the first game at St. Louis, the two clubs battled into the twelfth inning with the score tied, 5–5. With a runner on second, Schreck called on the idle Chief Bender to pinch-hit for the slumping Oldring. Bender jumped on the first pitch he saw and singled to center field, driving in the lead run. Rube Waddell, who came on in relief of Jimmy Dygert in the seventh, struck out the side in the bottom of the twelfth to preserve the victory. Bender took the mound the following afternoon as the starting pitcher and allowed only one run in a Philadelphia rout.[24]

Bender threw a masterful two-hitter in beating Big Ed Walsh and the Chicago White Sox, 2–0, in the first game of a doubleheader at Columbia Park on July 25. The Athletics reached the Pale Hose spitballer for two runs in the first inning of the opener and the two star hurlers were invincible after that.

"Mr. Bender, the polite young Carlisled son of the forest," wrote Charles Dryden, now working for the *Chicago Daily Tribune*, "bleached us with two blows, both doubles...." But each time the White Sox threatened to score "Bender put up an Indian sign and kept it working overtime. 'Ugh! Heap big war chief!'"[25]

By mid-season, the White Sox had fallen by the wayside and the pennant chase became a contest between the Athletics and Detroit's Tigers. The

Mackmen stayed on the heels of the Tigers through July and August, largely due to Bender's eleven consecutive complete game victories.

BENDER'S ELEVEN STRAIGHT
COMPLETE GAME VICTORIES

	opponent/pitcher	score	site
June 25	Washington/Charlie Smith	3–2	Columbia Park
July 4	New York/Al Orth	3–1	Hilltop Park
July 8	Chicago/Frank Owen	5–2	South Side Park
July 12	St. Louis/Cy Morgan	9–1	Sportsman's Park
July 18	Cleveland/Bob Rhoads	5–0	League Park
July 25	Chicago/Ed Walsh	2–0	Columbia Park
July 30	St. Louis/Jack Powell	2–1	Columbia Park
August 2	Cleveland/Bob Rhoads	9–1	Columbia Park
August 7	Detroit/Ed Killian	4–2	Columbia Park
August 10	Detroit/Bill Donovan	1–0	Columbia Park
August 15	Cleveland/Addie Joss	4–2	League Park

Bender's two victories over the first-place Tigers were especially sweet after they roughed him up earlier in the year. On August 10, 1907, at Columbia Park, Charles beat first-place Detroit, 1–0. Tigers hurler Bill Donovan allowed only three hits in the contest, but a first-inning base on balls proved his undoing. A walk, an error, a sacrifice and a wild pitch produced the only run of the game.

"Bender's pitching was remarkable and showed the splendid form he has reached," wrote the *Philadelphia Press*. "At all times he was master of himself and in addition to the three ragged hits which would not have been hits on a fast diamond, he did not permit a runner to reach third, and ... only one man got his base on balls. This was Jones in the ninth inning, Bender protesting and apparently correctly that Jones should have been called out on strikes."[26]

After the Sunday off-day, Rube Waddell beat the Tigers on Monday afternoon to push the Athletics into first place, a position they held in the standings until August 24.

On August 15, Bender won his eleventh straight complete game, defeating Cleveland's Addie Joss, 4–2. Charley's victory was especially notable in that he did not have his best stuff, pitched in and out of trouble all afternoon, and still prevailed against one of the best pitchers in baseball.

"Quiet Charles Edward [*sic*] Bender, the 'Chief of the Chippewas,' the 'human iceberg,' played leading roles with 'Socks,' " wrote Henry P. Edwards in the *Plain Dealer*. "The support accorded Bender at times would have driven many a young pitcher to the tall timber, but the fact that his teammates contributed five errors did not seem to worry the noble redskin in the least and he never let the Naps score until the ninth inning."[27]

Philadelphia carried a 4–0 lead into the ninth due to Bender's clutch pitching and the all-around play of Socks Seybold. The burly right fielder led the A's attack with two doubles and a single, drove in a run, scored another and made one of the best outfield plays of the year.

The Naps' Nig Clarke was on first base in the fourth inning when Bill Hinchman lifted a fly ball to short right field. It appeared Seybold had no chance to catch it, but he sprinted in and made a one-handed grab with his mitt an instant before the ball hit the ground. Socks kept right on running and beat the base runner back to the first sack to complete the unusual unassisted double play.

Cleveland did not go quietly against Bender in the ninth as two singles and an error led to a Naps run. With one out and a runner on third, Elmer Flick, one of the best hitters in the league and a former American League batting champion, crushed a pitch that appeared to be headed for the right field bleachers. It looked like a sure home run, but the wind pushed the ball to the right of the open seats. Seybold was off at the crack of the bat and hauled the ball in just short of the fence. The runner on third tagged up and scored to make it 4–2, but Bender fanned the light-hitting Rabbit Nill to settle the verdict.

After winning eleven consecutive starts, Bender won his twelfth game in a row in a relief effort against Cleveland on June 19. Joss started against Waddell and neither was effective. Rube lasted only one inning, relieved by Jimmy Dygert with the A's down, 3–0, and Joss blew up in the third when the Athletics scored six times. Dygert left after the seventh inning with the A's trailing, 8–7. Bender came into the game and, when the Athletics rallied for two runs in the eighth, he picked up the victory. The Chief allowed only one base runner, via a walk, and was the game's only effective pitcher in the 10–8 Philadelphia victory.[28]

Bender's personal winning streak finally ended on August 21 when he lost a pitching duel, 1–0, to Frank "Piano Mover" Smith in Chicago. The two hurlers put up eight scoreless innings, Bender allowing only a scratch hit by Dougherty and Sullivan's two-bagger. Smith gave up nine hits, but six came after two were out.

The Athletics almost took the lead in their half of the ninth. With one out, Bris Lord singled and moved up to second on a passed ball. Powers struck out, so it was up to Bender and he responded with a safety to center field. However, "a gallant heave" by Sox center fielder Fielder Jones just nipped Lord, who made a headlong dive for the plate.

Ed Hahn led off for Chicago in the last of the ninth and singled. Fielder Jones was up next and bunted the ball toward the pitcher. In his haste to retire the speedy Jones, Bender threw wild to first base. Harry Davis blocked the throw, but Jones was safe and Hahn sprinted to third. The A's brought the infield in and the Chief tried to pass Isbell, but the Rooster lunged for a wide pitch and meekly popped a foul ball that was corralled by Eddie Collins for the first out. It was only a temporary respite for Bender as Jigger Donohue ended the drama by chopping a bounder over the drawn-in shortstop to settle the contest.

Though the report of the affair in the *Daily Tribune* was not credited, it was classic Dryden. "While Joe Farrell's band blew holes in the air and Ed Heeman's rooting machine rumpled and wheezed; Charles Albert Bender strode toward the bench from whence his paleface pards had fled. Halfway in from the slab the Indian made a drop kick for goal with his glove. The swat of his toe raised the limp bunch of leather high in the air and as it fell Charles Albert passed on without looking back. One of his pals picked up the glove and will no doubt preserve it for Charles Albert to use another time."[29]

The Athletics moved into the top spot again on September 4 when Bender beat the New York Highlanders, 4–2, at Columbia Park. It was the Chief's second win over the Gotham team in less than a week, having pitched a three-hit, 3–0, shutout against Jack Chesbro in New York on August 31. After that game, the season turned sour for Bender and the A's.

On September 11, the Philadelphia castoff, Jack Knight, drove a long home run over the head of Rube Oldring in center field to make Boston a 5–4 winner over Bender. Three days later the Big Chief would pitch his final game for the A's in 1907. Though Philadelphia beat Boston, 7–6, Bender was obviously laboring by the sixth and had to be relieved an inning later when the Red Sox plated four runs to tie the score at six. The Athletics finished the day in first place, three games ahead of Detroit, but the loss of Bender for the remainder of the season due to a sore right arm may well have cost the Athletics a pennant. He was having his best season in the major leagues to that point — sixteen victories, four of them shutouts, against eight defeats and a 2.04 earned run average.

Bender did get into two games that September as a first baseman. On September 16 Charley pinch-hit for Harry Davis, who had to leave the game against New York because of a painful hip. Charley finished the game at the initial sack and the next day he played the entire game at first, though the experience was not among his shining moments as an Athletic.

A fifteen-minute rain shower in the second inning left the Columbia Park infield in poor condition and Bender struggled in the muck all afternoon, committing three errors. Worse yet, Jack Coombs, who was also battling a sore pitching arm, started for the A's and lasted only one-third of an inning, allowed two hits, a walk, and three runs. It became so hopeless for the home team, outfielder Bris Lord pitched the ninth inning for the Athletics and allowed the Highlanders' final two runs in the visitors' 11–3 rout.[30]

The Detroit club had a solid lineup that year, and their star center fielder

Ty Cobb, then twenty-one, made the Tigers a formidable foe. When the Tigers made their final visit of the season to Philadelphia for a three-game series starting on September 27, 1907, they were only a half-game behind the Athletics in the standings. Though the Tigers had won three more games than Philadelphia, the A's had a higher won-lost percentage due to rainouts that were not made up.

At this crucial juncture, the Athletics were having a difficult time finding healthy pitchers. Looking back on these events nearly four decades later, Mack told author Fred Lieb in his book, *Connie Mack: Grand Old Man of Baseball,* "Coombs injured his arm early, but what hurt us the most was that Bender's arm went absolutely lame at a time when we needed him most. Waddell had become unreliable, and I had to depend almost entirely on Plank and young Dygert, my little spitball pitcher."[31] Despite this discouraging situation, Mack remained optimistic. He remarked on the morning of the first game of the series with the Tigers that "If we beat them two out of three games, that should win it (the pennant) for us."

The first game pitted Eddie Plank against Detroit's George Mullin and the Athletics were able to score four runs early in the game off the Tigers' ace. Usually, four runs were enough for Plank to win, but the over-worked pitcher faded and Detroit came away with a 5–4 victory. Detroit now held first place and a half-game lead over the Athletics.

The little spitballer, Jimmy Dygert, was slated to start for the Athletics in Saturday's scheduled game, but it rained hard all day, causing a postponement. The off-day on Sunday gave the A's tired pitchers an extra two days of rest as the Saturday cancellation meant two games against Detroit would be played on September 30.

The citizens of Philadelphia turned out in record numbers for the Monday doubleheader. Trolley after trolley brought fans to Columbia Park, and long before the start of the first game, the stands and aisles were packed. The official paid attendance was 24,127, but it was estimated that 40,000 people gathered in and outside the ballpark. Many fans scaled the outfield fence to get inside the park and householders on adjacent streets were said to have charged from twenty-five cents to a dollar for standing room on the roofs. The gates to the grandstand were closed before one o'clock and an overflow crowd stood fifteen deep behind outfield ropes.

Despite an early 3–1 lead, Mack ordered Captain Davis to remove Jimmy Dygert with the bases loaded in the second inning. Mack later said that "Dygert made two errors and made a stupid play in the second inning. He seemed nervous; I had to get him out of there and called in Rube."[32]

Waddell escaped the second-inning jam and the Athletics teed off on Donovan to amass a six-run lead after six innings. With Plank scheduled to go in the second game of the twin bill, prospects for a sweep by the home team appeared a distinct possibility. However, Rube Oldring dropped a fly ball and one batter later A's shortstop Simon Nichols committed the error that set the stage for the Tigers to score four runs in the seventh to make the score 7–5.

The Athletics came back with a run in the bottom of the inning, giving Waddell a three-run cushion with two more innings to go. However, Rube faltered and the Tigers tied the score in the ninth when Waddell tried to sneak a 3–2 curveball past Ty Cobb with a runner on base. As soon as Cobb's mighty drive cleared the right field fence and landed on Twenty-ninth Street, Mack waved Waddell from the field and summoned Plank to take the mound. Plank and Donovan battled for five more innings with each team scoring a run in the eleventh. In the fourteenth inning an umpire's decision may have cost the Athletics the game.

With the Athletics at bat in that fateful inning, Harry Davis hit a long fly ball toward the crowd standing in front of the left-center field wall. As Sam Crawford went back to the edge of the crowd in an attempt to catch the ball, a policeman sitting on a soda box along the rope line rose from his seat to get out of the fielder's way. The ruling could have been a ground-rule double, but the Tigers complained that the officer interfered with Crawford. The Athletics insisted that the bluecoat was simply trying to get out of the Crawford's way. The *Philadelphia Inquirer* reported that Crawford reached the ball at a full run, but it dropped out of his glove. Therefore, there could have been no interference.[33]

When home plate umpire Silk O'Loughlin did not immediately signal a decision, the opposing players began to argue over the play while the crowd grew restless. After several minutes of pleas from the Tigers, Silk consulted with Tommy Connolly, the base umpire, who believed there was interference. In the meantime, the A's first base coach, Monte Cross, exchanged words with the much-larger Claude Rossman of the Tigers. When the fans saw Donovan shove Monte, several of them jumped the fence and headed for the assemblage of players on the field. Waddell rushed to the defense of his teammate and, with the assistance of some policemen, extricated Cross from the group of Tigers. After the field had been cleared of spectators, O'Loughlin announced Davis was out because of the policeman's interference. Now it was an incensed Connie Mack who was screaming at O'Loughlin, but his protests fell on deaf ears. Once the game resumed Danny Murphy hit a long single that would have easily scored Davis from second with the winning run. The game remained scoreless until darkness ended play following the seventeenth inning with the score still tied at 9–9. The game would not be completed and the second game of the doubleheader was never played.[34]

After the game, a livid Connie Mack accosted O'Loughlin in the umpire's room and demanded to know why he told the A's Tully Hartsel that he saw no interference and then called Davis out just minutes later. O'Loughlin did not answer.[35]

Mack issued an angry statement to the press. "In his umpiring Monday and in the game on Friday with Detroit, Umpire O'Loughlin demonstrated very clearly to me that he deliberately intended to rob the Athletics of the victory if he could. I have felt a long time he was just waiting the opportunity to give us a raw deal, and now I know that he did. I do not believe there was any money consideration involved in it whatever, but his motive was one of revenge alone."[36]

Connie Mack obtained affidavits from the policeman and persons in center field that there was no interference and sent them to American League president Ban Johnson. It was to no avail. Detroit left Philadelphia with a half-game lead over the Athletics in the standings. The Athletics could not close the gap and wound up in second place, 1 game behind the Tigers.

The Athletics ended the regular season with a doubleheader against Washington on October 5. In game one, A's starting pitcher Charlie Fritz faltered after only three innings and was relieved by Rube Waddell. Rube's first pitch was hit for a single. That one pitch was the last Waddell would throw as an employee of the Athletics.

Another of the A's Rubes, Harry "Rube" Vickers, eventually was the winning pitcher (4–2) in what turned out to be a fifteen-inning marathon with a spectacular twelve-inning relief effort. He came right back in the second game of the twin bill to throw a five-inning darkness-shortened 4–0 perfect game against the Nationals.

More than Waddell's inconsistency and O'Loughlin's umpiring, Chief Bender's sore arm probably cost the Athletics an American League championship. The 1907 season was a strange one for Bender. He finished with a record of 16 wins, 8 losses, but aside from the twelve-game winning streak, he went 4–8. Since 1905 though, Bender's number of walks allowed decreased each season. During the 1907 campaign he gave up only 34 bases on balls in 219 innings pitched.

When asked to what he contributed his great control, Bender said, "Practice! Constant practice. I must give Schreck a lot of credit, too. If you look back at the records, you will see that Plank and Rube also had fine control.

> Every day, Schreck would line the three of us up together, give each one a ball and hold his mitt at different spots. Each man would throw. Schreck would catch the ball in his glove hand and then turn and put it in his bare hand. He would wait until he had all three and then throw them all back at once. He never missed making a perfect return of the three balls, one to each man.
>
> Schreck was the greatest receiver I ever saw — and he could hit, too. If he hadn't liked his nip so much, he might have been the greatest catcher of all time. He could hit and I have never seen a man who could handle a mitt like he could.[37]

On October 7 the Athletics played an exhibition game against the New York Highlanders in Hartford, Connecticut, the proceeds to benefit the Tuberculosis Hospital. The A's lost, 8–0, then immediately left for a barn-storming tour through Pennsylvania. The traveling team was virtually the same as that of the regular season except for the absence of a couple of players.

The A's trip was uneventful until the barnstormers reached Williamsport, where they were to play a game on October 16. Trouble began when Osee Schreckengost decided he wanted some cash from his share of the receipts from the exhibitions. The players had agreed before they left home that shares would not be distributed until after the trip was completed. Schreck solicited his friend Rube Waddell to go to Captain Davis and insist the money be divided up then and there. Davis refused the demand, vowing to stick to the rule all the players had agreed to before their tour began.

"We had an argument in the lobby of the hotel there," Davis recalled many years later. "Rube threatened to hit me and I told him to go ahead and take the consequences. Chief Bender was itching to lay his hands on Rube. However, I decided it would be best to pay off Waddell. I think he received $70."[38]

Schreck wasn't in the lineup the next afternoon, much to the disappointment of the 1,500 people on hand to watch the A's play a team from Williamsport. Bender still was not able to pitch and played second base instead. The visitors' mound duties were shared by Waddell, Plank and Coombs while Rube Vickers pitched for the Williamsport nine. Vickers' regular-season teammates showed him little consideration in the 8–1 rout.[39]

That wasn't the end of the story as explained by Harry Davis. "We were scheduled to play the next day in Clearfield, Pennsylvania, and when we arrived, the sheriff showed me a telegram he had received from the Rube. It read: 'Don't go to the ball game tomorrow as I will not be with the club.'"[40]

Mack was fed up with Waddell after his performance during the 1907 season and his decision to get rid of the eccentric hurler was made easier the following February. "The boys came to me and said they didn't want the Rube around anymore," he related. "They couldn't play ball with him. There was no use having a big split on your club like that, so I had to let him go."[41]

When there were no takers when the A's offered Waddell in a trade, Mack sold him to the St. Louis Browns for $7,500 on February 8, 1908. Rube won 19 games for the Browns in his first year in St. Louis and then fell to a sub-.500 record a year later. While at bat during a Browns game in May 1910, Waddell's left elbow was broken by a pitch thrown by Eddie Cicotte of Boston. St. Louis released Rube that fall. George "Rube" Waddell died in April 1914, having contracted pneumonia while working at a flood site in Hickman, Kentucky. He was only thirty-seven years old.

By 1908, catcher Osee Schreckengost was nearly thirty-three and washed

Charles Bender warms up prior to a game at Columbia Park, Philadelphia. Although this image was used for a 1911 Turkey Red Cabinets card, the photograph had to have been taken prior to 1909 because of the style of the A's home uniform; also the configuration of the stands are Columbia Park, not Shibe Park (National Baseball Hall of Fame Library, Cooperstown, New York).

up. He was batting only .222 when Connie Mack unloaded him to Chicago late in the season. Schreck played only six games with the Sox and then was out of baseball for good. Osee lived only six more years, dying the same year as his friend, Rube Waddell.

In a break during the Philadelphia Athletics spring training of March 1908, Charley Bender and teammates Coombs, Plank, Powers and Nicholls went to the New Orleans City Park Gun Club for a morning round of trap with the expert marksmen from the U.M.C. and Remington squad, who were giving shooting exhibitions while on a tour of the South. Accompanying the traveling gunmen was the famous female shootist, Annie Oakley, formerly of the Buffalo Bill Wild West Show. Bender and Coombs hit better than 90 percent of their targets in the shoot. That afternoon, the Athletics played a game with the local Southern League club. During the course of the action, the contest was temporarily suspended due to a commotion when "Miss Oakley," escorted by Colby Jack Coombs, arrived.

"During the game," wrote a member of the entourage, "Annie Oakley, whose base ball education has been sadly neglected, but whose heart is in the right place, broke into the game at the wrong time with a bunch of applause, this when the New Orleans team put a run over the plate. Jack Coombs ... looked around with an injured expression, and Annie discovered she was 'in the wrong' and apologized."

Later, an A's batter drove a foul ball over the grandstand and Annie was delighted that the Athletics would get some runs before the ball could be retrieved. Again Jack straightened her out on baseball rules, but when she suggested the batter run directly from home to second base since it was much nearer than around by first base, Coombs gave up and remarked to her husband, Jack Butler, "We will let it go at that."[42]

The Athletics returned to frigid Philadelphia in early April 1908 for the annual city series against the Phillies, but three of the seven scheduled games were canceled because of bad weather. Newcomer Nick Carter won the first game of the series for the A's by a score of 5–0 and the American Leaguers went on to win the set, three games to one. Chief Bender got his final preseason tune up in the fourth and final game on a very cold Saturday the *Sporting News* described as "a mean kind of a day for base ball."

"Just to give Bender a chance to limber up after his recent illness, Manager Mack sent him in the firing line and Chief simply played horse with the Phillies," reported Philadelphia sports scribe Horace Fogel. "Bender was never so big and robust, and, in such great form this spring. The 12,000 spectators were surprised to see Bender cut up the way he did, as heretofore he has always been very old-womanish in his behavior during a game....

"A fine gale was blowing across the field and the thermometer was down to almost freezing point. It was, therefore, no wonder that Bender could control the ball so well, handicapped as he was by the strong wind blowing."[43]

The regular season began ominously at Hilltop Park in New York on April 14. During pre-game warm-ups, Philadelphia left fielder Tully Hartsel had his nose broken by an errant throw. Hartsel went ahead and played, mainly because pitcher Jack Coombs was already in the lineup as the right fielder due to an injury to Seybold and the illness of Oldring.

Athletics rookie spitballer Nick Carter made his regular-season debut and matched scoreless innings with the Highlanders' Slow Joe Doyle for eleven innings. In the twelfth, New York landed runners on first and third with a ground-rule double into the crowd and a single. A line drive to right fielder Coombs became the sacrifice fly that gave New York an Opening Day victory.[44]

Perhaps a result of the game he pitched against the Phillies a week earlier, Chief Bender was "under the weather" with a "very heavy" cold to start the season. He did not start on the mound until the Athletics' tenth game when he went twelve innings to beat the Highlanders, 3–2. Bender scored the winning run after he drew a walk and raced home on Simon Nichols' double. Despite a depleted outfield and a number of fresh faces on the pitching staff, Philadelphia stayed close to the top of the standings for the first six weeks of the season and actually held first place for a couple of days in early June.

In mid–May 1908, Rube Waddell visited Philadelphia for the first time as an opposing ballplayer. The Athletics won the first two games of their series with the Browns before Waddell and Chief Bender matched up in the finale on the nineteenth. A crowd of 28,000, the largest attendance for a mid-week game in Philadelphia history to that time, stormed small Columbia Park for the expected pitching duel. The crowd had to be let on the field and "all the windows in the neighborhood had occupants by the time Rube walked out to his old place of dominion, so had all the telegraph poles and many of the roofs."[45]

Waddell was cheered by the Philadelphia fans when he went out to warm up. When he came to bat in the third inning, the game was halted so Rube could accept a rifle and gun case from his rooters. The Athletics had decided the way to beat Waddell was to exploit his weakness in fielding bunts. The first Athletics batter, Tully Hartsel, beat out a bunt, but moments later he was picked off second base. In the third, Hartsel walked and went all the way to third when Waddell threw high to first after fielding Nicholls' bunt. However, Nicholls was thrown out before he made it to second and Hartsel was thrown out at the plate moments later on Collins' grounder. Harry Davis' base hit sent Eddie home with the A's second run, but the captain's single would be the last hit Waddell would allow.

Bender had an extra motivation for the game as well. The *North American* made it a point to note that "not less than half a dozen (of the A's) had announced after the barnstorming trip of last fall that they would quit the team if Waddell remained for another day. Included in this number was his swarthy rival in the box."[46]

The Chief appeared invincible in the early going. He struck out the side in the first inning and led 2–1 when the Browns came to bat in the top of the seventh. Suddenly Bender became hittable. When the dust settled, three singles and two doubles had produced four runs for the Browns. In the climatic ninth inning, Waddell struck out the three A's batters he faced to complete the 5–2 Browns victory. A crowd of about a thousand well-wishers surrounded Rube to shake his hand and pat him on the back. It took five minutes or so for the grinning pitcher to escape the bench and push his way through to the bus. The win was the first of Rube's three victories over the Athletics that season.[47]

Following a sluggish beginning that saw Bender win only one of his three starting assignments, Connie Mack decided to give Charley the final week in May off so he could attend the Pennsylvania State Sportsmen's Shooting Tournament at Bradford. Francis Richter of *Sporting Life* wrote that Mack made the move in the hope of improving the pitcher's "health and spirits."[48]

On June 9, Bender had perhaps his worse performance as a pitcher with the Athletics on a cold and windy day at Southside Park in Chicago. He gave up fourteen hits in a complete-game 10–0 loss to Ed Walsh and the White Sox. A few days later, the *Washington Post* speculated, "Bender seems to be all in, for he is being hit unmercifully hard."[49]

June 6 would be the last day Philadelphia would hold first place during the 1908 season. A day later, the Cleveland Naps replaced them at the top of the American League standings, and the day after that the White Sox took the American League lead for the first time. Within a week, the Athletics' losing streak reached seven games and they found themselves in fifth place.

Despite the Athletics' fast start, the club's season turned sour and 1908 became a rebuilding year for Connie Mack. That summer, Frank Baker and Jack Barry made their initial appearances in the infield and Eddie Collins became the regular second baseman, chasing Danny Murphy to right field. Another rookie to arrive in Philly that season was the highly touted Joe Jackson, a country boy from South Carolina who was deemed a "natural hitter" for his vicious line drives.

Bender pitched one of his best games for the year on September 4, yet he still lost to the Highlanders, 2–1. Charley allowed four hits and struck out ten opposing batters, but New York got an early run because of a throwing error by third baseman Scotty Barr, and the second run came as result of a walk and a hit batsman.

After losing to the Red Sox in the second game of a doubleheader on September 7, Bender did not start another game the remainder of the season. The 1908 season was his worst year as member of the Athletics. Charles pitched in only 18 games (17 as a starter) and finished with a record of eight wins and nine losses. He did throw two shutouts, both against the St. Louis Browns. The Chief's best stretch came in late summer when he put together a three-game winning streak with a 1–0 victory over the Browns on August 15, beat Doc White and the White Sox, 6–1, five days later, and polished off the Detroit Tigers in the nightcap of a doubleheader at Columbia Park on August 28.

Connie Mack left several regulars at home during the club's final road trip of the season in order to play some untried youngsters. Bender, Hartsel, Vickers, Dygert, Jimmy Collins, Schreck and catcher Bert Blue received three weeks off, beginning September 11 when the club started a long road trip. Unknowns Biff Schlitzer, Jack Flater and Gus Salve joined Coombs and Plank in the starting pitching rotation. Newly acquired rookie Jack Lapp got some work behind the plate, and Amos Strunk made his first appearance in Connie Mack's outfield on September 24.

While Charles Bender was conflicted about the future of his own professional baseball career, his brother John got thrown out of baseball, perhaps for good. John Bender had been a journeyman outfielder for several minor league clubs, including Fargo of the Northern League, Charleston, and Augusta, before he landed a job with the Columbia team of the South Atlantic League in 1908. Troublesome behavior by the outfielder surfaced a year earlier, and that August he was fined $20 and suspended indefinitely by Augusta manager Richard Crozier for violation of club rules.[50]

In July of 1908, John Bender was a member of the Columbia team traveling home aboard the steamship *Iroquois* after having completed a series in Jacksonville. About five hours out of port, manager Win Clark confronted Bender, who appeared to be intoxicated. The two men began to scuffle and Bender pulled a knife while Clark had only his bare hands to defend himself. Before the pair was separated, Clark suffered several knife wounds. John was placed in irons, hauled off to jail, and was eventually released on a bond of $1,000. The player was permanently suspended by league President Boyer, although the assault charges against Bender were dismissed by the U.S. District Court in Charleston a year later. John returned as coach of the College of Charleston baseball team in the spring, but he remained banned from Organized Baseball for more than two years.[51]

Philadelphia eventually finished a miserable sixth place in the 1908 American League standings, twenty-two games behind the Tigers, who repeated as champions by only .004 of a point ahead of Cleveland. In his final season with the Athletics, Socks Seybold played only 34 games in the outfield. Jack Coombs even filled in as an outfielder for 47 games, batted a respectable .255 and committed only one error. Nick Carter didn't pan out after so promising a spring, finishing with a record of two victories and five losses.

Chief Bender had more success at another pastime during the off-season, so reported the *Carlisle Sentinel*:

Charles A. Bender, the great Carlisle Indian pitcher for the Philadelphia Athletics, is also a marksman. "Chief" out shot a classy field of gunners who participated in Thursday's special live bird shoot at the Penrose Gun Club. The Indian was the only gunner to kill all his birds, bringing down the fifteen pigeons in decisive fashion, killing five of them with one barrel. Nine gunners entered the event, and although Bender had Fred Coleman, the ex-champion of Pennsylvania, to shoot against, he won by two birds.[52]

Trap shooting derives its name from the device that hurls the clay targets into the air. Trap simulates the flight of a game bird flushed ahead of the shooter and, in the original version of the sport, live birds were released from holes in the ground covered with silk top-hats. In the 1880s, clay targets were first developed. By the turn of the twentieth century, the sport was especially popular among ballplayers who participated in trap shooting during the off-season, much as modern athletes play golf for recreation. During the first decade of the century, two nationally circulated weekly newspapers, the *Sporting News* and *Sporting Life,* covered baseball, but also devoted space to the "traps." The Philadelphia-based *Sporting Life* ran a cover-page banner — "Base Ball, Trap Shooting and General Sports" — and the tabloid included a regular section devoted to trap shooting competitions.

Though many baseball players took up the sport, Bender became one of the best, perhaps only rivaled by Samuel Leever, a pitcher for the Pittsburgh Pirates and an expert shot. As the sport became more popular among major league baseball players in the ensuing years, such diamond stars as Honus Wagner, Tris Speaker, Joe Jackson and Joe Bush adopted trap shooting as a pastime. The *Washington Post* reported that Bender even "boosted his own bank account by betting on himself in several matches."[53]

In an article on Chief Bender for *Baseball Magazine,* Samuel Wesley Long called trap shooting "the sport that, more than any other, keeps eyes keen, steels the nerves and cultivates instant and accurate judgment of speed, distance, the effect of wind, etc., things that are invaluable to a pitcher.

"Hundreds of thousands of us know the Chief as he stands in the pitcher's box — A stolid giant with the unemotional characteristics of his race, yet comparatively few of the admirers of this wonderful mounds man know the other side of his personality as revealed when toeing the 'firing line' at a trap shooting club. Here, 'the boy in the man' asserts itself and a string of broken targets will make Bender as gleeful as a debutante who just received her first invitation to a dance."[54]

In February 1909, Charles Bender announced, "I have positively decided not to pitch any more, but in the future I will devote my time and attention to the match shooting business, in which I have been successful. I find that it has greatly improved my health."[55]

Upon hearing of his pitcher's remarks, an obviously irritated Connie Mack told the press, "I have done no business with Bender this winter. I do not think it is a question of money. He received the highest salary of his career last summer and his every demand was met. He did very little work for us last year and it is immaterial to me whether he pitches for the Athletics this season."[56]

Mack was quoted in *Sporting Life*, "Probably after Bender reads the salary clause in the contract I will tender him, he will feel like giving up pitching, if he had not already made up his mind to do so. The chances are that Bender has anticipated what is coming to him and to be first to have his say gave out the story of his retirement in the near future on that account."[57]

"But...," Manager Mack added, "if Bender signs at my figure, no matter how small, and then turns around and takes his regular turn next season, pitches well as he is capable of doing, and renders first-class services, I am willing to pay him the same salary next fall as I paid him last year. In other words, I will give him extra money as a present."[58]

When Bender received his 1909 Athletics contract in the mail, he found that Connie Mack had slashed his salary in half. Once spring came and attention turned to baseball, Bender had a change of heart and delivered his signed contract to Connie Mack less than a week before the club was to leave for spring training.[59]

Bender's struggle with the decision whether to quit or continue his baseball career and the lingering bad taste of the salary cut by Connie Mack may have factored in the Chippewa pitcher's response to a Carlisle Indian School questionnaire later that year. "I wouldn't advise any of the students at Carlisle to become a professional baseball player," he wrote. "It is a hard road to travel. Many temptations along the wayside."[60]

By the end of the 1909 season, Bender's performance on the baseball field would surpass his record of any previous season. As a reward, Connie Mack presented Charley with a bonus check that raised his salary to what his 1908 contract stipulated.[61]

◆ 7 ◆

Twenty-First and Lehigh

The 1909 baseball season ushered in a new era in Philadelphia sports history when Athletics principal owner Ben Shibe provided a new baseball palace for the team and fans. Connie Mack unveiled his new infield of Harry Davis, Eddie Collins, Jack Barry and Frank Baker to go with a pitching triumphant of Coombs, Plank and Bender. After his change of heart about a career change, Chief Bender had his best season on the mound to date and the Athletics would again do battle with the Detroit Tigers for supremacy of the American League.

Though Charles Bender let it be known he had no intention of giving up baseball for pigeon shooting or any other game, his Athletics contract remained unsigned and unreturned as the calendar changed to March. However, the A's last holdout relented and Bender was there in plenty of time to join the team before a "tremendous crowd" at Broad Street Station on March 8 for the send-off to spring training in New Orleans.[1]

During the training season, Connie Mack divided his team into two squads, the regulars and the "yannigans." The regulars were no match for the youngsters, who included among their number Collins, Baker, Barry, Joe Jackson, Stuffy McInnis and Amos Strunk. The split squads played their way north from Louisiana in a series of exhibition games. These contests not only allowed the A's to play themselves into shape, but the gate helped the club defray expenses. A casualty at the end of spring training was the homesick Joe Jackson, who was sent to Savannah of the South Atlantic League.

The newly christened Shibe Park was ready for the club's home opener that April. With the Athletics having long ago outgrown their first home, Columbia Park, Ben Shibe and minority stockholder Connie Mack decided it was time to build a bigger ballpark. As early as 1907 they quietly began the purchase of land in a largely isolated part of Philadelphia and made plans for a ballpark that would ultimately cost more than $315,000. It would become the first of eleven modern steel and concrete major league baseball parks that would be built over a five-year period.

Sod was removed from the existing Columbia Park surface to cover the new playing field and horse-drawn wagons carried 15,000 wagonloads of dirt to the new ballpark's site, which was bounded by Twenty-First Street, Lehigh Avenue, Twentieth Street, and Somerset Street. The field's dimensions would be a distant 515 feet from home plate to the flag pole in dead center field, 378 feet down the line in left, and 340 to the wall in right. Shibe Park would have seating for 23,000 and there were 200 parking spaces beneath the bleachers for the increasingly popular automobile.

The architectural style of Shibe Park was French Renaissance, constructed of red brick, with terra cotta columns, arches, ornamental scrollwork, and cornices. A cupola above the entrance housed the offices of team business manager John Shibe and manager Connie Mack. The double-decked grandstand evolved into bleachers down both outfield foul lines and club officials bragged that the park had no columns or posts that would interfere with a fan's view of the field.

The park had two sets of dressing rooms with twenty lockers each, shower baths, and a players' lounging room. On the way to the field, the players

Entrance to the newly completed Shibe Park at Lehigh Avenue and Twenty-First Street, 1909 (George Grantham Bain Collection, Library of Congress).

would not be exposed to the crowd as a tunnel took them directly from the dressing room to the bench.[2]

Prior to 1909, Connie Mack lived across the street from Columbia Park, but when the club relocated to Shibe Park, the manager moved to Ontario Street, seven blocks north of the new ballyard. Charles Bender also purchased a house nearby and several other players lived in the area near the ballpark.

Within a survey document for the Carlisle Indian School, Charles described his and Marie's new home seven blocks from Shibe Park at 3515 Judson Street. "A two-story brick home containing 9 rooms and bath," he wrote. "Terraced front porch. Gas and electric lights. Carry $5,000 endowment policy of 10 payments." Bender also indicated that he owned 160 acres of land on the White Earth Reservation.[3]

The first game at Shibe Park was played on April 12, 1909. A line began to form for tickets at seven A.M., and by the time the gates were opened, a line four and five abreast and a half-mile long extended down Lehigh Avenue from the main entrance located at the tower of the grandstand at Twenty-first and Lehigh. Depending on where their seats were located, 10,000 people spent fifty cents or one dollar to sit in the grandstand. Once inside the spacious lobby at the base of the tower, ticket holders were directed up a wide stairway to the main grandstand promenade. Ushers helped people locate their folding chair seats, a new feature for a baseball park. Two fourteen-foot-wide concourses beneath the grandstand took the 13,000 fans that paid a quarter to sit in the bleachers down either the first or third base lines.[4]

Sporting Life noted that for the inaugural game at least one-fourth of the grandstand spectators were women garbed in their Easter finery. The park offered no seating beyond the outfield wall, but for the first game 10,000 people paid to stand behind ropes on the terrace in the outfield. An hour before game time the last of the tickets were sold and the gates were closed. The disappointed crowd outside the park stormed the gates and pelted the ticket windows before police broke up the mob.

"A line of dangling legs spread around the fences," reported the *North American*. "The scoreboard platform, twenty-five feet in the air, filled up, and the roofs and porches of the houses on Twentieth Street were also chock a black."

One attraction at Shibe Park that became a hit with the club's patrons was John Shibe's large scoreboard that displayed the batting order of both teams and the scores by innings, not only of the local game, but all of the day's games in both the American and National leagues.[5]

Beginning at one o'clock, one of two regimental bands alternately provided entertainment for the fans, and at around 2:30 P.M., the crowd was led in the singing of "America." The Athletics, in their white and blue shirts, followed by the Boston Red Sox, marched behind the bands to center field where an American flag was raised by Ben Shibe and American League president Ban Johnson while "The Star-Spangled Banner" was played. The honor of throwing out the first ball to A's catcher Doc Powers went to mayor John Reyburn. John "Stuffy" McInnis ran to the shortstop position for his first appearance in a regular major league game.[6]

A baseball game still had to be played and the Athletics, behind the six-hit pitching of Eddie Plank, defeated the Red Sox, 8–1. In the late stages of the game, A's catcher Mike Powers began to suffer extreme abdominal pains. Taken to the hospital by ambulance, he was found to be suffering from gangrene of the intestines. An operation was performed and he briefly rallied, but two weeks later the veteran backstop was dead.

The paid attendance for Shibe Park's inaugural game was 31,162 and another 4,000 were guests of the club. The fans who made it to the ballpark on Opening Day were the first of 674,915 attendees at Shibe Park during the 1909 season. Over the ensuing years, the park underwent a variety of changes. In 1913, upper decks were added to the bleacher sections that extended down the left and right field foul lines, and bleachers in the outfield from the left field foul line to dead center field were added, raising the ballpark's seating capacity to 33,500.

Connie Mack's game ritual did not change just because of a new ballpark. He remained seated on the dugout bench throughout the game, always clad in his signature three-piece suit, and signaled his players by a complex wagging of his scorecard. One of his players said he looked like a deacon who had mistakenly wandered into Shibe Park. Mack rarely entered the clubhouse except for an occasional pre-game meeting.

Aesthetically, Connie Mack made a drastic change in his players' caps for the 1909 season. He dropped the traditional close-fitting cap and replaced it with a version of the 1800s, a cylindrical "cheese box" style adorned with four stripes. That season marked a change in the fortunes of the team on the field, and the superstitious manager was not about to change the cap style as long as his team continued to post winning records.

After four years of enduring Mack's caps, one disgruntled reporter, speaking for the traditionalists, editorialized, "The Mackmen continue to wear those atrocious looking caps, the style popular years ago. Nothing can induce the crafty Connie Mack to shift over to the style of base ball headgear worn these days."[7]

Chief Bender did not start a regular season game until April 26 in Washington. He took a one-hitter into the ninth inning against the Nationals and finished with 3–1 victory with a newcomer named Ira Thomas behind the plate. That day, the Athletics received word that Michael "Doc" Powers had died at age thirty-eight.

Powers' funeral the following Wednesday was one of the largest in the history of Philadelphia. Thousands passed by the fallen backstop at the funeral home and an estimated 10,000 people stood in the streets outside a packed church during the funeral service.

Though Connie Mack had Powers, Paddy Livingston and Jack Lapp among his stable of catchers going into the season, he had the foresight to purchase Ira Thomas from the Tigers. Hughie Jennings' club was well fortified behind the plate and Detroit was willing to give up Thomas, who was used in only twenty-nine games at catcher a year earlier.

Bender won his first five games in 1909 and became so confident with Thomas behind the plate, Ira became his favorite receiver. Once a game began, Bender refused to throw a ball to anyone but the catcher assigned to the game. Even if Thomas or Livingston was late getting to the box because they had to apply the catching gear after batting or running the bases, Charley would not throw to anyone else and risk jinxing himself.[8]

Bender's first encounter with Thomas was said to have been in 1906 when Ira was a twenty-five-year-old rookie with the New York Highlanders. In a previous game Bender had pitched against New York, an infielder named George Moriarity, on instructions from manager Clark Griffith, unmercifully badgered the Chief while he was pitching. Bender became so angry he swore he would get even when he got the chance. In a subsequent game that season, Thomas came up to bat against Bender as a pinch-hitter.

Moriarity, who was on the bench, recalled that Bender announced from his position atop the mound, "I've got you now!" Thomas did not pay much attention to the Athletics pitcher at first, but quickly realized something was afoot when Bender buzzed a pitch within inches of his head. A second pitch was just as close and sent the confused Thomas to the ground. Ira yelled to Bender that he was not who he thought he was, but the Chief threw two more close ones in an effort to hit the suddenly nimble catcher. The shaken Thomas took his walk and trotted to first base.

Moriarity added that "Bender didn't realize that it was a case of mistaken identity until a couple of weeks later when he happened to see me and Thomas together off the field. Then he laughed heartily and said that he was glad he hadn't killed Thomas and sorry that it hadn't been Moriarity up there at the plate when he was attempting murder."[9]

After Bender pitched so well in the first few weeks of the season, the *Washington Post* reported the Chief "announced he was through last February. But love for the game got Bender back, and when the season started he climbed into the striped uniform, much to the disgust of several players. Others thought Bender's pitching days were over, but after he finished off Detroit, 10 to 2, last week, the Tigers remarked that Bender had more speed than Walter Johnson."[10]

Ty Cobb usually hit Bender fairly well, compiling a .366 batting average in 82 career at-bats against the Chief.[11] But on that May 1909 afternoon in Detroit, Athletics infielder Simon Nicholls recalled that Bender made Cobb look bad. "In four times up all Cobb got was a slow grounder to Barry. The other times up he fanned."[12]

On May 29, Frank Baker hit the first fair ball out of Shibe Park. Horace Fogel wrote in the *Sporting News,* "It was believed when Shibe Park was opened that not for years, if ever, would any player hit a ball outside of that enclosure. It was a terrific smash, the ball sailing over the (right field) wall and going up against the wall of a dwelling house on the opposite side of the street with such force as to bounce almost back into the field again."[13]

Chief Bender suffered his first loss of the season on May 31 in the first game of a doubleheader at Shibe Park against the Red Sox. After he lost to Addie Joss in his next start, Fogel editorialized, "Joss, in the best exhibition of pitching I have ever seen since Mathewson's work in the 1905 World Series, shut the A's out with one hit." Bender had only one bad inning, when Cleveland managed to score the only two runs of the game.[14]

Bender rebounded in his next outing on June 12 when he held the Browns to four scattered hits and would have had a shutout but for errors by Davis and Baker. That victory sent the Chief on a personal four-game winning streak.

The talk of the town that summer was not about the Athletics veteran pitchers Plank and Bender, but involved a young southpaw who began a streak of ten straight victories, six of them shutouts, on May 8. That phenom was Harry "Lefty" Krause, a 1903 graduate of St. Mary's College in Oakland, California, who came to the Athletics in 1908 from an outlaw (not a member of Organized Baseball) team in San Jose. Krause finished the 1909 season in Philadelphia with 18 victories, only eight losses, and a league-leading 1.39 earned run average, a record low for an American League rookie.

In early June, Connie Mack obtained another starting pitcher for his already strong staff. Cy Morgan, a thirty-year-old spitball pitcher, came from the Red Sox for the rarely used Vic Schlitzer and $10,000. Morgan had been a starting pitcher for two seasons in Boston, but Cy's recent play had caused his manager to sour on him. On June 4, Morgan was pitching for the Red Sox in a game against the Tigers. Ty Cobb was on second base when the spit-baller uncorked a wild pitch. The aggressive Georgian did not slow down as he passed third base and charged on toward home plate. Morgan was there in plenty of time to make the tag, but he preferred to stand aside and attempt a swipe tag instead of blocking the plate. The Tigers star easily evaded the tag to score. Boston lost, 5–0, and the next day, Morgan was traded.

The trade quickly paid dividends for the Athletics when Cy pitched a three-hitter against St. Louis shortly after joining the club. Morgan won sixteen games in twenty-four decisions over the remainder of the season.

The Athletics took over first place the second week in August by taking three of four from the defending champion Tigers. They held that position until August 24.

On August 3, 1909, Eddie Plank and Chief Bender pitched the Athletics to a doubleheader sweep of the White Sox at Shibe Park. However, the fireworks for the day came courtesy of umpire Tim Hurst after Eddie Collins complained vigorously after being called out on a close play at second base. The umpire responded to Eddie's argument by spitting in the player's face. A near riot ensued and the police had to usher Hurst from the premises to save him from the enraged Philadelphia crowd.

That night, American League president Ban Johnson determined Hurst was the aggressor in the dispute with Collins and gave the umpire his release. Hurst had a reputation for his temper and had been suspended in 1906 for punching New York manager Clark Griffith in the mouth. On another occasion he was suspended for throwing a beer mug into the stands, breaking a fireman's nose.[15]

On August 17, Bender was scheduled to face the Nationals in Washington for the first game of a doubleheader. What made this contest notable was the Chief's pitching opponent, a tall, hard-throwing right-hander named Walter Johnson. In only his third major league season, Johnson was already establishing a reputation, but Walter was the only asset the Nationals had. At one point, Manager Cantillon was using the young hurler with only one day's rest. In fact, the young Washington ace had pitched five innings the day before his match-up with Chief Bender.

Johnson was wild for the first five innings but got out of trouble each time. The Athletics loaded the bases in the first inning, but Johnson escaped the one-out jam when Harry Davis grounded into a double play. Hartsel and Collins walked in the third, but George Browne made a great catch of Baker's drive to the fence and Jack Lelivelt made a sensational one-handed catch of Davis' long fly to center field.

Bender had his own defensive help, especially from catcher Paddy Livingston. In the third inning, Danny Murphy threw out Gabby Street at home plate when he attempted to score on Browne's single. Livingston then threw to first and nabbed the napping Browne. Livingston threw out two runners attempting to steal in the fourth and registered another caught stealing in the fifth. In the sixth inning, Germany Schaefer got a two-out single to left. He then stole second, and when Livingston's throw got past Collins, he kept on going, passed third and headed for home. Philadelphia outfielder Bob Ganley made a good throw to home, Livingston blocked the plate, and caught Schaefer "by a hair."

After the fifth inning, the two pitchers took control of the game. The first man to reach first base off Johnson after the fifth was Bender, when he singled in the tenth. Charley moved to second on a wild pitch, after which Hartsel sent a fly ball to center field. When Bender left second base before the ball was caught, he was doubled up.

The game continued through twelve tense innings. One report of the affair said Bender began to feel ill in the ninth inning, to the extent Harry Davis urged him to retire. Charley refused because he was confident his teammates would soon score and bring home the victory.[16]

The contest was finally settled in the Washington half of the twelfth. Lelivelt singled off Bender with one out and Wid Conroy was thrown out on a bunt, Lelivelt taking second. With two out, Manager Cantillon summoned Red Killifer from the coaching box to pinch-hit for Clyde Milan, who had already struck out three times in the game.

"He (Killifer) took his position at the plate with determination showing in every move," wrote J. Ed Grillo in the *Washington Post*. "There was a sneering smile playing on Bender's face, but it did not come from the heart. The Indian wanted to rattle the youngster."

Bender threw a fastball, but it never reached Livingston. Killifer swung, "there was a resounding whack, and as the ball was seen sailing on a line to center field a mighty cheer went up, which burst into pandemonium as Lelivelt slid over the plate in time to avoid the fast returning ball. The smile faded from the red man's face, the game was over, the day had been won."[17]

Walter Johnson allowed only four hits in topping Chief Bender, 1–0. Excessive overwork soon took its toll on Washington's young side-wheeler. He developed a sore arm and in his next two outings allowed 27 hits. Walter lost 25 games that season for the last-place Nationals. In ten of the losses, Washington was shut out.

One would think this classic pitching duel foretold many a match between two of the American League's most prominent hurlers. It wasn't to happen. Bender did get his revenge for the twelve-inning loss with a win over Walter at Shibe Park in 1910. After Johnson became the most dominant pitcher in baseball, Connie Mack seldom used one of his top pitchers against Washington's Big Train, choosing to use Bender and Plank against pitchers they were sure to beat.

On August 24, the Athletics visited Bennett Park in Detroit, leading the Tigers by mere percentage points in the standings. In the first inning, A's catcher Paddy Livingston threw out Ty Cobb who tried to steal third base during an intentional walk to Sam Crawford. The Athletics became enraged because they felt Cobb intentionally spiked third baseman Frank Baker on his bare hand. The Tigers won the game, 7–6, to take over first place. The Athletics would not see first place again after that as Plank and Bender lost on successive days and Detroit completed a sweep. Bender didn't make it out of the third inning in his losing effort.

After his 6–0 loss to George Mullin in the Detroit series, Bender came back strong, winning four straight games, including a 5–2 verdict over old teammate Rube Waddell in St. Louis and a 2–0 whitewash of the Washington Nationals. He struggled against New York on September 8 after striking out ten batters in six innings. With the A's leading by seven runs, the Highlanders reached the big Chippewa for six singles and narrowed the lead to 8–6. Charley finished the inning, but when Sweeney singled in the seventh, Dygert replaced Bender and saved the victory.

On September 16, Ty Cobb and the first-place Tigers came into Philadelphia with a three-and-a-half game lead over the Athletics. Prior to the series, the Tigers outfielder received death threats, stemming from the serious spiking of Frank Baker three weeks previous. A dozen threats intimated Cobb would be shot from the Twentieth Street roofs if he dared to play. More than 300 officers and special bodyguards were stationed about Shibe Park for the four games.

When Cobb stole third base in the second game, Baker shook his hand to break the tension. Then the fans cheered when Cobb dove into the roped-off area in right field to catch a foul ball. They cheered again when Cobb returned the next inning with $5 for the man whose straw hat he crushed while making the catch.

The A's and Tigers split the first two games of the series, Plank winning on Thursday and then Detroit beating Krause the next day. Chief Bender was to pitch the Saturday game, and he was an interested spectator as the Tigers ran wild against Krause and catcher Ira Thomas. The Tigers stole a total of seven bases, including three double steals in the final two innings.

The third game, played on Saturday, September 18, 1909, matched Bender against Detroit's Wild Bill Donovan before 35,409 fanatics, the largest paying crowd in American League history up to that time. About 10,000 spectators stood behind ropes in the outfield, the only open space being directly in line with home plate and the rubber in order not to obstruct the view of the batsmen. Thousands saw the game from the roofs and upper stories of the houses on surrounding streets. Others climbed telegraph poles to get a peek inside the park and hundreds simply scaled the concrete outfield fences and got to watch the game from there.

Detroit never came close to scoring in the contest and the *Philadelphia Inquirer* gave Bender the majority of the credit for the Athletics' 2–0 victory and noted that the Chief "kept such a close tab on the bases that the Tigers, who ran the bases wild on Friday, either hugged them closely or fell to Paddy Livingston's good throwing whip. Only two men — Tom Jones and Sam Crawford — attempted to go down and both were nailed."[18]

Wild Bill pitched well, too, but his own mistakes led to his undoing. The first Athletics run came on Collins' double, a sacrifice, and an error by

Donovan. When Harry Davis hit a grounder back to the mound, Collins was caught off third base. Eddie had started back to the bag, but Bill threw the ball over the third baseman's head and the runner jogged home. The second run scored when the Detroit pitcher's tardiness in covering first base allowed Collins to leg out a base hit. Donovan thought Collins was declared out by Umpire Perrine and casually walked toward the bench while Heitmuller scored all the way from second base without a throw to the plate.[19]

With one out in the ninth, Detroit's Matty McIntyre drew a pass, Bender's only base on balls in the contest. The big pitcher fell behind in the count to Donnie Bush but recovered to strike out the feisty shortstop. Ty Cobb was the final hope for the Tigers and he worked the count to three balls and two strikes. Bender's next pitch was in the strike zone but all "Tyrus the Great" could manage was a grounder to Eddie Collins, who threw him out at first.

"On Saturday, before the record crowd," wrote Francis Richter, "Bender pitched one of the greatest games of his career — one equaling his famous game against New York in the 1905 World Series."[20]

Bender's clutch three-hitter kept the Athletics in the pennant chase and reinforced his manager's confidence in him as a big game pitcher. Detroit left town only one and a half games in front, but that was as close as Philadelphia got.

Philadelphia played winning baseball for another week but couldn't gain any ground on the Tigers. The final nail was driven into the Athletics' coffin when they lost four times in a five-game series with the White Sox at Shibe Park between September 28 and October 1. The end-of-season swoon was blamed on the loss of shortstop Jack Barry due to a severe spiking and the absence of two catchers, Livingston and Thomas, due to injury. Furthermore, Danny Murphy and Harry Davis missed games because of "cholera."[21]

Though they won 14 of their 22 games with Detroit, the Athletics finished in second place, three and a half games behind the Tigers in the final standings. The Athletics won 95 games, a number that would have secured a pennant the previous four seasons, but the Tigers were victorious 98 times. However, the young Athletics stood on the threshold of their first dynasty.

Despite stomach problems during the season, Bender won 18 games and lost only eight, and had his lowest earned average to date, 1.66. The Chief had a career high in strikeouts with 161 and walked only 45 batters in 250 innings pitched. Among his losses was the one-hitter to Joss, the twelve-inning 1–0 loss to Walter Johnson, and a 1–0 loss to Chicago's "Death Valley Jim" Scott, who threw a two-hitter against the A's.

Following the regular season, the Athletics went on a two-month barnstorming tour across the nation, featuring games in California that November and early December. Connie Mack recruited Frank Bancroft, an ex–major league manager from the 1880s, to assemble an all-star team to oppose the

Athletics during the tour. Mack's team was dubbed the "All-Star Americans" and Bancroft's crew, which included several members of the New York Giants, was called the "All-Nationals." Marie Bender accompanied Charles Albert to Chicago for a game there and then she would travel to the West Coast to be with her husband during the two-month trip.

The two teams of barnstormers stopped on their way west to play exhibitions against the two Chicago major league clubs that had just completed their annual city series. On October 19, Chief Bender beat the Cubs, 2–0, allowing but two hits, a scratch by Joe Tinker and a single over second by the opposing pitcher, Ed Reulbach. At the game's conclusion, the touring clubs departed for the West Coast, with the A's taking along George McBride of Washington in place of the injured Jack Barry. Walter Johnson would hook up with the All-Nationals when they reached Seattle.

Bender pitched well in California, beating the Los Angeles Angels, 1–0, on November 6 and the Pacific Coast League-champion San Francisco Seals, 7–1, six days later. Cruising with a 3–0 lead over the All-Nationals in San Francisco on November 17, Bender faltered in the sixth and gave up four runs. His teammates bailed him out and the Chief held on for a 5–4 victory. Charley won all of his starts on the West Coast and threw six innings of shutout ball in relief of Krause in a 1–1 eleven-inning draw with the All-Nationals' Dolly Gray that was called because of darkness.

The final game of the West Coast tour was played on December 12 in what was advertised as "the first contest between major league teams ever played in Los Angeles." Bender was opposed by Johnson, and Charles came out a 4–3 winner after the All-Americans scored all of their runs off Walter in the eighth inning, three of them on errors.

The major leaguers' tour was a disappointment to Mack and the other promoters. The exhibition games scheduled in San Francisco were plagued by rain and poor attendance. The locals were used to 25-cent game tickets, but the major leaguers raised the price to 50 cents, which many fans were not willing to pay.[22]

The All-Stars were scheduled to play exhibitions in Arizona and Texas before the tour reached its final destination of New Orleans for a game on December 19. Even the game in New Orleans had to be cancelled due to rain and the players dispersed to their respective homes. In the end, the tour was deemed a failure. Twenty-five of the fifty scheduled games were cancelled because of cold or wet weather and the teams barely made expenses after leaving California.

◆ 8 ◆

A Stampede of
White Elephants

As the second decade of the century dawned, the pieces fell into place for Philadelphia's Athletics. The club was able to field one of the deepest pitching staffs and the best infield in baseball. There was no reason to think Chief Bender would not continue to build on the success he experienced the previous season, especially since he had developed a new pitch that resembled a fastball except that it broke late into a right-handed batter and outward to a lefty hitter. There was no name for the pitch, though it would become known as a "nickel-curve." Future generations came to know the pitch as a "slider."

One of the staples among hard-throwing pitchers of modern baseball, a slider differs from the fastball in that it is a bit slower and breaks in the opposite direction of a curveball. The best slider breaks late and quick.

During the pre-season city series against the Phillies, Bender showed he was ready for what turned out to be his best season in the major leagues. He threw five strong innings in a 6–1 Athletics victory, though the highlight of the day was the hitting of Frank Baker.

After the slugger's home run off the Phillies' Bob Ewing in the third inning, a scribe noted "Baker's blustery shot ... cleared the embattlements in right and broke up a party of roller skaters in Twentieth Street." The blast was only the second ball to be hit out of Shibe Park, the first being a Baker home run the previous May.[1]

The early 1900s saw a plethora of baseball team mascots who promised success, like Charles "Victory" Faust of the Giants, or ensured good fortune, such as Detroit's L'il Rastus and Alexander George Washington Rivers. Connie Mack hoped to ward off the bad luck of earlier seasons by hiring a teenage hunchback named Louis Van Zelst as the A's mascot for the 1910 season. According to a widely circulated story at that time, Van Zelst came to the attention of the Athletics one day late in the 1909 season when he asked for admittance to Shibe Park even though he had no pass. Louis produced a picture of Rube Oldring cut from a package of cigarettes, was allowed into the park, and took a seat in the grandstand near the players' bench. Connie Mack spotted the small disfigured boy and asked him if he would like to mind the bats for the day's game. Louis jumped at the offer, and that afternoon the A's ended a losing streak. The superstitious Mack engaged Van Zelst as the team's bat boy and mascot for the remainder of the season. The small boy with a spinal deformity became a sentimental favorite at Shibe Park, and before each game or at-bat, the superstitious ballplayers rubbed the hump his back for luck. Many claimed Van Zelst brought the champions good fortune while the Athletics won four pennants in five years.[2] After Louis died at the age of twenty from Bright's Disease in March 1915, the Athletics descended into last place for seven straight seasons.

President and Mrs. William Howard Taft, along with vice president James Sherman, surprised the Nationals and their home fans by showing up for Washington's season opener on April 14, 1910. Manager Jimmy McAleer suggested Taft throw out the first ball, and he became the first president to do so. Walter Johnson caught the symbolic pitch and then proceeded to strike out nine batters in a 3–0 pitching gem against Eddie Plank. An easy fly hit by Frank Baker into the overflow crowd, a ground-rule double, was the only blemish on Johnson's ledger.

The following afternoon, Bender pitched the Athletics to an 8–2 victory over the Nationals and also garnered three hits of his own. His next start came before a crowd of 15,000 in the Athletics' home opener at Shibe Park on April 20.

After two days of rain, the weather was perfect. The two teams, accompanied by a military-style band, paraded on the field and stood at attention as the stars and stripes were raised on the center field flagpole. Much of the contest was a pitching duel between Bender and New York's Slow Joe Doyle. The only run in the first seven innings came on Chief Bender's two-out single in the second that plated Harry Davis.

Doyle turned into a pumpkin in the eighth when six A's singles led to five runs and sealed the final verdict. Bender again contributed a key hit. His single sent two runners homeward and he took second on the throw to the plate. The Chief polished off the Yankees in the ninth to complete his 6–0 shutout.

A week later, Bender ran his personal winning streak to four games with a four hit, 3–0 whitewash of the White Sox. Then on May 12 he took the mound against a Cleveland club that arrived at Shibe Park riding a seven-game winning streak.

On that rainy May afternoon Charles Bender proceeded to pitch his only major league no-hitter in the A's 4–0 victory over Cleveland's young southpaw, Ed Linke. There were few difficult chances for Bender's fielders during the contest and the great Nap Lajoie was retired by Bender on three easy plays.

"There was nothing that looked like a base hit," remembered Rube Oldring, the Athletics' center fielder that day. "Frank Baker handled a hot drive by George Stovall in the eighth, and that was the hardest chance. The most spectacular play came in the sixth when Bris Lord sent a long foul fly in the direction of right field. Danny Murphy went after the ball at full speed and after catching it, had to vault over the wall into the stands to avoid a crash."[3]

Bender said he didn't realize he had a no-hitter until he returned to the bench in the middle of the seventh inning. "Then one of the players happened to mention it. Another shouted, 'Shut up! You'll break the spell.'"[4]

Chief narrowly missed a perfect game by allowing one base on balls. In the third inning, Terry Turner walked on a 3–2 pitch and then was thrown out by catcher Ira Thomas attempting to steal second base on a pitch out. "I'm sorry I got that walk," Turner told the *Cleveland Leader* after the game. "At the time I was glad to get on, but I felt different when I saw it robbed Bender of a perfect game."[5]

The crowd became greatly excited as the end of the game neared and the anxious fans watched each pitch with bated breath. Bender had a great fastball that day and it became his main weapon. He only struck out four but his rising speed ball led to eleven pop outs. The final batter he had to face was a future Hall of Famer named Elmer Flick, who was pinch-hitting for pitcher Linke.

Bender recalled that Flick "worked the count to 3 and 2 and then I turned loose with all I had on a fastball on the outside. He took a good cut, but lifted a little foul behind the plate. Ira circled around like a drunken sailor, but finally caught it — and I breathed a sigh of thankfulness."[6]

As soon as the final out was recorded, enthusiastic fans swarmed the Athletics' bench, attempting to shake the hand of the smiling pitcher. He didn't linger with the well-wishers, but grabbed his sweater, pushed past several teammates and headed for the dressing room.[7]

Bender's gem was the first no-hitter pitched in Shibe Park. A second game scheduled for that afternoon was canceled due to wet grounds.

The next day, Cy Morgan took a no-hitter against Cleveland into the eighth inning. There were two out in that frame when former Athletic Bris Lord tripled to center field to break up Cy's bid for immortality.

Bender followed up his no-hitter with another shutout on May 17. He allowed only four scattered hits in beating the White Sox, 3–0, and only one opposing player advanced past first base. When things were going Charley's way, he tended to do more talking than any other player on the team, joking and socializing with opposition players during the game.[8] In 1910, things were going the Chief's way.

Things were also going the Athletics' way, too. Bender's win marked the club's twelfth consecutive victory and seventeen wins out of twenty-one games played.

Bender finally lost for the first time on May 23 when Detroit's Bill Donovan escaped with a 4–3 victory at Shibe Park. Charley fell behind right off the bat when a Ty Cobb triple resulted in two first-inning runs. In the second inning, the Tigers' George Moriarity was awarded a walk on a very questionable ball four call and worked his way around to third on two infield outs.

While Bender was pitching to the opposing pitcher, he got into a verbal exchange with umpire John Kerin. The "Chief was moodily setting himself to pitch" when Moriarty, who was cheating down the third base line, made a dash for the plate. Bender threw the ball to Jack Lapp, but Moriarty executed a fade-away slide to evade the catcher for a clean steal of home. Donovan struck out on the next pitch from Bender.[9]

Donovan took a 4–1 lead into the ninth inning, but the Athletics rallied to score two runs. Murphy and Barry hit safely and with one out, Bender drove them home with a "herculean drive" to center field that fell for a double. Connie Mack, who had just returned to the club after a week-long illness, sent Ben Houser up to bat for Heitmuller. The pinch-hitter was easy for Donovan, and when he whipped the third strike over the plate, Bender made a dash for third base.

Catcher Stanage's throw was low and Moriarity dropped it, but the third baseman had so completely blocked the base runner's path with his body that he was able to recover the ball and tag Bender for a double play. James Isaminger wrote for the *North American*, "It wasn't Rittenhouse Square drawing room ethics but it probably saved the day for Detroit and a seemingly irresistible rally petered out like a piece of punk."[10]

Bender added two more hits to his seasonal total in the Detroit loss. At the end of May, the Chief's batting average in the nine games in which he pitched was a whopping .413, twelve hits in twenty-nine official at-bats. Though he would accumulate only thirteen more safeties during the regular season, Bender's .269 batting average in 1910 was his highest as an Athletic.

The loss to Detroit was only a temporary setback for Bender, but the club was suddenly beset by a number of injuries. In the game with Boston on May 29, third baseman Baker took a line drive off his shin that deflected into the stands for a home run and, a few days later, Frank had to leave the team to be with his wife, who had contracted typhoid.

During the course of the second game of a doubleheader in Boston on the final day of May, Bender's usual catcher, Ira Thomas, broke his thumb and was replaced by Jack Lapp. Lapp was Jack Coombs' personal catcher, but he now had to play every day because the club's other backstop, "Paddy" Livingston, also was ailing. With Heinie Heitmuller in center field for the injured Oldring and Morrie Rath in place of Baker, Bender polished off the Red Sox, 4–2, the next day. The Chief would run his record to ten wins against a sole defeat before he had an uncharacteristically bad outing in a 7–1 loss in Chicago on June 18.

The ailing Athletics lost their first four games in June and temporarily relinquished first place to the Highlanders. New York, Chicago and Philadelphia jockeyed for first place over the next two weeks, but after the Athletics took over the top spot on June 21, they would retain that position in the standings for the remainder of the season.

On July 8, Detroit came to town for a four-game series at Shibe Park, six and one-half games behind the Athletics in the standings. Mack tabbed Chief Bender to pitch the first game against the Bengals and he fell behind, 3–1, after three innings. It could have been worse had the first batter in the game, Davy Jones, not been thrown out by Hartsel when he tried to stretch a hit to left field into a double. Later in the inning, Cobb and Crawford reached Bender for successive doubles, but Charley got out of the opening frame down only 1–0.

After the Tigers scored two more runs in the third, Bender shut down the visitors' scoring machine. Meanwhile, the A's chipped away against Tigers pitcher George Mullin and scored the deciding run in the sixth after a crucial error by Donnie Bush. With two out, Bender lifted a high pop-up to the infield near the pitcher's mound. Mullin backed away from the play when he heard shortstop Bush call for the ball. However, Donnie muffed the easy fly and Bender was safe at first. Hartsel beat out an infield hit and Oldring's single to left sent Bender home with the eventual winning run. After the A's 4–3 first-game win, Philadelphia went on to sweep the series and effectively dash Detroit's hopes for a fourth consecutive pennant.

The Athletics' faithful didn't see Bender again for two weeks. "There was a little nervousness among the White Elephant rooters last week, when it was learned that Bender was ill in bed with an attack of stomach trouble," wrote William Weart of the *Press*. "This is no new thing for the 'Chief,' who does not appear to have a system that can stand hot weather. Fortunately, the illness did not prove as serious as it was feared and in three days the Indian was back in uniform."[11]

Bender's next mound appearance came on July 22 in the second game of a doubleheader against Cleveland at Shibe Park. The Chief and Fred Falkenberg of the Naps battled fifteen innings until the game was called because of darkness. Bender allowed only seven hits to the visitors' batsmen, but only got a no decision to show for a long day's work.

Philadelphia had a powerful lineup, except in left field where the skills of thirty-six-year-old Tully Hartsel had markedly declined. On July 25, Connie Mack traded the rights to South Carolina country boy Joe Jackson and reserve infielder Rath to Cleveland for Briscoe Lord, who returned to left field for the Athletics after a three-year absence. While he regretted the loss of Jackson, Mack felt the team needed immediate help in the outfield to secure the pennant. The Carolina rube went on to fame as the "Shoeless Joe" of baseball folklore.

The American League championship was virtually decided in the first week of August when the Athletics reeled off eight victories in a row at the same time second-place Boston was losing six consecutive games. Chief Bender achieved his first twenty-victory season on August 24 with a 3–1 victory over Cleveland in a game in which he struck out twelve Naps. Three days later Charley beat the Browns, 5–1, and again registered double digits in strikeouts, this time with eleven.

The young Athletics became the first American League club to win more than one hundred games in a season, finished with 102 victories, and took the pennant by 14 games ahead of second-place New York. Just before the end of the regular season, the players dipped into their future World Series shares and bought Connie Mack his first automobile.

After winning a ten-inning 2–1 verdict over Ray Collins and Boston on the seventh of September, Bender did not start another game during the regular season. The afternoon of September 14, Bender and A's scout Al Maul attended a Phillies doubleheader with the Chicago Cubs at National League Park. In preparation for the World Series, the pair was there to watch the presumptive National League champion Cubs play. Bender returned for the next two days and was said to have watched "Chance's men closely."[12]

"The Cubs are either not playing up to their true form," Charles remarked to the press, "or their reputed strength behind the plate, bases, and at bat, as compared to the Athletics, has been greatly exaggerated. If they play as I saw them play on several occasions, we will beat them easily in the world's series."[13]

The American League champion Philadelphia Athletics put up some pretty good numbers in 1910 — collectively and individually. Chief Bender achieved a career-best record with 23 victories and only five losses for a league-high winning percentage of .821. His 1.58 earned run average was a career low. The Athletics boasted .300 hitters in second baseman Eddie Collins and outfielders Rube Oldring and Danny Murphy, and a thirty-one-game winner in right-hander Jack Coombs, after his 12–12 record the previous season.

The American League season ended a week before the National League's. To keep his team sharp for the World Series, Mack asked his friend Jimmy

McAleer to assemble a team for a series of exhibitions with the A's. McAleer put together an all-star-caliber squad consisting of Clyde Milan, Gabby Street, George McBride and Kid Elberfield from Washington; Tris Speaker, Harry Hooper and Jake Stahl from Boston; and Ty Cobb from Detroit. The pitching staff was made up of Ed Walsh and Doc White from Chicago and Walter Johnson of Washington.

Johnson beat Bender, Plank and Coombs, 8–3, in the opener and the pennant-winning Athletics lost the first four games of the exhibition series before taking the finale. Chief Bender pitched the first three innings of four of the five games, but only in the fifth game did the A's bear down. On October 15, Bender, Plank and Krause combined to allow only three hits and shut out the All-Stars, 5–0. Ed Walsh pitched the entire game for the opposition.[14]

After the World Series, Mack claimed, "Those games with the American League All-Stars were the making of our team in its battle in the World Series with the Cubs. Those games, more than anything else, put the Athletics in a condition to outclass the National League champions."[15]

Unfortunately, the tune-up series cost the A's their center fielder. Rube Oldring batted a career-high .308 in 1910 and then broke his leg on the eve of the World Series.

"My spikes failed to hold while I was going for a line drive by Speaker and I fell and fractured a knee," Rube explained. "So I saw the Series from a box, with my knee in a cast."[16]

Rube's injury gave twenty-year-old outfielder Amos Strunk the chance to play center field. Strunk had only returned to the field in late September after missing four months due to "water on the knee."

Frank Chance's club had won the World Series against the Tigers in 1907 and 1908, and was the favorite to win again in 1910. The National Leaguers considered Mack's club to be a bunch of college kids and too inexperienced to compete against the rough and tumble Cubs. Furthermore, Oldring was out of the lineup and Plank was questionable for the Series because of a sore arm. However, Chicago manager Frank Chance didn't have a full complement of players for the World Series either. Star second baseman Johnny Evers was out of the games with a broken ankle.

While Philadelphia manager Connie Mack appeared at a disadvantage because of Plank's doubtful status, he still had Coombs and Bender — and that was enough. As it turned out, the Athletics did not miss Oldring either as Strunk collected a double, a triple, and three singles in the four games he played.

Strunk's play in the Series would prompt the *Sporting News* to report, "He played center field and showed the fans that he has lost none of his greyhound ability. The amount of territory this youth can cover is simply amazing."[17]

When it was learned that Chief Bender would oppose Chicago's Orval Overall in Game One of the Series at Shibe Park, the betting odds dropped from 12–10 Chicago would win to 7–5 the Athletics would be victorious.[18] The bookmakers were proved correct when Overall departed the game after giving up three runs on six hits in the first three innings.

The attendance for the opening game of the Series at Shibe Park would have been even greater if the police department had allowed standing room tickets for the aisles of the grandstand. Thousands of fans were turned away due to the inability to obtain tickets. The official count of those that got inside was 26,891 and the receipts for the day were $37,424, of which $20,209 was designated to be distributed among the players. Across the street from the outfield wall, owners of houses overlooking the playing field erected bleachers on their roofs and sold seats for $3 to $5 each.[19]

Crowds of people stood behind ropes in the outfield except for a short section in center field that was kept clear so that batters would have the green wall as a background. Frank Baker lost two triples because of a ground rule that declared any ball hit into the standees in the outfield would be a double.

Connie Mack decided to play a little gamesmanship and sent the ailing Eddie Plank out to warm up with Bender just to keep the opposition guessing. It wasn't until just before the first pitch that the identity of the A's starting pitcher was confirmed.

Before play could begin, Bender stood by idly while the umpires and Frank Chance argued about the motion picture cameras on the field. Eventually, umpire Hank O'Day ruled the newspaper photographers must leave the field and the "picture machines" could stay. When the photographers protested to Ban Johnson in his box, the American League president explained that the moving picture men had permission from the National Commission to film the game.[20]

When Bender finally made his slow walk to the mound, he was given a great ovation by the throng. The long delay did not appear to affect him, although the strikeout of the leadoff batter, Jimmy Sheckard, was followed by Frank Schulte's solid single to left field. When Schulte took off for second on Bender's first pitch to the next batter, Ira Thomas' perfect throw easily beat the runner to second. After Solly Hofman grounded out to end the first, the crowd gave Bender a resounding ovation.

Baker was the batting star for the day with three hits, each of which led to runs. Bender got into the act in the second inning when his two-out bad-hop single past second scored Danny Murphy.

At the end of every inning, Bender was cheered mightily, and after he retired Zimmerman and Steinfeldt on called strikes to conclude the fifth, "the mighty throng arose en masse and emitted a series of volcanic shouts in commendation of his performances."[21]

The contest was a mismatch for eight innings as Bender took a one-hit shutout into the final frame. Left-handed hitter Frank Schulte had been the only Cub to get to first base, on his first-inning single and on a base on balls in the fourth. He was thrown out trying to steal in both instances so by the time the ninth inning arrived, Bender had a four-run lead and had faced the minimum of twenty-four batters.

"The Cubs could not hit Bender," wrote Chicago columnist Hugh Fullerton. "He started with terrific speed and a fast breaking curve ... and he had the most perfect control any one ever saw. He was using his curveball in the pinches, pitching with the count three and two, not as a desperate resort, but to fool batters, having as good control of his curve as he had of his fast one."[22]

Ira Thomas' muff of Joe Tinker's little foul in the ninth inning cost Bender a World Series shutout. Thomas got both hands on the pop fly a few feet behind the catcher's box, but couldn't hold it. Tinker used the reprieve to drive a single to center and Strunk's fumble allowed the Cubs' shortstop to take second base. Joe then scored when Johnny Kling punched one of Bender's curveballs to center field for another single. The pitcher was due up next and Frank Chance called on Ginger Beaumont, a former National League batting champion, to pinch-hit. Beaumont smashed a hard bouncer toward right field that Eddie Collins ensnared and threw Ginger out at first. Bender reached back for something extra and struck out Jimmy Sheckard on a shoulder-high fastball for the second out, but he worked too carefully to Schulte and the Cubs' right fielder walked to reach base for the third time in the game. That meant Hofman, a .325 hitter during the regular season, would come to bat representing the tying run. Bender's first pitch was a fastball with something extra. Hofman took a mighty swing but could not catch up with it. On a one-and-two pitch, Solly hit a wicked grounder right to Frank Baker, who stepped on third base for the force out that gave the Athletics a 4–1 victory and a one-game lead in the Series.

Simultaneous to the final out, thousands of people left their seats in the grandstand and bleachers to make a mad rush onto the diamond. Before most of the players could escape, they were engulfed by the large jostling mob of baseball fans. As soon as Baker touched the bag for the final out, Bender raced to the players' bench and reached it only a few steps behind his elated third baseman. A new baseball had just been put in play before the Hofman at-bat and Bender called out to Baker, "Give me the ball." Frank hesitated for a moment and then tossed him the almost-pristine trophy, its only defect the mark made by Hofman's bat.[23]

Despite his ninth-inning trouble, Bender still finished the game with a three-hitter. "I knew I was about good enough to win after I pulled through the first inning," Bender told the press. "The Chicago batters tried to wait me out. I could tell that Chance gave his players those instructions by the way they acted at first.... I fooled the Cubs on an out drop curve, and of course I had plenty of speed behind it."[24]

Hugh Fullerton added, "There is nothing to be discouraged about defeat. Bender would have beaten any one on earth today. He had absolute control and he made the ball do whatever he wanted it to do.... The comfort remains that tonight, with the Cubs one game behind, the betting is 10 to 9 that Chicago wins the series. The gamblers are also betting 10 to 7 Bender does not win another game in the series."[25]

Jack Coombs gave the Athletics a 2–0 lead in Game Two of the Series, although he was far from impressive. In pitching a complete game, Coombs gave up eight hits and nine walks while staggering to a 9–3 triumph. The A's broke up a tight game with a six-run seventh, an inning that featured Murphy's two-run double off Cubs starting pitcher and loser Mordecai Brown.

On the travel day before the Series resumed in Chicago, an edition of one of that city's newspapers displayed two conspicuous boxes, which displayed the "alleged" salaries paid by the sixteen clubs of the respective major leagues. The Athletics were the lowest-paid team in either league and the Cubs had the highest salaries. The inequities revealed in the article were not lost on the Philadelphia players, but Connie Mack shrugged it off when asked about the validity of the figures.

"When shown the statements," wrote William Weart, "Manager Mack remarked that if he had the difference between the alleged salaries paid his players and what they actually received he would be willing to quit base ball for life."[26]

It took the Athletics' special train just over seventeen hours to reach Chicago. Crowds gathered at nearly every station along the route and cheered the two trains as they swept by.

After the A's arrived in the Windy City, Connie Mack and a group of his players attended a fete at the American Music Hall to honor an old-time Chicago baseball star, Bill Lange. As soon as the audience saw Chief Bender among the players proceeding down the aisle, the people "started to give Indian yells, in which Bender immediately joined." After the bizarre exchange, Bender felt compelled to bow several times before the Indian yells ceased.[27]

At West Side Grounds the next day, Mack surprisingly chose Coombs to oppose another of the Cubs' star pitchers. Unbeknownst to the players, a new cork core baseball, used by the National League, was substituted for the American League's old rubber center ball for the game. The batters on the two clubs exploded for 21 hits and 17 runs.

This time, the victim of the Athletics' bats was Ed Reulbach, who left for a pinch-hitter in the second inning after yielding three runs. Harry McIntire, so effective in the Series opener with five innings of one-hit relief pitching, took over in the third inning with the score tied, 3–3, and was shelled for four runs (three scoring on Murphy's home run into the right field bleachers) in only one-third of an inning. Before the end of the third, the Athletics tacked on a fifth run en route to a 12–5 romp. Coombs, pitching with only one day of rest, gave up six hits and the ex-outfielder helped himself at the plate with three hits and drove in three runs.

The Cubs, on the brink of elimination, turned away from the veterans of their pitching staff and entrusted the club's immediate fate to the right arm of rookie Leonard (King) Cole, who had a 20–4 regular season record, to oppose Bender in Game Four. Cole performed admirably, but Chicago trailed the Athletics, 3–2, when the twenty-four-year-old pitcher left for a pinch-hitter in the eighth inning.

The Athletics had plenty of chances to put the game away. In the sixth inning, the Athletics had men on first and third base with one out. Barry bounced a grounder to third baseman Steinfeldt, who jugged it for a moment but was still able to throw out Frank Baker when he attempted to score from third. Thomas singled to load the bases, but Bender lifted a high fly ball to right field for the third out.

The Athletics had another chance to score in the eighth when their first two batters reached base. A sacrifice and a hit batsman left the bases loaded with one out and weak-hitting catcher Ira Thomas due up.

When it came Thomas's turn to bat, Connie Mack told Tully Hartsel, a good hitter against a curveball pitcher, to prepare to bat. Mack knew the 5' 5" lefty pinch-hitter would be a difficult batter for Cubs right-hander Mordecai Brown.

Connie Mack later acknowledged that Thomas loudly objected to his eminent removal from the game. "Let me bat," he begged. "I'll start the runners on a hit-and-run play and push one through the hole. I know I can do it."[28]

Ira's pleas won his manager over, but instead of the hit-and-run, Thomas swung at the first pitch and hit the ball right back to the pitcher. Brown threw home for one out and a double play was easily completed at first on the slow-footed catcher.[29]

Though Bender had permitted only two runs, he did not have the sharp breaking curveball of Game One. The Cubs, down to what appeared to be their last gasp, gained new life in the bottom of the ninth inning when Frank Schulte drove a Bender curveball into the gap in right-center field for two bases. Hofman bunted the potential tying runner to third. Moments later, another of Bender's curveballs caught too much of the plate and Frank Chance hit a long drive to center field. Strunk appeared to lose the flight of the ball and it soared well over his head for a triple. The game was now tied, but Bender induced the next two batters to pop out and the game plunged into extra innings.

Philadelphia had their chance in the top of the tenth when Harry Davis doubled with one out. Shortstop Joe Tinker made a nice play on Murphy's grounder, but would have had a hard time throwing him out at first. However, Davis tried for third and Tinker's throw beat Harry to the bag. In the bottom of the inning, Chicago catcher Jimmy Archer hit a Bender fastball into the left field stands for an apparent game-winning home run. However, the umpires stopped him at second due to a ground rule instituted because of the crowd in front of the normal outfield wall. However, Sheckard came through with a two-out, game-scoring single to give the Cubs the 4–3 victory.[30]

Buoyed by their victory at West Side Grounds, the Cubs sent twenty-five-game winner Brown (the Game Four winning pitcher with two innings of scoreless relief) against Coombs the next day. After seven innings Philadelphia led only 2–1. The Athletics struck for five runs in the eighth and came out on top, 7–2.

Using only two pitchers, Bender and three-time winner Coombs, for the entire Series, the Athletics won their first World Series. Considering the youth on Connie Mack's team, Philadelphia appeared to be a team to be reckoned with for years to come.

Thousands of people lined the streets of downtown Philadelphia for the parade to honor the World Series championships. The event easily surpassed the 1905 festivities honoring the city's previous American League champions.

That November, the Athletics followed the New York Giants to Cuba for a nine-game series against the island's professional teams. Major league ball clubs began to make fall trips to the Caribbean island after the Cincinnati National League club first went there in 1908. The Reds quickly learned the Cubans would not be pushovers when a twenty-one-year-old pitcher named Jose Mendez shut them out twice and added a seven-inning scoreless relief stint against the big leaguers.

Each A's player was to get $500 for the Cuban series, but when Frank Baker and Eddie Collins passed on the trip, the Cuban promoters reduced the Athletics' guarantee to $5,000, only $357 for each player. Of course, Oldring would also be missing, so infielders McInnis and Derrick were substituted for the missing stars.[31] Mack did not go to Cuba either, but went on a honeymoon trip with his second wife, Katherine.

Philadelphia lost an exhibition game in Cuba against the Detroit Tigers and then played their first "official" game against the Havana Reds on December 6, 1910. The Athletics probably underestimated the Cubans, losing three of the first four games they played against Havana and Almendares, the two best teams on the island. The A's should have known better because the Cuban teams had already beaten a Detroit team that included Ty Cobb in eight out of twelve games. Plus, the Havana team had a quartet of ringers, four of the best African American players from the States in shortstop John Henry Lloyd, second baseman Home Run Johnson, outfielder Pete Hill and catcher Bruce Petway.

Bender lost to Havana, 2–0, in his first effort, and finished the trip with only one win out of four decisions. He did much better at the plate, leading the A's in batting (seven hits in 16 at-bats for a .368 average). Among the star African American players from the States, only Hill amassed as many hits as Bender. The great John Henry Lloyd batted .267 in his five games against the Athletics and Petway hit a paltry .120. The Athletics scrambled to take a four-to-three lead in games won and then dropped two games on their final day in Cuba; Plank lost to the Alemndares' Jose Mendez and Bender lost the second game, 6–2, to Havana.[32]

After earning post-season checks for almost as much as his regular-season salary, Charles Bender and wife Marie decided to winter in the South with the Hartsels and Mr. and Mrs. Harry Davis. The Benders spent the cold months in Atlanta where Charley spent his free time practicing a new obsession.

"Big Chief Bender, the prominent pitcher of the World Champions, has been wintering in Atlanta and has become a most enthusiastic golfer," reported the *American Golfer*. "Every day, when the weather would permit, he has been at East Lake playing at least 18 and sometime 36 holes. While he cannot yet be considered as good a golfer as he is a slab man, still, by constant practice, he has learned to make some wonderful shots from the rough and has become a genius in pitching his ball from a sand trap (by hand)."[33]

Upon Bender's arrival at the Athletics' Atlanta spring training camp in March of 1911, Connie Mack was impressed with the physical condition of the Chief. The manager didn't want to overwork his veteran pitchers during the early part of training and risk an arm injury. Though he was not a fan of golf, Mack decided to send Bender and Jack Coombs to the links for eighteen holes on a daily basis. Sometimes they were joined by Harry Davis and Eddie Collins, who were also golf enthusiasts. The program continued for the team's three-week stay in Atlanta, and the Athletics became the first club to use golf as part of the spring training regimen.[34]

Bender would also spend the next two winters in Atlanta perfecting his golf game. In March 1914, the *American Golfer* reported "Chief Bender, the famous Chippewa Indian pitcher, is really a very fine player, particularly with his irons."[35]

In the ensuing years, "C. A. Bender" became a frequent participant in golf tournaments in and around Philadelphia. Despite this new infatuation with the game of golf, Charley did not abandon his other off-season sport. The Chief delayed his return to Philadelphia that spring so he could participate in a shooting tournament in Savannah, Georgia.

♦ 9 ♦

"Who Can Hit a Pea?"

By all standards, 1911 should have been a great year for Charles Albert Bender. He played for a team that won its second consecutive world's championship, pitched two World Series victories, and he became a motion picture actor. However, it was also a year of tragedy for the Bender family.

Everything seemed to be in place for a Philadelphia Athletics dynasty in 1911. Eddie Collins and Jack Barry were only twenty-three, Frank Baker was twenty-four, Bender and Jack Coombs were twenty-seven, and promising young infielder Stuffy McInnis had just turned twenty. Even the seemingly old Connie Mack was a mere forty-six when he led the Athletics to the 1910 World Series crown.

In 1911 the Shibe's new and livelier cork center baseball was largely responsible for an increase in run production in the American League by almost twenty-four percent; home runs went up by twenty-five percent. Naturally, there were complaints by the old guard who claimed the new ball was corrupting the traditional game of pitching and strategy. Tom Shibe responded that "the cork center ball does not make base hits. It merely turns singles into doubles, doubles into three-baggers and three-baggers into home runs."[1]

Although there is no question about the increase in extra-base hits between 1910 and 1911, the largest leap was in batting average. The league's combined average was thirty points higher than the previous season.

Charles Bender was always stingy with the gopher ball, allowing only an average of one home run a season the previous four years. In 1911, the Chief gave up two four-baggers and then only a single homer a year later. By comparison, Walter Johnson and Jack Coombs each allowed eight home runs during the 1911 season.

Frank Baker captured the American League home run crown in 1911 with eleven round-trippers. With Baker driving home 115 runs, the Athletics batted a league-high .296, and once again dominated the American League with 101 wins. Outfielders Danny Murphy, Bris Lord and Rube Oldring batted a composite .312, while pitchers Jack Coombs, Eddie Plank, Chief Bender and Cy Morgan combined for 82 victories.

Another aspect of the game affected by the cork center ball was outfield play. Speedier outfielders became essential to corral harder hit balls and fans were thrilled by the sight of fielders making long runs to haul down well-hit fly balls.

The return of Rube Oldring from his injury of the previous fall meant that Amos Strunk was the odd man out. However, Mack wanted to get the talented Strunk and his outstanding defensive skills into the lineup. By shifting Oldring to left field, the A's managed to get Amos into center field for 47 games. A native Philadelphian, Strunk went to James G. Blaine Grammar School, only a few blocks from old Columbia Park, and attended Central Manual Training School at the same time as Connie Mack's son Roy. After Shibe Park opened, Amos lived with his sister some six blocks from the new ballpark.[2]

Bender received the Opening Day starting assignment at Shibe Park on April 12, 1911. Charles and New York's James Vaughan battled to a 1–1 deadlock through the first seven innings of the game. In the top of the eighth inning, shortstop John Barry's error allowed a Highlander runner to score and Bender lost, 2–1.

Before the game, Eddie Collins was presented with a new automobile for being named the A's best player in 1910. When he attempted to drive off in his new vehicle that had been placed outside Shibe Park, he discovered someone had driven a large nail into a tire. While a large crowd stood by, the car had to be towed into the park garage. Eddie had to pay a repair bill for $7.50 before he ever got a chance to use his award.[3]

The Athletics were in the cellar for the first two weeks of the season, and on May 19 Mack's men found themselves eleven games behind a surging Detroit team that won twenty-one of its first twenty-three games. The Mackmen won their next seven games to get within striking distance of the Tigers.

When Harry Davis was disabled because of back pain early that summer, John "Stuffy" McInnis assumed the first base position. Originally a middle infielder, McInnis bided his time on the Athletics' bench for two seasons after being signed as an eighteen-year-old high schooler out of Gloucester, Massachusetts. He is said to have acquired his nickname as a youngster in the Boston suburban leagues where his spectacular play brought shouts of "that's the stuff, kid."[4]

Once he got his opportunity, McInnis made the best of it. Stuffy got into 126 games, batted .321 for the 1911 season, and developed into arguably the best defensive first baseman of his day. He was the originator of the "knee stretch," whereby a first baseman did a full, ground-level split in reaching for a throw.[5] The press began calling McInnis, second baseman Eddie Collins, shortstop Jack Barry and third baseman Frank Baker "the million dollar infield."

The Athletics' game with the St. Louis Browns on June 12 at Shibe Park was designated a special day for the veteran captain, Harry Davis, who was rumored to be the next manager of the Cleveland Naps. Both clubs agreed to donate their share of the gate receipts to Davis, and a good crowd of 7,000 showed up for the game that would be preceded by several field events. More interesting was what happened after the silver cups were distributed to the winners of the athletic contests.

Eddie Collins, 1911 (Paul Thompson, photographer, Library of Congress).

Without fanfare, the A's players appeared on the field dressed in costumes and, according to *Sporting Life*, "went through a grotesque proceeding of trying to imitate the characters which they represented." Harry Davis was made up as Uncle Sam. Harry Krause was Little Lord Fauntleroy, Lapp was dressed as a Chinaman, and the keystone duo of Collins and Barry were "The Gold Dust Twins." Bender appeared dressed as a cowboy and his batterymate, Ira Thomas, played the "Indian." A lively round of baseball was played during which each participate assumed a position other than what he normally played.

During the course of the comedy, third baseman Rube Oldring, made up as a red-headed boy, received a split nose from a hard-hit bounder. The antics were concluded after about fifteen minutes and then everyone got ready for the regular scheduled contest.[6]

Despite his bloodied nose, Rube was able to play in the regular game, won by the Athletics, 1–0, on a ninth-inning run. Frank Baker, the "Mexican" from the pre-game farce, started the rally with a single, but when he attempted to go to second on short passed ball he was beaned by the catcher's throw. Derrick pinch-ran for the groggy third baseman and scored the winning run on a base hit by the "Irish Gentleman," Danny Murphy.

After a month lay-off because of a sore right shoulder, Chief Bender returned to the mound at Shibe Park against the Chicago White Sox on June 14. Bender and Ed Walsh matched up in a classic battle between two future Hall of Fame pitchers that took ten innings for one of them to come out on top.

The Athletics got a run in the first inning due to a misplay by a White Sox outfielder. Eddie Collins was on first base with two outs and was off at the crack of the bat when Frank Baker lifted a fly ball to right field. Right fielder Matty McIntyre backed up near the wall to make the catch, but the ball bounced off his hands and fell safely to the ground. Collins scored on the error and Baker made it to third, where he died when Walsh retired the next batter for the third out.

The visitors came right back to tie the score in their second at-bat. Two uncharacteristic walks by Bender cost him when a .220 lifetime hitter named Lee Tannehill singled in the tying run. After that, the game was scoreless through the ninth inning.

"It was a desperate battle, round after round," wrote Sam Weller, a reporter at the game, "with a crowd of eager spectators numbering 8,000 howling at every possible chance to get the needed run. As inning after inning was played it seemed the winning run never could be legitimately earned, and it was a question of which team would break first or which one luck would favor."[7]

It turned out that the weakest part of the Athletics' batting order brought victory to the home team. Leading off the bottom of the tenth inning, Jack Barry lined a clean single to left field. The White Sox guessed that light-hitting catcher Ira Thomas would try to bunt and a pitch-out was called. Walsh threw a pitch well outside the strike zone and Thomas pitched his bat at it. The bat made contact with the ball and it bounded erratically past the first baseman, who had charged in toward the plate to field the bunt. Barry ran to third and Philadelphia had two runners on base with none out.

The 8,000 rose in anticipation of the victory, but swooned when Bender bounced back to Walsh and Barry was run down between home and third. The next batter, Bris Lord, had been easy pickings for Walsh all day and the Sox infielders and outfielders moved in close for a potential play at home plate. Lord became the hero of the moment when he hit a line drive so hard it banged off the right field concrete wall on the fly. Bender trotted down and jumped on second base while the ecstatic crowd cheered their team's 2–1 victory over the great Ed Walsh.[8]

In a remarkable turn of events, the usually low-key Bender was ejected in each of his next two starting assignments. On June 19, Bender took a 6–1 lead into the last of the ninth inning after an especially porous Washington defense made seven errors behind Walter Johnson. Two singles and a walk with two out left the bases loaded with Nationals. Eddie Ainsmith batted for Johnson and beat Eddie Collins' throw to first by a hair. Bender kicked so strenuously at umpire John Sheridan's decision he was ordered out of the game. Krause took over the pitching duties with the speedy Clyde Milan due to bat. Milan flew out to center field, giving Bender and the Athletics the victory.

Four days later, Charley returned to the mound against Washington for the finale of the four-game series at Shibe Park. The Athletics were on the short end of a 2–1 score when Wid Conroy fouled a Bender pitch into the grandstand. While Charley was winding up to throw the next pitch, the earlier foul ball was tossed from the stands and rolled onto the diamond. Bender stopped during his windup, picked up the returned ball and threw it over the roof of the grandstand. Sheridan, noting a breach of the rules, signaled home plate umpire Jack Egan, who promptly thumbed Bender out of the game. Almost all the Philadelphia players surrounded Egan, but despite their procrastinations, the ejection stood. "Tiny" Leonard replaced the dispossessed Athletics hurler and Philadelphia went on to win the game anyway.[9]

On June 27, Bender made it through the entire ball game without running afoul of the umpires in a seemingly unremarkable game against the Red Sox at Huntington Avenue Grounds. However, the contest was marked by an unusual at-bat by Athletics first baseman Stuffy McInnis. The A's had built a sizable lead by the time they came to bat in the eighth inning. As Red Sox relief pitcher hurler Ed Karger was throwing a few warm-up pitches to his catcher, the scheduled batter, McInnis, stepped in and swung at one of the tosses. The ball shot into a vacated center field and McInnis raced around the bases while the bemused Boston outfielders were taking their positions.

When McInnis crossed the plate, Umpire Egan signaled "safe," and the run counted! Manager Patsy Donovan and the Boston players swarmed around the arbiter, but their appeals feel on deaf ears. Bender and the Athletics went ahead and won the game, 7–3.

Boston protested the game to American League president Ban Johnson on the grounds that two Philadelphia players were leaving the field and were in fair territory when McInnis swung at the practice pitch. Johnson denied the protest because of a recent American League rule that abolished warm-up pitches between innings in order to speed up games. Club owners were concerned about the length of games, some of which were lasting as long as two hours. Johnson's time-saving rule, stipulating that a pitcher should throw a pitch as soon as the hitter settled the batter's box, was shortly withdrawn.[10]

Philadelphia closed to within one and a half games of first-place Detroit before Ty Cobb ran wild in a four-game sweep of the Athletics the second week in July. Mack was all about match-ups and did not start Bender or Plank in the series, nor did Eddie Collins play, who was on the bench with an injured elbow.

In the third game, the A's mounted a four-run rally to take the lead in the eighth inning. The Tigers came right back to load the bases in the bottom of the frame before Bender was rushed in to replace Morgan. Bender fanned Schmidt for out number two and then had to face Davy Jones, the Tigers' pesky lefty-hitting left fielder.

Bender would later swear Jones was one of the most troublesome bat-ters he ever faced[11] and Davy bore that out when he slapped a single that sent two of the runners home to tie the score at 7–7. In the last of the ninth, Cobb led off with a hard-hit grounder that was too hot for second baseman Danny Murphy to handle. After Sam Crawford flied out, Jim Delehanty moved into the batter's box against Bender and punched one of the Chief's pitches into a vacated part of right field near the foul line.

A report of the affair read that Delehanty's single would only have been good enough to send an ordinary base runner to third at best. "But Cobb is not ordinary. He had a lead before Bender ever finished his windup and instead of sliding into second, as is his custom, his intuition responded to the crack of Delehanty's ash and the Bengal sensation continued on past third with ever increasing speed and slid in (to home) under Thomas seconds ahead of the ball. This run broke up the tie and incidentally the game."[12]

After Coombs was beaten badly for the second time in the series on July 14, the *Sporting News* suggested that "the disaster could not have been any more complete, and now it is going to be an awful uphill fight for Connie's men to again overtake the leaders."[13] The prediction was premature, for when the Tigers came to Philadelphia on July 28, the A's were within three and a half games of first place.

Charles Bender won seventeen games in 1911 and none of those wins was bigger than the 1–0 victory over Detroit's Ed Summers on July 28 in the opener of the pivotal five-game series with the Tigers. A throng, estimated at close to 32,000, squeezed into Shibe Park for the Saturday doubleheader and it was reported that scalpers charged $8 for $1 reserved seats. The park's gates had to be closed before the first game started at 1:15 P.M., leading several thou-sand disgruntled fans to storm the entrances and demand admission. They were only kept away by 200 policemen with drawn clubs. During the course of the second game that day, a thirty-three-year-old doctor reportedly died from the excitement.

A week earlier, Detroit scribe F. A. Beasley had written, "It is doubtful if there ever were in any league two clubs between which such bitter rivalry exists as now between the Tigers and the Elephants and evidence of personal enmity was plentiful in the recent series and combats between certain play-ers were expected at every turn."[14]

For eleven innings the fans in the bleachers megaphoned the game's results to the crowd outside. Detroit's Ed Summers allowed only one hit over the first nine innings, though he was supported by three outstanding catches by center fielder Cobb. Bender gave up eight hits but walked no one and was toughest on opposing batters when runners were on base. Summers brought about his own downfall when he walked the opposing pitcher leading off the home eleventh. Lord sacrificed Bender to second base, but Oldring went out harmlessly. With two out, Eddie Collins made the clutch single that sent Bender running home with the run that threw the huge crowd into delirium.[15]

Philadelphia won the second game of the Friday doubleheader and again on Saturday to pull with a half-game of first place, but Detroit came back to win the final two games of the long series. On August 2, Chief Bender shut out the Browns, 3–0, to move the A's within one game of first place, and the Athletics took over the top position for good with a doubleheader victory over St. Louis on August 4.

In the August 10 issue of the *Sporting News,* the Philadelphia correspondent wrote Mack "has nursed Bender along until the 'Chief' is now pitching the greatest ball of his career. Bender, in his last three games, has pitched 29 innings and has been so wonderful that he has not given a base on balls in these contests. Although the necessity was certainly great, Manager Mack would not send Bender in for repeaters in the series with Detroit, and he says the 'Chief' will not be used more than once in any series."[16]

A week later, the same reporter editorialized that "Bender is the only one of the crowd (of A's pitchers) who has not proved erratic during the team's home stand, the 'Chief' winning all five of his contests ... and had not Connie landed such a sterling rescuer as Danforth when he did the chances the Tigers would be in the lead."[17]

The Athletics reinforced their hold on first place with victories in the first four games of a five-game set with Chicago the second week of August. Rookie Athletics pitcher Dave Danforth made such a splash in the White Sox series, one was reminded of Harry Krause's remarkable winning streak two season's earlier.

The *Sporting News* was justifiably impressed:

Last Monday afternoon Dave Danforth, formerly of Baylor College, Texas, who reported here less than a fortnight ago, was rushed in Bender's relief in the fourteenth inning of a game with Chicago (won by Philadelphia). The next day, Danforth rescued Plank in the seventh inning with the score 0 to 0, three White Sox on the bases and one out. Dave had his nerve, for he fanned McIntyre and caused Harry Lord to give Eddie Collins an easy grounder, retiring the side without a score. On Wednesday, Danforth went to Coombs relief in the ninth inning and stopped a batting rally by the White Sox that threatened to overcome the home team's lead. On Friday, it was Harry Krause that needed assistance after five innings of twirling, and once more Danforth was called on.[18]

Danforth's star faded almost as soon as it emerged. He was back in the minor leagues a year later, though he returned to the major leagues and had a decent career with the White Sox and Browns, from 1916 through 1925.

After losing a game to the Tigers on August 1, the A's went 40–16 the remainder of the schedule and blew the Tigers away by 13 games. Bender ran his personal win streak to six straight before losing to the Tigers on August

27. He came right back with a 1–0 shutout against Ed Cicotte in Boston on September 1.

Chief Bender was recuperating from a bout of flu, called the "grippe" back then, when he received a wire from William "Deacon" White of the Edmonton, Canada, minor league baseball club. The telegram informed Charles of the death of his brother John Bender, an outfielder for the Edmonton team. It has been mistakenly written that John died while on the mound (or playing the outfield) during a baseball game. There have been many inaccuracies printed about John Bender's death, but the article from the *Edmonton Bulletin* of September 25, 1911, should set the record straight.

> Death came suddenly and without warning this morning to J. C. Bender, a professional baseball player, who was with the Edmonton team the latter part of the season just closed. The well known and popular athlete had just entered Lewis Bros. Cafe at 627 First Street and was on the point of ordering breakfast when he dropped dead at 9:15. He expired without saying a word.

The lengthy article noted "Bender joined the Edmonton team at Calgary last month and played right field. He arrived here August 27, when he registered at the Pendennis Hotel.... Deacon White first met him in Duluth, Minnesota, nine years ago, when he was with the Northern League, and has kept close tab on his work ever since. More recently Bender developed a bad case of heart disease, and this was the cause of his sudden taking off."[19]

If the news from Canada wasn't bad enough, the Bender family suffered another loss only four days after John's death. Anna Bender Sanders, younger sister of Charles, died on September 29, 1911. After graduating from the Hampton Normal & Agricultural Institute of Virginia, Annie completed business courses at Haskell Institute in 1908 and became a clerk at the Chemawa Indian boarding school in Oregon. She had married Reuben Saunders, a teacher at the school, only a year before her death.

It was feared Chief Bender might not be physically fit for the World Series because of influenza. However, when Connie Mack brought his twirler back to the mound on September 30, Charley pitched five solid innings, allowed five hits and walked only one batter. He departed after the fifth because Mack didn't want to risk overworking his pitcher before the Series.

For the off-week between the end of the season and the start of the World Series, Connie Mack again arranged for a tune-up against a team of American League stars. Johnny McAleer, who had recently resigned as manager of the Nationals, assembled the "all-stars" mostly from his former Washington club. There were a few additions, namely Ty Cobb, Hal Chase and Larry Gardner. The series was marred by controversy after the $275 each "all-star" player received from the Athletics was considerably less than the year before.[20]

The Athletics' World Series opponents were the New York Giants, setting up a rematch of the storied 1905 shutout classic that Mack's team lost to

McGraw's rowdies. The Giants of 1911 were a run-happy bunch, setting a modern major league record of 347 stolen bases. Christy Mathewson, who had thrown three shutouts against the Athletics in that earlier Series, was still McGraw's pitching ace, as reflected by his 26–13 regular-season record.

An emerging star for New York was twenty-one-year-old left-hander Rube Marquard, winner of 24 games. And the Giants had some good hitters, too, led by Larry Doyle, Fred Merkle and Chief Meyers.

John Tortes Meyers, a Cahuilla Indian from California who had attended Dartmouth College, had been the Giants' regular catcher since 1909. Meyers was also called "Chief" despite his disdain for the name.

"Back in the old days, ballplayers were considered rowdies and no decent hotels wanted them," Meyers once told an interviewer. "And to make matters worse, Indians were looked upon as foreigners. Anyway, McGraw saw to it that we lived at the best hotels on the road and things started looking up. McGraw was tough all right, but he fought for his players."[21]

Things did not always go smoothly for the Giants in their 99-victory season. Their ballpark, the Polo Grounds, burned to the ground in April and a new concrete double-decker, which seated 32,000, was not ready for games until late June. In the interim, the Giants played their home games at the park of the American League's New York Highlanders.

Several players who met in the 1905 Series were still among the opposing lineups, notably the starting pitchers Mathewson, Bender, Plank and Ames. Briscoe Lord, a rookie in 1905, was back in left field for Philadelphia after spending a couple of years in Cleveland. Philadelphia first baseman Stuffy McInnis would miss the 1911 World Series because of a broken hand sustained on a pitch thrown by George Mullin. That meant thirty-seven-year-old captain Harry Davis returned to first for one last hurrah in the Series and contributed a key double in Bender's fourth-game victory.

After his outstanding pitching down the stretch during the regular season, Chief Bender was the obvious choice to start the first game of the World Series against Christy Mathewson. Bender pitched in his last regular season game on October 3 and then had a tune-up against the American League all-stars.

Game One of the World Series was not played until October 14. (The late starting date was because the National League's regular season ran through Columbus Day.) The largest crowd ever to watch a major league ball game up to that time, announced at 38,281, squeezed into the Polo Grounds. The gate receipts were $77,379, also a Series record.

Fans lined up outside the stadium hours before the game began and hundreds gathered in a nearby auditorium to see the game "re-enacted" on a board. A hundred telegraphers were stationed in a special area behind home plate to send details of the game around the world. John McGraw again dressed his players in special black and white trimmed uniforms like the ones that apparently brought them so much luck in the 1905 World Series.[22]

Mathewson, winner over Bender in the Series finale six years earlier, prevailed again in a classic pitching duel. The A's seized a 1–0 lead in the second inning when Frank Baker singled, moved to second on a ground out, advanced to third on a passed ball, and scored on a single by Harry Davis. Mathewson claimed the game turned in New York's favor when the Giants changed their signs. McGraw was convinced Baker alerted Davis that a curveball was coming before he smacked his run-scoring hit. In the third inning, the Athletics put runners on first and second after two were out. Before Baker stepped up to bat, Mathewson and Meyers changed the signs. Whether or not the runner on second signaled Baker the pitches called for by Meyers, Frank struck out on three outside pitches.[23]

The Giants tied it in the fourth without benefit of a hit. With Snodgrass on third base, Buck Herzog scorched a grounder that Eddie Collins muffed and, before he could recover, the runner had scored. The Giants collected the game-winning run in the seventh when Bender's friend, Chief Meyers, did him in.

In a newspaper article attributed to Meyers, the Giants' catcher wrote that when he came to bat with one out against "my redskin friend Albert" the pair engaged in a bit of banter. Bender gave Meyers a laugh and then forewarned, "Good night for you, Chief."[24]

Meyers worked the count until he was able to get a fastball to his liking. His mighty swing sent the ball well over Lord's head and toward the left field stands, but it banged off the wall about four feet from the top. Meyers noted in his column that when he pulled up at second, it was his turn to laugh. Bender's response was to playfully shake his fist in retaliation.

Next up was Mathewson, who struck out, Bender's ninth victim of the day. Josh Devore had been easy for Bender in his previous at-bats, though he drew a walk on a full count in the third. The Chief whipped across two quick strikes on the little lefty hitter, then threw a ball. Devore swung late at the next pitch but made sufficient contact to hit a little fly ball over third base that rolled into foul territory and caromed off the stands. Meyers easily scored from second with the final run of the game.

Mathewson finished with a six-hitter in New York's 2–1 victory. The Giants' strategy had been to take a lot of pitches and wait for Bender's fastball to tire his arm out. Charles threw more than 130 pitches and walked four batters, but he fanned eleven and was still strong at the end, striking out two of the final five batters he faced.

Chief Meyers was among several players and managers solicited by news organizations that used the players' bylines for daily columns that appeared during the Series. The baseball men's words, or the words of their ghostwriters, were sent to local papers across the nation. It seems unlikely that Meyers would have used the word "redskin" or "Chief" to describe his friend, so it was more likely an eager ghostwriter may have added the distasteful words for embellishment.

"Albert Bender is a wonderful pitcher and had some of our boys standing on their heads," read Meyers' column. "I am glad to belong to the same race as that big fellow. But we will beat them surely and while — as I said before — Rube Marquard will win at least one game. In the end the thing that will win for us will be Matty and the wallop."[25]

Marquard and Plank matched Game One's starters with a low-scoring pitchers duel in the second game at Shibe Park. The score was 1–1 when the Athletics came to bat in the bottom of the sixth inning, and Marquard showed no signs of weakening as he retired Lord and Oldring. However, Eddie Collins followed with a double and clean-up hitter Frank Baker was next to hit. Baker walloped a 1-ball, 1-strike pitch from Rube over the right field wall for a two-run homer. Frank recalled that rounding second base to the thunderous ovation from the home fans was the greatest moment of his life. The smash proved the difference, as the A's held on for a 3–1 victory that tied the Series. The following morning, Christy Mathewson, or his ghostwriter, took Marquard to task in the *New York Herald*.

> Marquard made a poor pitch to Frank Baker on the latter's sixth-inning home run. There was no excuse for it. Prior to the game, John McGraw went over all of the Athletics' hitters in a clubhouse talk, and paid especial attention to the left-handed hitter, Frank Baker. We had scouted Baker, knew what pitches were difficult for him to hit.... Well, Rube pitched just what Baker likes.[26]

Before sundown, Marquard's ghostwriter, Frank Menke, would get his turn. In Game Three at the Polo Grounds, Mathewson took a 1–0 lead into the ninth inning. Collins led off the top of the ninth by grounding out and Matty needed just two outs for his fifth straight World Series victory over Mack's Athletics.

Mathewson had two strikes and a ball on Baker when the impossible happened. "There were two strikes called on Baker when the ball broke over with a curve shoulder high," wrote Grantland Rice. "For a brief second the gray ball seemed to hang in mid air.... Baker threw his war club into the argument, and as the ball sailed gracefully and swiftly far and deep in the right field stand, it spelled defeat."[27]

Frederick Lieb of the *New York Press* wrote of the great crowd of 27,216, "It was so quiet that those with especially good hearing could pick up the patter of Baker's feet as he romped joyfully around the bases."[28]

Baker's homer only tied the score, but it demoralized the Giants. In the top of the eleventh, the Athletics scored two runs off Matty with the aid of a pair of Giants errors, but McGraw's men fought back in their half of the

Eddie Plank and Chief Bender (right) during pre-game warm-ups, circa 1911 (George Grantham Bain Collection, Library of Congress).

eleventh against Coombs. Herzog singled and Meyers followed with a mighty smash into the left field bleachers. It was headed for fair territory, but a gust of wind caught it and blew the ball foul by inches. The New York catcher grounded out, but the Giants got a reprieve when Collins fumbled Beals Becker's roller and Herzog scored. With the Giants down one run, Becker attempted to steal second, but Lapp threw him out on a close play for his fifth caught-stealing victim of the day. McGraw screamed bloody murder, complaining that he had been robbed all day by Tom Connolly, the American League umpire at second. Coombs pitched the entire game for Philadelphia, permitting only three hits.

After the game, sportswriter Menke approached Mathewson. "Just what happened, Matty?" he is said to have asked. "What did Baker hit? It couldn't be that you grew careless, or did you?"[29]

At this point in the Series, the weather put the fourth game on indefinite hold. For six days, it rained. And rained! And rained! The Shibes and Mack had a crew of men at work drying the field by burning cans of gasoline. The fourth game was finally played on October 24, exactly a week after Game

Three. The break allowed the Athletics to get Oldring back in the lineup after he attended his sister's funeral on the twentieth. With almost a week's rest, Mathewson came back for McGraw while Chief Bender got another shot at the Giants' ace.

Several thousand New York fans were on hand at Shibe Park and cheered the Giants mightily when they took the field for batting practice. By the time the Athletics appeared, more than 20,000 people were already in the stands. They cheered their favorites for five minutes, "ringing bells, blowing whistles, twisting watchmen's rattles and pounding huge Chinese gongs."[30]

The crowd went into frenzy when Frank Baker came out for batting practice. The partisans began to cheer anew when Danforth grooved a batting practice fastball that Baker drove well above the right field fence and off an apartment house across the street. "Baker, Baker, the Giants' undertaker," shouted several Quakers through their megaphones. The Giants would hear this chant often during the afternoon each time the slugging third baseman came to bat.[31]

The next big demonstration by the fans came when Bender walked out to the mound. The crowd's cheers, the bells and gongs, drowned out the announcer who was shouting the names of the battery through his large megaphone. Within a few minutes the cheers turned to groans.

The Giants broke fast with two runs against Bender in the first inning. Josh Devore scratched a single past the mound and scored when Larry Doyle blasted a long drive into right-center. Center fielder Oldring slipped on the wet grass and the ball rolled to the fence for a triple. Snodgrass hit a long sacrifice fly to score Doyle and make it 2–0.

With Mathewson on the mound, there was no reason to think the two runs would not be enough. The Giants' "Big Six" struck out the three batters he faced in the first inning, Lord and Oldring on three pitches each. In the fourth inning, Mathewson suddenly and unexpectedly became hittable. It began with Baker, who had struck out swinging in the first. The count was one ball and one strike when one of Matty's fastballs drifted over the middle of the plate and Baker hit it on the sweet spot. The ball sailed deep into left-center field, out of the reach of Devore, who slipped in the mud as he made a lunge for it. After fouling a bunt attempt, Murphy doubled to score Baker. Harry Davis hit Matty's next pitch for Philly's third successive double and the score was now tied. A sacrifice fly plated the third run of the inning.

Now it was Bender's turn to shut the door on Mathewson and the Giants. The Athletics added another run in the fifth and the Chief did not allow the New Yorkers more than one base runner in any inning over the remainder of the contest. In the fifth inning, Chief Meyers doubled with one out. The Giants' catcher attempted to take third on a short passed ball, but Ira Thomas fired the ball to Baker in time to retire the opposing catcher.

After striking out in three straight times at bat, Fred Merkle doubled to lead off the visitor's ninth. Bender bore down and retired the next three batters. He got Meyers to ground out harmlessly to Collins for the final out of the game. Bender's 4–2 victory over Mathewson gave Philadelphia a Series lead of three games to one.

Josh Devore, New York's lead-off hitter, said of Bender, "The Chief makes the baseball look like a pea. Who can hit a pea when it goes by with the speed of lightning?"[32]

New York escaped elimination in Game Five, in which Philadelphia, behind Coombs, had a 3–0 edge after six innings. During the sixth inning, Coombs pulled a muscle in his groin when he caught his spikes in the space between the pitching rubber and the dirt. Twice Connie Mack sent Chief Bender out to the mound to make sure Jack was okay, but in spite of the pain Coombs had a 3–1 lead with one out in the Giants' ninth. On the verge of elimination, Art Fletcher doubled for the National Leaguers, moved to third on a ground out and scored on reliever Doc Crandall's double. Devore followed with a game-tying single. After Coombs beat out an infield hit in the top of the tenth inning, Mack put a pinch-runner in for the laboring pitcher. In the bottom of the inning, with Plank on in relief, Fred Snodgrass doubled and scored on a fly ball by Merkle. The Giants won, 4–3, and clung to life.[33]

Up to game time for Game Six, it was expected Connie Mack would pitch Plank because Bender rarely worked on only one day's rest. Before the game, both Plank and Bender began throwing as if each was going to pitch the day's game. When the umpires headed toward the A's bench to get the lineup from Mack, Bender turned to his manager and said, "Get a new ball out of the bag for me, Connie." Mack did not hesitate to give him the ball before he turned and told the arbiters Bender would be his pitcher.[34]

It was Red Ames instead of Mathewson that McGraw chose to oppose Bender before a diminished crowd of 20,485 in Philadelphia. Once again, the Giants started fast in the first inning against Bender. After Charley speared Devore's hot grounder with his bare hand and threw him out at first, Larry Doyle drove a ground-rule double into the overflow crowd in right field. Doyle then scored when right fielder Danny Murphy dropped Red Murray's fly ball. However, the Giants jubilance changed to sighs when Bender picked a napping Murray off first.

Murphy was distraught when he arrived at the bench between innings. The unflappable Bender sat down next to Danny and said, "All I ask boys is to get me that run back. The Giants may be able to tie us, but they never can win today."[35]

Ames managed to get through the first three innings with a 1–1 score, but in the bottom of the fourth, the Giants' bubble burst as Philadelphia scored four runs. The fun began after Baker scored from third base on Davis' grounder to second base when Larry Doyle hesitated and then threw late to the catcher. Next up was Barry, who in his attempt to sacrifice the two Philadelphia base runners, laid a little bunt down the first base line. Ames picked up the ball and heaved it toward first baseman Merkle. However, the ball bounced off Barry's head and rolled into foul territory down the right field line. Red Murray ran to the ball and made a "crazy peg" to second base in an effort to head off Barry. The wild throw flew into left field foul territory, and when Josh Devore slipped and fell when he attempted to pick up the ball, all three runners scored.

"Making the circuit of bases on a sacrifice hit is something new in baseball," noted the *New York Times* with undisguised sarcasm, "and the crowd almost died laughing — at the Giants."[36]

Hooks Wiltse replaced Ames and became the victim of a White Elephant seven-run stampede in the seventh, leading the *Times* to described the Giants' effort as "a rout which made the proud Manhattan team look like minor league tail enders."[37]

Bender's determination to win was demonstrated when he continued to pitch despite a bandaged right third finger after an injury to his hand early in the game. Charley pitched with pain and the digit bled intermittently throughout, but he never considered leaving the game.[38]

After he got the lead in the fourth inning, Bender forced the Giants to swing the bat, thus saving his arm. In the fourth he retired the side on just three pitches. From the fourth through the sixth inning Charley threw only eighteen pitches and only one was called a ball. The total was actually inflated by Josh Devore, who fouled off several pitches, and Bender had to make nine throws to get him out. The Chief allowed only three hits after the first inning and the Giants managed an unearned run in the ninth. The Athletics waltzed to a 13–2 victory and claimed their second successive World Series championship.[39]

The Giants' offense was impotent in the Series, with six regulars batting .190 or less (clean-up man Red Murray was 0-for-21). And after running at will against National League opponents during the regular season, the Giants stole only four bases in the World Series. Philadelphia's pitchers did their job in keeping base runners close to the bag so their catchers could throw the runners out when they attempted to steal. After New York second baseman Larry Doyle swiped second in the first inning of the first game, the Bender-Thomas battery did not allow another stolen base in the three games Charley pitched.

Bender, Coombs and Plank allowed New York only eight earned runs in the six games, but that Series is most remembered for the young slugger who made a name for himself because of his timely long-ball hitting. Frank Baker was thereafter known as "Home Run" Baker.

By this time in his life Chief Bender was a celebrity, having become one of the first major leaguers to appear in the new technology known as motion pictures, silent in those days. The melodrama was called *The Baseball Bug*. Bender and two of his A's teammates, Rube Oldring and Jack Coombs, appeared in the one-reel feature about the wife, played by Florence LaBadie, of a conceited small-town player (John W. Noble) whose limited baseball skills are exposed with the aid of the three major leaguers.[40]

Bender's movie career spanned just that one film, though he did appear in vaudeville. Late in the 1911 baseball season, Bender, Coombs, and Cy Morgan signed a contract to tour with the Pearl Sisters in an act entitled "Learning the Game." Their roles required the players to sing and dance on stage while wearing their baseball uniforms. Morgan was called "The Minstrel of the Diamond" and Coombs was known to have stage talent, but Bender's asset was said to be his smile.

The trio debuted in Atlantic City on November 6, which led the *Washington Post* to comment, "All three players appeared at ease, their singing and dancing being a credit to even seasoned stage professionals. The men have an excellent baseball sketch, replete with bright jokes, which they delivered in telling style."[41]

The sketch began with the entrance of Kathryn Pearl, who owns a major league team but has no knowledge about running it. Violet Pearl appears and, by coincidence, she had met the three best pitchers on the Philadelphia team and they had just arrived. With fanfare "Mister" Cy Morgan was introduced, followed by "Mister" Jack Coombs.

"And now," announced Violet Pearl, "I see coming none other than 'Chief Bender' himself, the man who conquered the whole Giant team!"

Amid a great fanfare from the orchestra, Bender's entrance provoked a loud demonstration by the audience. Charley made a dignified bow and then began his performance with the question "Why do we know the first baseball game was played in the Garden of Eden?"

The other cast members shrugged their shoulders and Bender replied in a very loud voice, "Because we read of the serpent a-scoring the first run."

The slide trombone sounded a mournful "ta-ta-ta-tah" that was echoed by the cornets and French horns. Once the applause died down, Morgan sang "Mr. Dream Man," after which each player gave a lecture about different pitches and demonstrated their delivery. After accepting flowers from the fans, each of them thanked the audience and departed the stage.[42]

"The heroes of the diamond, as soon as the last ball is hurled across the plate, make a home run in vaudeville," wrote Richard Henry Little, who reviewed the ballplayers' sketch when the troupe came to the Majestic Theater in Chicago. "Usually their acting is confined to coming out and leering shame-facedly at the audience and telling a funny story to the orchestra and the fortunate people in the first row of seats...."

"[W]hen the marvels of the diamond are posted on a vaudeville bill the theater always is so filled with devotees of baseball that even Edwin Booth, if he were to come back in the flesh and do Hamlet, there would be a distinct air of depression over the audience until the baseball heroes appeared."[43]

◆ 10 ◆

"Enough to Sour an Indian"

By 1912, Philadelphia's two-time World Series champions had earned a reputation as the smartest team of their generation. The veteran Chief Bender was such an intelligent player that he and Jack Coombs were usually employed by Manager Mack to coach the bases when not on the mound. Eddie Collins and Bender discussed fine points of play during much of their idle time, and de facto coaches Harry Davis and Tully Hartsel created the pre-game scouting report. No less than Ty Cobb called Bender the "brainiest pitcher" he ever saw.[1]

Ed Walsh had one of the best sharp-breaking spitballs in the game, but during a contest with the Athletics during the 1912 season opposition batters were lying off his wet ones and waiting for a fastball. The White Sox were convinced the A's knew the catcher's signs and changed them several times, but the results were the same. Chief Bender was in the third base coaching box, so Chicago manager Nixey Callahan and coach Kid Gleason began to concentrate on the coach. Bender intently watched Walsh before every pitch and the White Sox finally figured out how the Athletics knew when Walsh was going to throw a spitter. Bender noticed Walsh always put his hands to his mouth before delivering every pitch, but the big pitcher only wet his fingers for his spitball. Walsh also opened his mouth wider when he faked moistening his fingers, which caused the bill of his cap to rise. Thus, Bender was able to signal the batter when a spitter was coming. Once informed, Walsh corrected his routine and the spitter again became his most effective pitch.[2]

"Chief Bender and their own wits are the only signal tipping bureau the world's champion Athletics ever had," editorialized I. E. Sanborn of the *Chicago Daily Tribune,* "and that is no different from the system used by any other major league team, except that the Chief has inherited the traditional eagle eyesight of his ancestors, and there may be more wits working simultaneously on the Philadelphia bench than on other benches."[3]

"I know a lot of people believed we had some system of getting the pitcher's signs, but it is not true," declared pitcher Cy Morgan. "None of our boys wants the catcher's signs. But we do study the pitchers all the time, and whatever ideas we get about what is being pitched we get from them and not from the catcher's signs.

Chief Bender on the A's bench (circa 1911), his piercing eyes apparently studying the activities on the field (Paul Thompson, photographer, Library of Congress).

Chief Bender has wonderful eyes. I've been on the street with him and 'way off in the distance would see a small lettered sign which I could not make anything out of, and I have pretty good eyes. I'd point it out to Bender and he would read it easily. There are lots of little things almost unnoticeable about the motions different pitchers use in their delivery and most of those motions have a meaning. We sit there in a row on the bench and study the pitcher, and if we detect any difference in his motion we watch to see what kind of ball it means. Bender gets up on the coaching lines for a while, and if there is anything in it back he comes and tells what kind of a ball that motion means. Then we all know it and remember it. We watch the infielders and sometimes we get their signs, and we are always watching batsman or base runner for hit and run signs. But every team is doing that. It is part of the game, and a big part, too.[4]

The Athletics' keen observations of the opposition's signals did not always work out the way they planned. Eddie Collins told about the time Chief Bender figured out the opposing catcher's signals in a game being pitched by Walter Johnson. It was a very hot afternoon and about midway through the contest, Washington backstop Eddie Ainsmith removed his long-sleeved flannel undershirt between innings. From his post in the first base coach's box, Bender noticed that the muscles of the catcher's bare arm relaxed for some signals. Ainsmith wiggled his finger when he signaled for a curve and Charles noticed that when the muscles of the forearm moved, Johnson threw a curve and the rest of the time he threw fastballs. After watching the opposing catcher for an inning, Bender knew he had the Nationals' signals and began to tip off the A's batters. When Ainsmith realized batters were laying off Johnson's curveball, he changed the signals just before Jack Barry came to bat.[5]

"On the pitch, Bender gave Barry the tip and Jack stepped in to take a cut at the curve," recalled Collins. "The ball was not only fast but high, and it hit the side of the peak of Barry's cap and turned the cap halfway around. He got his base for being hit with a pitched ball. Jack's face was white as milk, partly with anger, as he went to first. When he reached there he spoke a piece to Bender, which the Chief still recalls as a grim smile spreads over his face."[6]

The Athletics' 1912 spring training in San Antonio, Texas, would be the team's first without Harry Davis since Charles Bender joined the club as a rookie in 1903. With Stuffy McInnis firmly planted at first base, Harry Davis was allowed to go to Cleveland as manager.

Jack Coombs beat Walter Johnson at Shibe Park on Opening Day and the Athletics won their first three games. Then the team slumped. By June 1, the A's had as many losses as wins and were already eight and a half games behind the Red Sox.

Bender did not pitch his first game of the championship season until April 25, and it took thirteen innings for him to emerge victorious over the New York Yankees, 5–4. "As the weather was not very warm that day," wrote William Weart, "the effect of the strain to which he subjected his arm may be felt by Bender, who has been troubled with rheumatism in his shoulder this spring."[7]

Only three weeks into the season, it was reported that "Chief Bender, of the World Champions' pitching staff, has caught cold in his valued pitching arm and will not be seen in action for some time."[8] After Charles suffered a tough one-run loss to the Yankees on May 1 despite striking out ten batters, he would not pitch again for more than three weeks.

Following the cancellation of four straight games at Shibe Park because of wet grounds, the Athletics finally returned to action on May 10 against Cleveland. The 1911 championship pennant was raised before 16,000, the big crowd being mostly a compliment to Harry Davis, who made his first appearance there in the role of an opposing manager. Harry assisted his successor as Athletics captain, Danny Murphy, in raising the pennant. Once the game got underway, Cy Morgan had a woeful outing on the mound as Cleveland pounded the Athletics, 11–3.

On May 14, on his second day with the Athletics, an eighteen-year-old pitcher named Herbert Pennock made his major league debut against the White Sox and gave up one hit in four innings. Four days later, he was used again in the final three innings of the famous 24–2 win over Detroit in which replacement players played in Tiger uniforms after the regulars went on strike to protest the suspension of Ty Cobb.

Like older players had done for him, Chief Bender mentored Connie Mack's coveted acquisition that spring and taught Pennock how to throw Christy Mathewson's "fade-away," variously known as a screwball.[9] However, Herb was thought too raw to be thrown in against the best hitting teams in the American League. Cy Morgan's 3–8 record to start the season and Harry Krause's sore arm led to the release of the two veteran pitchers at mid-season, which made the success of the big three — Plank, Coombs and Bender — even more crucial.

That August, the *Sporting News* noted, "Mack has only two twirlers who are in first class form, Coombs and Plank. Bender though, has recovered from his spell of illness, but he has not been able to go through an entire contest. In the Sunday game at Chicago, Coombs had to take Bender's place and here last Wednesday Houck was sent in as a relief pitcher for the Chief in time to save the game."[10]

On August 14, Bender took the mound in the first game of a doubleheader against Cleveland's Vean Gregg. Charley received the benefit of two inside-the-park home runs by Stuffy McInnis and pitched the Athletics to an 8–3 win over the Naps, though he had to have help from Byron Houck in the latter stages. When Philadelphia took the nightcap, 2–0, the A's winning streak reached seven games, but they still were eight and a half games behind Boston. Philadelphia then lost three straight games to Chicago, two as a result of catcher Jack Lapp's poor throwing.

Realizing his outfield was not delivering in 1912, Mack sought help for the pennant drive from Jack Dunn of the International League's Baltimore Orioles. Dunn had purchased the Baltimore franchise following the 1909 season with some financial assistance from Mack and the Shibe brothers, so there was always a close relationship between the two clubs. To acquire outfielders Jimmy Walsh and Eddie Murphy from Baltimore, the Athletics gave up $5,000, pitchers Dave Danforth and Dave Roth, catcher Ben Egan and shortstop Claude Derrick. As a condition of the deal, Mack would be able to acquire an additional player from the Baltimore club in 1913. The trade was finalized on August 24, the last day minor league players could be purchased for the current season.[11]

The Athletics reeled off five wins in the six games leading up to a do-or-die series with the first-place Red Sox scheduled to begin on August 29. Mack had rested Plank and Coombs so they would be ready for the key series in Boston.

The extra rest didn't help Eddie Plank as the lefty was soundly defeated, 5–1, in the first game of the Boston series. In game two, Coombs received the benefit of a four-run lead and then lost it. Bender was rushed in, but he wasn't effective either, giving up five hits in two innings, and Boston won again, 7–4. Coombs tried it again in the third game on August 31 and lost, 2–1. Now thirteen and a half games out of first place, Philadelphia's hopes for another title were finished. Behind Smoky Joe Wood's incredible pitching (he won 34 games and lost only five), Boston amassed 105 victories and finished fourteen games ahead of second-place Washington, fifteen ahead of Philadelphia.

The 1912 season was a poor one by Chief Bender's standards. He won only 13 games and lost eight. The Chief's earned run average was his highest since 1904 and only one of his wins came by shutout, a 2–0 whitewash of the White Sox on July 12. The lone bright spot was his control. He issued only 33 bases on balls to opposing batters for an American League low of 1.74 walks per nine innings.

Perhaps Bender's struggles could be attributed to the absence of Harry Davis. For nine seasons, Davis had been his mentor, friend and father figure through good times and bad. Connie Mack provided an example of the influence the "Captain" had on Bender.

"Bender's only bad habit on the mound was a tendency to relax when he felt he had the opposition under control," Mack recalled. "At such moments Harry Davis used to walk over from first base, berate the Chief in good, old fashioned language. Thus admonished, the Indian would bear down again."[12]

Davis' strict disciplinary tactics failed to inspire the Naps and he quit his job with Cleveland on the first of September when a record of 54-71 left his team in sixth place. Harry would return to the Athletics as a coach and non-playing captain until 1917.

On Monday, September 2, Bender relieved Plank in the eighth inning of a morning game at Washington and preserved the 3–2 victory for Eddie. Though he didn't know it at the time, that outing ended Charley's work on the mound for a month. Connie Mack became upset because of Bender's drinking habits.

F. C. Lane wrote for *Baseball Magazine*, "Even Mack loses his self control once in a while. It seems incredible that the lanky manager of the Athletics should ever relax his sad Abe Lincoln expression. But such is the case. Doubters need only to have been on hand at the Somerset Hotel ... when Chief Bender blew in after a somewhat prolonged dalliance with the fire water which the soul of the red man craveth. Brief but spirited remarks of the Athletic leader were a revelation."[13]

The final straw for the manager was when Bender and roommate Rube Oldring made the trip from Washington to New York on their own and showed up late at the team's hotel. Speaking many years later, Rube Oldring told Frank Yeutter of the *Philadelphia Bulletin* that before the team left Washington the evening of September 3, Connie Mack passed the word that any players who lived in or near New York could go directly there without stopping in Philadelphia. Chief Bender had the idea of having a friend bring his automobile to Wilmington, where he and Rube would detrain and drive to New York, stopping at "a couple of swell spots" along the way. Bender dropped Rube off at his Trenton home around 3 A.M. and then checked into a hotel. By the time the pair showed up at Hilltop Park in New York for the day's game against the Yankees, the rest of the players were preparing to warm up.

According to Oldring, Mack found out somehow that the pair had stayed out until the wee hours of the morning and told the tardy outfielder to remove his uniform.

As he left the clubhouse, Rube met Bender on his way in. "What's coming off?" asked the Chief. "Your clothes, I think, pretty soon," replied Rube. "Wait until the Old Man sees you."

Instead of going to the bench, Bender picked up a bat and commenced to hit a few fungos. "Then I saw his head turn around sharp like and he's over taking to Connie," recalled Oldring. "Pretty soon he headed for the dressing room and I knew he was out too."[14]

Bender and his running buddy Oldring were fined and suspended on Friday, September 6. Publically, the club said the two players were disciplined for not keeping in good condition. Privately, it was known that the real reason for the suspensions was the players' drinking habits. The fines were announced at $200 for Bender and $100 for Oldring.[15]

The *Philadelphia Telegraph* editorialized, "The suspensions of Bender and Oldring did not come as a surprise to those who have been hearing tales nearly all season of the doings of certain members of the Athletics. The only surprise was that Manager Mack did not act sooner."[16]

Many years later, Connie Mack told Arthur Daley of the *New York Times*, "I guess we could have won (the pennant) if I hadn't suspended Chief Bender and Rube Oldring for breaking training."[17] However, Mr. Mack's memory must have betrayed him because the Athletics were already fourteen games out of first place when the series with the Yankees began on September 4. In actuality, Mack did not have much choice. Had he suspended or released the pair while there was still hope for a championship, the A's had no capable replacements for the two stars.

If things weren't already bad enough for Bender, his wife fell down the stairs at their home in Philadelphia the morning of Charley's suspension. Marie was expecting a call from her husband in New York and hurried to answer the telephone downstairs. In her haste she tripped over a rug and tumbled down the stairway. After regaining consciousness, Mrs. Bender summoned help and was taken to the hospital, where she was found to have suffered a dislocated shoulder, contusions and possible internal injuries.[18]

Marie had undergone an operation two months earlier and the newspapers speculated the fall might cause series complications. Mrs. Bender was returned home at bed rest and eventually recovered. In an article "Enough to Sour an Indian," the *Sporting News'* Philadelphia correspondent wrote, "It was truly black Friday for Bender. At almost the same hour the man who has been an idol of the fans here for years was being disciplined, his wife was lying at her home seriously ill.[19]

Because the leagues and baseball's club owners strove to protect the public reputations of their "investments," the reasons for players' enforced absences due to alcoholism were described with coded terms, such as "out of condition" or "violation of training rules." The vague language was used to disguise the real reason a player was incapacitated, suspended, or unable to perform because of an alcohol problem.[20]

In the case of the suspensions of Bender and Oldring, noted sports columnist Hugh Fullerton was under no such constraints. In his column, "In the Wake of the News," for September 11, 1912, he wrote, "Chief Bender is in disgrace charged with guzzling firewater. The guzzling wasn't mentioned until the team failed behind him."[21]

Since the early days of professional baseball, players gained an unsavory reputation as heavy drinkers. Some were overt in their addictions, like Rube Waddell and Bugs Raymond. Native American players seemed to have suffered heaviest publicly because of that era's stereotype of the "drunken Indian." The drinking exploits of such Native American players as Sockalexis, Jim Thorpe and George "Chief" Johnson were widely publicized. Bender avoided this stigma for years and was considered a "sterling" citizen for much of his major league career.

Once Charles Bender's drinking problem began to affect his performance on the field, it became news. His name would be in the newspapers for additional alcohol-related incidents over the next twenty years. Bender's problem with alcohol appears to have developed over a period of time after joining the Athletics. Early on, he was not mentioned in the stories about the drinking sprees of teammates like Waddell and Schreckengost. However, Bender did admit going for a glass of beer to relax his nerves after a ball game.[22]

Though Charles became a prominent and visible citizen in the city of Philadelphia, he was still conscious of subtle racism because of his Native American blood. He also felt a responsibility to uphold the position as perhaps the most famous Indian in the country at the height of his baseball success. There too was the inner stress he experienced in performing his trade. He kept these stresses to himself, for Bender was not one to seek outside help. It is likely the pent-up anxiety contributed to his increasing dependence on alcohol for relief.

Chief Bender pitched one more time in the 1912 regular season, a three-inning stint against the Red Sox in the Athletics' final game. By pre-arrangement, he went the first three innings and threw scoreless ball against the team that would win the World Series a few days later. He also pitched the final six innings of the Athletics' 4–3 victory in the fourth game of the club's inter-league series against the Phillies.

Connie Mack had agreed with the Phillies to continue the post-season city series, but the Athletics' World Series appearances in 1910 and 1911 put the affair on hold until 1912. After the winning Athletics received only $82 per man (the losing Phillies each received $54) for the five games in 1912, the post-season city series was indefinitely suspended.[23]

The Athletics were also contracted to play a series of games in Cuba that November. In the charge of club secretary John Shibe and captain Danny Murphy, the team stopped off in several cities along the way south and picked up a little extra cash by playing exhibition games. Once the A's were in Cuba, Chief Bender won the first game against the island's best team in Havana on Sunday, November 3. While eight hits were made off his deliveries, the Chief's ability to stop the Almendares batters in the pinches enabled him pitch shutout baseball. With four hits off the renowned Jose Mendez in the first inning, Strunk, Oldring and Collins scored runs.[24]

Bender's victory was sweet revenge for the Athletics since Mendez had beaten Eddie Plank twice two years earlier when the Americans lost their series with the two top Cuban clubs, five games to four. Plank exacted further retribution the next day when he defeated Havana, 8–0.

The American League umpire assigned to the series had not arrived by the opening games in Havana, and a pair of the Cuban arbiters handled the job without controversy. Joe O'Brien arrived on the island in time for the game on November 7, but the crowd at Havana stadium became upset at the American umpire's decisions.

Eddie Collins indicated that O'Brien "was a little sickly, having just come off the boat. The natives started to rush the field, but the mounted cops got after them and there was no further trouble."[25]

Though the Americans won their first eight games with Cuba's two best teams, the Athletics had to scramble just to fill out the lineup. Right fielder Danny Murphy was unable to play in the first game and another outfielder, Rube Oldring, had to take over at third base after Baker was injured in a collision. When he wasn't pitching, Bender played the infield because John Barry developed a sore arm and then had to return to the States in the middle of the series because his sister was seriously injured in an automobile accident.

After the first eight contests, the *Cuban News* grumbled:

With the same players—almost—who were here before, two years ago, and who then got fearful drubbings at the hands of the local teams, the Philadelphia Athletics are here now just rubbing it in on our local teams, having played half their series and not yet lost a game. They have pounded the great Black Diamond all over the lot; been especially unkind to "No-Hit" Pedrosa.... The worst thing the Athletics have done, however, and for which they will never be forgiven, is that they have beaten the great Mendez twice—batted him out; slugged him' refused to fan the air for him; taken to his delivery like a boy takes a hot taffy.[26]

"Baker has killed the golden goose of the Cuban diamonds," reported *Sporting Life*. "Sunday's victory over the Almendares, the result of Bender's air-tight pitching and Baker's murderous slugging has completely broken the spirit of the Cubans." The Cuban fans expected a good showing by their clubs, but once their teams began to lose, they greeted the invaders with hoots and curses. That didn't bother the Athletics too much because none of them understood Spanish. On the eighteenth, the A's beat Havana, 10–5. When Baker slugged a double to score two runners, the crowd responded with dead silence.[27]

The Athletics won ten of their twelve contests during the Cuban excursion to gain a measure of vindication for the club's mediocre showing in November of 1910. Though they dominated their Cuban opponents on the field, nearly all the A's caught a severe cold while on the island. Plank was so ill he returned to Jacksonville several days in advance of the other players. In the final game on the island, the Athletics played a pitcher in the infield and another pitcher in the outfield. In the end, the trip to Cuba was a financial failure and John Shibe admitted the club was about $6,000 in arrears.

As usual, Bender was unsigned by the Athletics at the dawn of the new year, but his work in Cuba convinced Connie Mack that the Chief was repentant and sent the pitcher a contract for 1913. However, the salary offered by Mr. Mack was a drastic decrease compared to what he made in 1912.

"I sent Bender a contract for only $1,200," Connie Mack told columnist Arthur Daley almost thirty-eight years later. "Goodness gracious, but that was mean of me. His wife tore it up so he couldn't sign it."[28]

The reduction in pay should not have been a surprise to Bender since Mack had slashed his salary in half only three years earlier after Charley experienced a bad season in 1908 and then held out. On the first of February 1913, Charles Albert walked into Connie's office in Shibe Park's tower and told his pleased manager he was ready to sign a contract for the upcoming season.

A wire story reiterated the pitcher's problem of the previous year and reported his promise to remain sober during the upcoming baseball season. "Chief Bender, whose unruly conduct and consequent poor work was very costly to Connie Mack last season, has signed his Athletic contract for his eleventh consecutive season. 'Chief' has promised to stick high up on the 'water wagon' this year and personally assured Mack that he would be willing to work twice a week on the slab to make up for his 1912 slip up."[29]

"This winter Bender has spent nearly all the daylight hours automobiling and hunting in the South," a reporter noted after seeing the Chief that spring. "He looks stronger than ever and should do excellent service on the mound in the coming race."[30]

"Never before have the White Elephants looked as good in a preliminary series as they have against the Quakers this spring," William Weart wrote for the *Sporting News* in April 1913. "Instead of letting his men take things easy in the South, Manager Mack has put them through their paces and the men returned home ready to grapple with any team for American League honors."[31]

Mack started his young hurlers Wyckoff, Bush, Pennock and then Wyckoff again against the Phillies in the first four games of the inter-city series. In the fifth game, Boardwalk Brown pitched the entire eighteen innings for the A's in a game that was called after three hours of play because of darkness with the score tied at 2–2.

Following a sub-par 1912 season, during which the pitcher was ill and out of shape, the scribes and so-called experts predicted that the time of Chief Bender as a reliable starting pitcher was over. Even though he was beginning his eleventh year in the major leagues, one might tend to forget the Chief was still a few days shy of his twenty-ninth birthday when the season began.

Bender did little to dispel the doubters in the early days of the 1913 regular season. He had to be relieved by Joe Bush in a 6–5 victory over Boston at Shibe Park in the third game of the season. A day later, Bender came on in relief of Brown with the A's leading, 5–4. The Red Sox tallied four times and won the game, 8–5.

The Athletics won five of the six games against the defending World Series champions to open the season, Bender's blown save being the only loss. During the spring, Boston suffered a devastating blow to its chance of repeating as American League champions. While attempting to field a bunt in a game against Detroit, Smoky Joe Wood slipped on the wet grass, tried to brace the fall and broke the thumb on his pitching hand. Though the team rallied late in the season, Boston was never a factor in that season's pennant race.

The Athletics' Jack Coombs had his troubles, too. After his great season in 1910 and another big one (28–13) in 1911, he won twenty-one games in 1912. Without warning, Colby Jack was struck down with typhoid fever. The disease affected his spine, and for two years the pitcher was under treatment, during which he subjected himself to the torture of a rigging of his own making—"a contraption with weights hanging from feet and neck, to stretch the spine." The Philadelphia newspapers said Coombs was through and called him a "dangerously sick man, with physicians attending him day and night."[32]

The illnesses of Coombs and Herb Pennock forced the Athletics to bring twenty-year-old Leslie Ambrose "Joe" Bush up to the club earlier than Connie Mack wanted. The Minnesota native had won twenty-nine games with Missoula of the Union League in 1912 before pitching one game for the Athletics at the end of the season.

Bender and the Athletics' pitching staff also got a new receiver in 1913. Catcher Wally Schang was discovered in the sandlots of upstate New York by George Stallings (who went on to manage the "Miracle" Boston Braves of 1914). Schang became a catcher as a semi-pro when his team's regular catcher,

Wally's brother, broke a finger. He was an immediate sensation with Buffalo in 1912, batting .333 in his professional debut. Following only one year in the minors, the twenty-one-year-old joined the Philadelphia Athletics.

Jack Lapp had replaced Ira Thomas as the A's number one catcher the previous year, though the veteran began the 1913 season working in games that Bender pitched. As the season progressed, Schang was worked into the lineup as a late-inning replacement and eventually became Charley's personal receiver. The switch-hitting rookie became a favorite of Bender's, and Schang called the Chief the best right-hander he ever caught.

Bender's 4–1 win over New York at Shibe Park on April 24, 1913, put the Athletics into first place, a position they would not relinquish. Wrote William Weart, "Bender got a game in which he was hit safely eleven times and gave three passes. The beauty of this event was the fact that whenever the Chief had to let out an extra link or two he was right on the spot. He always had something in reserve, just as he did in the days when he was mowing down all teams with great regularity."[33]

On May 16 in Cleveland, Bender came into the game as a substitute pitcher in the seventh inning and preserved an 8–5 Philadelphia victory for Carroll "Boardwalk" Brown. Eight days later, the Chief relieved Brown again and protected the lead in a 4–2 win over Washington.

In the previous decade, managers like John McGraw and Frank Chance made relief pitching a prominent part of the game, not with the specialists relievers became in future decades, but with the club's premier pitcher who was available for a couple of innings between starting assignments. Connie Mack had employed Rube Waddell and Chief Bender in that capacity on many occasions. The press began applying phrases like "the heroic saver" to a substitute hurler who came into a game to preserve victory for his team.

Connie Mack explained his strategy for 1913. "Bender and Plank I used oftener than any manager had ever used two pitchers. I would put one of my youngsters in the box to start a game and then I would send Bender or Plank to save it."[34] That season, Mack's pitching staff registered the fewest complete games among major league teams.

Bender registered eighteen "saves" and posted ten victories in relief for the Athletics between 1903 and 1912. In 1913 Mack used him more in relief as the Chief started twenty-two games and relieved in twenty-six others. Bender registered a league-high twelve saves (retroactively computed because saves were not an official statistic at that time) and was the winning pitcher in six other games in which he replaced the starting pitcher.

Byron Houck, another of Connie Mack's collegians (University of Oregon), was sometimes unhittable and other times couldn't get the ball over the plate. However, pitching in the right situations got him eight victories as a substitute pitcher.

Though starting assignments were turned over more often to Eddie Plank and the youngsters, Brown and Joe Bush, Bender got enough opportunities to post his second twenty-plus winning season (21–10). Only one other American League pitcher, Reb Russell of the White Sox, appeared in more games on the mound in 1913 than Chief Bender.

Clark Griffith's Washington club emerged as Philadelphia's early competition for the pennant. When the Nationals arrived at Shibe Park on May 24 for a five-game series, the Capitol City team was only two and half games out of first.

The Athletics began a very long homestand by taking four of the five games against Washington to solidify their hold on first place. Connie Mack decided not to waste any of his front-line starting pitchers in the game against Walter Johnson and sent Texan Ball Taft to absorb the predictable loss. The next day, Mack came back with Plank and Bender in a doubleheader. The Nationals failed to score off Eddie and managed just one run off the Chief.

The double win on May 27 sent Philadelphia on a fifteen-game winning streak. In the midst of the streak, the Athletics ran into Walter Johnson again. Mack again chose not to use one of his first-line starters and pitched Bryon Houck. After Baker smacked a key home run in the fourth inning, the Athletics managed to scratch out a rare win over Johnson.

Cleveland became the next pretender to the crown by pulling to within one and a half games of the leaders in early June. The Naps were three games back when they came to Philadelphia for a four-game set at mid-month. Bender, who was "in wonderful form," pitched the second game on Friday. After the Athletics tallied a run in the first inning, Bender nursed the lead for eight innings, but Cleveland tied it in the ninth on Frank Baker's throwing error. Bender and George Kahler, who had relieved for the visitors in the ninth, matched zeros into the thirteenth inning. In the Philadelphia half of the frame, Jack Barry doubled and scored when Kahler made a wild throw on Schang's bunt to give Philadelphia a hard-won 2–1 victory.[35]

During the final game of the Cleveland series on Monday, the ominous specter of gambling raised its head at Shibe Park. By a pre-arranged signal, plain-clothes policemen swooped in to arrest thirty-eight gamblers in the stands.

One of Bender's six wins in relief came against Washington at National Park on June 26. In the second game of the day's doubleheader, Philadelphia's Boardwalk Brown loaded the bases with two out in the third inning. The Athletics were only up 3–2, so Connie Mack called on Bender to pitch despite his having thrown two and two-thirds innings of hitless ball in relief of Joe Bush the day before. The resilient Chippewa retired George McBride on a line drive to the center fielder for the third out of the inning. By the time the final stanza rolled around, Philadelphia had increased its lead to 10–2, and Bender was in complete control.

The Nationals finally scored against Bender in the ninth inning, though the pitcher assisted in Washington's run. With two out, catcher Eddie Ainsmith singled, and when the Athletics paid no attention to him on the bases, he stole second and then third. While Eddie was standing on third base, someone in the stands challenged him to finish the job by stealing home. As Bender started his wind-up, Ainsmith started for home plate. When the Chief saw the catcher lumbering down the line, he kept on winding up his right arm until Eddie slid safely across the plate. Ainsmith had tied a major league record with three stolen bases in one inning. When Bender finally delivered a pitch, pinch-hitter Rip Williams swung and flied out to end the game. The final score was 10–3.[36]

As Connie Mack had done the year before, he made a deal with Jack Dunn of the International League's Baltimore club to acquire an important addition for the pennant drive. In July, he sent four players to the Orioles and then used his pick of the Baltimore team, guaranteed the A's in the Eddie Murphy/Jimmy Walsh deal of the previous season, to acquire pitcher Bob Shawkey. Shawkey debuted for the Athletics on July 10 to begin a fifteen-year American League mound career.

By mid-season, Chief Bender had regained the respect of the Philadelphia press that lost faith in him the previous year. Philadelphia baseball scribe William Weart wrote in an article on July 24, "One of the real surprises of the American League season has been the numerous games in which Bender has figured. The Chief was not rated as an 'Iron Man' in the past, but he has certainly played a wonderful part as rescuer this year as well as taking a regular turn on the rubber."[37]

During the fourth inning of a game in Detroit on August 19, catcher Jack Lapp was hit by a foul tip that broke a finger, and he was replaced by Schang. Three innings later, Wally attempted to beat out a bunt and collided with the Tigers pitcher. The young catcher was badly spiked, but was bandaged up and finished the game behind the plate.

The *Washington Post* reported on August 25, 1913, that no fewer than eleven A's were on the hospital list. All three catchers were laid up and Harry Davis even had to squat behind the batter in a game two days pervious. Amos Strunk missed the first month of the season due to a sore throwing arm and then was sidelined with a severe ankle sprain in August. And when Jack Barry went down, Rube Oldring got into five games at shortstop before Mack engineered a deal with the Browns for John Lavan.

Chief Bender earned his twenty-first victory of the 1913 season on September 15 against Cleveland. He took the mound in the top of the seventh inning in relief of Houck with one out and the bases loaded. He got out of the jam with a strikeout of Doc Johnston and Terry Turner's pop-up to McInnis. Philadelphia took the lead in the bottom of the inning, and Bender faced the minimum number of batters over the final two innings, striking out four of the six Naps that stepped in the batter's box.

Despite the plethora of injuries and the league's sixth-best earned run average, the Athletics clinched the American League pennant on September 22. Philadelphia lost eight of its last nine games to allow second-place Washington to finish a more respectable six and a half games back.

The Giants' John McGraw, whose team had won the National League pennant by 12 games, had a trio of pitching aces—Rube Marquard, Christy Mathewson and Jeff Tesreau—whom he thought would be enough to overcome the Athletics, who had only two tested post-season hurlers in Bender and Plank. However, a World Series was not won on paper.

Playing for the Giants was a twenty-six-year-old rookie, Jim Thorpe, the Sac and Fox American Indian who arrived at Carlisle after Bender joined the Athletics. Thorpe was the sensation of the 1912 Olympics before it was discovered he had played baseball during the summer and received $25 for expenses. Jim was barred from amateur athletics and his Olympic medals had to be forfeited. McGraw signed the famous athlete to play the outfield and the Giants recouped the $9,000 signing bonus from the thousands of fans that flocked to the ballpark to see him play. The famous Olympian was a good fielder, but pitchers soon discovered he couldn't hit a curveball. After batting .143 in only 35 at-bats during the regular season, Jim did not see action against Bender and the A's during the World Series.

Before the World Series, a rumor made the rounds that a group of gamblers offered Chief Bender $25,000 to throw the games he would pitch against the Giants. No evidence to support the story was ever established, and Bender, Connie Mack and even John McGraw said the report was so ridiculous it deserved no comment.[38]

New York again won the coin toss for the first game and the Series opened at the Polo Grounds as it had in 1911. The Athletics arrived in New York the evening before the opening game and checked into the Hotel Somerset Hotel on West Forty-seventh Street around ten o'clock. The next morning, the A's prepared to depart for the stadium in five taxi cabs. To avoid scratching the freshly polished floor of their hotel, the players removed their spiked shoes and walked out onto the sidewalk in their stocking feet. Several hundred onlookers, mostly from Philadelphia, cheered the team as the players entered their cabs. "We'll be on the sidelines and we'll root for you," yelled a priest in the crowd.[39]

The day of the first game, elevated trains, traction cars, automobiles and all manner of conveyances brought thousands to the Giants' ball field. Despite threatening rain clouds, an announced crowd of 36,291 filled almost every seat in the house. As he had in 1910 and 1911, Connie Mack named the well-rested Chief Bender to pitch the opening game. Charley was the first of the

Athletics to get dressed in the clubhouse and then decided to get a look at the big crowd before the teams made their official entrance.

"There was a rousing cheer as the Athletics' pitching star popped his head out of the little doorway under the centerfield," recorded an observer. "Bender beamed at the crowd then disappeared."[40]

Shortly, the two teams trotted out onto the field and each took batting practice in turn. Instead of their road uniforms, the Athletics wore their home whites with purple stockings. Frank Baker posed for photographers by hitting an imaginary home run into the grandstand.

The Giants led the major leagues in stolen bases, but once play began the Athletics quickly served notice that the National Leaguers would not run free in this Series. After his single in the first inning, the Giants' Art Fletcher attempted to steal second and catcher Wally Schang threw him out by ten feet.

New York drew first blood with a run off Bender in the bottom of the third, but the Athletics came right back against Marquard. Eddie Collins led off the fourth with a triple and moments later scored the tying run. However, it appeared the Athletics would strand two runners after two outs when Schang lifted a fly ball to center field. Fred Snodgrass, the Giants' regular center fielder, had gone hitless against Bender in three games during the 1911 Series and McGraw benched him for the opener. Fred's substitute, Tillie Shafer, had only played seventeen games in the outfield during his four years in the National League. In going for Schang's fly ball, Shafer appeared to misjudge it at first and then leaped in the air while running backward. The ball went through Tillie's fingers and rolled all the way to the center field fence. Schang landed on third and two more runs scored.

Frank Baker homered into the right field bleachers with one out in the fifth to score Collins in front of him, but the Giants tagged Bender for three runs of their own in the home half of the inning to make the score 5–4. However, that was as close as New York would get.

The Giants threatened in the seventh when they put runners on first and third with one out. The rally died when Fletcher hit a grounder to Barry and the A's shortstop turned a double play. Amid an increasingly heavy drizzle, Bender set the Giants down in the final two innings with an infield single by Murray the only damage. Bender yielded eleven hits, but he was in command except for the fifth inning when three singles and a bad throw by Barry led to three Giants runs. Philadelphia won, 6–4.

Special correspondent Hugh Fullerton wrote of Bender's performance in that first game: "Someday, perhaps, you will hear the story of why Bender pitched and why he stuck there in the face of defeat. There were rumors started to damage him and which he was out there to refute, and at times the refuting seemed bad. He wasn't as great as he is sometimes, and his curve was attained with an effort. Yet he stuck, to disprove the stories the crooks had circulated, and, finally, with all the power in his body back of each ball, he fell back upon sheer speed."[41]

A *Washington Post* reporter was driven to hyperbole. "Chief Bender, more famous now than any of his painted forebears, conquered the white man in a war so clean and fine that there was honor even for those defeated."[42]

"Do you realize he has never failed me in a crisis?" Connie Mack asked Francis Richter. "Whenever there is a game that the fortunes of our club hinge on, I've gone to the Chief, and he has delivered every time."[43]

That evening aboard a train bound for Philadelphia, a newspaper reporter approached Bender in the team's parlor car. When the scribe asked Bender how he felt, Charley put his magazine down and pulled a three-year-old newspaper clipping from his wallet. The article prophesized the Cubs would win the World Series because "Bender was built for the Cubs." He then brought out a second clipping of recent vintage. Bender pointed out a line in the article he had underlined: "McGraw knows he can beat Bender, and hopes that Mack will start with the Indian."

"A friend of mine sent that a week ago," Bender explained. "And after I read it I knew that there couldn't be a chance for me to lose today. So when I got in the box I thought of the clipping, and that was enough. And the Giants will not beat me in this series."[44]

The Giants' best catcher, Chief Meyers, suffered a broken finger in pre-game practice before the first game. He struggled through the contest and was replaced by Larry McLean for the remainder of the Series.

Christy Mathewson, coming off his next-to-last twenty-victory season in the majors, was vintage Matty in Game Two at Shibe Park. The old Bucknell University star was matched against Eddie Plank and the result was the same old story. Mathewson broke a scoreless tie with a tenth-inning single, and New York went on to a 3–0 victory.

Joe Bush, a rookie who won fourteen games for Mack in 1913, shut down the Giants at the Polo Grounds in Game Three. Still several days short of his twenty-first birthday, Bush was the youngest player to pitch in a World Series game up to that time. The Philadelphia right-hander allowed only five hits and the A's batted New York's Jeff Tesreau around in an 8–2 triumph.

On the way downtown after the game, a taxi occupied by Bender, Danny Murphy and Stuffy McInnis was attacked by a crowd of "young hoodlums." Upon spying the Athletics in the vehicle, the thugs began hurling rocks, sticks and any other handy ammunition at the players. Policemen arrived on the scene and the shaken players escaped unharmed.[45]

Shibe Park was jammed to the brim when the Series returned to Philadelphia for Game Four as the weather was favorable despite the threat of rain early in the day. Sunshine frequently broke through the clouds and the playing field was comparatively dry and fast. Catcher Wally Schang drove in three runs with two singles and pushed Philadelphia off to a 6–0 lead after five innings. Fred Merkle fueled a Giants comeback bid with a three-run homer in the seventh, but Bender and the A's held on for a 6–5 victory.

With the Athletics ahead three games to one, Plank and Mathewson went at it in Game Five at the Polo Grounds. This time, Plank was the master. The A's lefty allowed only two hits—the first coming with one out in the fifth—in his 3–1 victory. Bender wasn't there to see it, left behind in Philadelphia to rest up in case the Series returned to Shibe Park for a sixth game.

The Giants had been out-manned and outplayed, losing in the World Series for the third consecutive year. Frank Baker led Philadelphia with a .450 batting average and drove in seven runs. Eddie Collins hit .421, while Schang knocked in six runs and registered a .357 batting average.

Fullerton wrote after the first game of the Series that Schang "stopped the Giants on the base paths, then held them up, and handled Bender's great bursts of speed as if they were easy. He marked himself as one of the greatest catchers of all time."[46]

Bender's conquests in games one and four boosted his Series victory total to six. Mathewson, pitching in what would be his final Series, wound up with a 5–5 lifetime record in the Fall Classic (he was 4–0 at one point) after splitting two decisions in 1913.

The day after the Athletics won the world's championship, captain Harry Davis' son, Harry, Jr., died suddenly. The youngster was well known to the A's players from the times he had worked out with the team and his death deeply affected everyone. The city's official celebration of the championship was postponed for a week because of the tragedy.

One of Bender's favorite anecdotes about Connie Mack came from the 1913 World Series. Just before the first game, Mack called Albert into his office on the second floor at Shibe Park and said he was depending on him to win two games in the Series. Mack then asked Bender how much he owed on the mortgage on his home. When Charles didn't feel comfortable disclosing such personal information, Mr. Mack replied, "All right. We'll talk about it later."

After Bender won the two games and the Athletics won the Series, Mr. Mack summoned the pitcher to his office and presented Charles with a check for $2,500, exactly what he owned on his home.[47]

"The oddest part about it," Mack later revealed, "is that I wound up paying him more money than I'd paid any ballplayer.... In fact I gave him something like $12,000 instead of the $1,200 he signed for. The Chief had kept his promise and had been outstanding."[48]

There is no way to discern exactly how much Bender actually received for his work with the Athletics that year, but after Mack restored the pitcher's salary to its 1912 level, added the $3,243.94 winning player's share for the

Series, and threw in the mortgage payment for beating the Giants twice, the Chief undoubtedly received the largest annual earnings to that point in his baseball career. One shouldn't feel too bad for Connie Mack as the club received a $69,333.79 check for the World Series championship.[49]

Predictably, Manager Mack and his players were in great demand for the stage and banquet circuit during the off-season. Following the World Series, Wally Schang and Joe Bush signed an agreement to appear on stage with a professional singer named Billy Gibson. The players made their first public appearance at a banquet for the 1913 champions. A couple of nights later the Bush-Schang-Gibson trio repeated the performance at a banquet given the Athletics by a moving picture company. Not to be outdone, Chief Bender put on a surprise performance of his own at the banquet celebrating the A's championship at the Bellevue-Stratford Hotel in Philadelphia.

"It wasn't Hiawatha or any other Indian ditty," wrote *Sporting Life*. "It was that bit that makes an Irishman want to cry: 'Where the River Shannon Flows.' And he sang it well: so well that they made him repeat it."[50]

After the customary parades and banquets, Bender went on a hunting trip with some of his teammates. In addition to his baseball accomplishments, ten days after the World Series Charles Bender was awarded the highest honor the Chippewa tribe could grant. When the White Earth Chippewa met in counsel, Bender and the tribal chief, Charles Rogers, were elected delegates to go to Washington, D.C., and secure legislation desired by the tribe.[51]

That November, Bender "walked the burning sands of the Mystic Shrine" when he gained membership in the Lu Lu Temple in Philadelphia. Members Harry Davis, Eddie Collins and Phillies second baseman Otto Knabe assisted in the initiation. Of course, as a Shriner Charles swore to comply with the principles of Masonic conduct and practices. After addressing the membership of the fraternal organization, Chief Bender remarked that he would "rather face 50,000 hostile fans as the pitcher in a baseball game than go through such an ordeal again."[52]

◆ 11 ◆

Seasons of Discontent

When Chicago businessman John A. Gilmore became president of the Federal League of Base Ball Clubs in July of 1913, it was still a minor league operating in the Midwest. Four months later the circuit proclaimed itself a full-fledged major league and became a serious rival to the monopoly enjoyed by the American and National leagues. The fledgling league awarded new franchises in the eastern United States and Gilmore recruited a number of wealthy men to run his more important clubs. In the fall of 1913, the Federal League declared war on Organized Baseball by directly challenging the major leagues with franchises in four cities and competing with top minor league clubs in four others.

The new league announced it would pay no attention to the reserve clause and sign any player whose contact had expired. The first well-known major league star to sign with the Federals was the Cincinnati Reds player/ manager Joe Tinker. At the National League's winter meeting of 1913, Garry Herrmann, the Cincinnati club president, sold Tinker to Brooklyn for $15,000. Joe balked at the deal and accepted the position of manager with the Chicago Federal League club. After a player of Tinker's stature went over to the Federal League, a number of other major leaguers made the plunge. In the seasons of 1914 and 1915, the upstarts employed 155 former major league players scattered throughout their rosters. It was estimated the established major leagues paid out $2,000,000 in those two years just to keep players under contract and prop up the American Association and International League.

Organized Baseball's magnates, unwilling to take defeat lying down, struck back. They amended the rules of the National Commission to specify a three-year suspension for reserve rule jumpers and a five-year suspension for contract breakers.

The Federal League threat forced major league club owners to pay unprecedented salaries in 1914 and 1915. Ty Cobb's annual pay check went from $11,332 after his holdout in 1913 to $20,000 in 1915. Walter Johnson was paid $7,000 in 1913, but he received a bump to $10,000 in the first year of the Federal League war. On the other hand, Mack and Shibe were in good shape for the war, at least for 1914, as most of the A's players were already under contract.[1]

Another problem for Organized Baseball was a suddenly activist players union. In 1912, former Philadelphia Athletics player and law school graduate Dave Fultz created the Baseball Players' Fraternity out of his effort to unionize professional baseball players. After the Federal League announced its intention to become a third major league, the Fraternity assumed a more aggressive stance. On November 8, 1913, baseball's ruling body, the National Commission, was handed a petition listing seventeen demands that was signed by nearly five hundred players who were pledged not to sign their 1914 contracts unless the petition was acted upon.

Although Ban Johnson declared the demands "blackmail" and called Fultz "a menace to the game," the owners agreed to eleven of the seventeen demands. Prior to 1914, ninety percent of major leaguers did not have copies of their own contracts, which was remedied. The organized major leagues agreed to publish waiver lists so players could learn of their potential dismissal, although Chief Bender found out this would not always be the case. Veterans of ten or more years of major league service could request their unconditional release, enabling them to negotiate a new contract. The owners also agreed to pay for uniforms and travel expenses to spring training, and henceforth would have to justify fines or suspensions in writing. In exchange for Organized Baseball's concessions, Fultz promised that the union would not take sides in the fight between the existing major leagues and the Federals.[2]

Chief Bender was not the only member of the Athletics who had taken a public stance in resistance to the club's substandard salary structure. In 1910 pitcher Clarence "Lefty" Russell held out all winter because Mack offered him only $1,800, less than the player made in the minors a year earlier. The Athletics finally gave in and agreed to pay the pitcher $2,400 a year, but the last laugh was on the club. Russell only won one game in three seasons with Philadelphia.[3]

Considering their recent success, the players on the 1914 Athletics were among the poorer compensated in the league. However, as members of the World Series champions in three of the previous seasons, the owners could point out that the A's players' yearly salaries were well augmented by their shares for their post-season victories.

Connie Mack had no problem using outside leverage to advance his own interests. Following the 1913 season, New York Highlanders owner Frank Farrell made Connie a considerable offer to manage his team. Ben Shibe quickly engineered a deal in which Mack acquired twenty-five percent of Athletics stock that had been farmed out to two newspaper men, Frank Hough and Sam Jones. Now, he and Shibe each had fifty percent of the club. It was agreed Shibe would retain complete control of the club's business activities, but now Mack would have full charge of the baseball side.[4]

Just as Connie Mack raided the Philadelphia Phillies for his new American League team in 1901 and 1902, the Federals looted the local National League club's roster in the spring of 1914. The Feds signed two of the Phillies' starting pitchers, the club's starting shortstop and second baseman, and a utility player. The Chicago Federal League club also signed the Phillies' catcher, Bill Killifer, but he jumped back to Philadelphia just before spring training when his salary was doubled.

When the Athletics opened spring training in Jacksonville, Florida, the only departure of any note was veteran outfielder Danny Murphy, who signed with the Brooklyn Federal League club after Mr. Mack shipped him to Jack Dunn's Baltimore Orioles. Murphy couldn't play the outfield anymore because of a lingering knee injury, and he had gone to bat only 80 times in 1913, mostly as a pinch-hitter. His loss would hardly be felt.

On Charles Bender's recommendation, Mack agreed to give an eighteen-year-old Chippewa named Joe Graves a tryout that spring. The young left-hander from Watcher, Minnesota, did not make the club.[5]

Another rookie pitcher in camp that year was nineteen-year-old Raymond Bressler. He took much the same route to the majors as Chief Bender, signed after having beaten Earle Mack's All-Stars while pitching for a Pennsylvania Railroad shop team. Nicknamed "Rube" because he was left-handed, Bressler told baseball historian Lawrence Ritter he held a very fond memory of his time with Charles Bender:

> Bender and Plank, the old war horses! When I got there in 1914, a nineteen-year-old kid, Bender had been with the A's for 11 years and Plank for 13. Hell, I'd been reading about those guys since I was in the third grade. And how do you think they treated me? Well, I'll tell you: wonderful. Just wonderful. Two of the finest guys who ever lived.
>
> I used to try to get near them and listen to what they were talking about, and every question I'd ask they'd pay attention and tell me what they thought.
>
> I roomed with Bender that first year; One of the kindest and finest men who ever lived. See, Connie roomed a youngster with a veteran. He didn't room two youngsters together, where they could cry on each other's shoulders and commiserate with each other. No sir. He had an old pitcher in there with a young one.[6]

Only a few days into 1914 season, the Cincinnati Reds' Native American pitcher George "Chief" Johnson jumped to Kansas City of the Federal League. Johnson, whose real name was George Howard, was a Winnebago from Nebraska. On April 18, Johnson pitched a losing game for the Reds against Pittsburgh. Five days later, he appeared on the mound in a Federal League game in Chicago.

Johnson took the ball for the Kansas City Packers on Opening Day at Chicago's brand-new Federal League Park on April 23. As the pitcher exited the field after completing the second inning, he was served with an injunction sought by the Cincinnati Reds restraining him from playing for the Federal League.

A more serious problem for Organized Baseball than increased payrolls for its clubs was the threat of court action to eliminate the ten-day clause. A standard feature of most baseball contracts then, the rule stipulated that a team was required to give a player to be released only ten days notice. According to Johnson's Federal League attorneys, the pitcher only joined Kansas City after giving ten days notice to the Reds, the same notice the Cincinnati club was required to give to him.[7] Major league club owners never anticipated that the clause might be used by a player (or a rival league) to get out of a contract with one of their teams.

After pitching in only three games for the A's in the first month of the season, pitcher Byron Houck was assigned to the Baltimore Orioles of the International League. Houck refused to report to Baltimore and signed with Brooklyn of the Federal League on May 19 at a significant increase over his $1,200 Philadelphia salary.

Once the regular season began, Bender did not pitch until his team's ninth game. Down to the New York Yankees, 4–2, Charley left for a pinch-hitter in the seventh inning. However, the Athletics rallied for three runs in the eighth to secure the victory. Because of the cool weather, the veterans Bender and Plank were used sparingly by Connie Mack over the first five weeks of the season. After the Chief was pounded for thirteen hits in a loss at Washington in his second effort, Stanley Milliken of the *Washington Post* wrote, "Bender did not look like the redskin who on more than one occasion has taken the scalp of not only the Nationals, but teams that have battled for the World Series title. The question is, has Bender gone back. Time alone will decide. One thing is certain; the Nationals hit him harder than they ever have done before. Bender was lucky more runs were not made off him."[8]

These assertions proved to be premature, though it would be several weeks before Bender's efforts would resemble his success of years past. On May 26, the Chief was pulled after four innings in a loss to the St. Louis Browns. After that defeat, his record stood at one win and two losses in six games pitched, three in relief.

Three days after his short outing against the Browns, Chief Bender pitched the first of his seven shutouts of the 1914 season in the second game of a doubleheader against the Yankees. About the only other thing of note in the game was a strange play in the fifth inning. Bender was the base runner at third base and Rube Oldring stood on second. Noting that Yankees pitcher Al Schulz was preoccupied on the mound, Oldring decided to steal third.

While the pitcher held the ball, Rube took off for third base and slid into the bag that was occupied by Bender. According to a reporter at the game, "The Indian was undoubtedly considerably surprised, but not a bit flurried when Oldring got up and dusted off his uniform, tapped him on the shoulder and called attention to the fact that the base would not hold two at the same time."[9]

Convinced that Bender wasn't going anywhere, Oldring headed back toward second. The Yankees' catcher and third baseman were yelling for Schulz to throw the ball, but he still didn't realize what was happening on the bases and delivered a pitch to the batter, Eddie Collins. Collins swung and hit an infield pop fly that stayed in the air just long enough for Rube to reach the safety of second base.

Bender's 3–0 shutout of the Yankees vaulted the Athletics into first place, and Philadelphia led the American League for the remainder of the season except for two days in June when Washington held the top position. However, Bender's season was put on hold after Charley pitched the first two innings of an exhibition game loss in Buffalo, New York, on June 5.

On June 15, William Weart wrote that "Bender, who was being reserved for the hot weather, was taken ill at Detroit and he was forced to take to his bed in Cleveland with an attack of tonsillitis."[10]

That same day, a bombshell hit the Athletics' club, courtesy of the *Chicago Daily Tribune*. The newspaper reported that Eddie Collins had been offered the largest salary ever given a ballplayer if he would join the Brooklyn team of the Federal League. "Collins, it is said, did not name the figure except to say that it was not less than $25,000 a year.... Collins also said he would not leave Philadelphia until the expiration of his contract, which holds to next October."[11]

Meanwhile, the Athletics had a pennant to win. On the A's way back east from St. Louis on June 23, Bender returned to the mound for the first time in more than two weeks when he pitched in a "draggy and featureless" exhibition game in Toledo, Ohio, before 12,000 employees of a large automobile manufacturing plant.[12] The travel-weary Athletics were scheduled to open a key series the next day with second-place Washington in the Capitol City. Connie Mack asked Clark Griffith of the Nationals to change the schedule and play only one game on Wednesday and then the doubleheader a day later. Griffith insisted the double-bill be played on the twenty-fourth as scheduled.

The Athletics' train arrived in Washington after 1 P.M. on the day of the doubleheader. The players rushed from the railway station to the park and arrived just in time to start the first game. The A's lost both games by one run, shrinking their hold on first place over Washington to two and a half games.

The next day's game was rained out, forcing the clubs to play another doubleheader on June 26. Philadelphia took a 2–0 lead in the first game before it ended with a controversial decision that may have cost Washington a game in the standings.

Newspaper accounts of the contest indicate rookie umpire Oliver Chill repeatedly called balls on Washington pitcher Engle after A's captain Ira Thomas complained that the hurler was not in contact with the rubber when he delivered a pitch. With the sacks full of Philadelphia base runners, Manager Griffith protested the umpire's actions and refused to order his men to resume play. Chill pulled out his watch and after a few minutes forfeited the game to the visitors.[13]

The second game was tied, 5–5, at the end of regulation. Chief Bender took the mound for Philadelphia in the top of the tenth and retired the Nationals without damage. Philadelphia scored a run in the bottom of the inning to gain the sweep and restore their four-and-a-half-game lead over Washington.

The Athletics finished off the Nationals on Saturday when Bender beat Walter Johnson, 4–2, in the final match-up ever between the two star hurlers. The A's scored all the runs they needed in the first inning with a rare four-run outburst against the "Big Train." Still seething from the previous day's forfeit, Stanley T. Milliken of the *Washington Post* blamed their star's failings on umpire Oliver Chill.

> "Guesser" Chill, champion of "Homers" handed out a few more of his weird decisions on balls and strikes this afternoon, mainly through his aid the Athletics were able to defeat the Nationals in the final game of the series.... Like the previous day, Chill picked the proper time to steal the scene. Instead of waiting, he decided that the first inning was the spot to "pull the stuff." He handed Murphy and Baker bases on balls, the last one forcing over a run. These, coupled with three hits off Walter Johnson and a successfully worked squeeze, put the Mackmen's sum total of tallies across.[14]

With Philadelphia leading, 4–1, in the second inning, Chill ejected the Washington first baseman, Chick Gandil, for throwing a ball toward the catcher that bounced and nearly hit the umpire. While the player and arbiter were arguing, the skies opened and the game was delayed for twenty minutes by the downpour.

Chief Bender nursed a 4–2 lead into the ninth inning and then hits by Johnson, Milan and Wally Smith loaded the bases for the Nationals with two out. As he did time after time, Bender was able to finish, inducing Howard Shanks to ground to Eddie Collins for the final out.[15]

Washington hung around in the pennant race and was only three games out on July 17 when Johnson not only lost a game to last-place Cleveland, but Clyde Milan, the Nationals' deer-footed center fielder, was lost for the pennant run when he suffered a broken jaw in a collision with his right fielder.

On July 3, Bender and Bob Shawkey pitched double shutouts against the Yankees, 2–0 and 1–0, at Shibe Park. Three days later, Bender came back with another 2–0 shutout of New York, this time against their best pitcher, Ray Caldwell. That victory was indicative of Bender's competitiveness, because he did not have his dominating stuff. Charley was unusually wild throughout the game, walking six batters.

In the sixth inning, Bender walked Caldwell and Truesdale. The Chief's former teammate, Tully Hartsel, attempted to sacrifice, but Bender's athleticism took over as he pounced on the bunt and forced the runner at third base. The next two batters were easy outs.

With one out and two New York runners on base in the eighth inning, Roger Peckinpaugh drove a low liner to left field, but Oldring snared the ball with a sensational diving catch. Truesdale, the runner at second, thought Rube had trapped the ball and was called out for not tagging up after the catch. Bender walked two more batters in the ninth before shortstop Jack Barry made a good stop on Luke Boone's grounder and threw him out to end the game.[16]

A week later, Philadelphia's victory in the second game of a doubleheader against the Browns started the Athletics on a twelve-game winning streak, which opened a six-game lead in the standings over second-place Boston. The Red Sox could not overcome a poor start, and a four-game sweep of the A's in early September still left Boston eight games behind Philadelphia.

A's right-hander Boardwalk Brown, a seventeen-game winner in 1913, had a horrible first half of the 1914 season and was sold to the Yankees on July 6. Brown's departure opened the door for Bender's rookie roommate Rube Bressler to join the starting rotation.

"You never could tell whether Bender won or lost," Bressler explained to Lawrence Ritter years later. Once after Rube suffered a particularly tough loss, Charley counseled the young pitcher, "'It's a matter of record now. Forget about that game. Win the next one.' That's all he said."[17]

After two months of legal wrangling, the case involving Chief Johnson was finally settled in favor of the Federal League on July 16, 1914. A Chicago appellate court held the ten-day clause in the ballplayer's contact null and void. On July 24, a petition of the Cincinnati club to grant a stay of dissolution to the injunction prohibiting Johnson from playing with the Federal League was denied by the court.[18]

Johnson pitched for the Kansas City Packers through 1915, but he never received another major league contract after that. Johnson was found shot to death in Des Moines, Iowa, on June 22, 1922. He was thirty-six years old.

Chief Bender was particularly strong in August when he threw four consecutive complete games, allowing a total of two runs in his four victories.

On August 15, he blanked the Griffmen from Washington, 6–0, and only one opposition base runner advanced as far as second base. In the sixth inning, Bender picked out a pitch from Grunting Jim Shaw and lined it to left field. The ball landed short of the Shibe Field fence, but took a bounce into the stands for a two-run home run.[19]

On September 7 Bender picked up another victory over Washington in a lackluster performance that saw him leave after the sixth inning with the Athletics ahead, 8–5. However, the win was noteworthy because it was Charley's fourteenth consecutive victory.

Bender's unbeaten string ended on September 12 at New York's Polo Grounds. In the ninth inning Bender was losing to the Yankees, 1–0, when a couple of Athletics reached base after two were out. With Oldring at bat, the base runners attempted a double steal. Catcher Ed Sweeney heaved the ball high over second base and Stuffy McInnis raced home with the tying run. Sweeney, the apparent goat of the day, was the first batter to face Bender in the bottom of the ninth. With the boos and taunts of the New York fans ringing in his ears, Sweeney's mighty swing made solid contact with a Bender pitch and the ball soared into the right-field stands for a game-winning home run.

"The crowd surged upon the field," reported the *New York Times*, "and when Sweeney rounded third base to come home, where Umpire Tommy Connolly was waiting, the big catcher was lost in the mob of hundreds of fans who made the trip with him."[20]

The loss was Bender's first since losing to the Browns on May 26. Between that loss and Sweeney's home run, Charley started fifteen games and relieved in five others without suffering a defeat. During that stretch, he won fourteen games, one in relief, and threw six shutouts.

In reality, Bender's fourteen-game winning streak in 1914 was not as remarkable as his twelve straight victories of 1907 in which he threw eleven complete-game victories in consecutive starts. During his 1914 streak, Bender was bailed out by his teammates on at least two occasions. On July 16 he gave up five runs before being relieved by Joe Bush in the fourth inning with the score tied. On August 4 Bender was down, 3–0, after two innings when he was relieved by Bressler. The Athletics rallied to win the game, 5–4, and saved the Chief from a loss.

In August, New York Yankees right-hander Ray Caldwell deserted his team following a dispute with manager Frank Chance. Caldwell openly negotiated with the Buffalo Federal League club, even sitting on the Buffeds' bench during a doubleheader on September 12. Frank Chance resigned as Yankees manager the same day and Ray rejoined the American League club. After earning $2,400 for the 1914 season, Caldwell signed a four-year contract with the Yankees for $8,000 a season.[21]

All of the defections and threats of defection could not be ignored by veteran ballplayers like Bender and Plank. Former Philadelphia Phillies hurler Tom Seaton, only in his third major league season, was being paid $8,500 by the Brooklyn Federals. (He made $2,500 when he won 27 games for the Phillies in 1913.)

Years later, Mack revealed his misgivings about the 1914 season.

> Thinking as I did at the time, I felt it was the most unhappy season of my baseball career. In view of conditions which existed on my ball club, the beating we took from the Braves in the World Series was not surprising.
>
> The Federal League was in the field that year, with several rich bankers, and all season long we were followed by agents of this independent league. What made it even a more bitter pill for me was that Danny Murphy, who had played on five of my championship clubs, was the Brooklyn scout.... He had the lavish Ward bankroll behind him and he was offering some of my players three and four times what we were paying them. We tore up some contracts, wrote new ones, and had three-year contracts with Eddie Collins, Baker and other key players. Still, the Feds kept raising their offers.[22]

Players dealing with the Federal League could have hardly been the reason the Athletics drew 225,000 fewer fans than in 1913. While the A's were winning their fourth pennant in five years, attendance was down at Shibe Park — from 571,896 in 1913 (second in the league) to 346,641 (fifth) in 1914. Even with no direct Federal League competition in Philadelphia, the A's had the lowest attendance of any American League pennant winner since 1907, and the club lost $60,000 that year despite going to the World Series.

Connie Mack refused to be pressured by his employees and he instituted a "no-beer pledge" for his players in the last few weeks of the regular season. Among the hard-drinking faction on the club, the policy further widened the rift between the manager and players. Years later, Charles Bender intimated that the pledge of temperance Mack extracted from the players led to their poor showing in the post-season.

> We got off to a great start that year and played fine ball to take a big lead. It looked like a cinch. Such a cinch that Connie called us together one morning to make plans for the rest of the season and the World's Series.
>
> "It looks like we are going to win," he said. — I can remember his words as if it were yesterday. — "And I want you to do something for me, I want you to give up drinking, even beer. I don't want the fans to be able to say one word against anyone."
>
> We all agreed and kept our promise. This meant that I, for example, who had been used to stopping on the way home from the ballpark for a glass of beer to relax my nerves, went straight home. The rest of the boys did the same.
>
> We became stale. Every athlete has to relax. If he doesn't, he goes into a slump; gets stale, can't do a thing.[23]

Chief Bender's 6–0 shutout of the Browns in St. Louis on September 27 clinched the American League pennant for the Athletics. He made his final regular season appearance at Shibe Park on October 6, 1914, working the first three innings against New York. The Chief appeared to be in good form, allowed but one hit, one run and struck out five in his tune-up for the World Series. In 1914 Bender started only twenty-three games on a very deep Athletics pitching staff, but he had a career high in shutouts with seven and led the staff with seventeen victories. Seven Athletics pitchers won ten or more games during the regular season.

The Athletics' opponents in the 1914 World Series were the "Miracle" Boston Braves, an outfit that went from last place in mid–July to win the National League title. The A's players took the Braves lightly — too lightly as it turned out. Mack had told Bender to scout the Braves in September when they played a series with the Giants at the Polo Grounds. Instead, Bender went on a fishing trip with some friends. However, Connie Mack heard that his pitcher was seen on a boat in Delaware Bay at the time he was supposed to be in New York.

Joe Villa reported that when Mack confronted the Chief after his return to Philadelphia, the "scout" disdainfully retorted, "I don't think it was worthwhile looking at that bunch of bush leaguers! There isn't a first-class hitter on the team, and everybody knows it."[24]

Though rumored to have listened to offers to play for the Federal League, Bender was slated to start the first game of the World Series as he had in 1910, 1911 and 1913. The Series began at Shibe Park on October 9 and a crowd estimated at 30,000 packed the stands or assembled on rooftops of buildings across the street from the outfield walls. All the players were on the field before one o'clock with the exception of Bender, who did not emerge from the dugout until fifteen minutes before game time. He warmed up slowly, stopping occasionally to oblige a photographer by posing for pictures.[25]

The game itself started harmlessly enough for Bender; Herbie Moran fouled out, Johnny Evers flied out to Eddie Collins and Joe Connolly struck out on three pitches. In the second, the Chief walked Possum Whitted, and after a fly ball out to Oldring, Boston's light-hitting catcher, Hank Gowdy, doubled home the first run. Gowdy then lumbered home on a single by Rabbit Maranville.

The A's scored a run in the bottom of the inning to pull within 2–1 and Bender regrouped in the third, retiring the Braves in order. Connolly led off the fourth with a single, but the next batter grounded back to Bender, who started a quick double play. Boston scored another run in the fifth inning that put them up 3–1, and then things fell apart for Bender in the sixth.

With a two-run lead, the Braves' players showed a "wonderful amount of pep." At the conclusion of each inning, they raced from the field for the opportunity to bat. Previous opponents, like the Giants, always walked on and off the field during their games while the Athletics were the team that displayed enthusiasm. On this day, though, observers commented the Athletics played the game with little attention and "without ginger."

With two Braves on base and one out in the sixth, Whitted hit Bender's second pitch between the outfielders into deep right-center field. The two base runners tallied to make the score 5–1, Boston. Butch Schmidt lined a rifle shot right through Barry at shortstop to send home yet another run. Coach Ira Thomas trudged to the mound to inform Bender that Wyckoff was to replace him.

"With head hanging low the stolid Indian stalked to the bench driven from the mound for the first time in a 'money series,'" noted the *Sporting News*.[26]

That day marked first time the Chief did not finish a World Series game he started. As he watched Bender walk to the dugout from the pitching mound, Mack couldn't help but exclaim, "Pretty good hitting for a bush league outfit."[27] Connie was especially angry because Bender did not appear at Shibe Park until thirty minutes before he was scheduled to pitch and then wasted several minutes with "horse play."[28]

The *Sporting News* later reported that Bender had so little respect for the Braves batting order that when Gowdy came to bat in the second inning, he thought it was third baseman Deal, a notably poor hitter. Manager George Stallings had switched Deal and Gowdy in the order and the latter was responsible for Boston's first two runs.[29]

The opposition team's captain, Johnny Evers, was not surprised the Braves were able to hit well against Bender. "I understand Bender has had a hard time getting in shape for this one supreme effort and he did not honestly believe he would ever get a chance to open another world's series. It is no secret of the profession that Bender has had to have his arm treated with electricity after every game he pitched during the season and for several days afterward to put life into it."[30]

The Athletics lost the Series in four straight games. After Plank lost Game Two, 1–0, Mack announced that he would use only his young pitchers in the remaining games. When a city official proposed a banquet for the American League champions, Mack and Shibe declined the invitation.

The last word on the Athletics' commitment in the 1914 World Series came from a twenty-one-year-old outfielder, James "Shag" Thompson, the last survivor from that team.

According to Mack biographer Norman Macht, "I interviewed the last survivor of the 1914 team, a rookie who played little but was there. He told me he didn't see it, but he heard that Oldring and Bender, who were drinking buddies, were out drinking till late the night before the series opener. Since they had been suspended by Mack for the same behavior in 1912, that I can believe."[31]

One story that made the rounds suggested the A's deliberately did not play well because of the fractionalization on the team. Frank Baker was so dissatisfied he sat out the entire 1915 season rather than play for the Athletics. Eddie Collins, who had discussions with the Federals, was sold to the White Sox.

Rube Oldring, who made only one hit in fifteen at-bats against the Braves, offered a unique excuse for his .067 batting average in the Series. Rube claimed his poor play was due to harassment from a woman who claimed to be his wife. If Connie Mack had any suspicions about Rube's poor performance during the Series, it would have been unlikely Oldring would have been retained by the A's in 1915.

Connie Mack, at approximately 50 years old (George Grantham Bain Collection, Library of Congress).

On October 31, 1914, Hugh Jennings, manager of the Detroit Tigers, leaked the news that Connie Mack had asked secret waivers on pitchers Eddie Plank, Jack Coombs, and Chief Bender. Plank supposedly had told the A's that he did not think the Philadelphia management would meet the salary offered him by the Federals.

"One of these men (Plank) has been doing business with the Federal League," said Mack, "and the other (Bender) is almost certain to, and when I learned of the salaries they wanted I decided that with six fine young pitchers—and I have beauties—it was out of the question for me to try to hold them, because I could not, and would not, pay them what they expect."

"I had hoped this would not become public because it hurts my plans," acknowledged Mack, "but as Hughey Jennings is a base ball manager only six months of the year and a vaudeville actor the other six you can't expect him to know the rules of organized ball."[32]

Mack told the newspapers he had to let Bender go because of his performance in the World Series. Blaming greed and intrigue for his players' discontent, which led to the loss of the World Series, Mack did not attempt to sell Plank and Bender to the highest bidder, but simply cut them loose.

Chandler Richter of *Sporting Life* reported that had the Federal League not been in the field, Mack would have been glad to give the pair their unconditional releases. When the Feds offered the players more money than they were worth, Mack's loyalty to the American League prompted him to ask for waivers in order that other clubs could clandestinely bid for their services and keep the pitchers in Organized Baseball. Hugh Jennings sabotaged that plan of action.

"I was pretty sore at the time — awfully sore," Connie Mack told Fred Lieb years later. "I felt the players were letting down both me and the club, and that we had paid them as good salaries as baseball then could afford and made it possible for them to get into four rich World Series. Today, over the perspective of the years, I feel a little differently.... I long have forgiven the players who gave me those 1914 headaches, and most of them have been back with me in some capacity."[33]

Speaking in his own defense some years later, Bender gave his explanation for the 1914 World Series loss:

> We went into the Series overconfident. We thought we'd take them in a breeze — just put on our suits and walk out on the field. I remember I was feeling ill — had vertigo and trouble with my gall bladder and stomach. I told Mr. Mack I didn't feel well. He merely smiled and said, "Oh, you can beat those fellows. Just warm up and go to the box."
>
> When I warmed up, I didn't have anything. I told him again, but he brushed my complaints aside. I went in and got my licking. I really didn't have much and it didn't take them long to find out. My control was bad, I was frequently in the hole with three and two and on the next pitch — wham!
>
> It has been said that we were flirting with the Federal League before the Series and weren't prepared to give our best, but that isn't true. Not one of us had been approached by the Federal League. The Braves beat us because they were the better club.[34]

Years after the fact, the story appeared that the 1914 World Series was thrown by some of the players on the Athletics. The tale about gamblers getting to Bender and perhaps other A's gained strength and hollow "validity" as it was repeated, even gaining inclusion in some mainstream publications. In the immediate days and months following the Series, there was no inference in contemporary reports that Connie Mack or anyone else suspected a fix in Game One or any of the other contests. Mack was livid about Chief Bender's lack of preparation and his not being in shape to pitch the first game, but he was able to forgive the pitcher for those transgressions and brought Charley back to the Athletics' family in 1939. It is doubtful Mack would ever have taken him back if he thought the Chief threw a World Series game. Norman Macht maintained in his landmark biography of Connie Mack that any idea the A's manager suspected any of his players of throwing the 1914 Series was a "ridiculous myth."[35]

One of the main contentions of the conspiracy theorists is that Bender had been so good in previous World Series starts for the Athletics, it was impossible for him to perform so badly in Game One unless he deliberately let up. Despite his 1914 pitching record, Bender experienced several bad outings during the season and Manager Mack carefully picked opposing pitchers and teams that the Chief would likely have success against. The fact was, Mack was convinced that Bender was an old thirty-year-old and he had issues with the pitcher's drinking habits.

William Weart, the *Sporting News'* correspondent in Philadelphia, wrote in the December 10, 1914, edition, "Unlike the average twirler, who works where told to do so by his manager, Bender was pretty much his own boss in this respect. The Chief almost invariably worked only when he felt absolutely certain that he was in first class form.

"During the past two seasons he did not pitch against Detroit and Boston which were rated as strong hitting combinations. Both Plank and Bender were 'nursed' along by Manager Mack and each was very successful against opponents chosen for him."[36]

Upon examination of the records, Bender did not start a game against Boston or Detroit during the 1914 season and his only appearances against either of those two clubs were a pair of one-inning relief efforts against the Tigers. Furthermore, only three of his twenty-three starting assignments came against teams that finished the season with winning records and seven of those starts came against a New York Yankees club that finished with the worst batting average among the twenty-four major league clubs.

Years later, Chief Bender said he only signed with the Federal League because Connie Mack released him following the 1914 World Series. "I was in the Texas Blockhouse in Williamsport, oiling my gun one morning, when Jerry Donovan dropped a paper in my lap. 'Hey, look at this Chief,' he said. Across the top of the sports page was the banner line: 'Mack Asks Waivers on Bender and Plank.' I felt as if someone had hit me with a sledgehammer."[37]

Two weeks after Charles learned of his release by the Athletics, he was injured in an automobile accident. Early the morning of Sunday, November 15, Bender and several friends were on the way to Sunbury when a small animal in the road caused the Chief to divert his automobile into a deep cut along the roadside and crash into the shrubbery. A report made the newspapers that Bender, who had been driving, was thrown into the windshield and was "half-carried, half dragged a distance of several miles to a hotel." Bender suffered cuts on his head, face, and hands, but escaped serious injury.[38]

"The big twirler's pitcher has adorned sports pages with the caption above stating the famous hurler was in a precarious condition as the result of an automobile accident," noted Chandler Richter in *Sporting Life*. "The 'Chief' was all but killed by the scribe, but upon arriving in Philly, Bender had nothing but a scratch on his cheek and said the machine was the only thing wrecked about the accident."[39]

Two weeks later, Bender was on the road again for a trip with his wife and two other women to Gettysburg, Pennsylvania. The group had lunch at Hotel Gettysburg and then proceeded to the home of Eddie Plank for a visit.

There is no doubt the former A's conversation focused on their future baseball options; seven days later Plank signed a contract to pitch for the Federal League in 1915.[40]

When Connie Mack was asked if he was sorry to see Plank go, the A's manager replied, "Oh, no. I was through with him. He was after the money and was quite willing to go to the Federals. He was a wonderful pitcher and he is a good one yet."[41]

The evening of December 5, 1914, Bender confirmed the reports that he had signed a contract to pitch in the Federal League, with either the Brooklyn or Baltimore clubs. Harry Goldman, treasurer of the Baltimore Federal League club, came to Philadelphia earlier in the day and the former A's pitcher wasted no time signing the agreement.

"The terms of the contract are very satisfactory, and it is the best thing I ever did in my life," Bender told reporters. "The contract is to run two years."[42]

> "I worked faithfully 12 years for the Athletics, gave them the best there was in me and do not think the summary way I was treated a month ago was the right kind of treatment for my years of labor. I feel sure that I directly drew to the box office thousands of dollars for the club, and during my service as a pitcher accomplished much to win a few pennants. Understand, I do not hold any resentment toward Connie Mack or anybody else connected with the club.... Connie and I parted the best of friends last fall and, while I have not seen him since, I do not hold any grudge against him over what has since transpired."[43]

It was later learned that Bender signed with the Feds for a $5,500 bonus and an annual salary of $8,500. The contract appeared to be a windfall for Bender, whose Athletics salary had been $5,000.[44] There were serious drawbacks though for the thirty-one-year-old hurler, who apparently had several major league seasons left in his arm. Organized Baseball had promised to blacklist any player who signed with the outlaw league and defecting players would have to sit out three years before they could return to the American or National leagues.

The Benders chose to retain their home in Philadelphia and Charley continued to pursue business interests there with the acquisition of a larger location for his sporting goods store. Chandler Richter reported that December that "Chief has an immense place on Arch Street west of Thirteenth now, and has placed three 'Skee Ball' alleys in the rear of the store. The game has become popular here and should net the Indian a neat sum aside from his regular business."[45]

The Benders had strong ties in Philadelphia. In addition to his sporting goods business, Charles was a member of the local Order of Eagles and Masonic Lodge, No. 487, along with close friends Harry Davis, Eddie Collins and Jack Coombs.[46]

Charles had maintained little contact with his folks back in Minnesota, but he did reconnect with two of his sisters after Elizabeth Bender came to the Carlisle Indian School as a teacher in 1915. She graduated from Hampton Normal & Agricultural Institute in Virginia, completed the post-graduate domestic science program and became a teacher in the United States Indian Service. That November a Carlisle newspaper reported that Elizabeth Bender and her sister Emma spent the weekend in Philadelphia with Charles and Marie.[47]

The following June, Elizabeth married the noted Winnebago educator Henry Roe Cloud, whom she had met at the 1914 Society of American Indians Conference in Madison, Wisconsin. The first American Indian to graduate from Yale University, Cloud founded the Roe Indian Institute (later renamed the American Indian Institute), became the first Native American president of the noted Haskell Institute, and served in the Office of Indian Affairs. Cloud's Chippewa wife helped him manage the institute. President Franklin D. Roosevelt appointed Mrs. Cloud as a delegate to the 1940 White House Conference on Children and Youth.[48]

Chief Bender did not neglect his passion for shooting and in December he appeared in a target shoot at Salem, New Jersey, the first trap shoot competition at night. "That the scheme is a great success is evident by the scores tallied," reported *Sporting Life*. The article noted that Charley broke 42 out of 50 targets under artificial light.[49] On January 31, the eagle-eye pitcher broke 94 out of 100 blue rocks to win the honors at the event held at the prestigious Beideman Gun Club at North Cramer Hill, New Jersey.[50]

When Charley reported to the Baltimore Terrapins' spring training site in Fayetteville, North Carolina, newspaper pictures showed the Chief in his old Philadelphia garb during throwing exercises with the other Federal League players. Baltimore finished only four and a half games out of first place in the 1914 Federal League pennant race and expected to contend in 1915. However, Bender was the only prominent addition to the team, while several other clubs made significant improvements. Eddie Plank went to last-place St. Louis and that team was in contention for the Federal League pennant until the next-to-last game of the season. Pittsburgh added the most defectors from the majors, but it was Chicago that won the flag. The Whales even had Walter Johnson's name on a Federal League contract for 1915, but the big hurler had a change of heart two weeks later and returned to Washington.

Bender found a few familiar faces when he joined the Terrapins. A fellow Shriner, second baseman-manager Otto Knabe, and slick-fielding shortstop Mickey Doolin were the keystone of the Philadelphia Phillies defense from 1907 until they jumped to the Federals prior to the 1914 campaign. Terps pitcher Jack Quinn, whose real name was John Quinn Picus, pitched for the New York Highlanders from 1909 through 1912 and had opposed Bender on the mound several times with little success.

Baltimore opened the season at Terrapin Park before 18,000 locals on April 10. Quinn, a 26-game winner the year before, was chased from the mound in a 7–5 loss to Newark. Bender made his debut as a Federal Leaguer three days later against the same club. Charley's mound counterpart was former Detroit Tiger George Mullin, who often opposed Bender when their former clubs battled for supremacy of the American League. Mullin won this particular game, 3–1, and matching Bender against well-known veteran pitchers would continue over the next few weeks. When the two clubs met again in Newark a week later, Bender lost a 5–1 game in bitterly cold weather to Ed Reulbach, a long-time star hurler with the Chicago Cubs who had pitched against the A's in the 1910 World Series.

The reunions with former pitching opponents continued on May 6, when Bender was matched against Three-Finger Brown of the Chicago Whales in a contest at Terrapins Park. Neither pitcher lasted past the sixth inning in a game Baltimore eventually won, 9–8.

Wrote Sam Weller, "Big Chief Bender, hero of many world's series when he wore the uniform of the Philadelphia Athletics, is merely a shadow of his former self and was no puzzle whatever to the Whales. They jumped on him unmercifully in the early innings, pounding out singles, doubles, triples and a home run (for eight runs) until they made him go to his tepee in disgrace."[51]

Charley finally broke into the win column for the first time as a Federal Leaguer in a game against St. Louis on May 11 at Terrapin Park. After he was touched for four runs in the first inning, Bender pitched well and drove in Baltimore's winning run with a double in the eighth. Four days later Charles came into a game against Brooklyn with one out, the bases loaded, and Baltimore leading, 10–6. He fanned Steve Evans and induced Claude Cooper to pop-up to end the threat. Bender polished off the Tip Tops in the ninth to complete the save. *Sporting Life* commented that Charley's two efforts on the homestand "made the fans believe that the big Chippewa is probably coming back into his own." It was a false hope.[52]

The inevitable match between Bender and Eddie Plank came in the first game of a Saturday doubleheader in Baltimore on June 26. The game featuring the two old war horses was heavily advertised and Baltimore's best crowd of the season turned out to see it. Bender pitched well enough to win, but Plank was better. The left-hander allowed only three hits in throwing a 2–0 shutout.[53] The pair met again, in St. Louis on July 20, and again Plank prevailed, 5–1. Gettysburg Eddie held Baltimore hitless until the seventh inning when the Terrapins scored their only run of the game on an error.

"Chief Bender is slipping," wrote Frank Menke in his syndicated column. "Once the most feared and most marvelous pitcher in baseball — now only an uncertainty on the mound.... The old speed has gone from the once mighty right arm; the curves no longer deceive. Bender has been batted from the box almost as many times this year as he was in all his years in the American League. And no man feels the tragedy of the fall of the one-time mighty Indian more keenly than does the Chief himself."[54]

Chief Bender won only four games for Baltimore. His best game came on June 21 when he struck out five in beating the eventual Federal League champion Chicago Whales, 7–2. On August 26, Bender started his final game as a Terrapin. The Chief lasted only one-third of an inning against Buffalo before he was removed, having allowed four hits and two runs. The Buffalo batters continued their assault on Quinn and Bailey, eventually thumping Baltimore, 11–9.

Pitching for a last-place club in Baltimore, Bender had a miserable season. In effect Connie Mack and Harry Davis weren't around to indulge the pitcher's idiosyncrasies and nurse him through the long baseball season. The Chief had a mound record of four wins and 16 losses when the Terps unceremoniously released him on August 30. Club president Carrol Rasin gave him the news. Bender wasn't the only one to go, as the financially strapped Terrapins traded or released most of their higher-salaried players.

Upon hearing the news of his former pitcher's release, Connie Mack was quoted as saying, "Bender still has a good deal of baseball left" and that he would not be surprised to see him back and show it. Connie intimated that the psychological effect of no fans in the stands to cheer him on hurt Bender.[55]

"After the 1914 season, my nerves reached such a pitch that I broke out in hives," Charley lamented. "My stomach still bothered me. I was weak and my pitching showed it. I spent hundreds of dollars on doctors and lost two big years."[56]

Two months following his release, Bender filed a suit in the Federal Court of Pittsburgh against the Federal League of Professional Baseball Clubs for breach of contract. The suit was directed against the league instead of the Baltimore club because his contract was with the Federal League and was signed by James Gilmore. The pitcher claimed he was owned $8,666.64, the balance of the money guaranteed him under the two-year contract he signed for $8,500 a year.[57]

Only two weeks after Bender's suit was filed, the organized major leagues and the Federal League reached an agreement that abolished the outlaws as an independent circuit. The price of peace with the Federals came high. First, the Feds insisted that their rivals assume the $385,000 worth of Federal League player contracts. Organized Baseball rejected the demand, but ultimately the clubs of the American and National leagues were forced to bid for the once-blacklisted players now available after the demise of the Federal League.

In effect, Organized Baseball bought out the Federal League. Terms of the agreement allowed the Feds' Charles Weeghman to buy the Chicago

National League club. Now that he owned the Cubs, "Lucky Charlie" moved their home from the West Side Grounds into his Federal League facility at the corner of Clark and Addison. The park would be renamed Wrigley Field several years later.

Phil Ball, the owner of the St. Louis Terriers, was permitted to buy the American League's St. Louis Browns. Weeghman and Ball then proceeded to merge their Federal League teams with the newly acquired major league clubs by taking the best players from each roster. The owners of major league baseball agreed to pay Brooklyn's Ward estate $400,000, while the Pittsburgh franchise was awarded $50,000 and the right to sell its players to the highest bidder. Harry Sinclair of the Newark club probably received the best financial settlement. The oil baron received a payment of $100,000 and was given the negotiating rights to Lee Magee, Benny Kauff, George Anderson, and the rosters of the Newark, Kansas City and Buffalo teams. Sinclair sold the players he controlled to Organized Baseball teams and then retired from the game.[58]

On January 19, 1916, Chief Bender's name appeared on a list of former Federal League players who, as result of the peace pact with Organized Baseball, were deemed to have little or no value in the open market. Essentially, Bender was now a free agent.

Organized Baseball offered the Baltimore club's stockholders a settlement of $50,000, but the club's investors wanted more. First, they wanted the right to purchase a major league franchise, which they planned to move to Baltimore. Denied, they then asked for an International League franchise in Baltimore, but were again rebuffed. Thus, the Baltimore interests preferred to pursue the matter in court.

In 1919, the Baltimore Federal League club was awarded $80,000 in damages that were tripled to $240,000 by the court. This decision was later reversed in an appellate court in 1921, and was reaffirmed by a Supreme Court decision in 1922. This was the famous Supreme Court ruling where Justice Oliver Wendell Holmes agreed with baseball's counsel, George Wharton Pepper, that the game was the national pastime, the actual games were not interstate commerce, which meant the anti-trust question did not need to be reviewed.[59]

The war between Organized Baseball and the Federal League exposed the inequity of the owner-player relationship. The temporary bargaining option the Federal League provided the players gave them a taste of freedom from the indentured servitude the oppressive reserve clause perpetuated. Additionally, the third major league provided an alternative to the National Agreement and gave the fledgling players' union leverage it needed to gain some concessions from the owners related to playing conditions and player contracts. Once the Federal League folded, salaries and players rights were rolled back to pre–1914 standards. The Players' Fraternity (union) was crushed after an abortive call for a strike in late 1916.

To showcase the interest that baseball players had in trap shooting, a tour was organized for the fall of 1915, the shooters to display the players' skills. In addition to Chief Bender, Christy Mathewson, Doc Crandall and Harry Davis were recruited. The players shot in seventeen cities in fifteen different states over a period of twenty days, each time performing against the best local trap shooters. Bender was far and away the best marksman of the group, averaging 92 breaks in every 100 targets. Crandall claimed to be a novice yet averaged 88 out of 100, while Christy averaged 71 and Davis 58. Bender's best performance was in Syracuse, New York, where he turned in 99 breaks out of the 100 targets.[60]

Samuel Wesley Long of *Baseball Magazine* interviewed Chief Bender for a trap shooting article that appeared in the April 1916 issue. "I have been shooting clay targets for about thirteen years and with every visit to a trap shooting club the hold of the sport on me grows," Bender admitted. "Always I find steady improvement in my shooting results.

"Lately I done the best work at the traps I have ever done. On four successive Saturdays my score was bettered, being as follows on 100 targets — 89, 94, 97, and 100 straight. And maybe I wasn't proud when I hung up that century."[61]

On George Washington's birthday Bender reunited with former teammates Bob Shawkey and Joe Bush for a three-cornered match at the Beidleman Club traps in Camden, New Jersey. Back in December, Bender had been at odds with Shawkey over a statement attributed to the young pitcher to the effect Plank and Bender were done and would never pitch winning baseball again in the American League. "I taught Shawkey all I knew about pitching," a disappointed Bender responded, "and then for him to come out with the statement credited to him is showing a spirit which actually startles me. I hardly believe it is true."[62]

Shawkey cut short his honeymoon to return to Philadelphia and tell Bender that the newspaper story was untrue. "I owe a lot to Bender, who has been good enough to teach me many things that have helped me to make good," swore Shawkey. "We have always been good friends and that interview which I was alleged to have given a scribe in Butler, Pa., is absolutely false.... I consider Bender about the best friend I had on the club, and he certainly did more for me and I would not want to lose his friendship for anything."[63]

With all forgiven, Charley went out to the line at Beidleman and shattered 90 targets to 86 for Bush and 84 for Shawkey.[64]

In between shooting matches during the baseball off-season, Charles Bender was a dealer in diamonds and other precious stones. He provided jewelry for many baseball players and kept a store in Conshohocken,

Pennsylvania. He also remained involved in the Chief Bender Sporting Goods Company in Philadelphia.[65]

Though baseball and trap shooting were Bender's livelihoods, and he was outstanding at golf and billiards, Charles found time for fishing and became an expert at fly and bait casting. On the surface, everything seemed to be going well in Bender's private life, but he needed to get control of his drinking issues and set his baseball career back on track. On February 11, 1916, Chief Bender signed a one-year contract during a conference with manager Pat Moran to pitch for the defending National League champion Philadelphia Phillies.

♦ 12 ♦

A Premature Eulogy

Charles Bender returned to the city of Brotherly Love in 1916, but he would not be pitching for the Athletics. In its baseball pre-season preview edition, *Baseball Magazine* proclaimed, "Chief Bender, the good old 'Injun,' has caught on with the Phillies."[1]

Obviously alluding to the vague reasoning behind the release of Bender by Baltimore for "being out of condition," Phillies manager Pat Moran told reporters, "I believe Bender will pitch great ball this year. He has seen the error of his ways and turned over a new leaf. The Indian has taken care of himself all winter and assures me he will report in fine shape."[2]

The origin of the Phillies could be traced back to 1883 when Al Reach purchased the Worcester, Massachusetts, franchise and transferred it to the National League. The club built a ballpark next to the Reading Railroad tracks where they crossed Broad Street at Lehigh. State of the art when it was built in 1887, tiny Baker Field had become by 1916 an opposing pitcher's nightmare with the advent of the livelier baseball.

When the Athletics captured the city's favor in 1902, the Phillies' fortunes sank as Connie Mack's soared. In 1911 the club was sold to William Baker, who established an even greater reputation as a "penny-pincher" than Mack. However, he did have the sense to promote a first-rate strategist in coach Pat Moran to manager in 1915.[3] Pat took a sixth-place team of the year before to the National League championship in his first season as field boss. The Phillies' best players were one of the greatest pitchers in the game's history, Grover Cleveland Alexander, and the National League's premier slugger, George "Gavvy" Cravath, who took advantage of the Baker Bowl's short fences to hit a National League-record twenty-four home runs during that pennant-winning season.

Bender was among the first group of seven Phillies to catch the steamer for Florida, where they would meet Manager Moran in camp at St. Petersburg. As the defending National League champions, the Phillies went into the new season with a deep pitching staff. Alexander was destined to win thirty-three games in 1916, including a record sixteen shutouts. Eppa Rixey won twenty-two games, and Al Demaree added another nineteen victories. However, Erskine Mayer, a twenty-one-game winner each of the two previous seasons, posted only a 7–7 mark. The Cherokee, Ben Tincup, was still with the Phillies when the team reported for spring training, but he would appear in only one game before being sold to Providence on April 15.

In addition to utilizing Bender as a reliever and spot starter, Moran was also interested in Charley's proficiency in the reading of the opposition's signals, and he would employ the veteran pitcher on the coaching lines as well. Bender made his initial National League appearance that April with one inning of relief work for Eppa Rixey against the Boston club he had failed so miserably against in his final game with the Athletics.

"Amid the cheers of the populace," wrote James Isaminger for the *North American*, "Chief Bender debuted for the Phils in the ninth. He saved the game, but the finish was goosefleshy."[4]

Philadelphia was up, 6–5, when Bender took the mound. The Braves' Zip Collins slapped a ball toward extra-base territory, but Milt Stock's sprawling stop of the smash held the runner at first. Moments later, a Bender pitch broke the left forearm of one of the Braves' best players, Sherry Magee. Following a sacrifice, the tying run stood on third with one out, and Moran had his infielders move in for a play at the plate. It paid off when Red Smith slapped a grounder to shortstop Dave Bancroft and Collins was tagged out trying to score. The next batter, Joe Connolly, took a mighty swing, but his bat only grazed the ball, which rolled about halfway to the mound. Bender rushed in, barehanded the ball, and made a blind throw that just nipped Joe at first to preserve the Phillies victory.

The most dramatic event of the 1916 season involving Chief Bender was a highly publicized pitching matchup against former teammate Jack Coombs, now with the Brooklyn Dodgers. In order to guarantee a good turnout, the Phillies announced two days in advance that the two former Athletics stars would pitch. On April 28, 8,000 fans, more than twice the usual turnout without the announcement, crowded tiny Baker Bowl that Friday to see the two former Mackmen go against each other.

The weather was cold and cloudy when the two teams took the field, and by the fifth inning it had begun to rain. Bender pitched seven innings and lost, 5–3, primarily because the breaks of the game did not go the Phillies' way. The Dodgers got one run when Phillies catcher Eddie Burns muffed a throw at the plate and two more scored after shortstop Dave Bancroft fell on the wet ground while running toward second base on what should have been an easy double play. One tally was produced by none other than Colby Jack, who greeted Chief with a hard-hit double in the second inning. Coombs ultimately scored on a scratch single by Jake Daubert.[5]

"Neither of the distinguished veterans was at his best," wrote Isaminger, "and both suffered the fate of being thumped off the tee, but in the archives of the league, it will officially be recorded as a conquest for the Colby alumnus and a defeat for the Chippewa."[6]

Bender got his first National League victory and complete game on May 14 when he pitched ten innings to beat Cincinnati, 4–3. He actually pitched better than the final result suggested as all three Cincinnati runs scored as the result of errors.

The Chief may have been more valuable to Pat Moran as a relief pitcher than as a starter. He served as a substitute pitcher fourteen times, posting two wins, losing one, and saving three others. For the second straight season, his overall record was well below his American League levels and he finished the season with a 7–7 record.

Bender's most impressive performance of 1916 came at the Polo Grounds against his old nemesis, John McGraw's New York Giants. The Giants' winning streak of seventeen straight games had been snapped the day before in the first game of a doubleheader, but New York came back to beat Grover Alexander in the nightcap. The next afternoon, New York touched Bender for a run in the first inning when Dave Bancroft made a wild throw in his attempt to complete a double play. In the top of the second, the Phillies came right back to take the lead for good against Pol Perritt on Dave Bancroft's three-run home run into the right field grandstand. Bender's two-out single in the fourth inning scored Bancroft with the Phillies' fourth run and the Chief's breaking pitches frustrated the Giants for the remainder of the contest, won by Philadelphia, 5–2.

Philadelphia held first place briefly in April and again moved into the top position early in September. Then the Giants, in the midst of a 26-game winning streak, beat the Phillies in four straight games.

On Saturday, September 9, thirty-five thousand noisy New York fans saw Pol Perritt pitch both games of a doubleheader against the league-leading Phillies. The lanky Giants right-hander beat Philadelphia, 3–1, in the opening act, then "changed his shirt" and threw a shutout in game two, besting Chief Bender, 3–0.

Later that month, Philadelphia went on a winning streak of seven games, and by beating Brooklyn in the first game of a doubleheader at Ebbets Field on September 30, the Phillies took first place again. They lost the top spot that afternoon when Brooklyn beat Alexander, 6–1. Except for a couple of scoreless innings in relief, Bender remained on the sidelines for the October stretch run as Philadelphia played itself out of the race by losing four of its final six games of the season to Boston. The Phillies actually won one more game than they had in 1915, but finished second behind the Dodgers.

With several players playing out of position, Philadelphia completed the

Chief Bender at Weeghman Field in Chicago, July 1916 (Chicago History Museum).

season with a meaningless game at the Baker Bowl that one newspaper called a "one-hand ball game." At a time when fielders made plays using both hands because of their pancake baseball gloves, for that one game "the players on both teams frequently made spectacular one-hand catches and one-hand stops."[7] In the course of the farce, Charley Bender replaced Bobby Byrne at third base, the Chief's only appearance at that position during his major league career. He went one-for-two at the plate and had two chances in the field.

On Saturday night, February 17, 1917, Charles Bender returned to Philadelphia by automobile after having participated in a clay bird shoot at Beiderman, New Jersey, earlier that day. As Charles drove down Broad Street, his car struck a pedestrian named John J. Curran, who was propelled against a pole. Newspaper reports indicate that a policeman happened to witness the accident and recorded the license number of the vehicle. In less than an hour Superintendent of Police James Robinson called off the search for the driver of the vehicle after Bender came to him and gave his version of the accident.[8]

A woman who lived on a first-floor apartment at 921 Broad told the *North American* she saw the accident and ran out to the car in time to recognize the driver as Chief Bender. Her account seemed to conflict with initial reports of the "hit-and-run" in which the driver did not stop, but turned the car around and sped north down Broad Street.[9]

Curran was rushed to St. Joseph's Hospital, but the thirty-year-old electrician died from a brain injury. Bender was placed into custody and then was released on bail.[10] A week later, the famous pitcher appeared before the coroner's jury.

At the time of the inquest, several things turned in Bender's favor. Bessie Curran, the wife of the deceased, claimed her husband was killed in the crosswalk, although he was apparently struck north of the crossing. Another witness said Curran appeared intoxicated shortly before the accident and the policeman on the scene remembered that Bender "had stopped" his car and then drove away a short time later.

"I was looking straight ahead at the time of the accident and was driving very slowly," testified Bender. "The man must have been hidden from my view by the shadows on the wet street for I did not see him until he was directly in the path of my car."[11]

The coroner's jury absolved Bender of any blame in Curran's death, but Charles still had to deal with the anguish of the incident as well as an $18,000 lawsuit filed by the victim's widow.[12]

Three days after the unfortunate accident, the Philadelphia Phillies unconditionally released Bender and the newspapers forecasted the end of the pitcher's major league career. Prior to his arrest, Charles was said to have been in contention for several managerial jobs, including Columbus, Indianapolis and Kansas City, but those positions were now out of the question.

"I've been pitching big league ball for fourteen consecutive seasons," he told sportswriter Grantland Rice only days before the accident, "and I'm ready to quit now without a kick when they think I'm through. In these fourteen years I've been on five pennant winning teams and have worked in five World Series. So I've had my share of the fun and the money with no kick at fate."[13]

With his baseball career in jeopardy, Bender immersed himself in his favorite diversion. Reported the *Sporting News* on March 1, "Bender's arm may have failed, but he still has the marvelous mental poise, nerve and eye that counted more than physical ability. The other day in a target shooting tournament, he killed his 99 birds out of 100 thrown. As a trap shooter he is always in demand and he loves this game above all others. It is said that a big powder company has offered him a flattering salary to become a professional at the traps and that he probably will accept."[14]

On March 29 Charles hit 97 of 100 targets at the opening event of the Laurel House Gun Club in Lakehurst, New Jersey. However, Bender was not ready to give up baseball just yet. He asked coach Roy Thomas (a former Phillies outfielder) of the University of Pennsylvania baseball team if he could work out with the school's pitchers during the spring. During practice at Franklin Field, the "Chief" acted as umpire and coached the Penn hurlers on how to approach each batter that came up to bat.[15] Bender also pitched a game or two a week for semi-pro teams in the area to keep in shape and also get a bit of cash.

Pat Moran listened to reports that Bender's arm was sound and invited the Chief to pitch batting practice to the Phillies. Convinced Charley was off the "merry mucilage" (yet another sportswriter's term for alcohol), wrote one reporter, Moran and the Phillies decided to take another chance on the thirty-three-year-old hurler.[16]

Without the benefit of formal spring training, Bender was brought along slowly, not pitching in a game until mid-season. He did become the focus of a complaint by Cubs manager Fred Mitchell, who maintained the Phillies, naming Chief Bender as the culprit, were using binoculars to steal the signals of their opponents from the Baker Bowl's clubhouse. Sportswriter William Weart pointed out Bender had been sitting in the stands behind the plate since he joined the club, making it impossible for him to be stealing the catcher's signs.[17]

Moran's Phillies did have a reputation for stealing the opposing team's signals and Bert Niehoff, Pat's regular second baseman from 1915 through 1917, commented in the spring of 1948 that "As soon as we got a man on base with less than two out, Pat would have him sacrificed to second so as he could get a look at the opposing catcher's signs."[18]

Behind the pitching of Alexander, the Phillies led the way in the National League pennant chase for two months. Then McGraw's New York Giants caught fire and blew past the Phillies on June 24. Charles spent a month coming into lost games just to mop up while the Phillies fell ten and a half games out of first place. Bender drew his first starting assignment against the St. Louis Cardinals on the final day of July and lost, 4–2, but he did well enough to warrant another chance five days later.

On August 5, the Chief beat Chicago at Weeghman Field, 6–2. Bender gave up six hits and walked three, but his teammates sealed the deal with a four-run sixth inning. The Cubs scored their only runs in the ninth inning.

On August 13, the veteran hurler posted his first shutout in three years when he blanked Boston, 3–0, on four hits. The game was a scoreless pitching duel between Bender and the Braves' Jesse Barnes until the seventh, when Dode Paskert's triple keyed a two-run inning for the Phillies. Bender was in trouble only in the fourth inning when Ray Powell doubled and Wally Rehg was hit by a pitch. Though no longer a power pitcher, the Chief fanned Joe Kelly and induced Ed Konetchy to fly out to left.

Four days later, the Chippewa shut out the Pittsburgh Pirates at Forbes Field, 3–0, in the first game of a doubleheader. Bender allowed just three singles and walked no one, though he did hit Max Carey with a pitch.

Following the two shutouts, the *Sporting News* retracted its eulogy for Bender's career of the previous winter. "It cannot be claimed for Bender that he has his old speed, but he certainly has his old cunning. His success though has not been due entirely to head work. Bender still has a lot of stuff and with doubleheaders pressing the Quakers will be mighty valuable."[19]

August 21, 1917, Bender pitched his third consecutive shutout, a one-hitter, winning, 6–0, over Chicago. No Cub managed to get as far as second base and the only Chicago batter to reach the Chief for a safety was Pete Kilduff. With two out in the second inning, Kilduff worked the count to three balls and two strikes. Bender threw a slow one that didn't break out of the hitting zone and Pete smacked it to center field, just out of the reach of Phillies shortstop Dave Bancroft. Bender was so dominant that no other ball was driven out of the infield until Charley Deal flied out with one down in the eighth. When Max Flack skied to center for the final out, the 8,000 fans in attendance at the Baker Bowl gave Bender a tremendous ovation. The delighted Chippewa sprinted off the field and Grover Alexander was one of the first to congratulate him.[20]

When the game with Cincinnati on Thursday, August 24, was postponed after four innings due to rain, the Phillies announced the contest would be made up as a doubleheader the following day. Grover Cleveland Alexander and Chief Bender would be the starting pitchers for the home team. A little drama was added to the twin-bill when Reds manager Christy Mathewson insisted that his pitchers, Fred Toney and Pete Schneider, could beat any pair the Phillies selected.[21]

On Friday, "all the stands were packed to capacity, the turn out being the biggest of the season." The crowd of 8,099 at the Baker Bowl was disappointed when the Reds beat Alexander in the first game of the doubleheader.

With his ball club desperate for a victory, Bender salvaged the nightcap, but he lost his shutout string when the Reds scored a sixth-inning run on Schneider's triple off the center field fence and a base hit by Heinie Groh. With Philadelphia up, 3–1, Cincinnati landed runners on second and third after two were out in the seventh. This time Schneider failed to deliver and

Grover Cleveland Alexander (center left) and manager Pat Moran of the Philadelphia Phillies (George Grantham Bain Collection, Library of Congress).

was retired on a harmless foul pop-up. Bender retired the side in order in each of the final two innings to secure the victory. By relying mostly on breaking pitches, the Chief scattered six hits and did not walk a batter nor did he strike out anyone. An oddity of the game was that Phillies catcher Bill Killefer did not record a put out, an assist or an error.

Charles Bender completed his remarkable August with a victory in the first game of a doubleheader against the Braves. He not only pitched the 4–3 victory, but the Chief also had two hits, one of them a long drive that bounced into the bleacher seats for a home run. The victory was not only Bender's sixth straight, Charley's contract stipulated he would receive a $50 bonus with each win. Though not officially wins, he also was awarded the extra money for the two games he saved.[22] Some baseball observers suggested Bender's rejuvenation was due to his use of an illegal pitch known as the "shine ball."

Even Connie Mack chimed in when asked about Bender's sudden success. "Whenever I hear of a pitcher coming back I always ask, 'What is he putting on the ball?' Old Chief Bender pitched three shutouts in a row in a remarkable come-back and I'll make a bet that he's got hold of the shine ball or something like it. The Chief is smart enough to master anything of the sort in a short while and it looks to me like that is what he's done."[23]

Bender's August bubble burst on September 5 in the opener of a crucial series at the Polo Grounds, site of the Chief's victory in the first game of the 1913 World Series. It was reported at the time "Bender was given the assignment for the first game though he was suffering with the old stomach trouble."[24]

Charles took the mound before a large Saturday crowd and pitched as well as he had ever pitched against the first-place Giants for seven innings. Bender fanned six and allowed only four hits through seven innings, and three times he stranded New York base runners after they reached third or second. McGraw did everything he could to rattle the veteran pitcher. The Giants complained so strenuously that Bender was defacing the baseball the umpire threw out five balls he was using. The baseballs were examined carefully for some sign of the shine but none was found.[25] The New York crowd began to applaud for Bender with increasing tendency as the game wore on.

Going into the eighth inning, Bender had a 2–0 lead, but things turned sour when Burns led off with a double to left and Buck Herzog's single drove him home. Next up was Benny Kauff. Bender had struck out Benny twice with runners on base, but this time Kauff "gave the ball a terrific smash and it soared high toward the grandstand, hitting the front of the upper-tier boxes."[26] The home run took the life out of the Philadelphia hitters, who went out meekly in the ninth. The demoralized Phillies also lost the second game to fall ten games behind New York in the pennant race.

Two days later, a friendly scuffle with Eppa Rixey nearly cost Bender the rest of his season. During the skirmish, Charley sustained a laceration when his arm went through a window pane. The Phillies' trainer bandaged the six-inch-long gash before Charles retired to his berth aboard a train taking the Phillies from New York to Boston. Bender awoke during the night in great pain, his arm swollen to twice its normal size. The episode was reported in various sources over the years, though the particulars vary somewhat from account to account. A reporter named Jack Smith recorded Bender's own recollection of the incident in 1942.[27]

"So I rolled out of my bunk and awakened Grover (Alexander)," Bender related during a wintry meeting of the hot stove league in Connie Mack's office. "I showed him the poisoning and offered him my knife. Old Pete said he wouldn't mind at all."

They sterilized the pocket knife in boiling water and applied a tourniquet. Alexander made an incision in the skin and drained the infected blood. For two hours the players kept the arm drained until Bender was able to see a doctor in Boston.

"Next day the doc told me he couldn't have done a better job himself," added Bender. "He said old Pete probably saved my life."[28] Less than three weeks after his injury, Charles was pitching again.

The incident was not picked up by the newspapers and the Phillies apparently did not offer an explanation for Bender's absence from the mound for three weeks. Charley returned to the mound on September 24 and pitched the first six innings in a 2–0 victory over the Pittsburgh Pirates. That same afternoon, Philadelphia was officially eliminated from the National League pennant race when McGraw's Giants defeated the Cardinals. Bender would make his final appearance in a major league game as a starting pitcher in St. Louis on September 30. After he allowed an unearned run in the first inning, the Chief threw scoreless ball through the sixth before he departed in favor of Rixey with the Phillies on top, 8–1.

During the 1917 campaign, Chief Bender showed signs of his former brilliance and put together a strong performance in what turned out to be his final season in the major leagues as an active player. Bender won eight games, lost only two, saved two others, and registered a 1.67 earned run average in 113 innings pitched. The Chief's August performance may well have been the best month of his career and was a remarkable effort for any pitcher. He had six consecutive victories, three by shutouts. During one stretch Bender pitched five times in six playing dates, twice for a full nine innings, which he won, and three times as a "rescue twirler."

Two weeks following the regular season, Bender picked up a tidy sum as a hired gun for a Pennsylvania town that hoped to win the championship of a semi-professional league. John Crozer, the backer of the Upland team in the Delaware County League, specifically recruited the famous hurler to pitch in the championship series against the town's biggest rival, Chester, Pennsylvania. Bender would once again be a teammate of Bris Lord, an Upland native who was the local team's center fielder.

In the end, Crozer's move didn't work out. In the deciding game of the five-game championship series on October 22, Bender was staked to a 3–0 lead in the top of the second inning. The Chester team chipped away at the lead and forged ahead when the eventual winning run raced home on an error by the Upland shortstop. Chester's "ringer," a star pitcher from Cuba named Oscar Tuero, came out on top in the duel with the great Chief Bender.[29]

During the 1917 baseball season, the Chief's former teammate of twelve seasons with the Athletics, Eddie Plank, hung up his glove for good. When Phil Ball acquired the St. Louis American League club after the Federal League folded, he transferred the Terrier players to the Browns. Eddie balked, claiming his lengthy tenure of service in the major leagues made him eligible for free agency. However, the National Commission disallowed Plank's request and the southpaw reported to the Browns. Eddie won sixteen games for St.

Louis in 1916, and, after losing an eleven-inning 1–0 game against Walter Johnson a year later, he quit baseball. Despite a 1.79 earned run average to that point in 1917, his record with the punchless Browns was only five wins against six losses. Eddie went home to Gettysburg with a record of 327 major league victories and did not again play professional baseball. In February 1926, Plank, one of baseball's greatest left-handed pitchers, suffered a stroke and died a short time later at his home.

The baseball fans of Philadelphia were stunned on November 11, 1917, when Phillies owner William F. Baker sold three-time thirty-game winner Grover Alexander and starting catcher Bill Killefer to the Cubs for two journeyman players and $60,000. The trio of Bender, Alexander and Eppa Rixey, who was lost to military service for the 1918 season, accounted for 54 of the second-place Phillies victories in 1917.

Chief Bender was one of several holdouts among the Phillies in the spring of 1918. Charley kept his arm in shape by pitching for semi-pro teams around Philadelphia in anticipation of returning to Moran's club. However, he could not come to terms with the club owner and just after the start of the regular season, Bender announced he would not return to the Phillies. The New York Yankees claimed the thirty-four-year-old pitcher off waivers, but gave up the rights after Bender declared he could not report to the club until after July 1.

Chief Bender pitched only one more inning in the major leagues after the 1917 season. Not including his post-season records, Charles Albert Bender finished his major league career with 212 wins against 127 losses, had 1,711 strikeouts, and posted a lifetime earned run average of 2.46. He appeared in 124 games in relief, winning 20 times and saving 36 others.

Though the entry of America into the World War had minimal effect on major league rosters in 1917, the impact of the war was significant a year later. In May 1918, the Provost Marshal, General Alvin Crowder, listed baseball among other "games, sports and amusements" that were nonessential to the war effort.

Charles Bender took a job in the shipyards because of the government's "work-or-fight order," a measure designed to force men with deferments into war-related occupations. It was said Bender tried to enlist in the Marine Corps but was sent back to the shipyard. Charles' younger brother Fred was already in Europe, having enlisted in the U.S. Army's machine gun corps in 1917.

In December 1918, Bender checked into a Philadelphia hospital, suffering from what was described as a "nervous breakdown." The reasons for the breakdown ranged from excessive hours and overwork to the illness of his wife.[30]

Charles lost a considerable amount of weight and the doctors told Bender he would be unable to return to work for three to four months, although he returned in a much shorter time. Just a few days after his release from the hospital, he appeared at a local gun club and "outscored many of the contestants."[31]

Charley claimed 1918 was the year he "found a cure" for the abdominal maladies that had plagued him for years. "I ran into a physician in Germantown who cured me for 25 cents," he later remarked. "He gave me soda mint tablets."[32]

Bender also attributed his job in war-related industries with improving his constitution. "I went to the shipyards and worked, pitching on Saturdays in Attleboro, Vermont, making $250 a game. It was tough work in the shipyards. I had charge of 23 men and swung a big sledge. It put me in great shape. I weighed 195 and was as hard as nails."[33]

Albert continued to pursue his alternate career in trap shooting. Bender joined several prominent Philadelphians with his membership in the prestigious Biedeman gun club on the eastern bank of the Delaware River. The trap house was supported by piers and extended into the river. The facility obviously impressed *Baseball Magazine*'s Samuel Long, who wrote, "The firing points are flanked on both sides by shade trees, but the unobstructed outlook up the Delaware River affords a perfect 'sky background' as the clay 'birds' go skimming over the water."[34]

In April 1919, the *New York Times* reported, "Charles Albert (Chief) Bender is possibly the best of the trap shooting ballplayers. During the off seasons Bender shoots on the Pennsylvania Railroad team in the Philadelphia Trapshooters' League and with the Biedeman Club of Camden, New Jersey. Bender is the only shooter who has broken 50 straight twice in a league series, and his average is about the best in the league."[35]

♦ 13 ♦

The Bush Leagues

In the days before baseball unions and pension plans, the end of a player's major league career did not necessarily mean his playing days were over. In the first half of the twentieth century, many an ex-major leaguer had a long minor league tenure after his days in the big leagues were done. Following his release from the New York Giants in 1908, "Iron Man" Joe McGinnity, owner of a 247-139 record in the majors, pitched for various minor league clubs through 1926, during which time he won another 207 games. Another Giants pitcher, Doc Crandall, who played against Bender in the 1911 and 1913 World Series, won 230 games and lost 151 in the Pacific Coast League after his ten-year major league career came to an end.

While working in the shipyard at Hogg Island in early 1919, thirty-five-year-old Charles Albert Bender became involved in negotiations with Cincinnati manager Pat Moran to pitch for the Reds when a more intriguing offer came his way. B. W. Wilson, president of the Class B Richmond Colts of the Virginia League, contacted Bender about managing and pitching for that club. After the Richmond team lost ten of its first fifteen games in the 1919 season, manager Frank Dobson was fired and Bender took over on May 29.[1] When he arrived in Richmond, the first-year manager found himself in charge of a young team with very little professional experience.

Without even having time to break in his uniform, Bender took the mound at Boulevard Field on his second day in the Virginia capital. The largest crowd to watch a Richmond baseball game to that time went home happy following the 8–4 victory by the Colts. Bender struck out eight Petersburg batters and gave up five hits, four of them in the eighth and ninth innings when the Goobers scored three of their four runs.[2]

The Chief took one day off then again defeated the Goobers in the first game of a Saturday doubleheader played before 3,000 fans. The *Richmond Times-Dispatch* exclaimed, "The big Redskin himself adorned the mound in the first encounter and toyed with the boys from across the way, allowing them only three singles, one of them a scratch."[3] On Monday, Bender's pinch-hit double drove home two runs to prevent a loss in a game that ended in a ten-inning deadlock. One day later, Charley got his third pitching victory in five games, a 2–0 shutout of the Suffolk team piloted by his old teammate Rube Oldring. After only six days in the Virginia capital, Bender had won three games and struck out twenty batters.

Bender's splendid work on the mound revived the city's interest in the team and was "bringing back to the ballpark hundreds of fans." The local scribes even began referring to the Richmond club as the "Indians" because of Bender.[4]

The Virginia League's thirteen-player limit for each team made it essential for Bender to take an occasional turn in the field. On June 13, the Colts manager put himself in left field for the game against the Truckers of Portsmouth and, in the second inning, Bender drove a pitch out of Boulevard Field for a home run. In the ninth inning, with two enemy runners on base and one out, the Chief took over the pitching duties and retired the final two batters to preserve a 7–6 Richmond victory.[5] The next day, "Big Chief hurled masterly" to persevere in a 3–2 Richmond win.

The streaking "Indians" were derailed on June 25 when Umpire Schaffer forfeited their game with Petersburg after Charles protested a play at second with Richmond leading, 1–0. Bender walked off the field, and after the umpire waited the allotted time for him to return to the mound, the game was forfeited to Petersburg.[6]

On July 12 Bender's team was down by a run to Suffolk when Richmond came to bat in the final frame. A runner was on base when Bender came to bat in the bottom of the ninth inning. The *Times-Dispatch* described the climatic end to the game.

"The Chief lifted one of Eckert's offerings far over the left field fence and trotted home behind Poole, who had doubled, bringing the contest to a close with the score board showing a tally of 8 to 7. Almost 3,000 enthusiastic fans rewarded Bender with the greatest ovation he has thus far received in Richmond and with three hats full of silver and currency gathered from the grand stand."[7]

Chief Bender won the first nine Virginia League games he pitched and then suffered his first loss to Oldring's Suffolk team, with Rube driving in the deciding tally. Bender would lose only one other game that season.

Several years later, Jim "Easy" Poole, a former major league first baseman who was the Colts' top hitter in 1919, related several stories about his time playing for Bender:

> This Chief was a funny kind of a fellow, but he was a good player. He used to go in about the eighth inning many a time and save the ball game for us. He'd stay in the clubhouse smoking cigarettes and come out about the seventh inning, look around and say, "Well, boys, how are you getting along?"

When we'd tell him that things weren't going so well, Chief would throw away a cigarette, trot out to the mound and win the ball game.

And Chief could play everything on the team. Once the center fielder got knocked out when we were playing in Norfolk. So Chief went out to take his place. The Norfolk outfield had grass growing in it about knee high. Chief went out there and lay down in the grass, and we couldn't see him from home plate. And he wouldn't get up. There were two or three balls knocked out there and the other fielders had to run their legs off to get over and catch them. Then Chief would get up, clap his hands and yell, "Atta boy! That's the way to play ball." But we went out and won the pennant, and Chief won lots of ball games. He kept the club going because he was always doing something that would relieve the tension and get the boys going well.[8]

The Virginia League used a split-season format in order to retain the interest of the fans for clubs that were hopelessly out of the championship race by mid-season. The clean slate gave the Indians a new lease on life, but Richmond's second-half record stood at only three wins and seven losses when Manager Bender took the mound against Petersburg at Boulevard Field on July 24. The Goobers loaded the bases in the first on three singles, but Charley struck out the next batter and got the third out on an infield grounder. At the end of nine innings, the contest was tied at one. The two teams plunged into extra innings with each team's pitcher going the route. Bender's Indians won the game in the bottom of the sixteenth on a throwing error by the opposing pitcher.[9] Bender took a day off and then went out and pitched Richmond to a 3–2 victory in the first game of a doubleheader sweep on Saturday.

On the final day of July, the Colts played a doubleheader at their home park against Portsmouth. After pitching the first-game victory, Bender relieved his second-game pitcher in the tenth inning. However, it appeared things would not go Richmond's way when the Truckers scored two runs off the Chief in the top of the twelfth. After the first Colt batter fanned in the bottom of the inning, many of the fans started for the exits. However, a walk to Bender and an infield hit caused them to pause. Another walk loaded the bases, and when Daughton drove a triple to deep right field, the bases were cleared and Richmond had the sweep. Richmond won again the next day to bring its record to 10 wins and 10 losses. Another doubleheader sweep on August 2 pulled the Colts into first place. Bender pitched a 4–0 shutout, struck out nine batters and walked no one in game one. The Chief contributed to the 4–3 second-game victory with a key pinch-hit single in a two-run ninth. The baseball fans of Richmond scheduled a special "Bender Day" the following Thursday to honor their manager and star pitcher.

After 3,000 enthusiastic fans gave Bender a rousing ovation at the conclusion of the "Bender Day" exercises, Charles took the mound and lost for only the second time in a Virginia League game. In their 5–2 victory, the Norfolk Tars bunched their hits in the second and fifth innings. "The left field fence was literally peppered with the swats of the Tars," noted the Richmond newspaper, "at least three of the hits rolling to the limit of the grounds before they could be fielded."[10]

Bender redeemed himself by throwing a shutout at Norfolk in the first game of a doubleheader at Boulevard Field on August 9. In fifth inning of the nightcap, "Bender created some surprise and enthusiasm when he took over Moran's place in the batting order in the home half," noted the *Times-Dispatch*. "But when he tripled to center he created real love in the hearts of the fans."[11]

Because Moran had to depart because of illness, the manager took over his place in left field when the teams switched sides for the top of the next inning. In the seventh, left fielder Bender "smashed a homer over the left field pickets." Norfolk tied the game on a home run of their own in the eighth, but Poole brought the home team victory with a run-producing double in the ninth inning.

At Newport News on August 11, Chief Bender pitched and won two complete games against the Shipbuilders, with whom the Colts were tied for first place. Bender protested the first game in the eighth inning. While the Newport News pitcher was warming up, Bender hit his toss for a triple. Umpire Larogue ordered the Chief to bat again because the umpire was "not ready" and the Builders' catcher was in the process of putting on his chest protector.[12] Ultimately, it did not matter as the "Indians" scored two runs to win the game, 2–1. Bender won the second game, 2–0, on a two-hitter.

In the stands that afternoon was a scout named Eugene McCann, dispatched by Manager Moran of Cincinnati. McCann tried to convince Bender to sign a contract to pitch with the first-place Reds right away, but the Chief declined. A few days later, the wire services distributed a story that Bender would join the National League club as soon as the Virginia League season ended on September 6. However, Bender would not be eligible for the World Series if he was not with the Cincinnati team by September 1.[13]

On August 16, Richmond and Newport News went at it again, this time with a substitute Colts infielder named O'Brien as the umpire after the two assigned arbiters failed to show up. "In the second inning," wrote the Richmond newspaper, "Fagan, who was cast off by the Indians, was pitching for the Builders and developed a streak of wildness, and one of his curves failed to break at the proper time and hit Chief Bender on the head. The Chippewa rolled over on the ground, but quickly recovered. He made a lunge for a bat with an attempt to attack Fagan, but the players of both teams restrained him, and the Chief cooled off and went to first without aid."[14] Despite the mishap, it was reported that Bender "had child's play with the Newport News' hitters." The Chief retired the first twelve men he faced and won easily, 6–1.

"Richmond fans are just awakening to a realization how hard the Chief has exerted himself to win ball games and put the club out front in the Virginia League race, and the high esteem in which they hold him is increasing every day," opined the *Post-Dispatch*. "Sport followers, looking back in later years over the baseball season of 1919, will recall how Bender pulled the club out of the hole in great style and put Richmond on the baseball map."

The same article put to rest the rumor that Bender would join the Cincinnati Reds at the end of the Virginia League season. The newspaper also reported, "He also declares that he has no idea of becoming manager of the New Haven club."[15]

On August 24 the large crowd at Richmond's ballpark overflowed onto the field until policeman forced them back into the stands. Bender won his twenty-fifth game with a 10–4 rout of the Suffolk team. The next day he came back with a 3–0 shutout in Norfolk despite a twenty-minute rain delay in the second inning. By this time the outcome of the second-half championship was a foregone conclusion. Bender's Indians finished with a 40–19 record, seven and a half games ahead of second-place Norfolk.

Richmond easily won the second half title despite having only one batter to hit over .300. On the mound, Bender proved to still be a durable hurler, pitching a league-high 280 innings while posting 29 victories against only two defeats. He led the Virginia League in strikeouts with 195 and had a minuscule earned run average of 1.06. He later called that season at Richmond his finest achievement in baseball.[16] Bender couldn't do it all alone, though, and the addition of Lefty Magalis (ten wins out of twelve decisions) at mid-season gave the pitching staff the impetus it needed for the pennant run.

There was supposed to be a seven-game championship series between Richmond and the first-half champion, Petersburg. However, the two clubs couldn't agree on the financial arrangements which, combined with a threatened strike by the Goobers, doomed the playoff. After splitting a couple of games with local amateur teams, the Colts/Indians disbanded.

The last Richmond saw of Chief Bender was on September 11, 1919, when he and Marie left for Philadelphia in their new roadster, purchased largely from the fund donated by Richmond fans in appreciation of his services. It was reported that Owner Wilson and other moneyed supporters of the club made up the difference.[17]

About his success that season, Bender once said, "I didn't have more stuff in 1919 than in 1905. I knew how to pitch and those minor leaguers didn't get one where they could bust it. I used to chuckle when I heard them say: 'Why, that fellow Bender never gives you a good ball to hit at.'"[18]

By early September, Pat Moran's Cincinnati club had a significant lead in the pennant race and was the prospective representative of the National League in the 1919 World Series. Moran asked Bender to be his bench coach during the Series to provide the Reds with information on the batting tendencies of the opposing Chicago batters, against whom the Chief had played. It was no secret that Charley was in the employ of the Reds when the first-place White Sox paid a visit to Philadelphia to play the Athletics on September 12. Bender not only scouted the American Leaguers during the series at Shibe Park, he even threw batting practice to the Sox hitters.[19]

The Reds' plan to use Bender as a special coach was nearly side-tracked when he suffered a left ankle injury while pitching for Millville in a semi-pro contest at Vineland, New Jersey. When Charley returned home to Philadelphia, he was cared for by his wife, who had broken her arm only three days earlier. However, he was on the bench when time came for the World Series opener in Cincinnati on October 1.

After the Reds beat Chicago in the Series, Bender was said to have abetted the National Leaguers victory by stealing signals. None other than Christy Mathewson came to the defense of his old foe.

Matty, who was serving as a special correspondent for the Series, said, "Bender is a student of baseball and a deeper student than many fans and writers are willing to admit. His presence on the bench or the coaching lines would naturally mean much to a ball club, for I have never met a player who could grasp situations as quickly as the Indian. Because he does grasp situations quickly however, it does not follow that he should be catalogued as a sharpshooter, nor should his motives be impugned until it is proven that he does actually steal signals."[20]

After only one season in Richmond, Bender moved to a higher classification minor league when he signed to pitch and manage at New Haven, Connecticut, (Eastern League) for the 1920 season. In 1919 the Eastern League moved up a classification to Class A, and the New Haven squad, now owned by local entrepreneur George Weiss, became known as the Weissmen. On July 24, 1920, Weiss dedicated a new stadium he called Weiss Park, located in an area bounded by Woodin, Murray, Helen, and Notkins streets in Hamden.[21]

"I went to New Haven as pitcher-manager for $8,500," recalled Charles in 1942. "I'll bet it was the highest salary George Weiss, owner of New Haven, now manager of the Yankee farm system, ever paid an Eastern Leaguer."[22]

Though Bender's best player at New Haven was outfielder Neal Ball, the Chief's most successful recruit was twenty-year-old catcher James Wilson, a semi-pro player from Philadelphia who was signed after a tip from Connie Mack. After three seasons at New Haven, Wilson went to the Philadelphia Phillies and spent the next eighteen seasons in the major leagues.

Chief Bender pitched his first game for the Weissmen on May 6 and lost a 1–0 decision to Waterbury's Herb McQuade. However, the veteran's performance was a harbinger of what was to come for the opposition during that season. In the first game of a Memorial Day doubleheader, Charley pitched New Haven into first place with a 6–2 victory over defending champion Bridgeport. Bender's Tribe went out and solidified their hold on the top spot with a 6–4 win over former White Sox star Ed Walsh that afternoon. Just one week to the day later, Bender struck out eleven Bridgeport batters while beating the Moosers, 8–3. However, Manager Walsh's Bridgeport club took the next two games to move within a half-game of first-place New Haven. Walsh pitched the 4–0 victory in the third game of the series.

Bender took the mound for the fourth and final game of the set at Bridgeport's Newfield Park on June 10. The Chief not only took a 4–0 lead into the ninth inning, he had not allowed a base hit. Charles retired the first two batters and then Ed Walsh strode to the plate, pinch-hitting for the Bridgeport pitcher.

Bender was a frequent after-dinner speaker in his later years and he liked to tell the story about Ed Walsh ruining his no-hitter. "He went in to pinch-hit in the ninth. I got two strikes on him then cut loose a duster. Walsh ducked, the ball hit his bat and sailed out as a high fly into left. Earl Stimpson, our left fielder, could have made the catch easily, but (he) stumbled, fell and the ball landed for a hit."[23]

Bridgeport's next batter singled to ruin Bender's shutout, though he went on to retire the side for a 4–1 victory. Later that season, the Chief would get another shot at Bridgeport.

With the hometown New Haven fans urging him on, Bender was almost perfect against the Moosers in the game of August 19. Charles allowed only one base runner, who reached on a walk and was immediately cut down when he tried to steal second. Though the Chief mowed the opposition down inning after inning, the outcome was in doubt for much of the contest. The Bridgeport pitcher also threw shutout baseball until New Haven broke through in the seventh with the first of their three runs. As in the earlier game, pinch-hitter Ed Walsh was the final batter Bender had to retire for a no-hitter. This time, though, it was the big Chippewa who was the master as Walsh "went out meekly."[24]

Bender's team went on to capture the 1920 Eastern League pennant with a 79-61 record, four games ahead of second-place Springfield, and on September 26 the Weissmen defeated the Boston Red Sox in an exhibition game in New Haven. Bender started on the mound for his club, but it did not appear that he would be around long when the Red Sox built a 9–0 lead after two innings. After that, Bender blanked the Bostons inning after inning while New Haven chipped away at the lead against three Red Sox pitchers. New Haven tied it in the ninth on Frank McGowan's home run and won it with a run in the thirteenth. After he was tagged for seven runs in the second inning, Bender pitched eleven scoreless innings against the major leaguers to gain the victory, 10–9.[25]

During his major league career, Bender was not perceived as a durable hurler, but after pitching in 34 games in only three months for Richmond a year earlier, the Chief threw 238 innings and won 22 games for the Weissmen. Several of the wins came in relief appearances between his regular turns on the mound. Besides his no-hitter, Bender had three two-hit victories, two four-hit wins and five five-hitters. He threw seven shutouts, had a twelve-game winning streak, pitched and won two doubleheaders and once secured victories on three consecutive days.[26]

When asked how he was able to pitch all those innings, Bender replied, "My arm feels fine this year, as good as it ever has felt. As a matter of fact, my arm never went back on me. I had stomach trouble for about two years, but it is all right now."

About keeping his arm in condition, the veteran hurler said, "I don't overwork it. I give it all the rest it needs. That's one of the reasons that pitchers spoil their arms. They overwork them. And in the winter months I give my arm a complete rest from baseball. Many pitchers tire their arms out by pitching in the winter."[27]

Following the 1920 baseball season, Bender accepted a position to manage the gun and ammunition department at the Winchester store in New Haven. Of course, he remained active in events staged by the New Haven Gun Club and also set aside time to coach the Yale University Gun Club. He became a member of the Winchester trap shooting team that toured the New England states that fall.

Following his managerial success in the minor leagues, Bender received opportunities to return to the major leagues as a coach, but he chose to stay at New Haven. As he told some friends, "I have had enough of the majors in my time. I sort of like this minor league stuff, helping the youngsters to get to the top. It's interesting to see them develop and it gives me a lot of satisfaction to be able to tell them of some of the finer points of the game."[28]

As part of his deal to remain in New Haven as manager and pitcher, Bender became a minority stockholder in the club along with the likes of Ty Cobb and Walter Johnson.[29] Charles and Marie sold their home on Judson Street in Philadelphia and established residence in New Haven.[30]

In 1921 the New Haven team was renamed "Indians" in honor of their star pitcher and manager. Bender posted a pitching record of 13–7 in his second season in Connecticut, but his club fell to fourth place in the final standings. Weiss and Bender were unable to secure replacements of the caliber of those players lost from the 1920 champions.

As a pitcher, Bender started out the season okay, getting three complete game wins in May, including a 4–3 victory over Worcester in which he hit a triple and a home run. After that first month, Charley often struggled, partly due to the shoddy defense behind him. He did have his highlights and posted a league-low 1.93 earned run average.[31] On July 9 Bender beat Hartford, 2–0, and on September 9, he shut out the Whalers again, despite walking six batters.

Other than himself and Frank Woodward, Bender had no depth in his pitching staff, and only Ball and catcher Wilson were batting anywhere near .300. In late July, he brought in his old friend Rube Oldring to improve the club's batting woes, but his team was never able to make a serious run for the pennant.

Bender's frustrations reached the boiling point that August. Outfielder Red McHugh, one of the team's best hitters, abruptly quit the team about the same time Charley suffered a meltdown during a game he pitched against Worchester on August 22. The contest had gone into the thirteenth inning with the score tied at three when Bender cost the Indians the game with two bad throws to first base. The frustrated pitcher rebuked his first baseman, but when he found the young collegian up to the challenge, Charley backed down.[32] A few days later, Jerry Kahn of Waterbury pitched a 5–0 shutout against New Haven, during which he did not allow a hit until two were out in the ninth inning when Ball's short fly fell safely among a crowd of waiting fielders.

The Indians' Frank Woodward pitched a no-hitter against Waterbury on August 31 to run his record to 23 victories against eight defeats. Since the club was already out of the pennant picture, George Weiss sold the New Haven ace to the Washington Senators.

On September 3, Manager Bender found himself without a second baseman for a doubleheader in Waterbury so he assumed the infield position for the entirety of both games. The Chief pitched in his final game for the New Haven Indians on September 22, 1921, and departed after only two innings with his club down, 3–0.

Though the Indians finished nine games above .500, Bender announced his resignation as manager following the season. In addition to his dissatisfaction with the team's performance, Bender was disappointed that the fans turned on the team when it began losing. Furthermore, his relationship with management had turned sour during the course of the season.

Bender's success in New Haven earned him a job in the International League for 1922. Meantime, the New Haven Indians captured another Eastern League championship under the management of Bender's former Detroit Tigers foe, Wild Bill Donovan, and then won the first-ever "junior world's series." In 1923 the New Haven club's nickname was again changed, this time to the "Profs." Donovan was killed in a train wreck on December 9, 1923, while on a business trip for the New Haven club.[33]

In 1922 Charles Bender became the fifth manager in four years for the Reading, Pennsylvania, International League club, and the Aces required a major overhaul just to field a competitive team. The Chief had a couple of ex-major league veterans he could count on—catcher Nig Clarke and outfielder Frank Gilhooley, a former New York Yankee whose .361 average would be the highest among International League batters with more than 400 at-bats. Bender's club got off to a good start in the spring, winning its first five exhibition games against minor league teams before losing to the Philadelphia Phillies, 2–1. Bender pitched the final two innings against the National Leaguers, striking out four of the six batters he faced.

On May 22 Bender displayed his old major league form on the mound at Syracuse when he and former Detroit Tigers hurler Jean Dubuc battled fourteen innings in one of the best minor league games of the decade. Before nearly 6,000 Syracuse fans, Dubuc set the visiting Aces down without a hit through eight innings. In addition, the hometown pitcher scored the runs that gave Syracuse its 2–0 lead by the time Reading came to bat in the ninth. Dubuc retired the first batter before Chief Bender strode to the batter's box.

Bender was known to banter with the opposition and this occasion was no different. "Great game so far, old boy," he shouted to his opposing number.

Dubuc grooved a fat pitch that Bender met with solid wood to send the ball on a line toward first base. Jim Bottomley managed to knock it down, but he had no chance to make a play on Charley. Although Bottomley yelled to reporters that he should be charged with an error, it was a clean single and Dubuc had lost his no-hitter. A double, an infield out, and a single later, the game was tied. Bender retired the side in the bottom of the frame and the game plunged into extra innings. The two veterans continued to pitch scoreless baseball through the top of the fourteenth inning.

Bender sat down the first two batters he faced in the fatal fourteenth then Dubuc came up to bat. Catcher Nig Clarke made the remark that the "kids" were out of luck. Dubuc laughed, and Bender reportedly chimed in with the comment, "I'm getting tired, how about you?"[34]

The *Syracuse Herald* reported that Dubuc swung so hard at Bender's first pitch that "the force of his swing carried him twice around and several steps toward first base." The batter stayed alive by fouling off a 2–2 pitch and then took a third ball.

The Chief's next pitch sailed into the danger zone just about even with the "S" on the Frenchman's shirt. Dubuc put all his force behind his swing and moments later the ball cleared the left field fence about ten feet inside of the foul line. Bender never turned his head to look and was already headed to the clubhouse when the ball sailed over the fence.

"I'll never forget the sound of that hit," Bender remarked a couple of years later. "There was a ball that was kissed. Size of the ballpark didn't mean a thing. That one would have been a home run in Gobi desert."[35]

The *Herald* editorialized that "the best game Syracuse fans have ever known in an International League contest was chalked down as a victory for Syracuse."[36]

Bender was just as sharp ten days later when he pitched a three-hit shutout against the Newark Bears. In his 2–0 masterpiece, Charley faced only twenty-nine batters, retiring the first seventeen in order, and he walked no one.

Later that month, Bender took the mound for the morning half of the Memorial Day doubleheader before 7,000 fans in Reading. Opposing him was the Baltimore Orioles twenty-two-year-old left-handed phenom named "Groves." Groves was wild, walking five batters in only two and a third innings of work. Though Bender said he was suffering from a slight case of tonsillitis, the Chief polished off the eventual 1922 International League champions, 6–1.[37]

The presence of Chief Bender on the bench and in the field caused an early-season spike in attendance at the Aces' games. The *Sporting News* wrote in early June that Bender "was the idol of the Reading populace" and by the end of the month the Aces were said to have drawn 4,000 more fans to watch them play than for the entire season of 1921.[38] However, the owners of the club were concerned.

Just a month later the same publication reported that "Charles Albert Bender is costing the backers of the Reading club a mint of money through changes in his team. Scarcely a day passes that does not record the bringing on of a new player and the release of one or several, and the new ones come from every neck of the woods regardless of transportation costs. That Reading club must have had 60 ballplayers on its roster so far.... Most of the men tried out had small chance to ever make good in a Class AA league."[39]

Among those going through Bender's revolving door were the ex–Senators clown/pitcher Al Schacht; teenage outfielder Floyd "Babe" Herman, who spent spring training with the Detroit Tigers; and Bill Barrett, an A's castoff who would begin an eight-season career in the American League a year after his Reading experience.

Pitcher Bender was sidelined much of the summer due to an injured hand and he posted only eight mound victories against thirteen losses for the season. However, his earned run average of 2.41 was the second-best mark in the International League. Reading finished in sixth place, which wasn't good enough to please the club's directors and Bender was not asked to return for 1923. The *Sporting News* surmised, "Bender was peerless leader again at Reading, had no team to speak of, (and) a board of directors willing to tell him when his men should and shouldn't sacrifice."[40]

Charles worked for an arms manufacturing company during the winter and in mid–March 1923, the Chief went to Annapolis, Maryland, where he would coach the pitchers on the United States Naval Academy's baseball team. On May 22, Middies head coach Victor Blakeslee was riding on the running board of a car when he was struck by a trolley and suffered a serious injury. Bender and another coach guided the Midshipmen through the remainder of the college baseball season.[41]

On May 28, the Washington Senators traveled to Annapolis for an exhibition game with the Midshipmen. The major leaguers built up a sizable lead and in the eighth inning Senators clown/coach Nick Altrock went in to pitch. Not to be outdone, Navy coach Chief Bender took the mound for the collegians. The Senators' sluggers showed no mercy for the rusty ex–Athletics star and scored six runs off his slants in the top of the ninth.[42]

Despite his poor performance against the Senators, Bender still felt he could be an effective pitcher in the professional ranks and listened to offers at the conclusion of the college baseball season. One offer that came his way was from one of the best baseball teams in the country, the Baltimore Orioles of the International League.

The 1920s were the "golden age" of minor league baseball in the United States, largely because of a 1919 dispute with the majors that led the minors to pull out of the National Agreement that governed Organized Baseball. Two

From left to right: Danny Murphy, Philadelphia Athletics coach; Joe Bush, New York Yankees; Chief Bender; and Bob Shawkey, New York Yankees, 1923 (George Grantham Bain Collection, Library of Congress).

years later, the minors rejoined Organized Baseball, but under the new agreement a minor league could choose to be exempt from the major leagues' draft of its players if that minor league's clubs relinquished their right to draft players from lower classified leagues. Though baseball commissioner Kenesaw Landis and the majors unilaterally scraped the new agreement and restored the draft, the International League held out until the end of 1924 when it agreed to a restricted draft.[43]

Astute owners like Jack Dunn in Baltimore were able to purchase major league quality talent, assemble strong teams, and occasionally sell a player to the major leagues at a large profit. Professor Harold Seymour wrote in his landmark *Baseball: The Golden Age* that Dunn realized nearly a million dollars in the 1920s from player sales. Since Dunn could not lose players to the major league draft, three important cogs in the Orioles lineup — pitcher Moses "Lefty" Grove, second baseman Max Bishop, and shortstop Joe Boley — remained in Baltimore from 1920 through 1923 as the club won 117, 119, 115 and 111 games over that period of four years.

In early June 1923 six straight losses by the Orioles caused owner/manager Dunn to become concerned that his club was falling too far behind in the standings to a strong Rochester team. When Dunn rejoined the Orioles following an absence due to the death of his son, one of the manager's first priorities was to find pitching help.

Chief Bender answered Dunn's summons, but took his time reporting to Baltimore and, upon his arrival, he was not in shape to pitch. Dunn was thinking both about the gate and the pennant when he decided to use Bender only on special occasions. The Chief found himself in familiar surroundings. Oriole Park was where Charley played during his one season with the Baltimore Terrapins. After the Federal League folded, Jack Dunn purchased Terrapin Park for $25,000 and it was home to the International League Orioles until it succumbed to fire in the 1940s.

Rochester eventually slipped in the standings and the Orioles moved into first place on June 20. Baltimore's new position atop the International League standings was quickly challenged in a key four-game series with second-place Rochester, starting June 23. After Moses "Lefty" Grove (the "Groves" Bender had pitched against and beat in 1922) lost the first game, Dunn selected thirty-nine-year-old Charley Bender to oppose Jack Wisner the next day.

The match between the rusty Chippewa and Rochester's best pitcher appeared to be a mismatch, but the Orioles' batters drove Wisner from the mound after only three innings and his veteran opponent went the distance. Bender allowed thirteen hits and won the contest, 13–6. Three of Rochester's runs came in the ninth inning against a tiring pitcher and after the verdict was assured. Baltimore won the next two games and maintained control of the pennant race thereafter.[44] Though the Tribe eventually won 101 games, Rochester never quite recovered from its mid-summer bad stretch.

While in Baltimore, Bender was a teammate of another eccentric hurler nicknamed Rube. The difference was this Rube was right-handed. Pennsylvania country boy James Arthur "Rube" Parnham pitched parts of the 1916 and 1917 seasons with the Philadelphia Athletics before he was released to Baltimore. In 1919 he won 28 games for Jack Dunn, then after a 5–0 start the following season, he jumped the club to pitch in an industrial league in Pennsylvania. Rube returned to the Orioles in 1922.

The *Sporting News* reported in July 1923 "Rube Parnham of the Baltimore Orioles went on another rampage last week and Jack Dunn again declared he was done with him, star though he may be. Parnham blamed Otis Lawry for failure to make a play and took a punch at the little fellow, who is about one-half the pitcher's size. Dunn suspended him on the spot and fined him $250. In a week's time, Rube was in there pitching as usual."[45]

Parnham had won eighteen straight games when he abruptly jumped the team with only one week left in the 1923 season. Rube showed up at the park on the final day of the regular season to pitch and won both games of a doubleheader against Jersey City to run his consecutive win streak to twenty.

Chief Bender pitched his last complete game in the International League on September 12, 1923, when he defeated his old club from Reading, 16–1. The Chief won six and lost three with the Orioles. Still a good hitter, the veteran batted .314 in 35 plate appearances and included a home run among his base knocks.

The Orioles won 111 games, lost only 53, and easily captured the International League championship. Future Hall of Fame flame-thrower Lefty Grove went 27–10 and set an International League record with 330 strikeouts. Parnham won 33 games, lost only seven, and set a twentieth century International League record for the most consecutive victories with twenty.

While Baltimore waited for the American Association season to conclude before the team would engage the Kansas City Blues in the Junior World Series, the Orioles played in several exhibition games. Three of the games came against the eventual participates in the 1923 World Series. After defeating the National League champion New York Giants, 4–3, in ten innings at Orioles Park, the Birds proceeded to whip the American League champion New York Yankees twice the following week. On October 2, three Baltimore pitchers shut out the Yankees, 4–0, in the second contest between the two clubs. After Grove threw hitless ball in his three innings against the champions, Bender came in to pitch and he too blanked the New Yorkers for three frames. However, the Chief did not finally get a chance to pitch to Babe Ruth, as the Bambino left after the first inning to rest his injured ankle.

After a day off, the Orioles played two games against Hartford, the Eastern League champions. Dunn felt the games were a no-win proposition for his club, but went forward because he had made the commitment. The Orioles went on to lose both games in Hartford.

The Orioles' magnificent 1923 season would end on a negative note when they lost the Junior World Series to the American Association champion Kansas City Blues, five games to four. Bender was not called upon to pitch during the series though he did warm up prior to a game that was ultimately started by Parnham. While the Chief stewed on the bench because Dunn was not using him in the series, the Orioles fell behind four games to three. In the eighth inning of the game on October 22, Bender created a disturbance when he went after a man in the stands who apparently was abusive toward the idle pitcher.[46]

That evening Bender and the Orioles' catcher that day, Lena Styles, had several drinks before they showed up at a banquet honoring the players that was attended by the Baltimore mayor, the city council and representatives of the other International League clubs. Newspaper reports indicated that both players had been drinking heavily and "made nuisances of themselves." Styles, it was said, was so drunk and unruly he had to be escorted from the hall.

Although Bender probably didn't figure in Baltimore's plans for 1924, Manager Dunn announced the indefinite suspension of Charles as well as Styles. Dunn also said the pair would be fined part of the money due them for their participation in the games against the New York clubs, Hartford, and the Junior World Series.

"I don't want these players ever to enter my park again," said an angry Jack Dunn. "They were the guests of the city and thirteen clubs, and according to reports which I have no reason to doubt, they were in an awful condition."[47]

Following the Naval Academy's 1924 baseball season, Bender returned to his old New Haven club to pitch for new manager Clyde Milan. The Chief made his return to the mound after only one day with the team in an Eastern League game against Waterbury on July 4. Bender threw six shutout innings, but after Waterbury scored two runs, he left for a pinch-hitter and New Haven lost the game in the eighth, 4–3. Bender posted a 6–4 record in the twelve games he pitched for the Profs.

A year later an old friend from the Athletics would bring Bender back to the major leagues for the first time since the 1919 World Series. Though he would return to the major leagues as a coach, Charles Albert Bender would continue to coach the U.S. Naval Academy baseball team for another four years.

In 1925 Eddie Collins, newly appointed manager of the Chicago White Sox, offered former teammate Charles Bender the job of pitching coach. Upon completion of his duties for the Naval Academy, Chief Bender returned to the major leagues on June 12. Charley's first challenge was to teach the White Sox hurlers how to throw a pitch known as the change-of-pace.

The new Chicago pitching coach also had plenty to say about the current state of the game in which batters had become the driving force as compared to the pitching-dominated era in which Bender played. "I guess they give all of their attention to the boys who are batting and are forgetting entirely about the development of pitchers," he said soon after joining the White Sox. "But taking batters a whole, bunching the entire lot, the pitcher who specializes on a low ball or a high ball will be successful....

"When I started pitching, I didn't need a college course to convince (me) that a batter could not get a solid wallop at a ball on the edge of the shoulder line.... Pitchers who feature curves should pick on the spot around the knees."[48]

As he watched the current stock of hurlers in the American League, the old Chief got the idea that he still had enough stuff to get major league hitters out. He was added to the Pale Hose roster just before a doubleheader at Comiskey Park against the Boston Red Sox on July 21. The Sox were down,

Chief Bender, as a coach of the Chicago White Sox, and umpire Harry Giesel, 1925 (Paul Thompson, photographer, Library of Congress).

4–3, in the first game when pitcher Sarge Connally, who had succeeded Red Faber, was pinch-hit for in the bottom of the eighth inning.

Bender walked to the mound for the start of the visitors' ninth amid cheers from the Chicago crowd. The Chief started off by walking the first man he faced then retired the next two batters. His return to the major leagues as a pitcher was ruined when he tried to sneak a fastball past Roy Carlyle and the Boston outfielder sent the ball on a long ride that ended in the top row of the right field bleachers. The forty-one-year-old pitching coach was able to retire the side, but he would not pitch in another major league game.[49]

Two days after his appearance in the official American League game, Bender took the mound again. The White Sox were thrashing the opposition in an exhibition game in Battle Creek, Michigan, when the fans began to chant for the Chief. They got their wish as Bender pitched the final three innings of the big leaguers' 8–1 victory. A week later, Charley did not do so well in Saginaw, where he gave up four hits and two runs at the end of Chicago's 4–3 victory.

The White Sox had not recovered from the effects of the "Black Sox" scandal of 1920 and finished fifth, although they were four games above .500.

With essentially the same pitching staff as in 1924, the White Sox hurlers posted a collective earned run average of 4.34, better than their American League–worst of 4.75 the previous year. Ted Lyons' record improved from a won-lost mark of 12–11 with a 4.87 ERA in '24 to 21–11 and 3.26. Ted Blankenship's 1925 record was 17–8 and 3.16, a substantial improvement from the 7–6 record and 5.17 earned run average of the previous season.

Bender could not return to the White Sox in 1926 until June 1 because of his commitment to the Naval Academy baseball team, but during spring training Eddie Collins gave his pitching coach all the credit for the remarkable progress made by Lyons and Blankenship in 1925. He added, "I regard Chief Bender as the smartest pitcher I have ever seen in action

Chief Bender, Chicago White Sox coach, 1924–1925 (National Baseball Hall of Fame Library, Cooperstown, New York).

during my major league career. I played with Bender on the Philadelphia Athletics when he was in his prime. I never saw him make a dumb move."[50]

After two fifth-place finishes, Eddie Collins was dismissed as manager of the White Sox on December 11, 1926. Two days later, new manager Ray Schalk hired Frank Roth as pitching coach, which spelled the end of the Chief's service with the club.

Bender was not without a baseball job for long after the 1927 college baseball season. President Harry Meehan of the Johnstown, Pennsylvania, club hired Bender to replace Babe Adams, who had just resigned as manager of the defending Middle Atlantic League champions. Bender assumed control of the club in Cumberland on Monday, June 9. Two days later, the Johnnies lost a doubleheader to Charleroi, during which Charley had to break up a fight between his catcher and first baseman after they collided while going after a pop fly. As he had done at Reading and New Haven, Bender cut several players and brought in new ones in an attempt to resurrect a faltering club. Among the six players released during Bender's purge in mid–July was pitcher Jimmy Devine, who had been with the Johnnies for two years.

With his hapless club in last place with a 9–25 record, Manager Bender decided to shake things up by pitching the game in Jeannette on June 20. The forty-three-year-old pitcher not only beat Jeanette's best pitcher, Chief Williams, he lost a no-hitter when his right fielder slipped in the mud to allow a fly ball to go for the only hit. The Jays managed only one other base runner, who reached on an error by Bender's first baseman.[51]

Next day, the Johnnies were shut out by the Jays' Elmer Knetzer, an ex-major league pitcher, but Bender's personnel moves soon began to pay off. By the end of the season's first half, the Johnnies had improved to 22 wins, 34 losses and got a new beginning with the start of the second half on July 7. One of Bender's new recruits was Frank Mottey, who had been coaching athletics at St. John's University. On July 14 the *Sporting News* reported that Mottey "is now regarded as one of the most dangerous hitters in the Middle Atlantic League and has shown unusual ability as a fielder, being the possessor of a fine throwing arm and having plenty of speed."[52] Motley would bat .347 in 48 games with the Johnnies.

Johnstown won the second half M. A. L. championship by three and a half games over second-place Scottdale. Manager Bender's pitching record was 7–3 with a masterful 1.33 earned run average that led the league. Furthermore, the Johnstown club drew record crowds both at home and on the road whenever Chief Bender took the mound. In opposition ballparks, however, even a venerated star like Chief Bender was not immune from hazing by the opposing fans.

During a game in Fairmont that August, Bender was constantly roasted by the local fans. In the final game of the series, a man procured a large megaphone and screamed insults at Bender from the bleachers. The Johnstown manager appealed to the umpire but the verbal abuse continued. In protest, Bender ordered his players to remain on the bench at the start of an inning. The umpire threatened to forfeit the game if the Johnnies did not take the field within five minutes, but one of the directors of the Fairmont club persuaded the fan to give up the megaphone.[53]

The season ended on a sour note as the Johnnies lost the post-season series to the first-half winners, the Cumberland Colts, four games to two. Bender pitched the opener of the series and lost, 5–3. The winning hurler for the Colts was Jimmy Devine, the pitcher cut by Bender back in June. Once the season was over, Bender decided he had pitched his last professional baseball game — almost!

Before the end of the Middle Atlantic League season, Bender signed a one-year contract to return to the Naval Academy as baseball coach in 1928. "Bender, as a man of baseball brains and coach, is held in high regard by Commander Jonas H. Ingram, director of athletics at the naval school," reported the *Washington Post*. Bender "has met with above average success here in consideration of the material available. Last season he developed a team that administered a severe drubbing to the rival West Point Cadets."[54]

Bender's Midshipmen had beaten the Cadets in three of the previous four years, but Navy lost its final game of the 1928 season to Army, 9–6, in a sloppily played affair. After the close of the collegiate baseball season, Charles signed to manage Richmond of the Virginia League again. It was hoped the presence of the Chief would revive baseball interest in the league's financially strapped clubs. By the time Bender joined the Colts on June 4, two clubs, Portsmouth and Petersburg, announced they were dropping out of the league. Bender managed two exhibition games against Norfolk before the remaining clubs in the league closed down for good.[55]

The following February, the Commander of the U.S. Naval Academy announced a new policy, which dictated that only graduates of the academy could serve as head coaches of athletic teams. Chief Bender found himself without a professional baseball job for the first time since 1918.[56]

In the meantime, things had turned around for Connie Mack and his Philadelphia A's, although Mack failed in his attempts to sign another "Chief." During the spring of 1928 "Chief Whitehorn," or Arthur Lee Daney, a Choctaw Indian and product of the Haskell Indian School, made the club as a pitcher. Daney, the star pitcher with a team that won the renowned *Denver Post* national baseball tournament a year earlier, recalled his first meeting with Bender's friend, ex-catcher Ira Thomas.

> One evening, while we were in Denver, someone knocked on the door of my hotel room. It was a scout from the Philadelphia Athletics, who was making some strides in the American League that summer. The scout's name was Ira

Thomas. He said he had been following me that summer and would I like to come to spring training with the Athletics ... he told me that Connie Mack, the Philadelphia manager, had been looking for an Indian pitcher since Chief Bender.... Of course I knew of Chief Bender.... I said I might not be as good as the Chief, but I would give it a try.[57]

Inevitably, Daney was given the nickname "Chief" even though he didn't turn out to be another Chief Bender. He pitched in only one inning for the A's, a relief appearance against the New York Yankees on May 25. The first batter Daney faced was Babe Ruth, who had already hit two home runs that afternoon. Daney induced the Bambino to hit a pop fly to the infield, but second baseman Bishop and shortstop Boley circled under the ball, collided, and it fell for a single. That was the only inning Arthur pitched in the major leagues, allowing that one hit and no runs.

There was no room for Daney on Mack's strong team that would win the World Series in 1929 and 1930. The leader of his pitching staff was Lefty Grove, a teammate of Bender with the 1923 Baltimore Orioles. Another pitcher on those teams was John Quinn. Though only one year younger than Bender, he won eleven games for the Athletics in 1929 and nine more a year later.

During the 1929 season it seemed natural that the city's sports scribes would go to Chief Bender for his comments about the A's juggernaut that was on its way to an American League pennant. "Remember Plank, Coombs, Bush, Shawkey and yours truly?" asked Bender. "This club has Grove, Walberg, Earnshaw, Quinn, Ehmke and Rommel. The present-day mounds men have more speed than we had, but in all around ability I think we had the edge. There is none of the present group except Quinn who can work on the batters. That is where we excelled."[58]

For the three seasons Bender was out of Organized Baseball, he became a celebrity pitching for semi-pro baseball teams in the four-state region of Pennsylvania, Maryland, Delaware and New Jersey. It was not a glamorous life driving his car to small towns to pitch in ramshackle ball yards on the weekend, returning to his home in Philadelphia after the game. He also wasn't always the hero on the mound as a report from McKinley, Pennsylvania, demonstrated. "Big Chief Bender was not so hot here yesterday against the South Philadelphia Hebrews who clouted him for 8 runs before he was yanked."[59]

On September 4, 1930, Charles Bender and his wife returned to Carlisle so the city could honor him for helping to bring renown to the Indian school as an athlete. The Benders were honored at a luncheon by the Carlisle Rotary Club. "It is 28 years since I pitched in Carlisle," Charles told the Rotarians. "My legs are gone and my arm is gone but my eyes are still good."[60]

After the festivities, Bender unpacked his old Philadelphia Athletics uniform and warmed up to pitch a baseball game for the Carlisle Community Athletic Association team before 2,000 fans that assembled to see the legendary Chippewa perform. Though Bender told an acquaintance on the bench that he had a sore arm, he went out and pitched seven strong innings against the Pennsylvania Railroad Division team, permitting only four hits while striking out seven batters. After he left the mound, Bender autographed a score of baseballs for the large number of youngsters who besieged their hero at the bench. Meantime, the Carlisle team went on to lose the game, 1–0.[61]

On occasion, Bender returned to a major league ballpark to participate in the popular old-timers games. On September 8, 1930, he joined Ty Cobb, Eddie Collins, Home Run Baker, Honus Wagner, and Jack Coombs on a team of old-time all-stars that defeated the former Boston baseball stars (including Cy Young, Tris Speaker and Smoky Joe Wood), 8–4, in a full nine-inning game that was played to benefit the Children's Hospital of Boston. The game at Braves Field brought together perhaps the finest assemblage of baseball greats ever. Sixteen of the old-time players would ultimately be voted into the National Baseball Hall of Fame in Cooperstown.

Bender officially returned to Organized Baseball in December 1930 when he was signed by his old adversary, John McGraw, as a pitching coach for the New York Giants. McGraw planned for the Chief to instruct pitchers in the spring and scout during the regular season. Among Charley's projects were pitcher Roy "Tarzan" Parmelee, a wild right-hander, and Joe Heving, who was struggling with a pick-off move. Bender also helped develop a young prospect named Harold Schumacher, a nineteen-year-old, 205-pound right-hander who won only one game in 1931 but would go on to win 158 major league games, all for the Giants.

When the Giants acquired Sam Mooney from Bridgeport late in the season, he was put in the care of Bender and the lefty won seven of his eight starting assignments. One move that didn't work out was the result of Bender's trip out west to scout the Pacific Coast League's pitchers. The Chief recommended a former Detroit Tigers hurler named Sam Gibson. The Giants purchased the right-hander from the San Francisco Seals, but Gibson would win only four more major league games. Led by the great screwball artist Carl Hubbell, the Giants' pitching staff led the National League in earned run average and complete games, but the club finished a distant second place to St. Louis in the pennant race.

On August 10, 1931, the Giants spent an off-day playing an exhibition game in Hartford, Connecticut, against the first-place club of the Eastern League. The crowd of 2,500 was treated to an appearance by Chief Bender, who pitched the final three innings for the major leaguers. He allowed four hits but no runs. On November 24, 1931, Coach Bender was released by the Giants for "various reasons," according to the *Sporting News*.

Chief Bender gives Giants rookie pitcher Harold Schumacher some pointers, 1931 (National Baseball Hall of Fame Library, Cooperstown, New York).

The Chief had only good things to say about McGraw during and after his tenure with the Giants. "Off the ball field he was the finest gentleman you could imagine," he said. "On the diamond he was tough."[62]

After a one-year absence, the Midwest's Class B Central League was reorganized in 1932, largely due to the efforts of Dayton attorney Frederick Howell, who became league president. The league would be affiliated with major league baseball, field six teams, and play night baseball.

On April 18, 1932, officials of the Central League's Erie, Pennsylvania, club announced that Chief Bender had signed a contract to manage their team for the upcoming minor league season. The Erie club had recently reached a working agreement with the New York American League club, and a photograph was widely circulated in newspapers across the nation that May with Charles Bender wearing a Yankees uniform. Erie's 140-game schedule would begin on May 4, and the Yankees sent a handful of capable prospects to Bender, including catcher Williard Hershberger, slugger Babe Hadder, and shortstop Eddie Leischman.

After watching his charges for a few games, Bender served notice that careless work would no longer be overlooked and he would "access fines on players who are guilty of sloppy play."[63] Charley was back at his old tricks early in the season as he released players and signed new ones on several occasions. However, the fortunes of the ball club changed in mid–May just before the Central League's rosters had to be reduced to the fourteen-player limit. The Erie club released three players to the Middle Atlantic League and acquired pitcher Marvin Duke from Scranton of the New York–Pennsylvania League.

On the evening of June 17, the House of David barnstorming baseball team came to Erie for a night game against the locals, four days after the Sailors played their first Central League game ever under the lights at Athletic Field. The star attraction for the bewhiskered ones was the clean-shaven Grover Cleveland Alexander, who was guaranteed to start the game.

Before the largest crowd to see a game in Erie that year, Alexander started the contest for the House of David and Bender threw the first three innings for his Sailors. Alex did not permit a hit in his two innings of work while Bender allowed four safeties, though he did strike out the side in the second. "The cheer that went up as the third man whiffed the ozone must have been heard downtown," reported Ray Preebles in the *Erie Dispatch-Herald*. "Bender used his curveball effectively, breaking it across the corners and at no stage of the proceedings did he give the hitters anything good."[64] Once the old-timers departed, the Sailors and the barnstormers went about settling the contest, won by Erie on a ninth-inning run, 5–4.

On June 25 Bender took the mound to save a game for the son of a good friend. When Erie pitcher Bob Walsh, youngest son of White Sox great Ed Walsh, weakened in the sixth inning of a game against South Bend, Bender "grabbed his glove and put down the uprising" with four innings of scoreless relief. The story didn't have a fairy tale ending because Walsh was given another chance in the second game of the doubleheader and left the game after allowing seven runs in four innings.[65]

During the course of the season, Bender continued to make significant changes in his pitching staff. On July 27, Hal Benne, another acquisition from Scranton, set an Organized Baseball record with eighteen strikeouts in a nine-inning game. Benne struck out thirteen of the first fourteen Fort Wayne batters he faced, but he ultimately lost the game, 4–3.

The undisputed ace of Bender's pitching staff in Erie was Georgia Tech southpaw Marvin Duke. On July 11 against Youngstown, Duke won his eleventh straight game to run his record to 14–1 for the season. During one nine-day stretch in July, Duke pitched and won four games against Dayton, one of them a one-hit shutout.

"Duke has a bullet-fast one," reported the *Sporting News* that August, "but under the direction of Chief Bender ... the youngster has been developing pitching finesse and device. He has a fine assortment of curves and a slow ball that he mixes in with the other equipment."[66]

Dick Peebles would one day be the sports editor of a major Texas newspaper, but in 1932 he was a ten-year-old in Erie who hung around the ballpark to get the chance to listen to Chief Bender's stories. Dick even decided to become a pitcher instead of an infielder after "the Chief had shown us with his own long, lean and brown fingers how to hold the ball for curve and how to hold it for a fastball."

Peebles wrote that Bender began to worry about his ball club and "he got to playing around with the firewater.... One time, fired up by the home brew, the gift of a grateful fan, the Chief ambled to home plate to dispute an umpire's decision and wound up sitting down on the plate and defying anyone and everyone to make him move. Two policemen finally persuaded the Chief to stake his claim back on the bench."[67]

Bender was popular among the Erie fans, but he missed a week during the summer because of his old stomach problems, and his drinking habits got him fired following a doubleheader against Dayton on July 24. "It was claimed Bender had been out on a party with two major league scouts the night before and continued celebrating throughout the initial tilt of the Sunday twin bill," wrote Edward Bierbauer in the *Sporting News*. Charley was ordered off the field when umpire Bruff Cleary asked to examine a ball being used by the Erie pitcher. Bender threw the baseball into the grandstand instead of turning it over to the arbiter.

While the umpire and Bender were arguing, fights broke out between some of the Erie and Dayton players. Several bleacherites came onto the field and began jostling with special policemen, who tried to push them back into the stands.[68]

Later that evening, a heated meeting between Bender and Erie club officials culminated with the dismissal of the manager. After he had time to cool down, the Chief met with the club's bosses and got his job back.

Marvin Duke chalked up his twentieth victory in the first game of a doubleheader against Youngstown on August 13. It would be the last game Manager Bender would see his young star win.

After two incidents in another doubleheader against Dayton on August 17, it was suggested that Bender had again "mixed pleasure with business." L. Frank Thayer wrote in the *Titusville Herald*, "The Sailor pilot was feeling mighty frisky and when things didn't suit him in the (fourth) inning he promptly called his team off the field and forfeited the contest."[69]

After umpire Con Daly ruled two Dayton base runners safe on a double steal in the first game, Bender ran out of the dugout and argued that the batter had interfered with his catcher's attempt to make the tag, which meant the runner should be called out. When the umpire refused the Chief's demand, Bender picked up his team's bats and instructed his players to follow him to their hotel. Dayton's president/manager Ducky Holmes, who had just completed a ten-day suspension for slugging Umpire Cleary, caught up with Bender at the gate of the ballpark and convinced him to return to the field, but by this time the game had been forfeited to the Ducks.[70]

During the second game, Bender taunted the umpire unmercifully and said "things unbecoming a manager of the Central League."[71] The Sailors went on to drop that game, 6–4, and in the process lost the club's hold on first place. The second instance of bad behavior by the manager in less than a month was too much for the Erie club's officials and Bender was fired as soon as they read the report of the game.

Just four days after he was given his walking papers by the Erie club, Chief Bender appeared on the mound during an old-timers game at Cincinnati's Redland Field. Among the old-time players who appeared in the exhibition were Tris Speaker, Honus Wagner, Cy Young, Dave Bancroft and Nick Altrock, who waved all his teammates off the field before he pitched to a batter.

"There was Chief Bender, Connie Mack's star of twenty years ago," read a report of the affair, "swinging an aged arm to whip the ball down in the way batters used to fear."[72]

During the spring of 1933, Charles assisted Frank McGowan, new manager of the Baltimore International League club, with the Orioles pitchers. Back in 1920 the manager of a semi-pro team in Branford, Connecticut, recommended McGowan, an eighteen-year-old outfielder, to New Haven owner George Weiss. The youngster tried out and was given a uniform by manager Chief Bender. The next day, Bender put the youngster in the starting lineup. "Maybe, because they had nobody else," McGowan later said. In his third trip to the plate, Frank came to bat with the bases loaded and stroked the hit that won the game. McGowan went on to play 134 games for Bender in 1920 then was peddled by Weiss to the International League after the season. By 1922, McGowan was in the major leagues with Connie Mack's Athletics. When he was named manager of the Baltimore Orioles in October 1932, McGowan didn't forget about what he learned from his old manager, Chief Bender.[73]

Bender appeared at the Baker Bowl in 1933 for another old-timers game and the celebration of the fiftieth anniversary of the Philadelphia Phillies' entrance in the National League. A few weeks later, the Chief was traveling with one of the most illustrious baseball teams in history. Charles was working for Wanamaker's Store in Philadelphia that summer when he received an offer from sports promoter Ray Doan to perform for the House of David touring baseball team. After signing a contract to play with the barnstormers for $350 a month on June 13, Bender was assigned to the eastern traveling team as manager and star attraction. Grover Cleveland Alexander would manage the western House of David team.

Benjamin Purnell and his wife Mary established the religious community known as the Israelite House of David in Benton Harbor, Michigan, in 1903. The purpose of this colony was to assemble the twelve lost tribes of Israel for an ingathering to await the millennium. Spurred by Purnell's love of athletics, the House of David began fielding baseball teams around 1913 as a weekend endeavor and within two years the colony's team was playing several games a week. By 1920, the team was barnstorming all around the country, scheduling games against the many semi-pro leagues that thrived during the twenties and thirties. The traveling team was originally comprised only of members of the colony, whose doctrine dictated that men wear beards and long hair. Though the House of David baseball team always drew large crowds and the team's fame spread over the decade, the colony began to recruit players not of the faith who were well known and would draw additional patrons to the ballparks. These star players, such as Bender and Alexander, were not required to grow the trademark beards.[74]

In their advance advertising, the House of David capitalized on Bender's fame by publicizing that the "Philadelphia Athletics Pitching Star and World's Series Hero will start the game." Joining Bender with the eastern traveling team was the first woman to ever sign a professional baseball contract, pitcher Jackie Mitchell.

In order to play games at night, the colony's teams used large flood lights on forty- to fifty-foot poles to illuminate the playing field. The power for the lighting came from a 150,000-watt generator with a 250-horsepower motor mounted on a truck. It took eight trucks just to carry the club's lighting system.[75]

On June 29, 1933, Bender was on tour, managing the eastern team in a game at Mount Carmel, Pennsylvania. The Chief was standing on the sideline, watching his team bat. When one of the players swung at a pitch, the bat slipped from his hands and struck Bender squarely on the right knee. An x-ray of the leg revealed Charles had suffered a fracture of his kneecap.[76] With Bender out of the picture, Jackie Mitchell, the Southern girl who once struck out Babe Ruth, became the eastern team's star attraction. A year later, Bender would sue the House of David in order to recover $700 for two months of salary due him from his 1933 contract after he was disabled by the fractured knee.[77]

After his 1933 stint with the House of David, Bender disappeared from the world of professional baseball and did not return for five and a half seasons. It wasn't by his choice.

◆ 14 ◆

A Philadelphia Athletic for Life

In February of 1934, Bill Dooly of the *Philadelphia Record* complained about Chief Bender's unofficial exile from Organized Baseball.

> It is a sweet mystery of life that sticks Charles Albert Bender behind a store counter, while every baseball caliph in the land is crying about the pitching problem, the same being in their most temperate description, horrible. This is one I can't come close to unraveling.
>
> This is even odder when I recall the many times I have listened to the old baseball boys tearing off a few reminiscences and bringing up the Chief as one of the "smartest" pitchers the craft has seen. They never forget the Chippewa brave when they bring up the old days.... So if I may be so bold, I am suggesting that some club owner or other give up the crying treatment and substitute Chief Bender. I'm willing to guarantee he'll get them results.[1]

By the 1930s, Bender had become content about his place in life. While he was out of Organized Baseball, Bender resolved his issues with drink and reconciled with Connie Mack. Unlike his early days with the Athletics, Bender became accommodating with newspaper reporters, who often sought him out for an opinion about the current state of the game. He was openly proud of his Native American heritage and even declared in his speeches that he spoke for "515 tribes."

His professional baseball career apparently over, Charles and his wife Marie remained in Philadelphia where he worked in the men's department at Gimbels Department Store downtown. During his years out of baseball, Bender remained close to the game and he continued to pitch for semi-pro teams in the Philadelphia area. He occasionally threw batting practice for the two Philadelphia major league clubs and worked with young pitchers at any opportunity.

After he became a star pitcher with the two-time National League champion Cincinnati Reds, Bucky Walters credited Bender with teaching him the slider in 1935 while he was with the Phillies. Walters said that Bender spent a lot of time hanging around the old Baker Bowl watching the pitchers. One day he stepped down from the stands and told the young Phillies pitcher he had a pitch he used to throw that Walters might be able to employ.

"He had no name for it, but it was a slider," recalled Bucky. "I'd throw it in the bull pen now and then but I never really used it until the 1940 World Series."[2] Walters began to use Bender's pitch against left-handed batters and it worked so well he added it to his pitching repertoire.

In addition to his work with young pitchers, Bender stayed close to the game through speaking engagements talking about his life in baseball. Very self-conscious about speaking in public when he first became a Philadelphia celebrity, Charles gained confidence through speaking engagements at high schools during his days as a pitcher. By the time his playing days ended, he had become an accomplished after-dinner speaker. In 1937 Charles even spent a week in Chicago participating in the radio broadcasts from Comiskey Park for General Foods Corporation.

Charles was always interested in new challenges, and once his baseball skills began to wane, he became an avid bowler. Back in January 1928, Bender organized a bowling team consisting of current and former A's Jimmy Dykes, Wally Schang, Bing Miller and Joe Bush.[3] Charles once said, "One thing that always helped me, though and I think it would help every pitcher without taking too much time, is bowling. You'd be surprised how it keeps the legs in shape, and the arm and shoulder muscles loose."[4]

Charles Bender, circa late 1930s, when he worked as a salesman of men's clothing at a Philadelphia department store (Cleveland Public Library).

The Chief delighted his Philadelphia neighbors by taking occasional turns on the mound in sandlot baseball games. "I ran the Gimbel baseball team in Philadelphia Industrial league and pitched several games for them," Bender wrote to a friend the fall of 1937. "My arm is still good, but my underpinning isn't so hot. Still, I managed to get by o.k. I resigned from the Gimbel force a few weeks ago, and went with Bond Clothiers."[5]

Charles Bender pitched his last formal game of baseball at the age of fifty-three on June 24, 1937, a 5–0 win over a semi-pro team.[6] That October Charles and Marie Bender celebrated their thirty-third wedding anniversary and the old ballplayer alluded to efforts to address his drinking problem. "She had one highball and I had two glasses of milk along with a chicken dinner," he wrote to an acquaintance. "Some celebration!"[7]

It was hard to be a baseball fan in Philadelphia during the late 1930s. After Connie Mack broke up his three-time American League championship club following the 1932 season, the Athletics descended deep into the second division and never recovered. The A's finished in either seventh or eighth place every season between 1935 and 1943. During that time, the team had only one legitimate star, outfielder Robert Lee Johnson. Johnson was the grandson of a full-blood Oklahoma Cherokee. "Indian Bob" or "Cherokee Bob," as he was alternately known, batted .307 in his ten years with the A's, knocked in 100 or more runs seven consecutive seasons, had nine straight twenty-plus home run years and scored more runs than any player in Philadelphia Athletics history. Five times he was selected to represent the Athletics in the All-Star Game.

Shibe Park acquired a new tenant in mid-season 1938 when the Phillies moved from their dreary home at the Baker Bowl, where they had played for fifty-one-and-a-half years. The move didn't improve the quality of baseball at Shibe Park, for the Phillies were just as bad or worse that the Athletics. In 1936, 1938, 1940, 1941, and 1942, both the A's and Phillies finished last in their respective leagues; the National League club did not place above seventh from 1933 through 1945.

Bender's dry humor made him a natural for the banquet circuit, and he was one of the most sought after speakers in the Philadelphia area. On the evening of March 11, 1936, Charles Bender spoke before the Sportsman's Dinner sponsored by the West Branch Y.M.C.A. in Philadelphia. The toastmaster was George Gilham, a journeyman third baseman who batted .221 when he played for Bender at Richmond in 1919. In his introduction, Gilham commented "the Chief was born 15 years too soon. Had he pitched today, he could have retired a well-to-do man."

On that occasion Bender said, "I signed with the Harrisburg A.C., a semi-pro team for $100 a month.... [T]he A's signed me for $1,800. Later I received $2,100 and finally $2,400."[8]

On other occasions Bender gave the more realistic figure of $5,000 as the highest salary he received with the A's. The $2,500 figure was more suitable for the banquet circuit, especially when he used one of his favorite clichés—"I don't know why they call me a 'money pitcher.' I never got any money!"[9]

Once he was out of the game, Bender was not shy about offering his opinion of modern day players in the major leagues. He told the newspapers in March 1938:

> There's no justice in (Bob) Feller getting $17,500. Nor is (Joe) DiMaggio justified in holding out for $40,000. DiMaggio is a great ballplayer, but he should be tickled to death to get $25,000 in his third year as an outfielder.... Don't get me

wrong, I believe in ballplayers getting as much as they can, but they should first prove they are worth their demand.

I see Lou Gehrig of the Yankees has signed for $30,000 for one year. Why, that's more than I got in my 12 years with the A's. I signed up for $1,800 in 1903 and in my last year, 1914, got $5,000. And it was like pulling teeth to get Connie to give me that. I guess I was born too soon.[10]

By 1937 any problem between Bender and Connie Mack had receded into the past. On December 23, Charley joined about a hundred of Mack's former players for the old manager's seventy-fifth birthday celebration at Shibe Park.

In June 1939, Connie Mack announced he had signed Chief Bender to scout for the Athletics. The former pitcher would take a leave of absence from his department store job and embark on a ten-week tour of the minor leagues to look for talent. Except for a brief term with the New York Yankees in the early 1940s, Bender remained on the A's payroll for the remainder of his life.

That September Charley joined many of his old teammates, including Eddie Collins, Frank Baker and Rube Oldring, for a special day at Shibe Park. Just before play began, the old-timers formed a crescent around home plate and Connie Mack shook hands with each one as their names were announced over the public address system. Between the games of a doubleheader featuring the A's and the Red Sox, members of the 1910–14 Athletics played a two-and-a-half-inning contest with the club's pennant winners of 1929–30. A crowd in excess of 23,000 watched the 1910 team win, 6–4. All of the old-timers played except Ira Thomas, who could not fit into one of the special uniforms provided for the occasion. The old Chief was a favorite of the autograph hounds.[11]

Following the 1939 baseball season, Mack named Bender manager of the A's newly acquired Wilmington, Delaware, franchise in the Inter-State League. Charley did not survive past Independence Day as pilot of the Blue Rocks and was replaced by former A's catcher Charlie Berry. Manager Connie Mack announced the change but the decision was apparently precipitated by the Wilmington club's stockholders, who wanted better than a fourth-place club. Bender immediately resumed his scouting duties for the Athletics.[12]

Bender managed the Athletics' Class C farm club at Newport News, Virginia, in 1941. After the club finished the season with a .500 record, Bender was not retained for the next campaign. Upon learning that Charley was negotiating with George Weiss, director of the New York Yankees farm system, Stan Baumgartner was led to write for the Sporting News, "Bender has always been an excellent manager, but was often a bit undiplomatic when talking to the big shots in the front office. He has not permitted any managing from behind closed doors. As a result, he has often lost out."[13]

Weiss, his old boss at New Haven, hired Bender as a scout for the New

York Yankees, but when several farm clubs were cut loose because of World War II, Bender found himself out of a baseball job.

Charles Bender was working at a retail clothing store in Germantown, Pennsylvania, when J. G. Taylor Spink interviewed the former Athletics star in late 1942 for an autobiographical article that was printed in the *Sporting News* that December.

> The tall, militarily erect Chippewa, heading for his fifty-ninth birthday with only a few gray hairs streaking his jet black hair, works in the Browning-King salesrooms at Chelten and Green Streets.... The years, we might add, set very lightly on the shoulders of the big Indian. He can still handle a gun with the best and beat almost anyone at the targets. For close work, reading, he uses glasses, but his eyes still have the piercing clearness that marked him as one of the finest shots in America. His memory is second to that of Connie Mack. He recalls dates, people, and incidents with the security of an encyclopedia.
>
> The Chief's activities and abilities spread beyond sports. As an off-season clothing salesman over a long span, he learned textiles and tailoring. In the jewelry trade he became known as an expert diamond appraiser. As an oil painter, he found a ready market for his landscapes. And if he had desired, he could have earned his livelihood as a tree-pruner or gardener.[14]

Right from the start, Bender straightened out the interviewer on some of the facts. "I was born May 5, 1884 — not 1883. Just got a copy of my birth certificate. See?" he added, pulling a slip of paper from his pocket. "Every year off helps these days."

"My father was of Dutch descent," Charles continued. "That's where the name Bender comes from. I never had an Indian name, like White Foot, or Red Feather, or anything as picturesque. My mother was half Indian — a Chippewa. That makes me a quarter Indian, doesn't it?" Spink added the notation "the Chief looks like a full-blooded redskin" to the final article. According to several sources, including the White Earth Reservation Land List (1911), Bender's mother, Pay-show-de-o-quay Bender, was of "full Indian blood."[15]

"There were 11 in our family, seven boys," Bender noted, "... and four girls. Three of my brothers are automobile mechanics, now working on the lathes in a defense plant in Detroit. One sister, Anne (he must have been referring to Emma), now Mrs. Huf, lives here in Philadelphia. She's a nurse."[16]

The former player went on to reminisce about his years at Carlisle, Connie Mack, pitching for the Athletics, Rube Waddell, and the 1914 World Series. In addition to the two-part article in the *Sporting News'* "Three and One: Looking them over with J. Taylor Spink," the tabloid also used the interviews for subsequent articles in the weekly baseball newspaper.

Bender was out of a job in baseball until Connie Mack called Charley in the fall of 1943 and offered his former pitcher a position as coach with the Athletics for the upcoming baseball season. Bender eagerly accepted. He worked with the team's young pitchers during spring training, and though he was officially employed as a scout, Charles continued to function as an informal coach during the regular season.

"Sixty-one-year-old Chief Bender puts in thirty to forty minutes a day as batting practice pitcher for the Athletics to ease the burden for Dave Keefe, the regular tosser," wrote a reporter during the 1944 season. "He admits he doesn't have much stuff left, but says, 'I'm out there to help the kids—not to throw it past them.'"[17]

On August 4, 1944, Chief Bender, Ira Thomas, and Joe Bush attended a celebration at Shibe Park to recognize Connie Mack's fifty years as a major league manager. The commemoration marked the date Mack was chosen for his first managerial assignment with the Pittsburgh Pirates of the National League in 1894. During that Friday afternoon, Connie Mack and numerous well wishers gathered at the Warwick Hotel for a dinner and then watched Mack cut a three-layer cake baked for the occasion.[18]

After beating the bushes for Connie Mack in 1945, Bender was given the opportunity to manage the Philadelphia Athletics Savannah farm club of the Class A South Atlantic League a year later. Savannah didn't have a very good team because the financially challenged Philadelphia A's just did not have any good prospects to send there.

After serving four years in the Air Corps during World War II, Frank Edde played his only season in professional baseball for Chief Bender at Savannah in 1946. The former minor league outfielder recalled his time with Bender some fifty-seven years later:

> I broke my foot rounding first after a hit, stepped into a hole, and that was the end of that. I knew Al Bender well, ya' know they used to call him Chief because he was an Indian. I don't remember much about that year, the memory is fading. He was still throwing batting practice then and he was in his 60's, too. He used to wear a pair of catcher's shin guards to the mound when he would throw batting practice.
> He was one of the nicest men I ever met. I just wished I'd have known what I know today, because I'd have had him sign a couple dozen baseballs and been set for a long time. I guess I could get a few thousand dollars each for them, that would have been nice.[19]

At the time Edde was speaking in 2003, the *Becket Guide* estimated that if a pristine autographed Bender baseball were available, it would go for around $4,000.

The highlight of the 1946 SALLY League season for the Indians was Randy Smith's no-hitter against Columbus on May 12. The lefty had won eight straight games for Bender at Newport News in 1941 and then spent the next four years in the United States Navy as a cook aboard an LST. After his no-hitter, Manager Bender bragged, "He's no flash in the pan. He wasn't lucky today. He's just a good pitcher."[20]

A week after Smith's no-hitter the Indians were in first place, but then they began to lose. By July the club landed in the cellar and stayed there for the remainder of the SALLY League season. Unfortunately, as the fortunes of the Savannah team fell, so did those of Smith. He won only one more game for Bender.

On July 3 Lena Blackburne temporarily assumed the club's managerial position while Bender took a leave of absence for surgery. The Chief returned to the helm three weeks later and suffered through loss after loss. Following his team's miserable 55-81 record, Bender's days as a professional baseball manager were over.

Chief Bender scouted for the Philadelphia Athletics from 1947 through 1950. He was involved with American Legion baseball and was named to the faculty of the Connie Mack Baseball School in West Palm Beach, Florida. The school operated in February and early March to provide training and tryouts for boys.

Over the years, Bender developed ten baseball "commandments" that he encouraged his pupils to adopt. "They are good points to teach youngsters learning the game and to remind those who have been playing for awhile," he explained.

CHARLES BENDER'S TEN BASEBALL COMMANDMENTS

1. Nobody ever becomes a ballplayer by walking after the ball.
2. You will never become a .300 hitter unless you take the bat off your shoulder.
3. If what you did yesterday still looks big to you, you haven't done much today.
4. Keep your head up and you may not have to keep it down.
5. When you start to slide, SLIDE. He who changes his mind may have to change a good leg for a bad one.
6. Do not alibi on bad hops.
7. Always run them out. You never can tell.
8. Never quit.
9. Do not find too much fault with the umpires. You cannot expect them to be as perfect as you are.
10. A pitcher who hasn't control hasn't anything.[6]

As early as 1908, *Baseball Magazine* used the term "hall of fame" to describe the list of pitchers who had thrown no-hit games. In preparations for the "100th anniversary of the origin of baseball" years later, a wealthy Cooperstown, New York, resident proposed the idea of a national baseball museum to National League president Ford Frick. Frick suggested the inclusion of a hall of fame for the game's greatest players, and the National Baseball Hall of Fame and Museum came to fruition. The first election of former players for the Hall of Fame was held in 1936, three years before the museum's official opening in Cooperstown. Members of the Baseball Writers of America (BBWAA) were given the authority to select players from the twentieth century while a special old-timers committee was to select deserving individuals from the nineteenth century. After the initial selections for the grand

Bender (right) and John M. Hoy in discussion on the evening of the Newville (Pennsylvania) Athletic Association Banquet, October 1951 (Cumberland County Historical Society).

opening of the hall in 1939, the voting and selections became erratic. The BBWAA elected only one player between 1939 and 1945 and the old-timers committee rarely met. Though he received votes at each election, the highest number of votes cast for Chief Bender was 39 in 1946, well below the required 75 percent required for selection.

In 1946, the Hall of Fame old-timers committee determined that the candidates from the early part of the century were not receiving enough support from the baseball writers to reach the necessary threshold of 75 percent. Because many younger writers were reluctant to vote for players about whom they had limited first-hand knowledge, the committee decided that players whose careers began after 1900 and extended through the 1910s needed to be removed from the BBWAA responsibility. That year the old-timers committee selected eleven players for induction. Two of the new Hall of Fame inductees were Bender's teammates with the A's, left-handed pitchers Eddie Plank and Rube Waddell. When only two veteran players were selected by the old-timers committee over the succeeding six years, it appeared Bender might not live to join former teammates Plank, Waddell, Eddie Collins, and Frank Baker in the hall.

After being on the road for most of his life, Bender returned home in 1951 as a full-time coach for the Athletics. Connie Mack was no longer manager of the team. He had retired at age eighty-eight following the 1950 season and the new manager was former A's infielder Jimmy Dykes.

As Ben Shibes' heirs died off, Connie Mack purchased additional shares in the club and by the mid–1930s, he had acquired majority ownership of the Athletics. After Connie retired, his sons, Roy and Earl, acquired the club by buying the shares of their half-brother, Connie Mack, Jr., and the surviving Shibe family members. In 1953, the new ownership officially changed the name of Shibe Park to Connie Mack Stadium.

The old pitching coach from the Deadball Era, Charley Bender, hurled batting practice for Jimmy Dykes' team and the Chief delighted in demonstrating his old routine on the mound. Bender made $2,400 for most of his years as a pitcher with the Athletics, but received more than double that as coach with the club in the 1950s.[22]

The Athletics' pitching staff improved its earned run average under Bender in 1951 to 4.47, more than a run better than the group of a year earlier. A smallish left-hander, Bobby Shantz, emerged as the A's ace with a remarkable record of 18–10 with a sixth-place club.

Less than one year after his return to the Athletics as coach, Bender was stricken with the disease that eventually killed him. He was forced to abandon the bullpen for the final two series of the season for what was described as a "minor operation." The Chief continued to coach for the A's but his days of throwing batting practice were over.

Bender was back with the A's when spring training came around in 1952. He convinced a pitching recruit named Harry Byrd to use a sidearm delivery. Byrd won fifteen games for the A's that season and just missed throwing a no-hitter against New York on September 3 when Irv Noren's double accounted for the Yankees' only hit.

Another pitcher the Chief helped was Joe Coleman, who had played on Bender's Newport News team in 1941 and became a mainstay on the Athletics pitching staff in 1948 and '49. By the spring of 1952 Coleman had fallen on hard times. His record of the previous season was a miserable 1–6 and the right-hander's career in baseball was in jeopardy.

Coleman recalled that Bender told him "to go out into center field and keep trying to throw the ball over the plate from 'way out there.' At first I thought he was kidding, but I tried it, anyway. And doggone if it didn't work. It strengthened my arm and improved my control."[23]

Bender underwent another operation in July, lost twenty pounds, and had to use a cane in order to get around. A special night for the Chief was planned for early August, but it had to be pushed back a month.

On September 4, 1952, the Philadelphia Athletics finally held a day to honor Charles Bender at Shibe Park and a crowd of 31,424 turned out to pay homage to the ailing coach. The Chief was presented a scroll of tribute signed by more than 150,000 fans as well as a check for $6,009.50 in coins collected from containers throughout greater Philadelphia. As a humble Charles Bender stood alongside his wife Marie, Connie Mack, Frank Baker, Rube Oldring and Ira Thomas, the throng in the stadium cheered after the Chief received assurance of a lifetime job with the A's.[24]

One of the most poignant tributes to the A's coach came from the star of the pitching staff, Bobby Shantz, who had written to the Chief when he was recuperating from an operation earlier that summer.

> We all certainly do miss you, Chief, and hope you can be back with us soon. Chief, I'd like to take this time to thank you for all the things you taught me about pitching. I'll probably never be the pitcher you were, but I'll always be there trying my best to do the things you taught me.
>
> It sure is a great asset to the club to have a man of your caliber around. I couldn't say this if I had to speak orally, but I can write pretty good. Guess I'll never learn to talk much.
>
> Best of luck and health to you and your wife, Chief. May God bless you.[25]

The little southpaw went on to win twenty-six games for the Athletics in 1952 and Shantz was named the American League's Most Valuable Player for that season. The club's fourth-place finish that year was only the third time the Athletics had ended the season in the first division of the American League since 1933.

Following his recent operation, Charles was told by his doctors that he had to give up hunting and golf. But that fall, the old pitching coach mustered enough stamina to go pheasant hunting, play sixteen holes of golf and hit 21 of 25 targets at sixteen yards in a trap shoot. Those would be his final tastes of the activities he enjoyed so much.[26]

Bender still had his garden. Like his other endeavors, Charles went at gardening whole heartedly. Since he didn't have room for a large garden at his home in North Philadelphia, a friend, John Burns, allowed Charley to plant his "farm" across the river in Haddon Heights. Bender raised all sorts of vegetables, tomatoes and strawberries. What the Benders couldn't eat themselves, they sold or gave away."[27]

Despite the constant pain he experienced, Bender remained active as an after-dinner speaker, representing the Athletics and recalling baseball anecdotes at club, community and industrial affairs. "I just figured that going out as a speaker will help and I like it," he said.[28]

When A's publicist Tommy Clark passed over the ailing Bender in early

1953 when lining up speakers for church, club and civic affairs, the Chief protested. "If I am going to die," he declared, "I can do it just as well on my feet, trying to make a few friends for the team."[29]

In late June Charley underwent a gallstone operation that was feared would end his life. He told friends he was ready for the third strike, but he rallied and was finally able to ambulate with the aid of a cane.

Through it all Chief Bender never lost his sense of humor. After a series of blood transfusions it was said he teased some friends with the remark, "I had no idea the blood of a white man could do so much good."[30]

In July 1953, an eleven-man Baseball Hall of Fame Committee on Baseball Veterans replaced the controversial old-timers committee. At the new group's initial meeting on September 28, Charles "Chief" Bender and five other old-timers were selected to join the Hall of Fame. An ailing Bender told the press, "I want to thank my friends, all the members of your Old-Timers' Committee that voted me into the Hall of Fame and all of the baseball writers who supported me."[31]

Bender stirred waves of applause with his speech at the Philadelphia Sports Writers dinner in January 1954. A month later, Bender ignored the advice of his physician and took off for A's spring training in West Palm Beach, Florida. The long drive, combined with his deteriorating condition, left the ill coach so weak he had to use a wheelchair after the first few days. Still, Bender sat near the dugout, studying his pitchers' every move and calling the young recruit pitchers over from time to time for personal instruction.[32]

On Bender's last day at the practice field in West Palm Beach, his wife Marie showed her new diamond wristwatch to some friends in the grandstand. When she pointed out the inscription on the back that read, "To Marie from Her Honey — 50th Anniversary," one of them exclaimed, "You've been married 50 years!"

"No," she said, "When he gave it to me, I told him, 'Honey you've made a mistake. We won't be married 50 years until next October.'

"He said, 'I haven't made a mistake. I wanted you to have this now. I won't be around for the 50th.'

"And how do you think he got the money to buy the watch? By saving what he sold out of the garden."[33]

Inevitably, Bender had to return to Philadelphia by train and was immediately hospitalized. The Chief constantly thought about the Athletics and followed them on radio, television and in the newspapers. He insisted Mrs. Bender leave his side to attend A's home games "so you can come back and tell me exactly what's going on."[34]

While under treatment for cancer at Graduate Hospital in Philadelphia, Bender received a letter from his pal, six-year-old Michael Burns, who helped him with the Haddon Heights garden. "The strawberries are good," he wrote. "Please get better soon. I miss you very much."[35] Bender did not see the garden or little Mike Burns again. He also did not live to see his formal admission to the Baseball Hall of Fame. Charles Albert Bender suffered a heart attack and died on Saturday, May 22, 1954.

Charles Bender's funeral was held in Philadelphia on May 27. Connie Mack and the Chief's former roommate, Andy Coakley, were in attendance. Pallbearers included some of the greats of Philadelphia baseball: Frank Baker, Lena Blackburne, Howard Ehmke, Hans Lobert, Bing Miller, Wally Moses, Amos Strunk, and Charley's old friend Rube Oldring.[36] Another close friend, Eddie Collins, had died three years earlier.

Charles Albert Bender is buried in Hillside Cemetery, Roslyn, Pennsylvania. The sobriquet "Chief" is engraved beneath his name on the grave stone. Marie Bender died in Philadelphia on February 28, 1961, and is buried next to her husband.

Marie Bender traveled to Cooperstown, New York, for her late husband's official induction into the National Baseball Hall of Fame on August 9, 1954. Mrs. Bender accepted a framed copy of her husband's Hall of Fame plaque that joined those of the other greats of the game in the museum gallery. Among the numerous former players, families and dignitaries in attendance were Roy and Earl Mack, representing the Mack family, the widow of John McGraw, and eighty-seven-year-old Cy Young, Bender's mound opponent in his first major league game.[37]

Upon their acquisition of the controlling shares of the Athletics, the Mack brothers assumed a large mortgage for Shibe Park. The owners' lack of personal wealth from non-baseball-related enterprises, weakness of the club's minor league system, and the increased popularity of the Phillies in the early 1950s contributed to the large numbers of empty seats at the ballpark whenever the Athletics played.

The brothers turned to the city for help with a new ballpark in a more desirable neighborhood. However, the Philadelphia mayor felt there were more pressing projects for the city to pursue. The debt load and the poor decision of the owners to sell the ballpark's concessions, a major source of income, led to the sale of the club to Arnold Johnson on November 5, 1954. Last-ditch attempts by local investors to save the club for Philadelphia were rejected by the Mack family and the American League.

Before the 1955 season, the Athletics were transferred to Kansas City, Missouri, where they performed even worse than they had in the previous twenty years in Philadelphia. For a while, Connie Mack, Sr., continued to use his old tower office with the consent of Connie Mack Stadium's sole tenant, the Phillies. But by this time, the aged man's health had greatly deteriorated and he died on February 8, 1956.

Charles Bender is not well known today except by the most devoted of fans of baseball history and the memorabilia collectors who realize that a "Chief Bender" autograph is one of the rarest in sports. Unlike many of his hard-drinking and profane contemporaries, Charley was not controversial and was generally a quiet and gracious man. He also was a student of the game of baseball and taught future generations a pitch that became known as the slider, a staple among hard-throwing major league pitchers of the twenty-first century. Few know that he an outstanding all-around athlete, "a natural," proficient at shooting, billiards and golf as well as baseball.

Chief Bender had the discipline to ignore the war whoops and racial aspersions to perform at a high level and dispel many of the myths of the time that the Indian did not have the intelligence to become successful in baseball at the highest level. He ignored politics and handled the bias of his time, not with anger, but with likability and intelligence. Though subtle racism persisted, success by a player of Bender's stature and the dignified manner in which he played the game helped to ease the way for future generations of Native American baseball stars like Rudy York, Allie Reynolds and Early Wynn.

During the late 1960s, Native Americans underwent a cultural change from a primal savage to the noble Indian that has much to offer white society. Anthony Raveni, professor in Native American Studies at Colgate University, wrote that they were no longer depicted as marauders, but "resisters of the white man's attempt to push them aside; they are sagacious and morally and environmentally sensitive as they struggle to retain their old ways."[38]

The despised "half-breed" was no more, as Caucasians came to believe it fashionable to be of Native American blood, no matter how small a degree. There was hardly any notice when Jacoby Ellsbury and Joba Chamberlain burst onto the national baseball scene in 2007, although both were of the same degree of Native American blood as Bender. Their Native American ancestry was rarely mentioned and there also was little comment from the Navajo Ellsbury or his family about the nickname "Chief," given him by his teammates.[39]

Born in Crow Wing County, Charles Bender was the lone Minnesota-born member of Baseball's Hall of Fame until Dave Winfield (a native of St. Paul) was inducted in 2001. In addition, Bender was installed in the Minnesota Sports Hall of Fame in Minneapolis on May 5, 1958, and into the American Indian Athletic Hall of Fame located at Haskell Indian Nations University in 1972. Other than his hall of fame plaques and a historical marker at Carlisle, there are few monuments dedicated to Charles "Chief" Bender. But in the first two decades of the twentieth century, Chief Bender became one of the legends of the game of baseball and perhaps the most famous Native American in the country.

Appendix:
Chief Bender's Pitching Record[*]

Year/Team	League	W	L	G	IP	H	BB	K	ERA
1903 Philadelphia	American	17	14	36	270	239	65	127	3.07
1904 Philadelphia	American	10	11	29	203.2	167	59	149	2.87
1905 Philadelphia	American	18	11	35	229	193	90	142	2.38
1906 Philadelphia	American	15	10	36	238.1	208	48	159	2.53
1907 Philadelphia	American	16	8	33	219.1	185	34	112	2.05
1908 Philadelphia	American	8	9	18	138.2	121	21	85	1.75
1909 Philadelphia	American	18	8	34	250	196	45	161	1.66
1910 Philadelphia	American	23	5	30	250	182	47	155	1.58
1911 Philadelphia	American	17	5	31	216.1	198	58	114	2.16
1912 Philadelphia	American	13	8	27	171	169	33	90	2.74
1913 Philadelphia	American	21	10	48	236.2	208	59	135	2.21
1914 Philadelphia	American	17	3	28	179	159	55	107	2.26
1915 Baltimore	Federal	4	16	26	178.1	198	37	89	3.99
1916 Philadelphia	National	7	7	27	122.2	137	34	43	3.74
1917 Philadelphia	National	8	2	20	113	84	26	43	1.67
1918 (Did not play)									
1919 Richmond	Virginia	29	2	34	280	209	22	195	1.06
1920 New Haven	Eastern	22	9	36	238	208	52	139	2.10
1921 New Haven	Eastern	13	7	36	196	168	59	131	1.93
1922 Reading	International	8	13	30	183	172	33	88	2.42
1923 Baltimore	International	6	3	18	93	109	30	44	5.03
1924 New Haven	Eastern	6	4	12	91	94	18	55	3.07
1925 Chicago	American	0	0	1	1	1	1	0	18.00
1926 Johnstown	Mid Atlantic	7	3	18	108	74	13	39	1.33
1932 Erie	Central	0	0	1	4	3	0	1	0.00
Major League totals	16 years	212	127	459	3017	2645	712	1711	2.46
Minor League totals	9 years	91	41	186	1194	1038	228	692	2.13
World Series totals	5 years	6	4	10	85	65	21	59	2.44

*Sources: Reicher, Joseph, ed. The Baseball Encyclopedia, 4th edition (New York: Macmillan, 1969, 1979); J. G. Taylor Spink, Paul Reichart and Ray Nemec, Daguerreotypes of Great Stars of Baseball (St. Louis, Charles C. Spink & Son, 1961); "Chief Bender" at www.baseball-reference.com; Sporting News, July 7, 1932.

Chapter Notes

Prologue

1. "Wanted to be a Pitcher," *Washington Post*, July 30, 1905.

2. *New York Times*, October 11, 1913.

3. Ibid., October 11, 1913.

4. "All Make a Hit," *Washington Post*, October 11, 1913.

5. "Barry and Schang Praised by 'Home Run' Baker," *Syracuse Herald*, October 11, 1913.

6. *New York Times*, October 11, 1913.

7. J. Taylor Spink, "Three and One, Looking Them Over with J. Taylor Spink: Chief Bender's Four Decades on the Mound" (Part II), *Sporting News*, December 31, 1942.

8. J. Taylor Spink, "Looping the Loops," *Sporting News*, December 30, 1953.

9. "Indians Watch Scoreboards," *Chicago Daily Tribune*, October 11, 1913.

10. "Daguerreotypes: Charles Albert Bender," *Sporting News*, October 21, 1937.

11. Spink, "Looping the Loops," December 30, 1953.

12. "On the Sporting Pike," *Lincoln Daily Star*, February 10, 1917.

13. "Lajoie Puts Bender Among Top Pitchers," *Janesville Daily Gazette*, December 21, 1916.

14. "Chief Bender Compares New and Old Pitching," *Galveston Daily News*, August 23, 1925.

15. Billy Evans, "Sports of All Sorts," *Port Arthur News*, December 17, 1925.

16. *Sporting News*, November 22, 1950.

17. Spink, "Three and One," December 24, 1942.

18. Spink, "Looping the Loops," December 30, 1953.

19. Ibid., September 30, 1953.

Chapter 1

1. Charles Bender's middle name may have actually been the German name "Albertus" rather than the Americanized "Albert." A reporter who did a first-hand biographical article on Bender during the summer of 1903 wrote, "His name is Charles Albertus Bender and all his life he has been called Al." "Baseball Gossip: Athletic Pitcher Bender Promises to Become a Celebrated Twirler," *Washington Post*, August 3, 1903.

2. "White Earth Reservation 1911 Land List ('individuals of full Indian Blood')," ftp://ftp.rootsweb.com/pub/usgenweb/mn/native/land/wereser6.txt.

3. Robert Tholkes of the Society for Baseball Research discovered that according to Charles' birth certificate, registered by his sister in 1942, his father's name was Albertus Bliss Bender. Robert Tholkes, "Chief Bender: The Early Years," *Baseball Research Journal* (SABR), 1983. "Albertus" Bender, age 20, appears in the 1880 U.S. Federal Census for McLeod County, Minnesota. He was a single farm laborer who gave his birthplace as Massachusetts. Some researchers have accepted this individual as the father of Charles Bender and maintain that "Albertus" was the elder Bender's given name instead of Albert. Census information is very problematic and should be considered very carefully and corroborated if at all possible. The entries are only as accurate as the individuals providing the information and the census official's competence. Often one might find the same individual in several censuses over a period of years, and it would not be unusual to find discrepancies in the spelling of family members' names, ages and even places of birth.

4. J. Taylor Spink, "Three and One, Looking Them Over with J. Taylor Spink: Over the Trail with Chief Bender" (Part I), *Sporting News*, December 24, 1942. Some baseball publications still use 1883 as Bender year of birth though Charles himself told Spink it was 1884.

5. Tholkes, "Chief Bender: The Early Years," Birthplace of Charles Albertus Bender came

from his birth certificate registered in 1942 by his sister Maud Seymour.

6. "Ojibwe History," http://www.tolatsga.org/ojib.html. The word Ojibwe came from the Algonquin word "otchipwa" which means "to roast till puckered up" (ojib "to pucker up" and ub-way "to roast").

7. *Our Documents: 100 Milestone Documents from the National Archives* (New York: Oxford University Press, 2003).

8. Spink, "Looping the Loops," *Sporting News*, September 30, 1953.

9. Spink, "Three and One," December 24, 1942.

10. *The News* (Frederick, Md.), March 23, 1944.

11. Tholkes, "Chief Bender: The Early Years."

12. Ibid.

13. From the prayer that preceded the school's charter. Tholkes, "Chief Bender: The Early Years."

14. Spink, "Three and One," December 24, 1942.

15. Ibid.

16. Ibid.

17. "First Person Accounts as Written by American Indian Students at Hampton Institute, 1878–1923," compiled and edited by John L. Brudvig, 1994 and 1996; http://www.twofrog.com/hampton.html.

18. *Chester Times*, June 17, 1940.

19. Spink, "Three and One," December 24, 1942.

20. Ibid.

21. Barbara Landis, "Carlisle Indian Industrial School History," 1996 at epix.net/~landis/history.html.

22. Barbara Landis, "A Virtual Tour of the Carlisle Indian Industrial School," 1996, epix.net/~landis tour.html.

23. Personal information on Bender from National Archives' student file #1327, folder 5453 (database compiled by Genevieve Bell), at "Benders at Carlisle," epix.net/~landis/bender.html.

24. Spink, "Three and One," Spink, December 24, 1942.

25. Jack Newcombe, *The Best of the Athletic Boys* (Garden City, NY: Doubleday, 1975).

26. Stoney McLinn, "Carlisle: Where Pop Warner Built First 'Color Team,'" *Sporting News*, January 7, 1943.

27. Spink, "Three and One," December 31, 1942.

28. Newcombe, *The Best of the Athletic Boys*.

29. *The Indian Helper, A Weekly Letter—* from the Indian Industrial School, Carlisle, Pa., June 30, 1899, reprinted at "Benders at Carlisle," epix.net/~landis/bender.html.

30. *American Indians in Football: Carlisle Indian School,* members.tripod.com/~johnny-rodgers/centrals qindian.html.

31. Spink, "Three and One," December 24, 1942.

32. Frederic Linch, "Charles Albert Bender," *Baseball Magazine*, May 1912.

33. Spink, "Three and One," December 24, 1942.

34. Linch, "Charles Albert Bender."

35. Spink, "Three and One," *Sporting News*, December 24, 1942.

36. *Carlisle Daily Herald*, May 2, 1901.

37. Spink, "Looping the Loops," *Sporting News*, December 30, 1953. Jeffrey Powers-Beck, *The American Indian Integration of Baseball* (Lincoln: University of Nebraska Press, 2004).

38. "Bloomsburg Loses to Carlisle," *Evening Volunteer*, June 22, 1901.

39. "Louis Leroy, Stockbridge," epix.net/~landis/leroy.html.

40. Ibid.

41. Newcombe, *The Best of the Athletic Boys*.

42. Powers-Beck, *The American Integration of Baseball*.

43. Spink, "Looping the Loops," December 30, 1953.

44. Ibid.

45. "Game Was One of the Prettiest Ever Witnessed at Carlisle," *Carlisle Daily Herald*, April 21, 1902.

46. Spink, "Three and One," December 31, 1942.

47. Spink, "Three and One," *Sporting News*, December 31, 1942.

48. *Harrisburg Telegraph*, June 16, 1902.

49. "Colts Defeat Harrisburg," *Chicago Daily Tribune*, June 18, 1902. "Bender Fooled Frank Selee," *Oakland Tribune*, April 26, 1908.

50. "Bender Fooled Selee," April 26, 1908.

51. "H.A.C. Should Have Won," *Harrisburg Telegram*, June 23, 1902.

52. "Lost in the Tenth Inning," *Harrisburg Telegram*, August 5, 1902.

53. Tholkes, "Chief Bender" The Early Years."

54. Spink, "Three and One," December 31, 1942.

55. Spink, "Three and One," December 31, 1942.

56. "Jimeson a Jewel," *Sporting News*, January 15, 1898; Powers-Beck, *The American Indian Integration of Baseball*.

57. Carlisle Alumni Who Played Major League Baseball: Charles Bender, Chippewa—Phil (AL) 1903–14, Balt (FL) 1915, Phil (NL) 1916–17, Chi (AL) 1925; Lou Bruce, Mohawk—Phil (AL) 1904; Louis LeRoy, Seneca—NY (AL) 1905–06, Bos (AL) 1910; Frank Jude, Chippewa—Cin (NL) 1906; Charlie Roy, Chippewa—Phil (NL) 1906; Mike Balenti, Cheyenne—Cin (NL) 1911, StL (AL) 1913; Jim

Thorpe, Fox & Sac — NY (NL) 1913–15, 1917–19, Cin (NL) 1917, Bos (NL) 1919.

Chapter 2

1. Connie Mack, *My 66 Years in the Big Leagues* (Philadelphia: John C. Winston, 1950).
2. Lawrence S. Ritter, *Lost Ballparks: A Celebration of Baseball's Legendary Fields* (New York: Viking Studio Books, 1992), p. 178. Michael Gershman, *Diamonds: The Evolution of the Ballpark* (New York: Houghton Mifflin, 1993).
3. Mack, *My 66 Years in the Big Leagues*.
4. Ibid.
5. Bob Warrington, "Connie Mack's Days as a Player, Part II: The Pittsburgh Years," philadelphiaathletics.org/history /Mack.html; Connie Mack, *My 66 Years in the Big Leagues*.
6. Norman Macht, "Connie Mack," http:// www.baseballlibrary.com.
7. Bob Warrington, "The Story of the 1902 American League Champion Athletics," phila delphiaathletics.org/history/1902champs.html.
8. "Senators Play Snappy Ball and Defeat Quakers," *Washington Post*, April 27, 1901.
9. Harry Davis obituary in *Sporting News*, August 20, 1947. Warrington, "The Story of the 1902 American League Champion Athletics," philadelphiaathletics.org.
10. Warrington, "The Story of the 1902 American League Champion Athletics."
11. "Telling Tales," *Sporting Life*, July 19, 1902.
12. "Mack Answers Mac," *Sporting Life*, July 19, 1902.
13. Mack, *My 66 Years in the Big Leagues*.
14. "Philly's Pennant," *Sporting Life*, September 27, 1902.
15. "Champions Honored," *Sporting Life*, October 4, 1902.
16. Ibid.
17. "Daguerreotypes: Charles Albert Bender," *Sporting News*, October 21, 1937.

Chapter 3

1. Spink, "Three and One, Looking Them Over with J. Taylor Spink: Over the Trail with Chief Bender" (Part I)."
2. Ibid.
3. Ibid.
4. *Philadelphia North American*, March 1, 1903; March 10, 1903.
5. Ibid.
6. "Baseball Gossip: Athletic Pitcher Bender Promises to Become a Celebrated Twirler," *Washington Post*, August 3, 1903.
7. "Bender Is Praised," *Philadelphia North American*, March 20, 1903.
8. *Sporting News*, April 25, 1903.
9. "Monte Cross Benched, Athletics Lose 6–5," *Philadelphia Inquirer*, April 10, 1903.
10. *Sporting Life*, April 18, 1903.
11. *Philadelphia North American,* April 11, 1903.
12. Spink, "Three and One," December 31, 1942.
13. "Philadelphia Teams Tie Boston Rivals," *Philadelphia North American*, April 11, 1903.
14. Ernest J. Lanigan, "Fight for Games," *Sporting News*, May 2, 1903.
15. Spink, "Three and One," December 31, 1942.
16. *New York World*, April 27, 1903.
17. *Philadelphia North American*, April 27, 1903.
18. *New York Times*, April 28, 1903.
19. *Sporting News*, May 9, 1903.
20. *Sporting News*, May 9, 1903.
21. *Washington Post*, June 8, 1903; Jeffrey Powers-Beck, *The American Indian Integration of Baseball*.
22. "Cartoonists Portray Doings of Athletics," *Philadelphia North American,* May 28, 1903.
23. Powers-Beck, *The American Integration of Baseball*.
24. "Athletic Pitcher Bender Promises to Become a Celebrated Twirler," *Washington Post*, August 3, 1903.
25. Roger Amsden, "D.A. Long Was Pioneer in Baseball and Journalism," *Weirs Times News Correspondent*, www.funspotnh.com/mws-tav ern.htm, the D. A. Long Tavern Web Page.
26. Catherine Davids, "A Season of Brilliance, Part II," 1977, www.aistm.org/sockbio 2.htm.
27. "Athletic Pitcher Bender Promises to Become a Celebrated Twirler," *Washington Post*, August 3, 1903.
28. Charles Dryden, "Bender and Henley Did Star Twirling," *Philadelphia North American*, July 22, 1903.
29. "Game Was a Tea Party, but Not for Boston," *Philadelphia North American*, August 7, 1903.
30. Alan H. Levy, *Rube Waddell: The Zany, Brilliant Life of a Strikeout Artist* (Jefferson, N.C.: McFarland, 2000).
31. Lee Allen, *The American League Story* (New York: Hill & Wang, 1962).
32. *Washington Post*, September 15, 1903.
33. Jeffrey Powers-Beck, "'Chief': The American Indian Integration of Baseball, 1897–1945," (University of Nebraska Press, The American Indian Quarterly, Volume 25, Number 4, Fall 2001).
34. Spink, "Three and One," December 31, 1942.
35. *Oakland Tribune*, September 24, 1907; *Philadelphia North American*, August 17, 1903.

36. "Billy Evans Says," *The Bee*, Danville, Va., November 17, 1925.

37. C. B. Rothwell, "Only the Ball Was Dead: Conversations with Connie Mack's White Elephants," codelikethewind.com. This document was found among receipts, contracts and other miscellaneous papers in a cardboard box, stored in a warehouse after Shibe Park was demolished. Interestingly, the questions are not included, only the players' answers. The interviewer is also unknown.

38. *Sporting News*, October 10, 1903.

39. Norman L. Macht, *Connie Mack and the Early Years of Connie Mack* (Lincoln: University of Nebraska Press, 2007).

40. Spink, "Three and One," December 31, 1942.

41. "Bender a Billiard Expert," *Carlisle American Volunteer*, February 27, 1904.

42. *Washington Post*, March 13, 1904.

43. Frank G. Menke, "Big Chief Bender Cures Himself Without Services of Physician," *New Castle News*, April 30, 1914.

44. *Sporting News*, October 15, 1904.

45. *Sporting News*, October 10, 1903; Bill Weiss and Marshall Wright, "The 1902 Toronto Maple Leafs," www.minorleaguebaseball.com.

46. *Sporting News*, June 18, 1904.

47. *Sporting News*, July 23, 1904.

48. Ibid., July 23, 1904; "White Coat for the Sox," *Chicago Daily Tribune*, July 14, 1904.

49. *Sporting Life*, July 23, 1904.

50. Ibid.

51. *Sporting News*, October 1, 1904.

52. "Clever Indian Player Found Wife in Detroit," *The Titusville (Pa.) Herald*, October 10, 1904. According to United States census records, Marie Bender's father was born in France and her mother was German.

53. *Washington Post*, October 8, 1904.

54. Ed Pollock, "A Wife's Memories of Chief Bender," *Philadelphia Evening Bulletin*, May 24, 1954.

55. *Syracuse Post-Standard*, December 17, 1904.

56. Rich Westcott, "Columbia Park Was the First Home of the Athletics," *Philadelphia Athletics Historical Society*.

57. "Bender Praised," *Sporting Life*, November 25, 1905.

Chapter 4

1. "First Person Accounts as Written by American Indian Students at Hampton Institute, 1878–1923."

2. Francis Richter, "Philadelphia News," *Sporting Life*, August 5, 1905.

3. H. C. Hamiton, "Chief Bender Is About Thru," *Waterloo Evening Courier and Reporter*, March 10, 1917.

4. J. Taylor Spink, *Sporting News*, February 19, 1931.

5. *Philadelphia North American*, April 11, 1903.

6. "Charles Dryden Dies," *New York Times*, February 13, 1931.

7. "Athletics Won Opener after 9th Inning Scare," *Philadelphia North American*, April 15, 1905.

8. *Sporting Life*, May 26, 1906.

9. *Washington Post*, June 30, 1906.

10. *New York Times*, September 4, 1908.

11. *Waterloo Evening Courier*, September 17, 1910.

12. "Athletics Are the Champions," *New York Times*, October 27, 1911.

13. "Career of 'Chief' Charles Albert Bender, The 'Good Indian' of Baseball," *Chicago Daily News*, May 11, 1913.

14. "A Just Protest," *Sporting Life*, April 6, 1907.

15. "Bender Is Bad Indian When His Blood Is Up," *Atlanta Constitution*, April 9, 1908.

16. "This Was Different," *Sporting Life*, November 25, 1911.

17. Nick Jaska, "Louis Sockalexis: An Analysis of the Media Coverage Given to Baseball's First Native American," (Thesis) University of North Carolina at Asheville, November 2003.

18. David Fleitz, *Louis Sockalexis: The First Cleveland Indian* (Jefferson, N.C., McFarland, 2002).

19. Jaska, "Louis Sockalexis."

20. Davids, "A Season of Brilliance," Part I, www.aistm.org/sockbio2.htm.

21. *Sporting News*, May 1, 1897.

22. Sockalexis a Big Chief," *Washington Post*, May 2, 1897.

23. "Sockalexis in Trouble," *Chicago Daily Tribune*, July 15, 1897.

24. "Sockalexis Likes Firewater," *Washington Post*, July 31, 1897.

25. "'Ugh!' Was All Sockalexis Said," *Fort Wayne Gazette*, August 3, 1897.

26. *Cleveland Plain Dealer*, January 17, 1915.

27. *Cleveland Plain Dealer*, January 18, 1915.

28. "Baseball Gossip: Athletic Pitcher Bender Promises to Become a Celebrated Twirler," *Washington Post*, August 3, 1903.

29. "Wanted To Be a Pitcher," *Washington Post*, July 30, 1905.

30. "Evans Says," *Port Arthur News*, February 3, 1925.

31. Ibid.

32. Patty Loew, "Tinker to Evers to Chief: Baseball from Indian Country," *Wisconsin Magazine of History* (Spring 2004).

33. "Wanted to be a Pitcher," *Washington Post*, July 30, 1905.

34. "About Chief Bender," *St. Louis Star*

Chronicle (reprinted in *The Arrow*), September 13, 1907.

35. Warren Goldstein, "Bender, Chief," *Encyclopedia of North American Indians* (Boston: Houghton Mifflin, 1996), http://college.hmco.com/history/readers comp/naind/html/na_00 3500_benderchief.htm.

36. Lawrence Ritter, "Rube Bressler" in *The Glory of Their Times* (New York: Macmillan, 1966).

Chapter 5

1. "Chief Bender Compares Two Great Teams," *Portsmouth Herald*, July 11, 1929.

2. "Recalls with Relish Pitching Mastery of Rube Waddell," *Kansas City Star*, March 29, 1942.

3. Spink, "Three and One," December 31, 1942.

4. Levy, *Rube Waddell*.

5. Ibid.

6. *Sporting News,* February 18, 1905.

7. "Quaker Quips," Frances Richter, *Sporting Life*, March 11, 1905.

8. *Sporting News,* March 18, 1905.

9. *Sporting Life*, April 8, 1905.

10. "Quakers Hit Young Hard, but the Safeties Are Scattered," *Philadelphia North American*, April 15, 1905.

11. "Athletics Won Opener After 9th Inning Scare," *Philadelphia North American*, April 15, 1905.

12. "Wanted to Be a Pitcher," *Washington Post*, July 30, 1905.

13. Levy, *Rube Waddell*.

14. "Waddell with Bender's Help Beat 'Cy' Young," *Philadelphia North American*, July 8, 1905.

15. "Athletics Split Doubleheader with Boston Before Largest Crowd in Local Baseball History," *Philadelphia North American*, July 9, 1905.

16. "Quaker Public Is Mad with Joy," *Chicago Daily Tribune*, September 30, 1905.

17. Ibid.

18. "Bender Takes Scalps," *Chicago Daily Tribune*, September 30, 1905.

19. Charles Dryden, "Two Scalps for Bender," *Sporting News*, October 14, 1905.

20. "Indian Pitcher Hero in Double Victory," *Washington Post*, October 6, 1905.

21. Allan Sangree, "Hail Mathewson, the Champion of All Pitchers," *New York World*, October 9, 1905.

22. Geoffrey C. Ward and Ken Burns, *Baseball: An Illustrated History* (New York: Alfred A. Knopf, 1994).

23. J. Taylor Spink, "How Disaster Befell a Great Pitcher, *Sporting News*, December 10, 1942; Levy, *Rube Waddell*.

24. Frank Graham, *The New York Giants: An Informal History* (New York: Putnam's, 1952).

25. Allen Sangree, "Hail Mathewson the Champion of All Pitchers," *New York World*, October 9, 1905.

26. "Giants Triumph, 3–0, in Inter-League Game," *New York Times*, October 10, 1905.

27. John J. McGraw, *My Thirty Years in Baseball* (Lincoln: University of Nebraska Press, 1995).

28. Allan Sangree, "Hail Mathewson the Champion of all Pitchers," *New York World*, October 9, 1905.

29. "Giants Triumph, 3–0, in Inter-League Game," *New York Times*, October 10, 1905.

30. *New York Times*, October 11, 1905.

31. Bozeman Bulger, "Like Mathewson, Bender Was Too Good for Giants," *New York Evening World*, October 10, 1905.

32. *New York Times*, October 11, 1905.

33. Ibid.

34. "Bender Baffles New Yorks," *New York Sun*, October 11, 1905.

35. Spink, "Three and One," *Sporting News*, December 31, 1942.

36. Graham, *The New York Giants: An Informal History*.

37. McGraw, *My Thirty Years in Baseball*.

38. "Players Rewarded," *Sporting Life*, October 21, 1905.

39. *Washington Post,* September 5, 1909.

40. Francis C. Richter, "Philadelphia News," *Sporting Life*, October 28, 1905.

41. "A's Tiptop Days with Topsy Recalled by Harsell's Death," *Sporting News*, October 26, 1944; Francis C. Richter, "Philadelphia News," *Sporting Life*, October 28, 1905. The Philadelphia Mummers were social clubs that practiced the old world tradition of parading in costume much like that at *Mardi Gras*.

Chapter 6

1. *The Sporting News*, March 10, 1906.

2. Rube Oldring, Jr., "Rube Oldring: 'The Pride of the Left Field Stands,'" philadelphi-aathletics.org/museum/ rube.html.

3. *Sporting News*, April 14, 1906.

4. *Sporting News,* September 20, 1961.

5. "Without Equal," *Sporting News*, May 12, 1906.

6. *New York Times*, September 23, 1905.

7. *New York Evening World*, May 4, 1906.

8. "Hogg Batted Out of Box," *New York Times*, May 6, 1906.

9. Herb Rogoff, "The Mighty Bender," *Baseball Magazine*, September 2003.

10. *Cleveland Plain Dealer*, May 22, 1906.

11. "Recalls with Relish Pitching Mastery of Rube Waddell," *Kansas City Star*, March 29, 1942.

12. Bert McGrane, "'Ironman Jack' Coombs Set Records That Still Stand" *Des Moines Register,* April 8, 1956.

13. *Sporting News,* July 28, 1906.

14. *Philadelphia Inquirer,* March 18, 1907.

15. *Sporting News,* September 20, 1961.

16. Ibid., September 20, 1961.

17. Oldring, "Rube Oldring: 'The Pride of the Left Field Stands.'"

18. *Sporting News,* April 13, 1907.

19. "Barred from New Orleans," *Sporting News,* April 13, 1907.

20. *Sporting News,* April 20, 1907.

21. *Sporting Life,* April 27, 1907.

22. *Washington Post,* April 30, 1907; *Washington Herald,* April 30, 1907.

23. *Washington Herald,* August 26, 1907.

24. Levy, *Rube Waddell.*

25. "Indian Sign on the Sox?" *Chicago Daily Tribune,* July 26, 1907.

26. "Bender's Great Game," *The Arrow,* August 23, 1907 (reprinted from the *Philadelphia Press*).

27. *Cleveland Plain Dealer,* August 15, 1907.

28. "Philly Proud," *Sporting Life,* August 24, 1907; *Sporting Life,* August 31, 1907.

29. *Chicago Daily Tribune,* August 22, 1907.

30. "Athletics, in Slump, Are Beaten by Poor Pitching," *Philadelphia North American,* September 18, 1907.

31. Frederick Lieb, *Connie Mack: Grand Old Man of Baseball* (New York: Putnam's, 1945).

32. Bob Warrington, "We Wuz Robbed! The Pennant Race of 1907," Philadelphia Athletics Historical Society, philadelphiaathletics.org/history/1907.html; *New York Times,* October 1, 1907.

33. "Athletics Foozle It in the Seventh," *Philadelphia Inquirer,* October 1, 1907.

34. Ibid.

35. Macht, *Connie Mack.*

36. *Racine Daily Journal,* October 3, 1907.

37. "Three and One," *Sporting News,* December 31, 1942.

38. Dan Basenfelder, "Harry Davis ... Keeps in Contact with Athletics, His Old Team, at 69," *Sporting News,* January 7, 1943.

39. *Gazette and Bulletin,* October 17, 1907.

40. Basenfelder, "Harry Davis..."

41. John Kieran, "Chatting with Connie Mack," *New York Times,* June 29, 1938; "St. Louis Buys Waddell," *The Washington Post,* February 8, 1908.

42. Tom A. Hamilton, "Work in South" *Sporting Life,* March 28, 1908.

43. *Sporting News,* April 16, 1908.

44. *Sporting News,* April 30, 1908.

45. "Waddell Hero Again; Beats Athletics, 5–2," *Philadelphia North American,* May 20, 1908.

46. Ibid.

47. Ibid.

48. *Sporting Life,* June 6, 1908.

49. *Washington Post,* June 14, 1908.

50. *Sporting Life,* August 17, 1907. Article incorrectly stated that James Bender played with Jacksonville.

51. "Wm Clark Stabbed," *San Antonio Light,* July 25, 1908. "Bursting an Old Bubble," *Archives de Colby Cosh,* colbycosh.com/old/march03,html; "South Atlantic League," *Sporting Life,* March 27, 1909.

52. "Carlisle Indian Is a Great Marksman," *The Arrow,* December 18, 1908 (reprinted from the *Carlisle Sentinel*).

53. *Washington Post,* June 6, 1909.

54. Samuel Wesley Long, "Chief Bender Goes Back to O.B.," *Baseball Magazine,* April 1916.

55. *Washington Post,* February 21, 1909.

56. Ibid., February 21, 1909.

57. *Sporting Life,* February 27, 1909.

58. Ibid.

59. "Mack Suspends Two of His Men," *Washington Post,* September 7, 1912.

60. Tholkes, "Chief Bender: The Early Years."

61. "Mack Suspends Two of His Men," *Washington Post,* September 7, 1912.

Chapter 7

1. *Sporting Life,* March 13, 1909.

2. Bruce Kuklick, *To Every Thing a Season: Shibe Park and Urban Philadelphia* (Princeton, N.J.: Princeton University Press, 1991), p. 28; Francis Richter, "New Century Event in Old Philadelphia," *Sporting Life,* April 17, 1909.

3. Tholkes, "Chief Bender: The Early Years."

4. Kuklick, *To Every Thing a Season: Shibe Park and Urban Philadelphia*; Richter, "New Century Event in Old Philadelphia."

5. Francis Richter, "Quaker Quips," *Sporting Life,* May 15, 1909.

6. "Great Throng Sees Athletics Start Season Victorious," *Philadelphia North American,* April 13, 1909.

7. *Sporting News,* May 8, 1913.

8. "Star Pitchers' Superstitious About Their Battery Partners," *Anaconda Standard,* November 20, 1910.

9. "The World of Sport," *Lincoln Daily News,* May 15, 1913.

10. *Washington Post,* June 6, 1909.

11. Richard Bak, *Ty Cobb: His Tumultuous Life and Times* (Dallas: Taylor, 1994).

12. "No Weak Spot in Ty Cobb, Great Slugger," *New Castle News,* April 22, 1910.

13. *Sporting News,* June 9, 1909.

14. *Sporting News,* June 17, 1909.

15. Allen, *The American League.*

16. William Peet, "Win Out in Twelfth," *Washington Herald,* August 18, 1909.

17. *Washington Post,* August 18, 1909.

18. "Bender in Fettle: Cops Third Game from Detroiters," *Philadelphia Inquirer,* September 19, 1909.

19. *Sporting Life,* September 25, 1909.

20. Francis Richter, "The Athletics Grand Triumph," *Sporting Life,* September 25, 1909.

21. *Sporting News,* October 7, 1909.

22. "Ten Games More Then Coast Barn-Stormers Will Hie Away Home," *Sporting News,* December 9, 1909; Henry W. Thomas, *Walter Johnson: Baseball's Big Train* (Washington D.C.: Phenom Press, Washington D.C., 1995).

Chapter 8

1. *Washington Post,* April 7, 1910.

2. "Mack's Mascot Paid $50 Per Month," *New Castle News,* November 2, 1910.

3. Kuklick, *To Everything a Season.*

4. Spink, "Looping the Loops," *Sporting News,* December 30, 1953.

5. Brown Holmes, "Turner's Base on Balls Mars Chief's Record," *Cleveland Leader,* May 13, 1910.

6. Spink, "Three and One," *Sporting News,* December 31, 1942.

7. Holmes, "Turner's Base on Balls Mars Chief's Record," May 13, 1910.

8. Ibid., p. 6; "Three and One," *Sporting News,* December 31, 1942.

9. "Mackmen's Spurt in Ninth Suddenly Ends; Lose 4–3," *Philadelphia North American,* May 24, 1910.

10. Ibid.

11. *Sporting News,* July 21, 1910.

12. *Sporting News,* September 22, 1910.

13. *Waterloo Evening Courier,* September 7, 1910.

14. *Sporting News,* October 20, 1910.

15. Thomas, *Walter Johnson: Baseball's Big Train.*

16. *Sporting News,* September 20, 1961.

17. *Sporting News,* October 16, 1910.

18. "Twirling Tells Tale," *Washington Post,* October 18, 1910.

19. "Injun Pitcher All Too Merry," *Post-Standard* (Syracuse, N.Y.), October 18, 1910.

20. "Athletics Draw First Blood, *Galveston Daily News,* October 18, 1910.

21. *New York Times,* October 18, 1910.

22. "Twirling Tells Tale," *Washington Post,* October 18, 1910.

23. *New York Times,* October 18, 1910.

24. "Views from Rival Camps After the Battle," *Chicago Daily Tribune,* October 18, 1910.

25. "Twirling Tells Tale," *Washington Post,* October 18, 1910.

26. *Sporting News,* November 14, 1912.

27. *Chicago Daily Tribune,* October 21, 1910.

28. "My Fifty Years in Baseball by Connie Mack," *Salt Lake Tribune,* October 7, 1930.

29. Ibid.

30. *Washington Post,* October 23, 1910; *Chicago Daily Tribune,* October 21, 1910.

31. *Sporting Life,* January 14, 1911.

32. John B. Holway, *Blackball Stars: Negro League Pioneers* (New York: Carroll & Graf, 1992); "Athletics' Cuban Trip," *Sporting Life,* January 21, 1911.

33. "From the South," *The American Golfer,* March 1911, No. 2.

34. "From the South," *The American Golfer,* December 1911, No. 2.

35. "From the South," *The American Golfer,* January 1913, No. 3; March 1913, No. 5.

Chapter 9

1. *Sporting News,* June 1, 1911.

2. Kuklick, *To Every Thing a Season: Shibe Park and Urban Philadelphia.*

3. *Sporting News,* April 20, 1911.

4. Mack, *My 66 Years in the Big Leagues;* Shatzkin and Holtje, *The Ballplayers.*

5. Bill James, *The Historic Baseball Abstract* (New York: Villard, 1988).

6. Francis Richter, "Quaker Quips," *Sporting Life,* June 17, 1911.

7. "Wasn't It Tire Trouble That Beat the Hare in the Tortoise Match," *Chicago Daily Tribune,* June 15, 1911.

8. Ibid.

9. *Washington Post,* June 23, 1911.

10. Bill McCurdy, Philadelphia Athletics Historical Society: Fact of the Day, philadelphia athletics.org/history/ mcinnis.html.

11. Spink, "Looping the Loops," December 30, 1953.

12. "Cobb Goes One Better, He Beats Athletics," *San Antonio Light,* July 14, 1911.

13. *Sporting News,* July 20, 1911.

14. *Sporting News,* July 20, 1911.

15. "Shibe Park Goes Mad," *Washington Post,* July 29, 1911.

16. *Sporting News,* August 10, 1911.

17. *Sporting News,* August 17, 1911.

18. Ibid.

19. "Baseball Player Dropped Dead," *Edmonton Bulletin,* September 25, 1911.

20. Thomas, *Walter Johnson: Baseball's Big Train.*

21. *Sporting News,* August 14, 1971.

22. Robert Smith, *World Series: The Games And The Players* (New York: Doubleday, 1967). "Giants Battery Gives Views on First Game," *Washington Post,* October 15, 1911.

24. "Giants Great Backstop Predicts Series Victory," *Syracuse Herald,* October 15, 1911.

25. Ibid.

26. Fred Lieb, *Baseball as I Have Known It*

(New York: Coward, McCann & Geoghegan, 1977).

27. Grantland Rice, "Baker Slams Second Home Run in Two Days and Athletics Win," *Trenton Evening Times*, October 18, 1911.

28. Lieb, *Baseball as I Have Known It*.

29. Graham, *The New York Giants: An Informal History*.

30. "Athletics Pound Out Their Third Victory in the World's Series," *Syracuse Herald*, October 25, 1911.

31. Ibid.

32. Lieb, *Baseball as I Have Known It*.

33. *Sporting News*, April 24, 1957.

34. James Isaminger, "World Series Hero," *Sporting Life*, March 9, 1912. Ty Cobb, "Athletics Earn Right to Title," *Chicago Daily Tribune*, October 28, 1911.

35. James Isaminger, "World Series Hero," *Sporting Life*, March 9, 1912.

36. "How the Giants Lost," *New York Times*, October 28, 1911.

37. "Athletics Are Champions," *New York Times*, October 28, 1911.

38. *Sporting Life*, November 4, 1911.

39. *Washington Post*, October 27, 1911; Cohen, Neft, and Deutsch, *The World Series*.

40. James Mote, *Everything Baseball* (New York: Prentice Hall, 1989).

41. *Washington Post*, November 11, 1911.

42. Richard Henry Little, "The Idols of the Diamond," *Chicago Daily Tribune*, December 6, 1911.

43. Ibid.

Chapter 10

1. Bak, *Ty Cobb*.

2. James Cruisenberry, "Secrets of Winning a Championship," *Baseball Magazine*, April 1914.

3. I. E. Sanborn, "Bender Eyes of the Team," *Chicago Daily Tribune*, December 3, 1911.

4. Ibid.

5. Joe Williams, "Del Baker Signal Hawk for Hank Greenberg," *Sporting News*, April 9, 1936. The Ainsmith story was retold many times with basically the same details except for the batter, who was variously said to have been Oldring, McInnis or Barry.

6. Thomas, *Walter Johnson: Baseball's Big Train*.

7. *Sporting News*, May 2, 1912.

8. *Washington Post*, May 17, 1912.

9. Frank Vaccaro, "Herb Pennock," *SABR's Baseball Biography Project*, http://www.bioproj.sabr.org.

10. *Sporting News*, August 22, 1912.

11. *Sporting News*, January 15, 1931.

12. "Connie Mack's Fifty Years in Baseball," *Gettysburg Times*, September 23, 1930.

13. F. C. Lane, "Greatest Manager in Organized Baseball," *Baseball Magazine*, May 1913, vol. X, no 7.

14. Frank Yeutter, "When a Few Beers Cost A's Flag" (condensed from *Philadelphia Bulletin*), *Baseball Digest*, January 1951, Vol. 10, No. 1, pp. 61–62.

15. "Mack suspends Two of His Men," *Washington Post*, September 7, 1912; *Van Wert Daily Bulletin*, September 8, 1912.

16. "The Fallen Stars of 1912," *Sporting Life*, September 2, 1912.

17. Arthur Daley, "Sports of the Times," *New York Times*, March 6, 1950.

18. "Chief Bender's Wife Seriously Injured," *Syracuse Herald*, September 9, 1912.

19. "Enough to Sour an Indian," *Sporting News*, September 12, 1912.

20. Seymour, *Baseball, The Golden Age*.

21. "In the Wake of the News," *Chicago Daily Tribune*, September 11, 1912.

22. Spink, "Three and One," *Sporting News*, December 31, 1942.

23. *Sporting News*, October 24, 1912.

24. Victor Munoz, "Athletics Are Out to Retrieve Reputations," *Sporting News*, November 14, 1912.

25. *Sporting Life*, December 14, 1912.

26. *Sporting Life*, November 30, 1912.

27. "Baker's Bat," *Sporting Life*, November 30, 1912.

28. Daley, "Sports of the Times," March 6, 1950.

29. "Baseball Notes," *Lowell Sun*, February 6, 1913.

30. *Washington Post*, February 2, 1913.

31. *Sporting News*, April 17, 1913.

32. Bruce McGrane, "'Ironman Jack' Coombs Set Records That Still Stand," *Des Moines Register*, April 8, 1956.

33. *Sporting News*, May 1, 1913.

34. Mack, *My 66 Years in the Big Leagues*.

35. *Sporting News*, June 19, 1913.

36. *Sporting Life*, July 5, 1913; *Washington Post*, June 27, 1913. According to a story introduced by Billy Evans in his newspaper column a few years later, Bender concluded his windup by delivering a pitch to the batter, who swung and hit a harmless fly ball. Immediately, Bender made a mild protest to Umpire Evans. "Naturally, the run doesn't count," he insisted. Evans realized there were two out when the play began and announced, "You're right. The run doesn't count. I have to give the decision on the pitch and the pitch starts with the windup." However, the record books credit Eddie Ainsmith with three stolen bases in one inning. Arthur Daily, "Sports of the Time," *New York Times*, May 28, 1954; unidentified newspaper, Bender player file, National Baseball Hall of Fame Library.

37. *Sporting News,* July 24, 1913.

38. "Deny Rumor that Chief Bender Was Bought," *Daily Northwestern* (Oshkosh, Wis.), October 7, 1913.

39. *Sporting News,* October 16, 1913.

40. "Athletics Trim Giants, 6 to 4," *Lowell Sun,* October 7, 1913.

41. *New York Times,* October 8, 1913.

42. *Washington Post,* October 10, 1913.

43. Allen, *The American League Story.*

44. Gordon Mackay, "What Spurred Bender to Supreme Efforts," *Sporting Life,* November 22, 1913.

45. *New York Times,* October 8, 1913.

46. "The Indian's Triumph," *Washington Post,* October 8, 1913.

47. "Chief Bender Answers Call to Happy Hunting Grounds," *Sporting News,* June 2, 1954; "Charles A. Bender," Associated Press article, May 15, 1942, player file, National Baseball Hall of Fame Library."

48. Daley, "Sports of the Times," March 6, 1950.

49. *Sporting Life,* October 25, 1913.

50. "Honor for the Athletics," *Sporting Life,* November 1, 1913.

51. "Big Chief Bender Is Honored," *Lima Daily News,* October 21, 1913.

52. *Sporting News,* November 13, 1913; *Sporting Life,* November 22, 1913.

Chapter 11

1. Seymour, *Baseball: The Golden Age.*

2. Ibid.

3. Ibid.

4. Kuklick, *To Every Thing a Season: Shibe Park and Urban Philadelphia.*

5. *Washington Post,* February 22, 1914.

6. Ritter, *The Glory of Their Times.*

7. *New York Times,* April 14, 1914; Seymour, *Baseball: The Golden Age.*

8. "Bender Severely Pounded...," *Washington Post,* May 8, 1914.

9. "Yanks Give Mack a Helping Hand," *New York Times,* May 30, 1914.

10. *Sporting News,* June 18, 1914.

11. *Chicago Daily Tribune,* June 15, 1914.

12. *New York Times,* June 24, 1914.

13. *New York Times,* June 25, 1914, *Sporting News,* July 2, 1914.

14. *Washington Post,* June 28, 1914.

15. Ibid.

16. *New York Times,* July 7, 1914.

17. Ritter, *The Glory of Their Times.*

18. *Washington Post,* July 17, 1914.

19. "Griffmen Are Helpless Before 'Chief' Bender," *Washington Post,* August 16, 1914.

20. "Sweeney's Homer Beats Athletics," *New York Times,* September 13, 1914.

21. *New York Times,* September 13, 1914.

22. Frederick G. Lieb "Inside the Games Most Famous Deals," *Sporting News,* October 28, 1943.

23. Spink, "Three and One," December 31, 1942.

24. Joe Villa, "The Athletics Downfall," *Sporting Life,* October 24, 1914.

25. *Sporting News,* December 5, 1914.

26. *Sporting News,* October 15, 1914.

27. *Sporting News,* October 22, 1914.

28. *Sporting News,* November 5, 1914.

29. *Sporting News,* November 5, 1914.

30. Lieb, "Inside the Games Most Famous Deals," October 28, 1943.

31. Notes from the *Shadows of Cooperstown,* #289, Norman Macht, Society for American Baseball Research (SABR), March 4, 2003.

32. "Athletic Housecleaning," *Sporting Life,* November 7, 1914.

33. Lieb, *Connie Mack: Grand Old Man of Baseball.*

34. *Sporting News,* October 6, 1948.

35. Macht, *Connie Mack and the Early Years of Baseball.*

36. *Sporting News,* December 10, 1914.

37. Spink, "Three and One," *Sporting News,* December 31, 1942.

38. *Sporting News,* November 19, 1914.

39. *Sporting Life,* November 28,1914.

40. *Star and Sentinel* (Gettysburg, Pa.), November 27, 1914.

41. *New York Times,* December 2, 1914.

42. *New York Times,* December 6, 1914.

43. "Bender's Statement," *Sporting Life,* December 12, 1914.

44. "$5000 Most Bender Drew, *San Antonio Light,* March 16, 1938; Spink, "Three and One," *Sporting News.*

45. *Sporting Life,* December 19, 1914.

46. *Sporting Life,* May 18, 1912.

47. *Carlisle Arrow,* November 12, 1915.

48. Brudvig, "Hampton Normal & Agricultural Institutes American Indian Students, 1878–1923"; Jason Tetzloff, "Cloud, Henry Roe" in the *Encyclopedia of North American Indians* (Boston: Houghton Mifflin, 1996). http://college. hmco.com/history/readers.com.

49. *Sporting Life,* December 19, 1914.

50. *Syracuse Herald,* February 1, 1915.

51. *Chicago Daily Tribune,* May 7, 1915.

52. "The Terrapins' Trouble," *Sporting Life,* May 22, 1915.

53. *New York Times,* June 27, 1914; *Sporting News,* July 1, 1914.

54. *Lincoln Sunday Star,* August 22, 1915.

55. *Sporting News,* September 5, 1915.

56. "Three and One," *Sporting News,* December 31, 1942.

57. *New York Times,* November 30, 1915. Bender's suit never made it to court as an

undisclosed settlement was apparently reached with the Baltimore stockholders.

58. Seymour, *Baseball: The Golden Age.*

59. Ibid.

60. "Many Ball Players Are Excellent Trap Shots," *Atlanta Constitution*, March 5, 1916.

61. "What a Famous Pitcher Thinks of Trap Shooting," *Baseball Magazine*, April 1916.

62. "Bender's Statement," *Sporting Life*, December 12, 1914.

63. *Sporting Life*, December 26, 1914.

64. "Many Ball Players Are Excellent Trap Shots," *Atlanta Constitution*, March 5, 1916.

65. Bob Warrington, "Charles 'Chief' Bender," philadelphiaathletics.org/history/bender.html.

Chapter 12

1. William A. Phelon, "A Chapter from Current Baseball History," *Baseball Magazine*, April 1916.

2. "Believes in Bender, *Sandusky Star-Journal*, March 14, 1916.

3. Pat Levitt, "Pat Moran" at *The Baseball Biography Project*, www.bioproj.sabr.org.

4. *Philadelphia North American*, April 20, 1916.

5. *New York Times*, April 19, 1916; *Sporting News*, May 4, 1916.

6. "Coombs Beats Bender, but Neither Pitcher Lasts," *Philadelphia North American*, April 19, 1916.

7. "Play One-Hand Ball in Game Braves Win," *Washington Post*, October 6, 1916.

8. "Bender Is Motorist Who Ran Away When His Car Killed a Man," *Philadelphia North American*, February 19, 1917; "Chief Bender Is Arrested," *Los Angeles Times*, February 19, 1917.

9. "Bender Is Motorist Who Ran Away When His Car Killed a Man," *Philadelphia North American*, February 19, 1917.

10. *New York Times*, February 22, 1917.

11. "'Chief' Bender Exonerated," *Evening Bulletin*, February 26, 1917.

12. *Washington Post*, February 26, 1917.

13. "On the Sporting Pike," *Lincoln Daily Star*, February 10, 1917.

14. *Sporting News*, March 1, 1917.

15. "Chief Gives Pointers to Penn Hurlers," *New Castle News*, March 27, 1917.

16. "'Chief Bender May be Moran's Best Bet Next Season," *San Antonio Light*, January 21, 1918.

17. *Sporting News*, June 28, 1917.

18. Tom Meany, *Baseball's Greatest Teams* (New York: A. S. Barnes, 1949).

19. *Sporting News*, August 23, 1917.

20. "Chief Bender Hold Cubs to One Hit," *Philadelphia North American*, August 22, 1917.

21. *Philadelphia North American*, August 26, 1917.

22. *Lincoln Daily Star*, September 24, 1917.

23. Pitchers Are the Only Come-Backs," *Oakland Tribune*, October 29, 1917.

24. *Sporting News*, September 13, 1917.

25. *Lincoln Daily Star*, September 24, 1917.

26. *New York Times, New York Times*, September 6, 1917.

27. Accounts vary as to when Bender's injury initially occurred and in a few other minor details. Bender seems to be confused about the time frame because he stated in 1942 that the incision and drainage of the arm occurred "three weeks later on another train (and) my arm swelled up like the head of a rookie pitcher after a no-hit game." This account just does not fit the time frame from this period, as Bender was pitching again in a National League game seventeen days after the injury. More likely, Alexander's surgical intervention occurred on the trip from New York to Boston on September 6 as indicated in Raymond Hill's account in the *Evening Bulletin* on June 11, 1931.

28. "'Fit and Able' Thanks to Old Pete's Pocket Knife," *Galveston Daily News*, February 27, 1942; Raymond A. Hill, "Alexander Saved Chief Bender's Life by Pen Knife Operation on Train," *Philadelphia Evening Bulletin*, June 11, 1931.

29. "Chester Clubbers Win Championship," *Trenton Evening Times*, October 22, 1917.

30. "Chief Bender Deserves Boost," *New Castle News*, February 1, 1919.

31. "Bender Fools Doctors," *Washington Post*, December 15, 1918.

32. Spink, "Three and One," *Sporting News*, December 31, 1942.

33. Ibid., December 31, 1942.

34. Samuel Wesley Long, "De Luxe Trapshooting," *Baseball Magazine*, January 1917.

35. *New York Times*, April 28, 1919.

Chapter 13

1. Spink, "Three and One," December 31, 1942; W. Harrison Daniel and Scott P. Mayer, *Baseball and Richmond* (Jefferson, N.C.: McFarland, 2003).

2. *Richmond Times-Dispatch*, May 31, 1919.

3. *Richmond Times-Dispatch*, June 2, 1919.

4. *Sporting News*, June 12, 1919, June 19, 1919.

5. *Richmond Times-Dispatch*, June 14, 1919.

6. *Richmond Times-Dispatch*, June 26, 1919.

7. *Richmond Times-Dispatch*, July 13, 1919.

8. "'Yes Sir, Chief Bender Was a Real Player,' Says Poole," *Atlanta Constitution*, April 8, 1928.

9. "Burnham's Error Loses Game for

Petersburg," *Richmond Times-Dispatch*, July 25, 1919.

10. "Culloton's Pitching and Hitting Defeats Indians," *Richmond Times-Dispatch*, August 8, 1919.

11. "Chief Hurls and Slugs Indians to Double Win," *Richmond Times-Dispatch*, August 10, 1919.

12. "Shipbuilders Fall Easy Victims Before Bender," *Richmond Times-Dispatch*, August 12, 1919.

13. "Bender to Join Reds," *Times-Democrat* (Lima, Ohio), August 16, 1919.

14. "Indians Take Series by Winning Double-header," *Richmond Times-Dispatch*, August 17, 1919.

15. *Richmond Times-Dispatch,* August 18, 1919.

16. Spink, "Three and One," December 31, 1942.

17. "Richmond Club Disbands," *Richmond Times-Dispatch*, September 11, 1919.

18. "Chief Bender Compares New and Old Pitching," *Galveston Daily News*, August 23, 1925.

19. *Chicago Daily Tribune*, September 16, 1919.

20. "Bender Did Not Steal Signals, Say His Friends," *Atlanta Constitution*, December 9, 1919.

21. Robert Obojski, *Bush League: A History of Minor League Baseball* (New York: Macmillan, 1975).

22. Spink, "Three and One," *Sporting News*, December 31, 1942.

23. Ibid.; "Big Ed Doubles in Ninth and Robs Bender of No-Hit Game," *Bridgeport Telegram*, June 11, 1920.

24. "The Dream of the Baseball Pitcher...," *Bridgeport Telegram*, August 20, 1920.

25. *Bridgeport Telegram*, September 27, 1920; *Washington Post*, September 27, 1920.

26. C. Ford Sawyer, "Chief Bender at 37 Still Pitches No-Hit, No-Run Games," *Boston Daily Globe*, September 26, 1920.

27. Ibid.

28. "Bender Prefers Minors as Manager, He Asserts," *Sandusky Star-Journal,* June 6, 1921.

29. *Sporting News*, December 23, 1920.

30. *Sporting News*, November 3, 1921.

31. Spink, *Daguerreo-Types.*

32. *Sporting News*, September 1, 1921.

33. Tom Marchitto, "New Haven's Minor League Clubs," www.ldeo.columbia.edu/~t marchit/rec/.

34. "Daguerreotypes: Charles Albert Bender," *Sporting News*, October 21, 1937.

35. *Syracuse Herald*, July 6, 1931.

36. *Syracuse Herald*, May 15, 1922.

37. *Reading Eagle*, May 31, 1922.

38. *Sporting News*, June 8, 1922; *Sporting News*, July 6, 1922.

39. *Sporting News*, July 6, 1922.

40. "Daguerreotypes: Charles Albert Bender," *Sporting News*, October 21, 1937.

41. *Washington Post,* May 23, 1923.

42. "Nats Show Fondness for Navy Pitching," *Washington Post*, May 29, 1923.

43. Seymour, *Baseball: The Golden Age.*

44. *Sporting News*, June 24, 1923.

45. Bill Weiss and Marshall Wright, "The 1923 Baltimore Orioles," www.minorleague baseball.com.

46. *Frederick Post*, October 23, 1923; "Baltimore Made It a Battle to the Finish," *Sporting News*, November 1, 1923.

47. "Chief Bender and Styles Disgraced Club, Says Dunn," *Bridgeport Telegram*, October 29, 1923. "Dunn suspended both players for their actions in disgracing the team at the very time when they should be on their best behavior," wrote Charles J. Foreman in his column for the *Sporting News*, "and he is so wrathful that it isn't likely either will ever don an Oriole uniform again. Both have been sources of trouble before, being forgiven each time.... When Lena's batting helped the Birds win the seventh game he, with Bender, who was peeved at not being used on the mound, put on a celebration before attending the banquet, where they nearly broke up the party"; *Sporting News*, November 1, 1923.

48. "Chief Bender Compares New and Old Pitching," *Galveston Daily News*, August 23, 1925.

49. "Daguerreotypes: Charles Albert Bender," *Sporting News*, October 21, 1937.

50. "Eddie Praises Bender," *Lethbridge Daily Herald*, March 17, 1926.

51. "Chief Bender Hold Jays to One Hit and Johnnies Shake Off Losing Streak," *Johnstown Daily Tribune*, June 21, 1927.

52. "Chief Bender Gets Results," *Sporting News*, July 14, 1927.

53. Article from unidentified newspaper, August 30, 1928, Bender player file, National Baseball Hal of Fame.

54. "Bender Again Hired to Coach Navy Nine," *Washington Post*, August 28, 1927.

55. Daniel and Mayer, *Baseball and Richmond.*

56. *Washington Post*, February 29, 1929.

57. "Arthur Lee Daney," submitted by Dru Pain in the *Scottsdale Progress*, March 17, 1979.

58. "Chief Bender Compares Two Great Teams," *Portsmouth Herald*, July 11, 1929.

59. *Chester Times*, September 15, 1930.

60. *East Berlin News Comet*, "Along the Way," September 5, 1930.

61. *Carlisle Evening Sentinel*, August 29, 1930.

62. "Sport Shorts," *Chester* (Pa.) *Times*, November 21, 1946.

63. *Sporting News*, May 19, 1932.

64. Ray Preebles, "Bender, Alexander Thrill Crowd with Great Exhibitions," *Erie Dispatch-Herald*, June 18, 1932.

65. "Chief Bender in Come Back Role," *Chicago Daily Tribune*, June 26, 1932. The four-inning stint by Bender against South Bend is not included within his statistics in most record books, but the official box score confirms the appearance. *Sporting News*, July 7, 1932.

66. *Sporting News*, August 25, 1932.

67. Dick Peebles, "From a Seat on the Knee of the Chief," *San Antonio Express*, May 25, 1954.

68. "Chief Bender Is Fired and Re-Hired by Erie Within the Space of Few Hours," *Sporting News*, August 4, 1932.

69. L. Frank Thayer, "From the Fence," *Titusville Herald*, August 19, 1932.

70. "McCorry Succeeds Bender, *Sporting News*, August 25, 1932.

71. Thayer, "From the Fence," August 19, 1932.

72. "Creak! Old Ball Players Try It Again," *Chicago Daily Tribune*, August 22, 1932.

73. *Sporting News*, October 20, 1932; *Sporting News*, April 6, 1933.

74. Joel Hawkins and Terry Bertolino, *The House of David Baseball Team* (Chicago: Arcadia, 2000).

75. *Middletown Times Herald*, July 8, 1933.

76. *Washington Post*, July 4, 1933.

77. *Evening Sentinel, Carlisle*, August 2, 1934.

Chapter 14

1. *Sporting News*, February 8, 1934.

2. *Sporting News*, November 30, 1955.

3. *Philadelphia Evening Sentinel*, January 28, 1928 (loose article, Bender file, Cumberland County Historical Society).

4. Spink, "Looping the Loops," December 30, 1953.

5. *Gastonia* (N.C.) *Daily Gazette*, January 31, 1938.

6. *Sporting News*, December 12, 1942.

7. *Gastonia* (N.C.) *Daily Gazette*, January 31, 1938.

8. "$2400 Highest Pay for Chief Bender," *Philadelphia Inquirer*, March 12, 1936.

9. Ed Pollock, "Playing the Game," *Philadelphia Evening Bulletin*, May 24, 1954.

10. "$5000 Most Bender Drew," *San Antonio Light*, March 16, 1938.

11. "Ghosts of the Past Frolic in Shibe Park," *Sporting News*, September 14, 1939.

12. *Sporting News*, June 22, 1939, November 23, 1939.

13. *Sporting News*, January 15, 1942.

14. Spink, "Three and One," December 24, 1942.

15. "White Earth Reservation 1911 Land List," ftp://ftp.rootsweb.com/pub/usgenweb/mn/native/land/wereser6.txt.

16. Spink, "Three and One," December 24, 1942.

17. *Frederick Post*, September 8, 1944.

18. Bob Warrington, "A 1944 Tribute to Connie Mack," philadelphiaathletics.org/history/.

19. Bob Brill, "Hobby Notes," *Maine Antique Digest*, 1996, beckett.com.

20. "Four No-hitters in Four Minor Loops in Three Days," *Sporting News*, May 23, 1946.

21. *Baseball Digest*, April 1970.

22. "Chief Bender Dies," *New York Times*, May 23, 1954.

23. "Chief Gets Joe Right," *San Antonio Light*, May 12, 1954.

24. *Sporting News*, September 17, 1952.

25. "Prize Pupil Shantz Paid Glowing Tribute to Chief," *Sporting News*, September 30, 1953.

26. "Chief Bender Shows Fine Comeback After Surgery," *Sporting News*, January 21, 1953.

27. Pollock, "A Wife's Memories of Chief Bender," May 24, 1954.

28. Spink, "Looping the Loops," *Sporting News*, December 30, 1953.

29. Ibid.

30. "Chippewa Chief Bender Goes Back to Baseball at Age of 69," *Washington Post*, January 18, 1953.

31. Spink, "Looping the Loops," *Sporting News*, December 30, 1953.

32. "Chief Bender Answers Call to Happy Hunting Grounds," *Sporting News*, June 2, 1954.

33. Pollock, "A Wife's Memories of Chief Bender," May 24, 1954.

34. "Chief Bender Answers Call to Happy Hunting Grounds," *Sporting News*, June 2, 1954.

35. Pollock, "A Wife's Memories of Chief Bender," May 24, 1954.

36. *Sporting News*, June 9, 1954. At the time of his death, Chief Bender and his wife lived at 5431 North Twelfth Street in Philadelphia. He was survived by five of his siblings—two brothers, James and George of Detroit, and sisters Elizabeth Roe Cloud, Maude Seymour and Emma Huf.

37. *Sporting News*, August 18, 1954.

38. Anthony Raveni, "The Noble Savage Then and Now," *The Journal of the Colonial Williamsburg Foundation*, Summer 2008.

39. Gordon Edes, "Ellsbury a Rare Talent: In Him, Sox Nation Meets Navajo Nation," *Boston Globe*, March 11, 2007, http://www.boston.com/sports/baseball/redsox/articles.

Bibliography

Newspapers & Periodicals

The American Golfer
The American Indian Quarterly
The Anaconda (Mont.) Standard
The Arrow, Carlisle Indian Industrial School
Atlanta Constitution
Baseball Digest
Baseball Research Journal (SABR)
Boston Daily Globe
Bridgeport Telegram
Carlisle American Volunteer
The Carlisle Arrow
Carlisle Daily Herald
Chester (Pa.) Times
Chicago Daily News
Chicago Daily Tribune
The Cleveland Leader
The Cleveland Plain Dealer
Danville Bee
De Moines Register
Edmonton Bulletin
Erie Dispatch-Herald
Fort Wayne Gazette
The Frederick News
Galveston Daily News
Gastonia (N.C.) Daily Gazette
The Gettysburg Times
Harrisburg Telegram
The Janesville Daily Gazette
The Journal of the Colonial Williamsburg
    Foundation
Kansas City Star
Lethbridge Daily Herald
The Lincoln Daily Star
Los Angeles Times
The Lowell Sun
Mansfield News
Middletown Times Herald
New York Sun
New York Times
The New York World
Oakland Tribune
The Daily Northwestern, Oshkosh, Wis.
Philadelphia Evening Bulletin
The Philadelphia Inquirer
Philadelphia North American
The Port Arthur News
The Portsmouth Herald
Reading Eagle
Richmond Times-Dispatch
St. Louis Globe-Democrat
St. Louis Post-Dispatch
The Salt Lake Tribune
San Antonio Light
Sandusky Star-Journal
Scottsdale Progress
Sporting Life
Syracuse Herald
The Sporting News
The Titusville (Pa.) Herald
Trenton Evening Times
Van Wert Daily Bulletin
The Washington Herald
Washington Post
Waterloo Evening Courier
Weirs Times News Correspondent
Wisconsin Magazine of History
Gazette and Bulletin, Williamsport, Pa.

Books

Alexander, Charles. John McGraw. Lincoln:
    University of Nebraska Press, 1995.

Allen, Lee. *The American League Story*. New York: Hill & Wang, 1962.

Bak, Richard. *Ty Cobb: His Tumultuous Life and Times*. Dallas: Taylor Publishing, 1994.

Charlton, James, ed. *The Baseball Chronology: Complete History of the Most Important Events in the Game of Baseball*. New York: Macmillan, 1991.

Cohen, Richard, David S. Neft, and Jordan A. Deutsch, ed. *The World Series*. New York: Dial Press, 1979.

Fleitz, David. *Louis Sockalexis: The First Cleveland Indian*. Jefferson, N.C.: McFarland, 2002.

Gershman, Michael. *Diamonds: The Evolution of the Ballpark*. Boston: Houghton Mifflin, 1993.

Graham, Frank. *The New York Giants: An Informal History*. New York: Putnam's, 1952.

Daniel, Harrison W., and Scott P. Mayer. *Baseball and Richmond*. Jefferson, N.C.: McFarland, 2003.

Hawkins, Joel, and Terry Bertolino. *The House of David Baseball Team*. Chicago: Arcadia, 2000.

Holway, John B. *Blackball Stars: Negro League Pioneers*. New York: Carroll & Graf, 1992.

James, Bill. *Bill James Historic Baseball Abstract*. New York: Villard, 1988.

Kuklick, Bruce. *To Every Thing A Season: Shibe Park and Urban Philadelphia*. Princeton, N.J.: Princeton University Press, 1991.

Levy, Alan H. *Rube Waddell: The Zany, Brilliant Life of a Strikeout Artist*. Jefferson, N.C.: McFarland, 2000.

Lieb, Frederick. *The Baltimore Orioles*. Carbondale: Southern Illinois Press, 2005.

_____. *Baseball As I Have Known It*. New York: Coward, McCann & Georghegan, 1996.

_____. *Connie Mack: Grand Old Man of Baseball*. New York: Putnam's, 1945.

Macht, Norman L. *Connie Mack and the Early Years of Baseball*. Lincoln: University of Nebraska Press, 2007.

Mack, Connie. *My 66 Years in the Big Leagues*. Philadelphia: John C. Winston, 1950.

McGraw, John J. *My Thirty Years in Baseball*. Lincoln: University of Nebraska Press, 1995.

Meany, Tom. *Baseball's Greatest Teams*. New York: A. S. Barnes, 1949.

Mote, James. *Everything Baseball*. New York: Prentice Hall, 1989.

Newcome, Jack. *The Best of the Athletic Boys*. Garden City, NY: Doubleday, 1975.

Obojski, Robert. *Bush League: A History of Minor League Baseball*. New York: Macmillan, 1975.

Okkonen, Marc. *Baseball Memories: 1900– 1909*. New York: Sterling, 1992.

_____. *The Federal League of 1914–1915: Baseball's Third Major League*. Garrett Park, MD: Society for American Baseball Research, 1989.

Our Documents: 100 Milestone Documents from the National Archives. New York: Oxford University Press, 2003.

Povich, Shirley. *The Washington Senators: An Informal History*. New York: Putnam's, 1954.

Powers-Beck, Jeffery. *The American Indian Integration of Baseball*. Lincoln: University of Nebraska Press, 2004.

Reicher, Joseph, ed. *The Baseball Encyclopedia*, 4th ed. New York: Macmillan, 1979.

Riley, James A. *The Biographical Encyclopedia of the Negro Baseball Leagues*. New York: Carroll & Graf, 1994.

Ritter, Lawrence S. *The Glory of Their Times*. New York: Macmillan, 1966.

_____. *Lost Ballparks: A Celebration of Baseball's Legendary Fields*. New York: Viking, 1992.

Rossi, John P. *The National Game: Baseball and American Culture*. Chicago: Ivan R. Dee, 2000.

Seymour, Harold. *Baseball: The Golden Age*. New York: Oxford University Press, 1971.

Simon, Tom, ed. *Deadball Stars of the National League*. Washington, D.C.: Brassey's, 2004.

Smith, Robert. *World Series: The Games and The Players*. New York: Doubleday, 1967.

Spink, J. G. Taylor. *Judge Landis and 25 Years of Baseball*. St. Louis: Sporting News, 1974.

_____, Paul Reichart, and Ray Nemec. *Daguerreotypes of Great Stars of Baseball.* St. Louis: Charles C. Spink & Son, 1961.

Sullivan, Dean, ed. *Middle Innings: A Documentary History of Baseball, 1900–1948.* Lincoln: University of Nebraska Press, 2001.

Thomas, Henry W. *Walter Johnson: Baseball's Big Train.* Washington, D.C.: Phenom Press, 1995.

Thorn, John, Pete Palmer, Michael Gershman and David Pietrusza. *Total Baseball: The Official Encyclopedia of Major League Baseball,* 6th ed. New York: Total Sports, 1999.

Voight, David Quentin. *American Baseball: From the Commissioners to Continental Expansion.* University Park: Penn State University Press, 1983.

Ward, Geoffrey C., and Ken Burns. *Baseball: An Illustrated History.* New York: Alfred A. Knopf, 1994.

Wright, Russell O. *Dominating the Diamond: The 19 Baseball Teams with the Most Dominant Single Season, 1901–2000.* Jefferson N.C.: McFarland, 2002.

Web Sites

www.aistm.org/sockbio2.htm (Catherine Davids, "A Season Of Brilliance, Part II," 1977).

www.baseball-almanac.com/players

www.baseballhalloffame.org

www.baseball-reference.com

www.baseballlibrary.com

www.beckett.com. Bob Brill ("Hobby Notes," *Maine Antique Digest,* 1996).

http://bioproj.sabr.org. (The Baseball Biography Project).

http://www.loc.gov/chroniclingamerica/home (Historic American Newspapers).

http://www.loc.gov/rr/print/catalog.html (Library of Congress prints and photographs).

www.colbycosh.com/old/march03.html "Bursting an Old Bubble" (Archives de Colby Cosh).

http://college.hmco.com/history/readers.com (*Encyclopedia of North American Indians,* Houghton Mifflin).

www.ldeo.columbia.edu/~tmarchit/rec (Tom Marchitto, "New Haven's Minor League Clubs').

http://epix.net/~landis/history.html (Barbara Landis, "Carlisle Indian Industrial School History").

http://epix.net/~landis/bender.html ("Benders at Carlisle").

http://www.twofrog.com/hampton.html ("First Person Accounts as Written by American Indian Students at Hampton Institute, 1878–1923," compiled and edited by John L. Brudvig, 1994 and 1996).

www.historicbaseball.com/scplayers/jacksonmedia.html

www.kc.rr.com/starrpower/sports/history.hym#baseball

http://www.la84foundation.org

http://www.loc.gov/chroniclingamerica

www. marylandmissing.com

www.members.tripod.com/~johnny rodgers/centrals qindian.html (American Indians in Football: Carlisle Indian School).

www.minorleaguebaseball.com

www.newspaperarchive.com

http://www.ourfutureourpast.ca/news papr/ (Alberta Newspaper Collection).

http://www.paperofrecord.com

www.philadelphiaathletics.org (Philadelphia Athletics Historical Society).

www.retrosheet.org/

http://ftp.rootsweb.com/pub/usgenweb/ mn/native/land/wereser6.txt (White Earth 1911 Land List).

www.sabr.org (SABR-ZINE).

http://www.tolatsga.org/ojib.html (Ojibwe History).

Index

Numbers in **bold italics** indicate pages with photographs.